THE SIGNS OF THE TIMES

UNDERSTANDING THE CHURCH SINCE VATICAN II

BY FR. RICHARD W. GILSDORF

EDITOR: PATRICK F. BENO

STAR OF THE BAY PRESS

Published by Star of the Bay Press
2345 Sunrise Court
Green Bay, Wisconsin 54302
www.esto-vir.org

Nihil Obstat: Rev. Fr. Alfred McBride, O.Praem
Imprimatur: Rev. Fr. John F. Doerfler, STD, JCL, delegate of the Most Reverend
Timothy M. Dolan, apostolic administrator of the Diocese of Green Bay

The Scripture verses herein are taken from several translations.

Library of Congress Control Number: 2008923159

Editors: Patrick Beno, Sr., Brian O'Neel

Interior Design: Michael Fontecchio

Cover Design: Ted Schluenderfritz, Five Sparrows Media (www.5sparrows.com)

Printed in the United States of America
ISBN 978-0-615-18489-0

*Dedicated to my family: My wife Joanne, and
my children Dan, Tim, Mary, Fr. Patrick Charles, and
especially to my daughter Elizabeth, whose expertise
on the computer assisted me in compiling this compendium.*

*Also to all Catholic priests loyal to the Faith and the papacy
who unselfishly dedicate their lives to our Savior Jesus Christ.*

Acknowledgments

My thanks to editors of the publications in which the material herein originally appeared for permission to reprint Fr. Gilsdorf's work. Thank you also to Kate Vrazel, Lisa Terasa, Valerie Striker, and Sarah Rozman for their excellent proofreading work, which made this an even better book.

I also wish to acknowledge that I, Patrick F. Beno, am singularly responsible for all errors—theological or otherwise—that may become known.

This work of compiling Fr. Gilsdorf's valuable gifts to the Church has been a joy and a blessing in my life. Please pray that his loyalty, fidelity, and lifetime of love for the Person of Jesus Christ are now being rewarded in the kingdom of God.

Praise be Jesus Christ!

TABLE OF CONTENTS

TESTIMONIALS

During the six years I had the privilege to serve as bishop of the Diocese of Green Bay, Wisconsin (1984-90), I came to know Fr. Richard Gilsdorf as a holy priest, a Scripture scholar, teacher, and pastor. I proudly add that he was also a friend and confidant, someone whose opinion and insights I valued. I especially appreciated the fact that he was faithful and loyal to the teachings of the Church and had a zeal for communicating the Faith to others. I have no doubt this collection of his columns, articles, essays, and other reviews will be both inspiring and challenging for any reader. He always stretched my thinking and enlarged my heart; I trust he will do the same for you in these pages.

~ Adam Cardinal Maida
Cardinal Archbishop of Detroit

Fr. Gilsdorf was a priest's priest, a pastor, spiritual counselor, scholar, and lecturer. He was one of the first to grasp the crisis that gripped the Church after the Council. With insight and tact, he exposed dissent and stood as a kind crusader for Catholic truth as contained in Scripture, Tradition, and the Magisterium. Father was a champion of orthodoxy and readers of this volume will find a unique perspective on the struggles of these past 40 years.

He wrote an article for my magazine called "The Plight of the Papist Priest" (included in this book). Its impact was so great that it was translated into five languages, and people requested it for over 20 years. In it, he pinpointed the problem of priests trying to be faithful to the Pope and the Magisterium who are ordered by their bishop to do something less. Proof that he was on target is this: Priests from three different parts of the country told me they were sure the anonymous author was in their diocese.

~ Fr. Kenneth Baker, SJ
Editor, *Homiletic and Pastoral Review* magazine

1

When scholars write the history of the post-conciliar Church in America, one remarkable priest will finally receive the honor due him for his fearless defense of the Faith. Fr. Gilsdorf stood up against the attacks, maligning, and subverting of the Church. He was a true pastor of souls and was among those heroic priests who came to the aid of Catholic parents who saw the faith of their children endangered by "false teachers" with "itching ears" who would no longer endure sound doctrine (cf. 2 Tim 4:3). He was a man of God who labored in and suffered for the Church during the crisis of faith afflicting the Church. He was a great friend of the laity who sought to deepen their faith and help them fulfill their true role in the Church. May his memory be eternal!

~ James Likoudis
Publisher emeritus, *Lay Witness* magazine

This book is a treasure. It preserves the crucial work of an exemplary pastor who courageously and charitably defended the Faith against those who distorted and hijacked Vatican II. Fr. Gilsdorf provides here a goldmine of insight into problems of the '60s and the following decades, which I predict will have its greatest impact in the coming years.

~ Dr. Charles E. Rice
Author, *50 Questions on the Natural Law* (Ignatius Press)

Through prayer, zeal for genuine evangelization, towering intellect, and superlative apologetic skill, Fr. Gilsdorf played a significant role in my life. His wise counsel and adept academic assistance were invaluable assets in my formation and education. There are no adequate words to express the breadth and depth of my gratitude.

This book provides numerous examples of Fr. Gilsdorf's immense value to the Church during a period of great turmoil. It shows how his exemplary cooperation with Divine Grace enabled him to eclipse the adversity dealt to him, which benefited countless souls. I have been blessed beyond measure to stand among them.

~ Deacon Robert F. Ellis
Diocese of Green Bay

INTRODUCTION

About six months before Fr. Richard Gilsdorf passed away, we spoke at his small cottage on the shores of Green Bay, which he called *Stella Sinus*, Latin for Star of the Bay (a reference to Our Lady, and hence the name for the publishing house that has published this book).

At that time, he hesitatingly asked me if I would approve of being included in his will. In addition to taking charge of his extensive library, he wanted me to clean out his files, which consisted of about 20 standard file cabinets jammed full of personal correspondence and copies of various writings, speeches, book reviews, and unpublished articles. These he wanted to become a book for publication.

This wasn't for vainglorious reasons. Father was a humble man. However, he had recorded the troublesome times the Church had confronted from 1960 through 2000. He wanted his life's work documenting these trends and events preserved for posterity.

Thus, what follows in this book best exhibits what he accomplished. They demonstrate the historical and theological points of division in the Church that arose in the past few decades. After finishing this book, the reader will understand what caused the many distortions and misapplications of the Second Vatican Council's (Vatican II) teachings.

As the reader will also discover, the works Fr. Gilsdorf produced were a heroic effort that projected his great love for the Church.

For instance, one of the many gems I discovered was "Signs of the Times," the series of columns he wrote for Green Bay's diocesan newspaper. Each one began with this quote from the Gospel of Matthew (16:3), "You know then how to read the face of the sky, but you cannot read the signs of the times."

Fr. Gilsdorf was a priest who accurately read the signs of the times.

Father wrote these columns in the first 15 years of his priesthood. At that time, many considered him quite a progressive priest, especially because of his excitement over the work of Vatican II and its efforts to further Christian unity.

As one reads these columns, however, it becomes easy to perceive how his excitement grew more and more tempered by his discovery of the misuse and distortions of conciliar teachings that began to surface shortly after the close of the Council in 1965. The reader will notice a growing disenchantment with the many academics who twisted the Vatican II documents to promote an agenda he believed would greatly harm the Church. The record of these past 40 years proves that his sense of concern was truly prophetic. The remainder of the works included in this volume also testify to his foresight.

However, for all of Fr. Gilsdorf's brilliance, his writing is sometimes difficult. I beg of you to do as I did: persevere. Read with the thought in mind that you are sitting with him in his living room listening intently as he explains these awesome insights. If you do, you will benefit immensely.

That said, to make some of the theological concepts herein more intelligible to the average reader, we have provided a glossary and explanatory footnotes.

Patrick F. Beno, editor

FOREWORD

Two important things happened to me while editing this book. Because of this, Pat Beno, a man whom I have come to greatly admire, invited me to write about the profound impact *The Signs of the Times* has had on me, and which I pray it will have on you.

The first thing that happened is that I gained a new hero and teacher in Fr. Richard Gilsdorf. As you will learn in these pages, many contemptuously ridiculed and marginalized Father simply because he was a Catholic priest who did his best to remain faithful to the Church.

In the face of this adversity, he could have bemoaned the state of things and given up. He could have joined the many others who simply swam with the tide. Instead, he chose to make a positive difference by standing his ground and fighting for the Church and her teachings. He did everything possible to ensure his own tiny flock remained faithful Catholics. Furthermore, he valiantly sought to help others in the wider Church understand what was happening around them. In this, he gave us a heroic example to follow. I think you will agree after reading this book that he deserves to be better known than he is.

That leads me to the second thing.

For the first time since I decided to dedicate myself to my faith, I understood the reasons for the things that have confused, disappointed, and even angered me over the previous 10 years. Simply put, the things Father writes about led me to an epiphany, to the scales falling from the eyes. No longer did I, in the words of St. Paul, "see through a glass darkly."

To convey the significance of this, I need to give a bit of background.

By and large, the people of my generation learned little of our faith growing up. As noted scholar Francis Beckwith puts it, we grew up "during a time in which well-meaning Catholic leaders were testing all sorts of innovations in the Church, many of which were deleterious to the proper formation of young people." As a result, what we did learn came by way of felt banners, atonal music featuring diluted, sometimes misleading lyrics, and homiletics without real substance.

For me, that began to change in my late twenties when I read Dr. Scott Hahn's conversion story. Like thousands of others, his explanation of the truths of the Faith electrified me. My whole outlook on the Church was transformed overnight. I became convinced of her moral authority, and I feverishly desired to learn as much as possible about her teachings. As a result, I have spent much of the time since then reading and studying whatever I could get my hands on.

Along the way, however, I also discovered the various crises affecting the Church, particularly the crisis of dissent. And what I learned greatly disturbed me.

It disturbed me because, in the process of all this exploring and learning, I had come to love the teachings of my Church. Therefore, I could not fathom how anyone who called themselves Catholic and knew the Faith could disagree with its tenets, much less actively seek to change them. I was bewildered, and I know many others shared this feeling. Indeed, this level of dissent had not existed for at least 400 years. What happened to cause it? I could not understand.

So I read even more to find answers, from the perspectives of traditionalists who had separated themselves from the Church because of her alleged lapse into "Vatican II heresy" to the so-called "progressive" dissenters and everything in between. None of this, however, helped me understand.

That changed as I edited Fr. Gilsdorf's important book. I not only learned more about theology and philosophy, but I grew to appreciate Fr. Gilsdorf's profound insights into the Faith, and, most importantly, I finally began to *understand*.

For instance, he writes about the *Dutch Catechism*, which is a major hinge on which the dissent of the last 45 years pivots. And yet before reading this book, most people will have never heard of it.

Then there are names like Bultmann, Brown, and Rahner. While some Catholics have heard these names in passing, how many know the monumental role they played in creating the theological confusion of the past few decades?

To read this book, then, is to understand the crises afflicting the Church. It is to understand why catechesis has lacked substance and been so ineffective, why some diocesan newspapers still feature dissenting columnists, and why some diocesan chanceries employ those who dissent from and finesse away Church teachings.

Furthermore, to understand the problems and the crisis of faith these have created is to understand how to *solve* the crisis. Fr. Gilsdorf isn't content to curse the darkness. Rather, he shows us where to find the light switch so we will find our way out again.

It is true that things have become somewhat better since the time Father wrote. For this reason, as Pope Benedict XVI affirms in *Spe Salvi*, we have much for which to hope. Indeed, this is largely due to the efforts of Benedict, John Paul II, Fr. Gilsdorf, and many others. They have blessed us with the map and compass we need to navigate how to get confidently toward the hoped-for springtime.

No one can pretend we are there yet, however. Souls are still gravely at stake because a whole generation has been practically lost to secularism, fundamentalism, and other "isms." Despite their having 12 years of education in Catholic parochial schools, we still have students graduating who don't know the Ten Commandments or their basic prayers, much less essential dogmas. There are more non-practicing Catholics in this nation than ever before. As a result, Mass attendance figures are pitiful relative to their historic levels. Many have only a vague awareness of the Rosary.

Additionally, surveys show that average Catholics not only dissent from moral teachings such as contraception, they don't believe in Christ's Real Presence in the Eucharist, either. The antidote to this crisis is not more of the same of what has brought us to this point. We need a *metanoia*, a turning around, now, not tomorrow.

Thankfully, Fr. Gilsdorf describes what is necessary for that to happen. Best yet, he gives us great hope that it not only *can* happen, but that it *will* happen. He even gives us the tools to *make* it happen. In this and many other ways, he has had much to teach me. I hope you find he has much to teach you, as well.

Brian K. O'Neel

The Life of Fr. Richard Gilsdorf

Fr. Richard Gilsdorf was born to Wilbert and Gladys Gilsdorf on January 24, 1930, in Green Bay, Wisconsin. He attended that city's Central Catholic High School and then the St. Lawrence Minor Seminary in Mount Calvary, Wisconsin.

He received his BA at St. Norbert College in DePere, Wisconsin, in 1952, and then studied Theology at St. Meinrad Seminary in St. Meinrad, Indiana, after which he received Holy Orders to the priesthood at the hands of Bishop Stanislaus V. Bona at Green Bay's St. Francis Xavier Cathedral on May 26, 1956.

He served his first appointment at St. John Church in Little Chute, Wisconsin, for two years, and then received assignment to the faculty of Sacred Heart Minor Seminary near Green Bay.

From 1960-61 he took a leave of absence to pursue advanced studies in classical languages at Columbia University in New York City, where he received his master's in Greek in 1961. He then attended the Sorbonne in Paris where he earned his *Certificat du Cours Supérieur* in 1963.

In 1970 he received a second master's degree in Scripture from St. Louis University, and he completed his doctoral studies in Scripture in 1973.

He served at a number of parishes in the Green Bay diocese, was active in the diocesan migrant worker apostolate, and taught summer courses in Scripture at the Pontifical Catechetical Institute in Beaverton, Oregon, for four straight years.

During then-Bishop Adam Maida's tenure as ordinary for the Green Bay diocese, Fr. Gilsdorf served as a member of the Presbyteral Council and the College of Consultors.

He was founder and, from 1994-99, president of the Confraternity of Catholic Clergy, an organization of priests, deacons, and seminarians promoting loyalty to the Holy Father and the authoritative teachings of the Catholic Church.

For the final 23 years of his priestly life he served as pastor of Holy Trinity Church in Casco, Wisconsin. "Fr. Gilsdorf gave all his time to his parish helping people spiritually. I needed his help many times, and he was always there. His example caused me to start thinking about the priesthood," former parishioner Rory Cravillion once told the Green Bay diocese's newspaper, *The Compass*. "He [led] a simple life and [was] close to God by the way he [lived]. That [inspired] me."

After several years of serious illness and much suffering, Father passed to his eternal reward on May 4, 2005, and was buried at St. John the Baptist Cemetery in Howard, Wisconsin, near his father's and mother's tombs. His talks are still available from KeeptheFaith. org.

The following prayer appeared on his ordination announcement:

Thou art a Priest Forever

To live in the midst of the world without wishing for its pleasures;

To be a member of every family, yet belonging to none;

To share all sufferings;

To penetrate all secrets;

To heal all wounds;

To daily go from men to God and offer Him their petitions;

To return from God to men to bring pardon and hope;

To have a heart of fire for charity and a heart of bronze for chastity;

To teach and to pardon, console and bless always, My God, what a life!

And it is yours, O Priest of Jesus Christ.

J.B. Henri Lacordaire, OP

PART I

Fr. Gilsdorf's Early Writings

CHAPTER 1

THAT ALL MAY BE ONE[1]

"Religion" is a word we take for granted. When we speak of the various religions in the world, when we hear of the Christian religions, or "organized" religion, or the "old-time" religion, we feel sure we know what religion means.

However, perhaps we should stop for a moment to test this common word. Just what is religion? What does the word itself mean?

In the beginning, at the dawn of time, God made all things from nothing. That is the basic reason for religion. Man also makes things, but he makes some things from something, and that something is already in existence. Yet even in this limited way, the things a man makes belong to him, depend on him, and may be used or disposed of at his will. If this is true of man, what, then, is the case between God, Who creates, and all those things He has created?

Certainly all creation (and man pre-eminently, who is the crown and culmination of God's creative act) stands in total subjection to God's will and depends on Him for their very being. This dependence is not merely "in the beginning." Rather, from moment to moment, from breath to breath, from pulse to pulse, we depend upon the attentive and consenting will of God to hold us from a lapse into the nothingness from whence He called us. We belong to God far more than the crude products of our hands belong to us.

We must submit, then, with love, with humility, with abandonment to the mind and the will of God. Our life must be— above all other concerns—alert, attentive, receptive, and searching in respect to God Who sustains us. If and when He speaks to us, our feeble minds must absorb this wisdom and revelation with hunger and humility. If and when He commands, our weak wills must embrace these tests of our love with ardor and surrender.

This sum of the relations between God the Creator and man, His creature—made in His own image and likeness (i.e., with intellect and free will)—this is religion. The word itself means "a bondage."[i] Religion is the bond that binds us back to the very source of being, of knowledge, and of love.

Total surrender

The form religion must take depends entirely on the initiative of the Creator, not upon the discretion and whims of the creature. Our sole posture in religion must be a continuous receptivity of whatsoever issues from God. We cannot select, we cannot dictate. We must be as parched earth yearning for the life-giving moisture that comes only from above. We must offer God an unconditional surrender of our entire being. This is worship or adoration. It is not worship merely to sing to God or even to shout to God—"not every one who cries 'Lord, Lord' shall enter the kingdom of heaven."[2]

We must also totally surrender our mind and our will and all aspects of our life to the mind and will of God—"but he who hears the word of God and fulfills it." The Psalm beautifully pictures religion: "As the eyes of the serving girl are fastened on her master, so our eyes are turned always on Thee, O Lord."[3]

Christ is the Word. He is the perfect expression of the Father. The divine Word takes on human flesh and dwells among us.[4] He, God, communicates His deep mysteries through human words with human lips to human minds. In the Person of Christ, we possess the fullness of truth. "I am the Truth."[5] When we accept this, then our religion advances to the necessity of embracing Christ—not with emotion alone, not with qualifications, but with exactly the same unconditional surrender we owe to our Creator.

---

[i]   Latin: *religare*, to bind back

"The Father and I are one."[6] We must seek nothing more than to learn from the lips of Christ His precise teachings, His revelation, His will toward us as expressed in His commands and precepts. "If you love Me, keep My commandments."[7] We must put on the mind and will of Christ—this is religion in its true and genuine sense.

Unity: A necessity

As Christ is but one Person, so the mind and will of Christ are one. Nor is He deceived or mistaken or fallible. Christ is Truth; Christ is the Way.

Therefore, we blaspheme if we attribute contradictions, inconsistencies, and divisions to the Mind and Will of the divine Word. The revealed teachings, the plans and designs that flow from the lips of Christ, *must* be ordered and unified. In a word, as defined and taught by Christ in His gospel, religion must be one, without contradiction, and without division.

Yet today we face the anomaly. There are hundreds of religious bodies all claiming to represent to mankind the mind and will of Christ, and each one represents it in a different way. As Martin Luther once deplored, "*Tot capita, quot sententiae.*"[ii]

From all that we have considered thus far, the honest mind draws a conclusion: Either every one of these groups are wrong, or else one and only one is true, and all the others are consequently in error. While this is a disturbing statement, it is the key to salvation and the first step toward clearing the scandal of "divided Christianity."

Furthermore, if every follower of Christ would constantly and firmly believe and pray over this thought, we would have gone far toward realizing the promise of Christ: "... and there shall be one fold and one shepherd."[8]

If five bank clerks mentally add the same column of figures, and all return different sums, no responsible person would smile and say all these answers are good in their own way, that it really makes no

---

[ii]   "There are as many opinions as there are heads."

difference. We are far more prudent in the values of this carnal life than we are in the means to obtain eternal life. Only the truth will make the bank clerks free to proceed in their work.

Similarly, only the truth will make us free in our relationship to Christ. And so we put to rest the fear we feel as we first realize that not all Christian bodies can be the true Church of Christ.

Our love for Christ and discovering the truth can only liberate us to love Him, serve Him, and embrace Him more fully. If we detect we are in error and hesitate to advance to newly discovered truth, then our love is not so much for Christ as it is for our vanity and ourselves. Here the surrender that is the essence of religion and worship meets its greatest challenge. It is not easy to find that we are mistaken; it is heroic to admit it; but it would be ridiculous and disastrous to place our poor mental powers above those of God—Lucifer already tried that.

So we state the obvious choice again: Either all Christian bodies are false, or only one is true, and the rest are in error. It is essential to salvation that we completely satisfy our conscience that we are in possession of the true teaching of Christ. Those who seek and, through no fault of their own, never discover the full will of God for them are certainly pleasing to God.

Nevertheless, Christianity as a whole must be stirred up, must be made restless until the contradiction has been resolved. For that mind that is in Christ Jesus must be the single mind and the single direction of His one Body, the Church. And the Spirit of Truth who has come to teach us all truth must no longer suffer the blasphemy of being named the source of contradictory teachings.

No less is it blasphemous for myriads of men to sit in judgment upon that totality of truth—"all truth"—which the Spirit of Truth reveals to mankind, dissecting strand from strand, thread from thread, as some do, labeling one doctrine as essential, "fundamental," and another as unessential. *All truth is essential.*

This duty of satisfying one's conscience falls heavily upon each lover of Christ, but the burden crushes upon the conscience of the leaders of Christianity whose duty it is to test their credentials.

They are responsible for those whose limited abilities cannot easily untangle the mesh of contradiction and division. Indeed, some of these leaders are shepherds of the flock of Christ, and just as surely, all the rest are intruders whose credentials are not sustained by authority from Christ.

Let us pray that soon there will be but one flock and shepherd. The Apostle Peter received such authority when Christ commissioned him, when He said, "Feed My lambs... Feed My sheep."[9] In turn, Peter commissioned others. Upon whom does this line of authority fall in our world today? Either the leaders of no church are so authorized or else only the leaders of one church. Again, we cannot evade or pass off this principle: "How shall they preach, unless they be sent?"[10]

Christ and unity

We would not be wrong in supposing that the most pressing desires and thoughts of a person will come forward in the hours immediately preceding an anticipated death. The late hours of Holy Thursday, the discourse of the Christ to His apostles at the Last Supper, are laden with the urgent need for oneness: "That they all may be one, as Thou Father are in Me and I in Thee. That they also may be one in Us, that the world may believe that Thou has sent Me..."[11]

Christ always describes His Church, His kingdom on earth, as a unit, one that is visibly, perceptibly, and organically one. It is a living vine with but a single life, a universal tree that has developed from a single seed, a fishing net that catches all fish, good and bad. It serves as an assimilating leaven that transforms and unites all into a single unit. It is a flock where the truant must be reclaimed at all costs and where a single shepherd leads and feeds with but one direction and one purpose.

In this latter case, Christ, the Good Shepherd who lays down His life for His sheep, evokes in the minds of His hearers the resounding theme of the Prophets: The Messiah is to be the Great Shepherd!

Christ, too, refers to the robbers whose own the sheep are not, who enter in by stealth, and whose voice the sheep know not. Later, before lifting His bodily presence from the earth, He commissions Peter to feed His lambs and His sheep.[12]

His entire flock is now in the care of a visible vicar on earth, but the lambs and the sheep are ever "*My* lambs," "*My* sheep." In this same theme, Christ pleads for and promises unity: "Other sheep I have which are not of this fold. These also I must gather, and there shall be but one fold and one shepherd."

Christ also strongly condemns even the smallest change or deviation from His teaching. He berates those who would alter a jot or tittle even one of the slightest nuances of the divine meaning which came from His lips "and teach it thus to men."[13]

To His apostles, as an authorized college of teachers, He declares, "He who hears you, hears Me. He who despises you, despises Me. He who despises you, despises Him who sent Me."[14] "As the Father has sent Me, I also send you… Go, therefore, make disciples of all the nations, teaching them to observe all things whatsoever I have commanded you, baptizing them in the name of the Father and of the Son and of the Holy Spirit. And behold, I am with you all days even unto the consummation of the world."[15]

The apostles

As the Father sends the divine Word to mirror the mind of God to men, and just as Christ is "the great teacher come from God,"[16] so also our Lord sends His apostles as teachers to all nations. They—as Christ—neither add nor subtract; they mirror. They "pass on that which they also have received."

The apostles, then, all proposing the same single doctrine, persistently reiterate Christ's demand for unity. They frequently anathematize deviations from the received teaching of Christ, the "deposit of the faith." Their letters are replete with fulminations against the "false teachers" of their day.

The following sketchy examples only skim the surface of Scripture, but they bring forth the mind of the apostles, men whom Jesus sent by commission.[iii] "I am amazed that so quickly you have passed over from the gospel which called you unto the grace of Christ into another one, which is not another gospel at all, but there are certain men who disturb you and wish to change[iv] the gospel of Christ. But though we or even an angel from heaven should teach you a gospel other than that which we have already taught you, let him be anathema. As we have said before, so I say now again: If anyone teach you other than that which you have already received, let him be accursed."[17] "Hold fast to the deposit of faith..."[18]

"For I have passed unto you, that which I also have received from Christ Jesus."[19] "One Body and one Spirit, even as you have been called in one hope of your vocation. One Lord, one faith, one Baptism. One God and Father of us all ... until we all run fully into the unity of faith and of knowledge of the Son of God ... no longer as tottering children tossed about by every wind of doctrine by the wickedness of cunning men unto the bypaths of error..."[20]

Paul warns us that false teachers will come one day, men of "itching ears," men who cannot bear "sound doctrine," wafted about easily by each new and fitful gust of doctrinal wind. The phrase "sound doctrine" (*he didaskalia he hygiainouse*) resounds as a theme throughout the teaching of the apostles and of the earliest Christian writers.[21]

The profound Pauline allegory of the Body of Christ, the Church, presents truly organic unity (a unity of life of mind, vivifying and directing the diverse operations of the one body) as essential. And the Last Supper unites and nourishes this unblemished and undivided Body. "All we who are nourished by the same Bread are of the same Body."[22] For other expressions of these thoughts, one need only page the Holy Scriptures.[23]

[iii]   Greek: *apostellein*—to send.

[iv]   Greek: *metastrepsai*—one can also translate this as "distort," "reverse," or "pervert," in the sense of to turn something into its opposite.

All this, then, is most certain: Adherence to Christ with complete abandon and surrender to His person must result in the singleness of thought and mind of those who love the same Person. The unity of the followers is the working of the Holy Spirit, Who proceeds from the Father and the Son: "I will send you the Spirit of truth and He will teach you all truth."[24] The Church, therefore, built upon Peter, the apostolic rock, against which the gates of hell shall never prevail, and in whose human hands are placed the keys of the kingdom of heaven, to bind and loose on earth with the authority of heaven itself—this Church is "the pillar and the groundwork of the truth."[25]

Twenty centuries later

If this be the case, then it is still Christ's prayer "that they all may be one." The ardent plea of St. Paul rings out as a challenge to our times, "One Lord, one faith, one baptism!"[26] We must apply the principles of unity—that all who claim to love and follow the unique Shepherd should constitute but a single flock, following their Master in a single direction. All should be joined as in the same, single Body of Christ with a single life, a single center of thought, a single movement of love, a single growth and development, a single direction of activity, though many in its functions, yet of a single purpose. St. Paul asks the seemingly ridiculous question, "Shall the hand rebel against the foot?"[27]

If a divided Christianity were the will of God, this "absurdity" would be an actuality attributable to God Himself. The union of the Body is realized only by the formula, "Let this mind be in you, which was also in Christ Jesus."[28] All who profess to love Christ must enter into such a union—this is the condition of our love. Where in our world today is this compact body, this Church against which Christ promises that the gates of hell, the gates of error and falsehood, will never prevail? Where is that city on a hill that is visible to all and built upon the Rock? Where is that great tree, in the branches of which all the varied species of birds take rest and build their nests and the shadow of which falls upon every nation of the earth?

This kingdom is the pearl of great price, and we must sell and cast aside all without regret or afterthought in order to procure it. Accordingly, all Christians must halt to consider: Is Lutheranism in the fold of Christ? If so, all must adhere to this faith. If her teachings are the mind of Christ, we cannot rest until we have that mind. Is Methodism the true vine of Christ? If so, no consideration must prevent us from grafting ourselves unto her. Are Presbyterianism or Christian Science or Congregationalism the Church of which Christ declared, "He who listens not to the Church is to be regarded as the heathen and the publican"?[29] Are the Baptist Churches that unique Body of Christ?

If so, we must not rebel against the Body, but we must incorporate ourselves into its ordered growth and life, for, severed and divided from the Body, there is only death and corruption. Is Anglicanism the kingdom of Christ? Despite all difficulties and barriers, we must give allegiance to her. Is the Catholic Church the true fold of Christ?

Again, let us abandon all our prior judgments and attachments and band ourselves with the Shepherd of our souls, who remarks— sadly—"he who does not gather with Me, scatters."[30] We dare not remain deliberately or culpably distant and unattached. For either all these hundreds of religious bodies are false, or one and only one is true.

One of the basic norms of logic, a principle without which there could be no normalcy in any of our human endeavors, is the principal of contradiction; namely, which means that two contradictory statements on the same subject cannot both be true. Were we to ignore this principle in mathematics, in science, in medicine, in finance, in business, in jurisprudence, or in government, there would result a strangling anarchy—the world would revert to hermitages; social life would be inconceivable. To deny this principle is to commit intellectual suicide—without it, one cannot progress along any avenue of thought. One cannot even begin to think.

Such a primitive picture of life seems absurd to us. Who could ever deny this first principle of reasoning? Yet here is the enormity of it all: In the most critical field of human thinking—religion— here alone we discard the principle of contradiction. Every breeze of opinion, though contradictorily opposed to scores of other opinions on the same subject, is indulgently labeled as "equally good," of no consequence, as not "fundamental." This suicide, this prostitution of human reason cries aloud for resolution.

Why should it be that we ignore the first principle in the theological science alone? We find the reason in the spiritual nature, the spiritual consequences of such anarchy—our world only fights back against things that are of discomfiture to flesh and blood. The calamity of the rebellion in religion is seen adequately only after death, and then it is already an eternal calamity. The divisions, the ideological and philosophical conflicts in the world are the secondary results of this folly. But though massed together, no consequences on earth, no losses on earth could approach the everlasting loss of one immortal soul. Surely the time has come to be as kind to our spirit as to our flesh. Surely the time has come to return to sanity and logic in religion.

Approaches

From all these considerations, there follow several practical resolutions.

For instance, if I am reasonably and thoroughly convinced that I already belong to the true Church of Christ, then my duty is one of boundless charity and zeal for those whom I believe to be less fortunate—those "other sheep" whom Christ must gather. I must pray for them earnestly and incessantly, for they are in a state of jeopardy to their souls. The fullness of revelation does not illumine them, the fullness of Christ's dispensation of grace does not fortify them, the framework of Christ's religious establishment does not guide them. I must strive to understand them, to appreciate their problems, to help them by explanation and encouragement. Above all, I must love them as my own soul and regard them as precious beyond measure since the sacred Blood of Christ has redeemed them. I must never deliberately malign them, never delight in or exploit scandals. After all, "it is necessary that scandals come,"[31] and scandals do not touch upon the merits or claims of a religious institution (except in someone who claims a new and extraordinary divine mission).

Above all, there must reign charity for all outside the one Church I am convinced is the true Church of Christ. Humility must reign alongside charity, for I know that nothing I possess is due to my merits, but is the free gift of God.

If, on the other hand, I am not certain whether my present religious affiliation can claim or does claim to have authority from Christ, then with earnest prayer and sincere investigation, I must search for the truth. It is no shame not to have been born in the truth. It is, however, a shame not to seek for and accept it when and where discovered. It would be an eternal, infinite *tragedy* to die in error, but an equally great *triumph* to arrive at the truth by the hard road of humility, prayer, study, and God's grace.

If all the world would advance only so far as this realization leads us, if all souls would stand in a state of either possessing the truth or openly and eagerly searching for it, then the walls of division would soon crumble. We would then have but one fold and one Shepherd. The facetious but fatal fallacy that dams back the flood of such a movement is the irrational axiom that all religions—though mutually contradictory—are all equally true, all equally good, all equally pleasing to God. We must explode such a blasphemy against the Spirit of Truth. Now is the time for the walls of separation to fall and the nets of contradiction to disintegrate. No man dares shrug off religious doubts and uncertainties, for religion is the road to eternal life, and God has charted the route.

Finally, let every soul on earth—whether convinced or uncertain but seeking—pray. This is the one thing we can do in unity. Let us all pray to Christ that He unite all Christians and us lead us in the same direction along the same path, to feed us with the same nourishment, to instruct us with the same doctrine, to order us with the same commands, in a word, to make our minds His Mind, to conform our wills to His will, and the mind and the will of Christ are one. It is not slavery to surrender to Christ, for only the Truth can make us free. In ardent charity, tempered by humility and understanding, with no taint of animosity or of prejudice, let us beg the Holy Spirit to teach us all truth, to show us the established and secure road to the eternal vision of God, which is the eternal destiny of every soul.

Some religious groups have an eight-day period of special prayer for this purpose, from January 18 through January 25 each year.[v] Let us join them by making this a universal octave of prayer by all Christians. No harm can befall us if we beg that all may know the truth and have unity in that truth. If we already are in the truth, the others will join us—if the others possessed the truth, we would join them. But every day also, let us enter into the spirit of the dying prayer of Christ, the prayer of His heart: "That they all may be one, as Thou, Father, in Me, and I in Thee; that they also may be one in Us, that the world may know that Thou has sent Me ..."[32]

---

[v]   Prayer for Christian unity was encouraged by Leo XIII, and was further endorsed by St. Pius X (cf. http://www.weekofprayer2008.org/about-milestones.html). The Week of Prayer for Christian Unity as we know it now had its origins in 1908, and was started by Rev. Paul Wattson, an Anglican clergyman. He believed unity could only be achieved by the separated Christian communions returning to the Church, and he later became Catholic. The Church has officially marked this octave since 1986.

Chapter 2

Tension in the Manger[1]

When a child is born, his parents wonder at the awesome mystery of the love that gave it existence. This new being becomes the object of their contemplation, and disturbing thoughts assail them: "How shall we help it to attain the fullness and maturity of its manhood?"

The child is born for a purpose. We must know that purpose in order to educate and raise him.

When Mary and Joseph beheld the Child in the manger, they not only asked the previously mentioned question but also, "Who is this child whose birth was so unlike every other birth?"

We know the answer that His parents also sensed: This Child is destined to bring life to a race of new men, a new people, a new world, a new cosmic body.

Now, every man must look to the stable and contemplate this Child in Whom all life must henceforth subsist. After all, God the Father desired to reconcile all things in heaven and on earth in Him.

The first Christian centuries sought to comprehend the mystery lodged in the Flesh and Blood of this Baby lying in a food trough in the "House of Bread."[i] The first questions of the early Church had to be the questions of Christmas, for the answers to these queries would determine the pilgrimage, mission, and destiny of all that came after.

---

[i] The name Bethlehem means "House of Bread," fitting as it was the first town to house the Bread of Life.

This is why the Christmas liturgy represents the mystery of the birth of the Word Incarnate each year. And this is not merely an exercise of intellect or recall: By existential anamnesis,[ii] in other words by entering into and poignantly recalling the Event, we become present to it and it to us: "Let us go over to Bethlehem, and see ..."[2]

Perhaps this year recollection is needed more than ever with the tension we see in the Church today. Infectious enthusiasm tends to sweep us all into militant camps of the far right or the far left.

Only in the Nativity do we find our problem's sorely needed resolution. For if we look with the eyes of faith, we will see that the Child, Prince of Peace, presents in the oneness of His Person not the peace of static, but the peace of dynamic. The manger is the eye of the universal hurricane. It births the serenely potent harmony of cosmic tensions. The supreme analogue of all tension (Divinity-Humanity) is polarized in this little Body, the Church.

The tortured word "tension" comes from the Greek *teno*,[iii] from which in turn derives the noun "tone," the "tone" of sound muscular tissue, the "tone" of tautly harmonious vocal cords. The Word made Flesh—the supreme harmony, a polarity that can nonetheless reconcile seeming opposites—dwells among us, and we dwell in Him precisely to recapitulate [i.e., concisely repeat] all the analogous "tensions" we now face. The Infant effects moderation, but He does not do so in the sense of compromise or indifference. Instead, we find in Him the only perfect state of genuine and productive dynamism.

The current fad is to reject this incarnational moderation. One must be either liberal or conservative; free or obedient; institutional or charismatic. The Germanic *entweder-oder*,[iv] heir to ancient Persian dualism,[v] is ruthlessly and witlessly imposed.

---

ii   Existential means of or relating to human existence, and anamnesis means a recalling or recollection of an experience.

iii   i.e., "stretch"

iv   A German term meaning "either/or."

v   This is likely a reference to the notion of dualism in the Zoroastrian religion. As the 1913 *Catholic Encyclopedia* notes, "the name [dualism] has been

Yet a deep and faithful contemplation of Bethlehem shows clearly that these pairs are not exclusive and contradictory opposites. Rather, they are polarities. The answer found in the Manger is not the excesses of either/or, nor even the self-destructive thesis/antithesis of Hegel, but rather the dynamic harmony of *both/and*.[vi]

And as this Babe is both true God and true Man, hypostatically[vii] harmonized in a Divine Person, so His Body the Church is both

---

used to denote the religious or theological system which would explain the universe as the outcome of two eternally opposed and coexisting principles, conceived as good and evil, light and darkness, or some other form of conflicting powers. We find this theory widely prevalent in the East, and especially in Persia, for several centuries before the Christian Era. The Zend-Avesta, ascribed to Zoroaster, who probably lived in the sixth century BC and is supposed to be the founder or reformer of the Medo-Persian religion, explains the world as the outcome of the struggle between Ormuzd and Ahriman. Ormuzd is infinite light, supreme wisdom, and the author of all good; Ahriman is the principle of darkness and of all evil."

[vi] Georg Wilhelm Friedrich Hegel (1770-1831) was a hugely influential philosopher and was one of the so-called "German idealists." According to the 1913 *Catholic Encyclopedia*, "'The rational alone is real' was a favorite motto of Hegel. It means that all reality is capable of being expressed in rational categories. This is a gnosticism more detrimental to Christian conceptions than the agnosticism of Huxley and Spencer. It implies that God, being a reality, must be capable of comprehension by the finite mind. It implies, moreover, as Hegel himself admits, that God is only in so far as He is conceived under the category of Becoming; God is a process. It is by this doctrine (which is at once so out of place in a great system of metaphysics and so utterly repugnant to the Christian mind) that Hegel's philosophy is to be judged. Hegel attempted the impossible. A complete synthesis of reality in terms of reason is possible only to an infinite mind. Man, whose mental power is finite, must be content with a partially complete synthesis of reality and learn in his failure to attain completeness that God, Who evades his rational synthesis and defies the limitations of his categories, is the object of faith as well as of knowledge."

[vii] This word derives from "hypostasis," meaning the substance, essence, or underlying reality of a thing or person. So we talk about the "hypostatic union" in Jesus, meaning His two natures (divine and human) are united in the one Person and are not separate.

truly divine and truly human. It is in this Christic bipolarity that the pairs of the "tensions" exist, and in it alone can they be resolved.

Let me stress again: The theological meditation on the mystery of Christmas is far from a sterile intellectual project. The dogmas of the great Christological Councils are not exercises in futility. [In other words, this all matters for the average person in the pew.] Dogmas led to "pragmas,"viii ideas lead to deeds. The future of Jesus' Church depends upon our understanding of Him.

The man who today seeks to reconcile both poles of tension is doomed to obscurity. Often, he is ridiculed. More often, he is brusquely dismissed as a compromiser, as one who straddles fences. Those our age considers champions are those who out-pull the latest extremist. They crave and receive instant status with a feckless willingness to abandon either the past or the future. They sell their birthright for a mess of popularity.

On one side we see the "neo-Judaizers" who are intransigent and Parmenidean,ix and who refuse to burst through the cocoons of historical circumstance. On the other we see the "neo-gnostics" who flit from password to password, reserving salvation to an illuminated esoteric circle.x Who will lionize the moderate?

But is this not the lesson of the Manger? The Infant is, in a surpassing sense, the great revolutionary Moderator, the cosmic Straddler of fences Who constantly labors to break down the walls of partition. This moderation is not a do-nothing mediocrity. As Christ is true God and true Man, He is also the perfection of progressivism and the perfection of conservatism.

---

viii   A Greek word whose root meaning is "that which has been done, an act, a deed, a fact." It is also the root of our word "pragmatic."

ix   This comes from the ancient Greek philosopher Parmenides, who depreciated sense-knowledge and held that change, motion, and multiplicity are illusions.

x   Gnosticism is the theory of salvation by knowledge, mostly secret knowledge available only to the few. Father is comparing gnosticism, therefore, to a secret society with secret handshakes, passwords, and the like.

The Fathers of the Church ascribed to Christ the formula, *Quod erat permansit; quod non erat assumpsit.*[xi] As Cardinal Suhard[xii] so brilliantly expounded, this applies also to the Mystical Body of Christ [i.e., the Church], which is the continuance and fulfillment of the incarnational bridgehead.[xiii]

This dictum likewise applies to the recent ecumenical council [i.e., the Second Vatican Council]. It initiated many changes. Because of this, it is important that all of us understand what is elementary: Some things the Church can, should, and must change, while it cannot change in substance other things (and here we must further distinguish between changing teachings versus changing their formulation or explication).

"What the Church was, it remains; what it was not, it assumes." The Church's greatest present need is to clearly discern between the divinely immutable [i.e., the things of God that can't change] and the

---

[xi]   "That which He was, He remained; that which He was not, He assumed."

[xii] Emmanuel Célestin Cardinal Suhard served as archbishop of Paris from 1940 until his death in 1949. During World War II, the Nazis held him under house arrest for a time, which did not keep him from being seen as too sympathetic to the puppet Vichy regime. Indeed, upon his entering Paris, General Charles de Gaulle refused to enter Notre-Dame Cathedral until Suhard had left. Despite this, His Eminence openly protested the deportation of Jews to concentration camps (in what the *New York Times* called a "spirited written protest against racial and religious persecution") and young workers to forced labor in German concentration camps. When his protests failed on the latter point, he sent clandestine priests to minister to those who had been forcibly taken. During the latter part of his life, he became a forceful and somewhat prophetic speaker on what Christians need to do to truly be Christians in the world. His powerful and eminently quotable style garnered him many disciples of a sort, and several of his works were translated into English. It is not certain to which statement Fr. Gilsdorf is referencing here, but the most likely is "Growth or Decline?" taken from *The Church Today: Collected Writings of Emmanuel Cardinal Suhard* (Chicago, IL: Fides, 1953). He is buried in the crypt at Notre-Dame.

[xiii] The sense of bridgehead here is that of beachhead, i.e., a preparation or foothold for a larger action at some later time. In other words, the Incarnation began the work that He ultimately left the Church to continue.

humanly transient [i.e., the human things that can change]. Only a more-than-human guidance can preserve us from disastrous errors. Ultimately, this guarantee resides in the college of bishops in union with Christ's vicar.

The Incarnation allows for and demands progress and change, after all. And, again, in the light of Bethlehem, this growth is that of a Person. Since the Body of Christ is an organism, the growth must stand in substantial continuity with its past. It must be coordinated, organized, and unified in harmony throughout the entire Body. Consensus is important for sound growth and adaptation. In Council, the Church crystallizes a harmony and thus approximates the ideal of the Incarnation. For example, the Church in the United States is now buffeted by tensions and thus needs a Plenary Council where a whole People of God will achieve harmony. The sooner the easier, but sooner or later we will need an American Council.

The Incarnation also demands an immutable but dynamic essence. It embraces, requires, and harmonizes both of these poles. Adapting to historical contingencies, the Body of Christ does at times rally toward one pole or the other in order to preserve its total health. However, it always seeks its normal balance as the crisis passes. To exaggerate the correctives of Vatican II would prove to be as much a disaster as was the exaggeration and over-persistence of the correctives of Vatican I.

A few concrete applications of our meditation on the Manger: Catholics (and most acutely the religious) are currently struggling with the legitimate search for "freedom." This search is not opposed to genuine obedience, which is, in fact, one of the most insistent Gospel descriptions of the Christ Child. "In the [beginning] of the book it is written of me: that I should do Thy will, O God."[3]

From His youth to the cross, He humbled Himself, was subject, and became obedient unto death.[4] His meat was to do the will of His Father.[5] Yet who is more "free" than Christ? Who could justly aspire to more freedom than the paradoxically sovereign but suffering Servant, the Master-Minister?

Again, Bethlehem gives a key: This is a Son! The obedience He gives is thus filial. In our own father-son relations, we have all hopefully experienced a shadow of the fearlessly free and loving obedience that has its perfection in Christ.

In the liturgy, which makes Christ present to us in His mysteries, we have the humanly changeable and the divinely unchangeable. It is as serious a departure from the Incarnation to never adapt anything as it is to seek to change everything. With the latter, we will grow so preoccupied with experiments on externals and accidentals that reverence and awe for the essence will become forgotten or even obscured by reckless gimmickry. This will engender a far more devastating irrelevance than the rushed mumbling of yesterday. The last state could be worse than the first.

Then there is Scripture. In exegesis, we must avoid and/or correct the tendency to "demythologize" the Bible, especially in passages such as the Nativity. In their attempt to do the valid and required work of criticism, some engage in the Bultmannian[xiv] excess of over-intellectualizing, of coming up with easy, pat answers to resolve difficult or hard to resolve facts or passages.

The Gospels, however, are not a collection of myths. Rather, as the Council's *Dei Verbum* and Pius XII's encyclical on the study of Scripture (*Divino Afflante Spiritu*) stress, they are historically reliable. Thus, the Gospels are a magnificent example of the Word made Flesh living among us. The exegete must be conscious of the fact of Christ and His transcendent presence in Scripture, the words of the Word, that Christ's presence in Scripture was both historical and eternal. There is both *kairos*[xv] and *chronos*.[xvi]

We all, then, must go up to Bethlehem and see. We must regain the balance that can derive only from a spiritual life of union and

---

[xiv] This refers to Rudolf Bultmann, a Lutheran theologian from Germany who taught New Testament at the University of Marburg. It seems his principle goal was "demythologizing the New Testament mythology."

[xv] Greek word meaning "the right moment" or "God's time."

[xvi] The Greek personification of time, from which we get the words "chronology," "chronicle," and so on.

growth with, in, and through this Child unto the full measure of His manhood. The closer our union with Him, the more we will realize the harmony of a sound, polarized tension in each and all of us. We begin by believing into Christ, as the Gospel of John suggests.[6] (Not the "believe on" of King James or the weakened "believe in" of the usual translation, but the "believe into," *pisteuein eis*.) This act of faith (which is both an existential and a personal act of love) enables the whole man to enter into the life of the whole Christ. And once we are one with this Babe (who is the Father of the age to come), we have entered into His Body, the Church.

As a whole, the Church must resolve its tensions by union with Christ in mind, heart, will, humanity, and divinity. Only then can we become a Bethlehem for a world still alienated, a world full of untempered tensions gone berserk. This turbulent world can only be recapitulated if the Church is visibly and cogently a sign of the harmony of the Manger, the stability of the Stable.

The Babe ages a day, a week, a year, and He passes through the unheralded but wondrous mystery of 30 years. By the temper of our days, some would have voiced the challenge, "Why did He remain silent so long? Why—with all His power—did He fail to speak out, to act, to save? To what purpose is this waste?"

Eventually, the Babe grows into a man and enters into the midst of His three years of intensive mission. Encircled by a clashing storm of acceptance and rejection, love and hate, He climbs into a boat with His apostles and ventures out into the Sea of Galilee. As they strike out to the depths, a violent and sudden storm surrounds them. The apostles huddle as the boat pitches under the tensions of the sea's tempest. But ever the eye of the hurricane, Christ rests in serene peace in His manger-boat.

The waves lashing and the winds buffeting the fragile earthly timber represent tensions such as we have discussed, along with many more we have yet to experience. And with us all days, in our very midst—*if only we believe*—is Emmanuel. In Him all is harmonized, all is overcome, all is recapitulated, all is pacified. He is living, but silently He sleeps like a Babe.

The apostles should have known that this sleep of God was not oblivion, abandonment, or impotence, much less death. Christ was "in the same boat" they were. Their lots were inseparable. Their real fault lay in forgetting in a moment of human panic that their faith in this Person would overcome the winds and tides of the world. The harmony within would harmonize and reconcile all without—all, even the cosmic elements.

For the apostles, as for us, salvation lies in huddling close to and embracing Christ in faith, hope, and love, sharing in His life, so that we are not only in the same boat, but in the same Body. Strained by our tensions, we call out, "Save us, Lord, we perish!" And He will recall us to the power of our Faith, echoing again the message heard over the waters and winds of Galilee and the manger of Bethlehem: "Peace! Be still! To all men on this earth be peace and glory to God in the highest."

PART II

SIGNS OF THE TIMES

CHAPTER 3

SIGNS OF THE TIMES[1]

"You know then how to read the face of the sky, but you cannot read the signs of the times" (Matt 16:3).

One of my greatest peeves—and that is saying a lot these days—is that one must often read Catholic columnists with an exacting eye in order to discover where the writer stands. Some such as Greeley[i] defy analysis.

Therefore, before initiating a series on biblical topics in this "Signs of the Times" series, I want to simply state where I stand. This way, those who dislike my position and are not at all curious as to why I hold to it can spare their eyes, minds, and emotions the inevitable pain.

Before anything else, I am a Roman Catholic priest, proud of and delighted with every part of the title. I am a "Vatican II liberal," and I will explain what I mean by that before the end of this article. I am in full sympathy of mind and heart with Pope Paul.[ii] I embrace without any equivocation the *Credo of the People of God*.[iii]

I love the Church as my Mother. I love her as she was, as she is now, and as she will develop. As any mother, she has some human defects. I have noticed these, but they have not made me cynical or driven me to anything like rebellion. Nor have I ever had the urge to

---

[i] This would be Fr. Andrew Greeley, sociologist and priest, who many hold to be heterodox.

[ii] At the time Fr. Gilsdorf wrote this column, Paul VI (1963-78) sat on the Chair of Peter.

[iii] *Solemni Hac Liturgia*, *motu proprio*, Paul VI, June 30, 1968. Available (and worth reading) on the Vatican website.

run around the neighborhood of the world broadcasting her human faults. I haven't the slightest shame of her, although I have much shame that I am not worthy of her.

I am intensely grateful for all the Church has given me: at home, in the parish, in the old-fashioned Sisters' school, in the seminary, and in my 13 years of priesthood. I see no discontinuity or contradiction in my faith through all these wonderful years. Nor do I hesitate to look with optimism to the future as long as I remain firmly and lovingly attached to the Church and move with her apostolic leadership.

I believe the Church needs action and requires changes. Just as intensely, however, I believe prayer, spiritual life, and adherence to the essential doctrines of the Church represent the only conditions under which action and change can be successful and saving. I believe some of my fellow Catholics are in grave danger of eventually and imperceptibly losing their faith and, in the process, of shattering the hopes of the Council.

I was taught in the seminary that it was an expression of love to follow the Church's laws, even in the small rubrics of the liturgy. I also learned that this expression would permit me to act in the name of Christ and show forth His glory and grace. I believe what the Church has taught me, and I have no desire to act in my own name or to parade my ingenuity (i.e., vanity) when I approach the altar of God.

I am convinced of the divine wisdom of the sacrament of penance, and although I will eagerly accept the expected new directives giving a more communal expression to the sacrament, I am convinced from years of experience as penitent and as confessor that the living Christ works His miracles of healing in the sacrament as the Church practices it now. As Pope John XXIII clearly taught, I believe frequent confession is to be greatly encouraged.

I believe in devotion to Mary. I believe in the power and splendor of the Holy Rosary. I believe in Fátima and its message.

I believe the Church's doctrines are the precious, saving words of Christ. Not for a moment can I feel free to throw them up for grabs or submit them to systematic doubt. Nor can I subscribe to the irrational, agnostic know-nothingism that abhors "content" in favor of vague "life experiences" untouched by divine revelation. I must admit at this point that this is not from a lack of scholarship. But in all my studies and reading (probably more of it from Protestant and liberal Catholic sources than from the "safer" authors), I have yet to find anything that can lead me to doubts or to hesitation on the list of beliefs I present here.

In fact, everything has led to a confirmation and deepening of the faith I learned from my penny catechism and the faith I professed at my ordination. Whenever I weigh the sanctity, the intellect, the scope of information, the moral heroism, the charismatic endowments—not to mention the authority—of Pope Paul against the credentials of his critics, I wonder why the "experts" ever bothered to stand up. I wonder even more why anyone ever chose to sit at the errant feet of such self-appointed "experts."

During the years of the sessions of the Council, I followed with the greatest alacrity and prayer every action of the Fathers. I rejoiced at the victories of the progressives. I accept the Council without reserve and hope to see it produce the fruits of hope it has sown in the world. I am, then, a Vatican II liberal.

But there are many who would deny me this title after reading what I have stated above. The reasons for this are several, but the primary reason is that we have seen a dramatic semantic shift in the last few years.

The current abusers of the tags "liberal" and "conservative" have completely altered their meanings without consulting the rest of us. In many circles today, "conservative" means "orthodox," and I dread to think what this does to "liberal." This is a frightening fact, and if anyone *insists* that orthodoxy is conservatism, then I will not hesitate to accept the label, not for a moment.

As I will explain later, however, a Catholic must be both liberal *and* conservative (in the older, pre-Vatican II sense). I, for one, am as conservative as Pope Paul is and as liberal as he is. For me, his teaching charism is a supreme test.

I fully sympathize with the Jesuit theologian Henri de Lubac,[iv] who remarked this summer in a lecture at St. Louis University that he ran the risk of being classified as conservative or a reactionary or "outdated" simply because he attacked the "negative self-criticism" in the Church. Yet he said he believed people must speak thus in order to lead the Church out of the "web of ambiguity that is smothering us."

One final whimsical question: How many are we?

I am almost positive that the vast majority of the faithful would subscribe to what I have listed above. That said, it is in the very nature of people like us that we do not speak out until we believe ourselves compelled to do so. Maybe this is a weakness, and maybe we could have safely indulged this weakness in former times. Today, however, I think that with so much at stake, we must give witness to our faith whatever the cost. No one is asking us to shed our blood, but we should not hesitate to shed human estimation. The man of faith is often ridiculed and ostracized, for the wise of this world hold that the wisdom of God is foolishness, a scandal, a stumbling block.

---

iv   Henri Cardinal de Lubac stood among the most influential twentieth century theologians, and his work strongly influenced the course of the Second Vatican Council. He was considered a liberal theologian and was a principal proponent of the so-called "New Theology." For all of that, however, he became disillusioned with the disordered turn of events after the Council, and he wrote several post-conciliar works on what Vatican II had truly meant to accomplish. In 1983, at age 87, John Paul II created him cardinal deacon of Santa Maria in Domnica. Cardinal de Lubac passed away in 1991.

CHAPTER 4

RELEVANCE AND/OR FAITH[1]

*"You know then how to read the face of the sky, but
cannot read the signs of the times" (Matt 16:3).*

Those who have any love for language had better quickly mount
a protest movement (or is it already too late?).

Edwin Newman recently recited a litany of grievances over
people using words to mean things they don't.[i] But if the abuses are
merely annoying in secular vocabulary, they are lethal in the context
of religion.

Terms such as fulfillment, identity, freedom, encounter,
conscience, commitment, renewal, structures, democracy, collegiality,
the spirit of Vatican II, liberal, conservative, and a host of others have
become completely fluid. They can mean anything, and, therefore,
they mean nothing.

Beyond being maddening, however, the death of semantic
meaning in the jungle of popular theology is a symptom of the
deepest spiritual crisis.

Here semantic death may well lead many a soul to eternal
death, for it bars the communication of revealed truth. Thus, it is a
desperately crucial attack against the very pediments of the gospel
of Christ.

---

[i]   Newman (b. 1919) was a long-time newsman for NBC who was well-known
for his being something of a one-man language police force. In 1984, he
even hosted *Saturday Night Live*, and in one sketch poked fun at himself by
playing a suicide hotline counselor who kept correcting the callers' grammar.
He wrote two books on the proper use of English.

The day is not far off (or may be already upon us) when a Catholic congregation may recite the Creed with individuals present using the same words to understand a radically different faith, differing not only from one another but from 20 centuries of Catholicism.

One of the abused words is "relevance." It nauseates me even to type the blasted word. Where is the emesis basin?[ii]

Really, my disgust extends only to the current pop theology usage. The word in itself is wholesome and perfectly applicable to sound Catholic faith.

But for my feelings about the counterfeit, "disgust" is too superficial a word. When I hear fellow Catholics screaming frantically about the need for "relevance," I feel a profound chill of horror pass through me. To the degree that the person is frantic about this need, to that degree I sense his faith is ebbing away. That time of disenchantment may be longer or shorter, but ultimately that person will wake up one day and realize he no longer believes. After all, in its true sense, relevance comes primarily from within. Indeed, this is true of meaningfulness in any order.

Granted, there should be an orderly and systematic monogram to establish certain external and conventional signs to facilitate true relevance. The Council made giant strides in this direction. We can take pride in how our diocese has led the way in this ecclesial labor.

But when experiments in the name of a false relevance are introduced on individual whimsy and then excessively multiplied, it is an admission that something is seriously defective inside.

Furthermore, it becomes increasingly imperative for persons engaged in such experiments to innovate, and correspondingly impossible for them to find satisfaction in their souls. Flying from high to high, they end up being turned on by nothing.

For instance, take the priest who feels compelled to create a bootleg liturgy (despite the generous flexibility of normative liturgical rules). Inch-by-inch, he progressively moves to the most

---

ii   A basin into which people vomit.

bizarre efforts to display his personal message through his self-starred showmanship, all in the name of being "relevant."

The debacle in Milwaukee of recent unhappy memory is a stark proof.[iii] The ineffable communication of the presence of the Master in His saving acts becomes increasingly obscured in favor of the "servant," who drowns out this presence by the cacophony of sounds and gyrations (which, at their root, are symbolic of the dionysiac element of this world). As a result, the Holy Mass becomes a plaything, a recreation period.

The underlying problem with this is that it misses the point, doesn't it? For making the Divine Liturgy one's own personal theater can never enable us to penetrate to the living presence of Christ the Savior Who has died, is risen, and will come again. Only faith can do this, and if we have no faith, then no amount of histrionics or innovation or invention will make the Mass "relevant."

For instance, our level of faith will automatically dictate many manners of acting, of speaking, of expression at Mass. Faith will lead the soul into peace, harmony, and interior light that one can only attain within the framework of the prescriptions given by the total Church (and which cannot be found with the coteries of separatists).

If, on the other hand, this interior experience of faith is present, the mania for showmanship reveals itself for the demonic obsession and empty vanity that it is.

Many of these innovations have raised barriers to total community worship and have wounded and plagued sincere consciences. And innovation in the liturgy is only one example of where this mad quest for "relevance" has led us.

---

iii   While Father's precise meaning here is unclear, he probably is making a reference to the bizarre liturgical situation that was common under Archbishop William Cousins at the time. Things such as clown Masses, polka Masses, rock Masses, and the like proliferated. Indeed, Milwaukee was known for its anything goes liturgical atmosphere.

One of the Council's most inspirational moments came when the Fathers decided to begin their deliberations on the liturgy. Soon their consensus became visible, and the genuine spirit of the Council was gradually grasped.

Sacrosanctum Concilium (Constitution on the Sacred Liturgy) strongly influenced and colored all the other acts of the Council, including the key document *Lumen Gentium* (Dogmatic Constitution on the Church). Why? Because the old adage "the norm of prayer is the norm of belief" had proved itself once more.

The Council Fathers understood the intimate, interacting bond between the inspired words of Scripture, the revealed words of doctrine, and the existential words of worship.

Now understanding this and before going any further, consider that whenever there have been deviations in liturgy in the Church's history, there have been deviations in biblical exegesis.

And since the liturgy is an external expression of interior faith, it is the most immediate target for the charge of irrelevance. Again, however, this charge is but a symptom of the erosion of faith within.

We must always face the truth that the words of Scripture, of revelation, and of liturgy are all words of the Word. If we love the Word, we will keep and cherish His words. For this Word "became flesh and dwelt among us."[2]

And by faith "we have seen His glory—glory as of the only-begotten of the Father—full of grace and truth ... and of His fullness we have all received."[3]

This Word is the true Light that, coming into this world, enlightens every man. He has come unto His own, but some who cannot see with the eyes of faith have complained that He is not relevant, that the words and deeds and precepts of the Creator are meaningless in the Space Age, and therefore some of His own receive Him not.

But to as many as receive Him as the ultimate revelation, as the key to all meaning, to these He gives the power of becoming sons of God. And who are these who receive Him? "Those who believe in His Name."[iv]

CHAPTER 5

CORINTH: THE SECULAR CITY[1]

"You know then how to read the face of the sky, but you cannot read the signs of the times" (Matt 16:3).

When St. Paul's First Letter to the Corinthians is mentioned to those who know it, great blazing images seem to flash to the mind. We recall its references to the Exodus and Passover as types of our life "in Christ," the Lord's "tradition" of the Eucharist, the doctrine of the Church as the Body of Christ, the majestic hymn of charity, the witness to the Resurrection.

But quite frankly, Paul had a practical reason for mentioning all of these. He was provoked to do so by grave problems and disorders within a troubled Christian community. Thus, the more thoroughly one reads the epistle, the more convinced one becomes that First Corinthians is eminently applicable to our own situation.

In fact, Paul seems very much like the modern bishop of a city in 1969: His most thorny problems, his deepest daily anxieties, even the worst ingratitude and abuse come to him from within a confused, faction-ridden, sophisticated flock.

Located on the slender neck of land between the Aegean and the Adriatic Seas and a major port of commerce, Corinth was in many ways a symbol of our modern cities and, indeed, of "City" in the generic sense of modern civilization and culture. Boats were loaded, unloaded, and dragged along the fabled rails from one harbor to the other. And, as was the case in those days, with the boats came not only sailors but imperial officials, philosophers, and religious heralds.

However, there was also something else about this city. The very name "Corinth" brought a smirk to the lips. It was the vice capital of the ancient world. The temple of the love-goddess Aphrodite, where prostitution constituted worship, dominated the city from its perch on the Acrocorinth.[i]

There were at least 10 other major cults of the Greek pantheon popular here, as well as wild new gods of the mystery cults. Wisdom and *gnosis* were in the air.[ii] These produced a kind of intellectual snobbism because their adherents claimed that their "wisdom" gave them a special key to salvation. Salvation of this kind was quite separate from the ethical standards of the older systems.

---

[i]   This was the acropolis of Corinth.

[ii]   "Wisdom" here is another word for philosophy. For some people in first century Corinth, being wise (defined as intimately knowing some philosophical system that gave its adherents the secret answers to all of life's questions) was akin to having a nice car or a state-of-the-art sound system today. In other words, it was a way of counting yourself better than others, a mode of being a snob. Gnosticism was the height of this phenomenon because not only did the gnostics have knowledge, they had secret knowledge. Furthermore, the mere fact that they had this knowledge meant that these people had attained salvation. Christians were not immune to gnosticism's allure. As Fr. John Hardon, SJ, notes in his Pocket Catholic Dictionary, "Already in the first century of the Christian era, there were Gnostics who claimed to know the mysteries of the universe. They were disciples of the various pantheistic sects that existed before Christ. The Gnostics borrowed what suited their purpose from the Gospels, wrote new gospels of their own [e.g., the Gospel of Thomas, the Gospel of Peter, the Gospel of Judas, and so on], and in general proposed a dualistic system of belief. Matter was said to be hostile to the spirit, and the universe was held to be a depravation of the Deity. Although extinct as an organized religion, gnosticism is the invariable element in every Christian heresy, by its denial of an objective revelation that was completed in the apostolic age and its disclaimer that Christ established in the Church a teaching authority to interpret decisively the meaning of the revealed word of God."

Besides religion, there were also the "in" philosophies of stoicism,[iii] cynicism,[iv] and epicureanism.[v]

It was into this hub of profligate sin, esoteric "wisdom," and fatalistic sophistry that Paul entered. He was one more herald (*keryx*) of a new spiritual manifesto (*kerygma*).[vi] The wonder is that he succeeded as much as he did. The little flock grew like a flower in the municipal dump.

After Paul moved on to Ephesus, however, reports began coming to him from Corinth that became more and more alarming. It was not a healthy Church.

In First Corinthians, Paul addresses the serious problems orally reported to him by delegations, and he also responds to questions sent to him in a letter from Corinth. The list he tackles is long, and the issues are often extremely complicated (we may never understand some of them). For now, we will have to satisfy ourselves with noting some of the major problems and how closely they parallel our own.

[iii] Stoicism taught the development of self-control, fortitude, and detachment from distracting emotions. It held that indifference to pleasure or pain allows one to become a clear thinker, level-headed, and unbiased. A primary aspect of stoicism involved improving the individual's spiritual well-being.

[iv] Cynicism held that virtue was the only necessity for happiness, and that it was entirely sufficient for attaining happiness. The cynics followed this philosophy to the extent of neglecting everything that did not further their perfection of virtue and attainment of happiness. Thus, the title "cynics" was assigned to them because they lived like dogs—neglecting society, personal hygiene, family obligations, pursuing money, and so on—to lead entirely virtuous and, thus, happy lives ("cynic" is derived from the Greek word *kuon*, "dog" in English).

[v] This philosophical system is simply hedonism wrapped up in an intellectually attractive package. Epicureanism holds the greatest good is to seek modest pleasures in order to attain a state of tranquility and freedom from fear as well as absence of bodily pain through knowledge of the workings of the world and the limits of our desires. The combination of these two states is supposed to constitute happiness in its highest form.

[vi] As stated, a *keryx* was a herald, someone who proclaimed something. The *kerygma* was that which he proclaimed.

The root of the ills within the Church at Corinth was intellectual pride. For historical reasons peculiar to the time, "wisdom" was as tempting to the minority Jew as to the majority Gentile. Slogans and false charisms were the source of factions and errors. As is usual with gnostic enthusiasts, a few adherents became rigorists while the vast majority excused themselves from the common laws of morality. They appealed with slogans and special insights to their illuminated consciences to justify the most scandalous laxity of morals and discipline.

To these, Paul (like today's beleaguered Magisterium) insists on the Cross: Foolishness to the Gentiles, a stumbling blocks to the Jews, but to us the true wisdom of God.

"When I came to you, I did not come with pretentious speech or wisdom... I determined not to know anything among you, except Jesus Christ and Him crucified... And my speech and preaching were not in the persuasive words of wisdom, but in the demonstration of the Spirit and of power, that your faith might rest, not on the sophistry of men, but on the power of God."[2]

Paul is blunt when he attacks the sexual scandals in the backsliding Church. Throughout the text, one can detect a series of slogans some used to justify this conduct. Pride of intellect, besides causing factions, invariably leads to moral deviation. One sees a whole system of "situation ethics" in First Corinthians. Paul ruthlessly and fearlessly rips the foil off these specious arguments to expose the naked corruption for what it is: a pollution of the Temple of the Spirit, an apostasy from the pure Body of Christ. Read the text! Paul acted much like the Paul of our day.[vii] And whether we like it or not, the stance of Paul—excommunications included—is not unlike that of the Archbishop of Washington.[viii]

[vii]   i.e., Pope Paul VI.

[viii] Patrick Cardinal O'Boyle, archbishop of Washington, DC, from 1947-73, who was at the center of the dissent aroused by Paul VI's encyclical *Humanae Vitae*. Catholic University of America is in Washington, and several theology professors there—namely Fathers Charles Curran, Robert Hunt, and Daniel McGuire—issued a statement, signed by more than 80 other

In Chapter 7 of the epistle, we see the heights of holiness in marriage as well as in celibacy. Léon-Dufour[ix] has brilliantly commented on this chapter, concluding that the institutions of marriage and celibacy are inseparable partners in dialogue.

Paul's words, however, afford little comfort for the "flesh-bound." He wishes that all be like himself, free for the service of the Lord and of the brethren. He is thereby all the more a Father, having begotten sons in the gospel of Christ. Doubtless some were arguing that you could not find life fulfilling or be a whole man without marriage.

Ever hear those lines?[x]

Chapter 11 begins Paul's withering condemnation of eucharistic and liturgical abuses. (Tempting as it may be to open a few cans of worms, I will heroically make no comments on the first things discussed: women

---

American theologians (which number eventually grew to over 600) who dissented from *Humanae Vitae*. Cardinal O'Boyle disciplined the clerics. The dissenters then appealed to the Vatican for redress, and the Vatican later sided with them against the Cardinal. Thus was born Cafeteria Catholicism. George Weigel has called the Vatican's inaction "The Truce of 1968," which he said "taught theologians, priests, and other Church professionals that dissent from authoritative teaching was, essentially, cost-free. The Truce of 1968 taught bishops inclined to defend authoritative Catholic teaching vigorously that they should think twice about doing so, if controversy were likely to follow; Rome, fearing schism, was nervous about public action against dissent. The result was that 'a generation of Catholic bishops came to think of themselves less as authoritative teachers than as moderators of an ongoing dialogue whose primary responsibility was to keep everyone in the conversation and in play.' And Catholic lay people learned 'that virtually everything in the Church was questionable: doctrine, morals, the priesthood, the episcopate, the lot.'"

[ix]   Fr. Xavier Léon-Dufour, SJ, French professor of Scripture.

[x]   Indeed, we are still hearing them today. On October 19, 2007, dissident theologian Fr. Richard McBrien told conferees at a Voice of the Faithful convention, "Can you imagine what kind of candidates we would attract to the US Senate, for example, or to any other high-ranking political, corporate or academic office if a commitment to lifelong celibacy were an essential, non-negotiable requirement?" Of course, look at all the people it hasn't stopped, people whom the Church now considers saints, people even in our own age.

without head coverings in the assembly and boys wearing long hair...) Attributing all aberrations to a failure "to discern the Body" (meaning the Eucharist and the Church), Paul counteracts with a crystal-clear "tradition" he gained from the Lord. Beyond the Mass, he indicts the dangers of charismatic illusions and Pentecostal-like disorders. The final criterion for order at worship is that if any self-styled charismatic does not listen to Paul's authentic apostolic judgment, he is to be ushered out.

Relevant, isn't it?

I urge all to carefully and prayerfully read this most modern epistle. During the next few weeks we will apply it to our secular city. Here we will not only find the exposure of evil but solutions—and how greatly we need these! Paul leads us to the genuine experience of the Cross, to spirituality "in Christ," to eucharistic unity and growth, to genuine and orderly worship, to the "foolish" wisdom of God, to a fully eschatological worldview, to a constant and full sense of corporate solidarity in the one Body of Christ Jesus, and Him crucified.[xi]

Perhaps we should also allow the nagging thought to take germ in our confused minds and turbulent hearts that God has indeed raised up another Paul in our days, an apostle to the Gentiles, a man on the move, a severe but exalted teacher "in spirit and power." He is severe with the severity of a true Father, not with the indulgent permissiveness of the "many pedagogues" (1 Cor 4:15), one reviled and despised, held up as foolish, as a stumbling block.[xii] However, for those who are true sons of God, he is a genuine dispenser of the mysteries of God, a true herald of Christ's gospel. But perhaps now (as in Corinth and throughout history) we will have to get much worse and much more miserable before we become humble enough to turn to apostolic authority.

[xi]   An eschatological worldview is a view of creation (i.e., the world) that is mindful of why God ultimately created the world and of His intention to engage Himself and us in an effort to realize that purpose.

[xii]   This is a reference to 1 Cor 1:23, which contains this phrase. The Greek word for "stumbling block" is *skandalon*, from which we get our word "scandal."

CHAPTER 6

FIRST CORINTHIANS 7: PROCREATION AND THE NEW CREATION[1]

"You know then how to read the face of the sky, but you cannot read the signs of the times" (Matt 16:3).

In some epistles, notably Ephesians and the pastorals,[i] St. Paul treats separately the topics of marriage, consecrated widowhood, and celibacy. But only in First Corinthians 7 do we find marriage and celibacy considered together in their close theological relationship.

Here we will discuss only what the apostle discussed. His conclusions: Celibacy is a state that is not only desirable but also essential to the Church in the Messianic era. And while marriage is a holy and wholly lawful—indeed the ordinary—state of life, St. Paul nevertheless recommends that "apostles" (in the broader Pauline sense) remain unmarried.

Since our present and ancient law of clerical celibacy was not yet a historical question for Paul, this is as far as he goes. He warmly recommends and gives profound theological bases for such a discipline. So "Pastoral Renewal" (a euphemism for a clutch of aging bachelors plotting to gracefully break their solemn vows) will not get its precise question posed in Chapter 7.[ii] Yet, given his stand on apostolic authority, there is little doubt what Paul would say today.

---

i   St. Paul's so-called "pastoral epistles" are First and Second Timothy and his Letter to Titus.

ii   This is a reference to the National Association for Pastoral Renewal, which was a group of priests (many of whom had left or were in the process of leaving the priesthood) who agitated for scrapping the Church's discipline

Remember, the Corinthian Church had grave divisions within it. In the area of sexual conduct, one side had opted for laxity and even license, using sophistries that would make Fr. Curran and his less gifted imitators look unimaginative.[iii] Paul completely devastates the party countenancing laxity in two powerful images:

1. "Know you not that your bodies are members of Christ? Shall I then take the members of Christ and make them members of a harlot" (6:15)?
2. "Know you not that your members are the temple of the Holy Spirit, who is in you... For you have been bought at a great price. Glorify God and bear Him in your body" (6:19-20).

The other side insisted (a bit prematurely) on the elimination of sex for all Christians in view of the Second Coming (*parousia*). This alarming view, called by the Greeks *encratism* [from their word for self-discipline], used for its slogan St. Paul's words, "It is good for man not to touch a woman" (7:1). The Adventism[iv] that prompted this doctrine is much the same as the error of those Thessalonians who merely sat and prayed, neglecting daily work and activity, waiting hour by hour for Christ's imminent return. (Recall how Paul had also resolutely condemned the false Adventism at Thessalonica.)

Rigorism of this type, as medieval Catharists such as the Albigensians have shown, is subversive of society itself.[v] The great

---

on celibacy. It was very active in the late 1960s and early 1970s. From all appearances, the group is now defunct.

iii   Fr. Charles Curran, dissident Catholic theologian best known for spearheading the dissent against *Humanae Vitae* in 1968. In 1986, the Congregation for the Doctrine of the Faith, headed by then-Joseph Cardinal Ratzinger, revoked his eligibility to teach Catholic theology.

iv   i.e., a belief that the *parousia* was about to happen.

v   According to the 1913 *Catholic Encyclopedia*, the Catharists were "(From the Greek *katharos*, pure), literally 'puritans,' a name specifically applied to, or used by, several sects at various periods. The essential characteristic of the

surprise is that Paul is not as ruthless toward the rigorists as he was toward the laxists. In fact, a superficial reading of Chapter 7 might lead to the false conclusion that Paul himself deprecates marriage as a necessary evil ("It is better to marry than to burn" in 7:9, and so on).

It is true he regards celibacy and continence as an ideal sign of the Messianic Age, but this is also the same Paul who wrote Ephesians 5. He well knows that marriage is an essential institution, a sacramental "mystery" blessed and instituted by the Lord. Nor is he a naïve "imminent eschatologist," turning his back on life with its ordinary secular states and duties. Such an assessment—now discredited— formerly held sway in scholarly circles. Paul probably expected Christ to return rather soon, but certainly not immediately. (To prove this would require a linguistic study of the Greek text that is beyond our scope here.)

As a rabbi, Paul had learned to see the procreative role of husband and wife as the continuation of creation. The rabbis held that voluntary celibacy was tantamount to the shedding of blood. To see the radical revolution in Paul's thought, we need only compare Genesis 2:18 ("It is not good that man be alone") with 1 Corinthians 7:8 ("But I say to the unmarried and to widows, it is good for them if they so remain, even as I").

Catharist faith was Dualism, i.e. the belief in a good and an evil principle, of whom the former created the invisible and spiritual universe, while the latter was the author of the material world." The Albigensians were latter-day Catharists. They taught that man "is a living contradiction. Hence, the liberation of the soul from its captivity in the body is the true end of our being. To attain this, suicide is commendable; it was customary among them in the form of the *endura* (starvation). The extinction of bodily life on the largest scale consistent with human existence is also a perfect aim. As generation propagates the slavery of the soul to the body, perpetual chastity should be practiced. Matrimonial intercourse is unlawful; concubinage, being of a less permanent nature, is preferable to marriage. Abandonment of his wife by the husband, or vice versa, is desirable. Generation [i.e., procreation] was abhorred by the Albigenses even in the animal kingdom. Consequently, abstention from all animal food, except fish, was enjoined."

What had caused Paul's shockingly new judgment? He had seen Jesus the Risen Messiah, the Lord of time Who had entered history. With this "intrusion," time itself has been profoundly altered. In Christ, there has been a new *creation*. "The schema [i.e., frame, present form] of this world is passing" (7:31). The old creation is continued by the successors of the first Adam and the first Eve. In the "new creation," the new Adam, Christ, begets sons of His spouse the Church—not of "blood," not of the will of the flesh, nor of the will of man (cf. John 1:13, Matt 19:12, and Gal 3:28). Paul, "an Apostle sent by Christ" and united with Him in the life of grace, boldly proclaims the new paternity, which remains the glory and the potency of the celibate priest: "Little children, in the gospel I have begotten you."

In Ephesians 5, Paul will later explain the difference between the animal "love" of Corinth (and our own secular city) and the genuine love we have "in Christ." The essence of true love is sacrifice; it is surrender of self for the beloved.

And so again, we return to the key to Paul's gospel: the Cross. "Husbands, love your wives, just as Christ also loved the Church and delivered Himself up for her" (Eph 5:25). Is sexual union—though lawful and holy—a more perfect expression of love than the spiritual union of sacrifice? Ask couples who have grown old together. Ask young married people who must abstain at times for motives of love. Ask the celibate Christ, Who on the Cross "loved His own unto the end."[2]

Paul shows a remarkable insight into the intimate relation of body and soul in marriage (cf. 7:3-5). There is a relation between the sexual and the sacred. In a commentary, the Jesuit Léon-Dufour abundantly corroborates what is said here. He shows how Paul teaches there must be a "symphonic" union of the souls of the spouses, beyond the union of the bodies. Marriage must have *une ouverture vers le haut*, in other words "an opening upwards," a "vertical dimension."

> Each partner joined to the Lord of the two; beyond body, beyond soul. To admit this helps to recognize within the bosom of marriage itself what constitutes the

> essence of virginity, which is an immediate meeting of
> the soul and its Lord. Only reference to the Lord makes
> marriage stable... The celibate is a visible type of this
> vertical encounter essential to every soul.[3]

Thus, Paul never speaks of marriage without celibacy in 1 Corinthians 7. He conserves the values of marriage and especially its indissolubility (7:10), but the weight of his esteem goes to continence as a charism. Procreation has now lost its absolute character. To maintain intact its own properly Christian order, marriage demands the charism of voluntary non-marriage at its side in a constant dialogue that harmonizes the eschatological tensions of the Messianic Age. Of this age of the "end-time," celibacy is the seal and the sign. It is the true fertility of the New Creation; it is *regenerative*, not merely generative. Indeed, a complete doctrine of Christian marriage will concomitantly relate itself to celibacy.

It is another of those heart-crushing inconsistencies so typical of today's do-it-yourself theologians that while they overstress the fullness of the celibate Christ's humanity to what approximates a denial of His divinity, they just as loudly proclaim that a celibate cannot truly and fully be a man!

What a boon for vocations and priestly perseverance it would be if priests would profess the teaching of St. Paul (instead of engaging in unblushing whining for bodily fulfillment). Marriage is an image of Christ's union to His spouse, the Church, which is at once immaculate virgin and mother of all the living. Would a man marry a woman if he did not love her with all his heart and soul? The disciples of Jesus (seminarians and religious postulants) must be led to so love the Church that they, too, will courageously and permanently "deliver themselves up for her."

Indeed, what is true for seminarians and postulants is true for all of us—married or celibate.

CHAPTER 7

FIRST CORINTHIANS: WORLDS APART[1]

"You know then how to read the face of the sky, but you cannot read the signs of the times" (Matt 16:3).

In reading First Corinthians, you may have already noticed that St. Paul often uses the term "world" in a very bad sense. In First Corinthians, we read the "wisdom" and the "rulers" of this world are passing away (2:6). Even the schema (or form) of this world is passing away (7:31). The "saints" will judge this world (6:2). The spirit of this world is opposed to the spirit that is from God (2:12).

We could multiply such examples, and this attitude is consistent through all his letters. At one point, Paul exclaims, "The world is crucified to me, and I to the world."[2]

Yet there are other places where he uses the word "world" in a perfectly friendly, commendatory sense (e.g., as an object of love, of mission, or of restoring in Christ).

How can these statements be reconciled? I am well aware of the rabbinic doctrine underlying the problem. I have done considerable homework on the tannaitic doctrine[i] of *ha-'olam ha zeh*[ii] and *ha-'olam ha-ba'*.[iii] I mention this to forestall any suspicion that I have overlooked the subtleties. I am convinced, however, that my greatly simplified statement of the case is justified and accurate.

So—fine points aside—the New Testament's divinely inspired authors agree substantially regarding their uses of the word "world."

---

[i] A school of *Mishna* (i.e., Torah) interpretation.

[ii] i.e., the present age.

[iii] i.e., the age to come.

The reader of Paul and the Gospels (especially that of John) must understand, "world" has two opposed meanings! The same word does not mean the same thing every time it is used.

Most often "world" (especially "this world") stresses the fallen side of creation that is under the sway and influence of Satan, who works out his "mystery of iniquity." "This world" is the enemy of Christ, the arena of the anti-Christ, the antagonist of God's kingdom, a dangerous peril and seduction to the disciples.

"World" is also the creation of God who saw that "it was good."[3] It is to be redeemed, restored, and "recapitulated in Christ."[4] The disciples have a divine commission to transform it into the kingdom. God so loved *this* world that He gave His only begotten Son.[5]

We see this opposed double meaning sharply in John's Gospel. Christ's kingdom is in this world, but not of this world.[6] The disciples are in this world, but not of this world.[7] Christ has overcome the world.[8] At times, Scripture tells us to love this world and, even more often, its bids us to flee it. This tension is always with us. It has continued throughout Church history with some eras opting for Martha, others for Mary.

This scriptural distinction is *critically* important for interpreting Vatican II. Here one can see how crucial sound doctrine is. Ideas lead to action; doctrine determines practice. In reading the conciliar texts, if we do not *distinctly* evaluate both meanings of "world," the most pernicious errors result.

Let's face it—in some cases this is precisely what has happened. Some are embracing the world without heeding the biblical and conciliar distinction. This way lies disaster—and damnation.

These errors have an intimate connection with the doctrine of the "secular city." This catchall term is linked to Dr. Harvey Cox,[iv] who is himself indebted to Friedrich Gogarten.[v] Addressing the Latin

---

iv   Liberal Protestant theologian and long-time faculty member of the Harvard Divinity School.

v   Lutheran German who taught dialectic theology at the University of Göttingen until his death in 1967. His thought was closely aligned with that

American hierarchy in Colombia last spring,[vi] Pope Paul singled out by name *The Secular City*'s theory as the deepest root of many grave disorders in the Church.[vii] Later, at a congress on non-believers held in Rome,[viii] the Pope met Cox.

I quote an Associated Press (AP) release dated March 27, 1969:

> Among the first the Pope shook hands with was black-bearded Harvey Cox, professor at the Harvard Divinity School and author of the book *The Secular City*. The book concerns what Cox calls a new freedom where men can choose to accept or reject religion independent of family and other such influences.
>
> Cox says Pope Paul apparently has understood his book to mean a rejection of the supernatural.
>
> The Pope smiled and said, "We are fighting against you, but we read you with great interest."

So Cox has denied the Pope's assessment of his thought. I can't vouch for the master, but I surely know a few of his disciples. The point is that whether or not Cox can somehow deny in theory that he rules out the supernatural order, his devotees—including a number of priests and religious—have evidently not shared the finesse and

---

of both Karl Barth and Rudolf Bultmann, especially the latter's attempts to remove "myth" from the New Testament.

vi   August 22-25, 1968.

vii   *The Secular City* is a book written by Dr. Cox in 1965. In it, he argued "that the Church is primarily a people of faith and action, rather than an institution." He argued "'God is just as present in the secular as the religious realms of life.' Far from being a protective religious community, [he said] the Church should be in the forefront of change in society, celebrating the new ways religiosity is finding expression in the world." Many saw phrases such as "intrinsic conservatism prevents the denominational churches from leaving their palaces behind and stepping into God's permanent revolution in history" as embracing the social revolution of the 1960s.

viii This was the First International Symposium on Belief, held March 22-27, 1969, a sponsor of which was the Vatican Secretariat for Non-Believers. The Holy See later suppressed this dicastery.

verbal gymnastics required to avoid such a position. Whether they say it or not, they profess a flagrant secularism in the practical order by their words and deeds that is nothing more than a warmed-up Pelagianism.[ix] One can verify this by the resultant attacks—big and small—against the doctrine of the Fall (i.e., original sin).

In case some have read this far and still doubt the concrete consequences of naïvely sucking in the whole bait of secularism, let me list just a few of the many disastrous effects.

Regarding liturgy, we have seen what can happen when no distinction is made between the sacred and the secular, between the cultic and the profane, between worship and recreation (and we may still have yet to watch it carried to the blackest limits of desecration).

And as we pray, so we believe. In doctrine, we see a similar effort by some to eviscerate all content, to bypass articles of revealed truth, to discard any reference to the supernatural acts of God, to mute the divine mysteries, to smother the otherworldly asceticism of the Cross.

In its place, we are immersed in humanistic, worldly "life experiences" and purely social platitudes. In the name of secular relevance, our ears are bombarded by sloganism. The objection here is not to new methodology in catechesis, but to what is really a "new" gospel, a worldly un-doctrine.

[ix]   This is "the belief that original sin did not taint human nature (which, being created from God, was divine), and that mortal will is still capable of choosing good or evil without Divine aid. Thus, Adam's sin was 'to set a bad example' for his progeny, but his actions did not have the other consequences imputed to original sin. Pelagianism views the role of Jesus as 'setting a good example' for the rest of humanity (thus counteracting Adam's bad example). In short, humanity has full control, and thus full responsibility, for its own salvation in addition to full responsibility for every sin (the latter insisted upon by both proponents and opponents of Pelagianism). Since humanity is no longer in need of any of God's graces beyond the creation of will, Jesus' sacrifice is devoid of its redemptive quality."

Without a transcendent God Who establishes an objective moral law, situation ethics[x] poisons the ethical atmosphere of the modern world with absolute subjectivism and a chaotic appeal to the sovereign self-sufficiency of the conscience of Everyman. The traditional and perennial allowance for diminishing or aggravating circumstances and the "voluntary" of a given human act has been isolated and elevated to the only norm. Since it suffers no divine guidance, grace, or Magisterium, self reigns supreme.

This new theory reduces the visible Church, as established by God the Son, to a merely human organization. It judges the bishops and the pope as mere politicians. It sees the People of God not as the Family of God, nor even as the Body of Christ in this world, but as just another worldly socio-political aggregation.

The new theorists and activists demand—contrary to Christ's constitution—that the Church function as an absolute democracy (which could easily become the worst type of tyranny). They would promote unionism and politicking, pitting "labor" (i.e., bishops, priests, people) versus "management" (i.e., pope, bishop, pastor). This is not the collegiality of the Council. Rather, it is a secularism that denies the "otherness" (i.e., the transcendence) of the Church.

In religious life, we see the heart-rending spectacle of some monasteries and convents rushing to "identify" with this world, as if the word had only one meaning in the vocabulary of Jesus and His Church. Such souls have made the *saeculum* their *sacrum*.[xi] Precisely in this most painful and sensitive area we see how some have reversed the entire thrust of the Incarnation. Is not the mission of consecrated souls to transform the world by imitating Christ?

Moreover, how in the name of the Incarnation can anyone ever claim the Church should be transformed by the world? The Incarnation inserts the divine into the human. It thus acts like leaven in the mass of dough in order to transform and raise it to a higher

---

[x]   The belief that situations dictate what is ethical in any given situation, not objective moral norms or the Natural Law.

[xi] In other words, they have made the age what is holy to them.

subsistence, a higher level. The point is not to let oneself be dragged to a lower level, not to be overcome by fallen nature, not to succumb to the "flesh."

"They who belong to Christ have crucified their flesh with its passions and desires."[9] The world is crucified to Paul and he to the world.[10]

The new secularism, then, is a demonic promotion of original sin. It is diametrically opposed to the saving, redeeming, and transforming mission of Jesus the Christ, true God and true Man.

Most firmly do I believe—as we must all believe—that the gates of hell will never prevail against the Church. Yet, humanly speaking, if the powers-that-be allow the present course of secularism to infect the People of God, hell would indeed prevail. Therefore, we have confidence and fervently pray that by the example and the teaching of courageous men and women of God who understand the biblical paradox of loving the world and fleeing it, the Church will soon check this desacralization.

The Apostle Paul saw the cosmos, our beloved but fallen world, as a vast missionary arena. He labored and died for its potential conversion to the Lord. He reminded us to love the world as Christ loved it, by evangelizing it and transforming it.

CHAPTER 8

"I Am, Indeed, a King!"[1]

"You know then how to read the face of the sky, but you cannot read the signs of the times" (Matt 16:3).

On the verge of what seemed to be the ultimate defeat, a condemned man had the most unlikely question in history posed to him: "Are you then a king?"

Then came the even more unlikely reply: "You yourself say so: I am a king."[2] Only a faithful few at that moment of crisis believed that the carpenter's son was more than a condemned man.

Since he never calls Him "King," it might seem on the surface that Paul, whose Corinthian correspondence we have discussed, has little or nothing to say of Christ's kingship.

Nothing could be further from the truth. Paul prefers a different word, *Kyrios* (Lord). This was the title of the Roman emperor, whose worship, as we read in the early Church Fathers, was summarized by the acclamation, *"Kyrios Kaiser!"*[i]

No true Christian could accept this.

From the earliest days, the heroic counter-confession *"Kyrios Iesous Christos!"* affirmed the universal kingship of Christ.[3] Moreover, this title *Kyrios* connoted divinity. The Septuagint consistently translates the Hebrew term for the Lord God *Yahweh-Adonai* as *Kyrios*.

Thus the phrase "Jesus is Lord," which seems so common to us today was in reality revolutionary: "Jesus, the crucified and risen, is Emperor-King! He is God!"

---

[i]   Lord-Emperor.

Therefore, in the New Testament, the titles *Basileus* (King) and *Kyrios* (Lord) confess Christ's dominion. "Kingdom" in the New Testament (as Schnackenburg has thoroughly documented in his book *The Church in the New Testament*)[ii] refers primarily to the Church. The title "king," then, evokes the thought of Christ as ruler of the Church, the new Israel. "Lord," however, more appropriately describes the dominion of Christ over the whole universe, over all visible and invisible creation, including the angelic "princes" of the nations. There is no doubt that Paul teaches both of these overlapping extensions of kingship.

Let us isolate just a few of the remarkable characteristics of Jesus' kingdom. First, "My kingdom is not of this world." At the opening of the Synod last week,[iii] Pope Paul said one cannot identify the Church with any earthly form of government. He specifically corrected those who claim collegiality must precisely mean what "democracy" means. As with worldly kingdoms, the transcendent kingdom-Church is a visible, structured, and hierarchical institution with juridical, legal, and executive powers. But how different, how "other"!

In earthly kingdoms, external conformism satisfies the law. We must do certain things (pay taxes); we must not do certain others (bomb the offices of the Internal Revenue Service). No earthly rule could presume more (at least successfully). Yet the law of Christ, a law that is pure love and freedom, demands an unconditional surrender of the whole person. It penetrates to the inner citadel, and governs the internal forum of mind, heart, soul, will, and even emotions.

There are no limits to this dominion. Thus, in *Lumen Gentium* (Dogmatic Constitution on the Church), the Council demands that all Catholics give internal assent to the ordinary Magisterium of the pope. Is it any wonder, then, why those who do not understand the biblical nature of the kingdom rebel against the rule of the vicar?

---

ii   Rudolf Schnackenburg, twentieth century professor of New Testament exegesis at the University of Würzburg in Germany.

iii   First Extraordinary Assembly of the Synod of Bishops, September 11-October 28, 1969.

One clearly sees how in the person of the Holy Father all ecclesial authority participates in the mystery of Christ: The higher the authority, the more one becomes a suffering servant obedient unto death.

No one is more fully bound to obedience than the pope, who bears the keys to bind and loose. This is one reason why he cannot give into the demands and whims of the multitude.

The enforcement powers and sanctions of this greatest of all kingdoms are not material or physical, but simply moral. Love is the adhesive "force" of the kingdom, and this love is also transcendent. It is the sacrificial love exemplified by the Cross.

Hence, the crisis today: The love that is in the air is no longer the love of Christ, but the "love" of earthly power, humanism, and secularism, and this cannot hold the Church together. As the Holy Father asked last spring, "Where is love for the Church?"[iv]

[iv]   The talk actually took place in September 1968 at Castel Gandolfo. Here is the quote in context: "A spirit of corrosive criticism has become fashionable in certain sectors of Catholic life. Some want to go beyond what the solemn assemblies of the Church have authorized, envisaging not only reforms but upheavals, which they think they themselves can authorize and which they consider all the more clever the less they are faithful to tradition. Where is the consistency and dignity that belong to true Christians? Where is love for the Church?"

CHAPTER 9

FIRST CORINTHIANS 12: WE ARE ONE BODY[1]

"You know then how to read the face of the sky, but you cannot read the signs of the times" (Matt 16:3).

Volumes have been written on the theology of the Mystical Body of Christ (i.e., the Church). Pius XII summarized much of this studious reflection in his masterful encyclical, *Mystici Corporis Christi* (On the Mystical Body of Christ). In the face of all this, any thought of condensing the unfathomable image of the Church as Christ's mystical Body into a few paragraphs is indeed a mission impossible.

A less presumptuous approach, then, is to look at and single out some very specific points St. Paul makes on this topic. This is a fine example of the form-critical approach that stressed the "situation in life" (*Sitz im Leben*).[i] Paul develops the theme of Body throughout the epistles and notably in Ephesians 4:15 and Colossians 1:18. But what specifically is the situation, the real, existential life context of First Corinthians 12?

We began our consideration of First Corinthians with the assertion that it is strikingly modern. Ancient Corinth had factions, and so do we. Corinth had liturgical abuses, and so do we. Corinth had charismatic chaos and Pentecostalist pandemonium, and— perhaps with sympathetic vibrations from Fr. MacNutt[ii]—we may

---

i   A German phrase meaning "setting in life." It deals with the events and thus context that gave rise to various biblical passages.

ii   Fr. Francis MacNutt, OP, who claims to have been baptized in the Spirit in 1967, after which he helped found the Catholic charismatic movement. He left the priesthood to marry in 1980, which caused the Church to

have even more. First Corinthians 12-14 zeros in on the mixed blessings of charismatic expression.

During the apostolic age, the Holy Spirit lavished wonders of grace on individual Christians for the benefit of the whole community. The Holy Spirit gave these "pentecostal" graces not so much for the sake of the individual as for the foundation and edification of the nascent Church. The functions of prophecy, tongues, interpretation, and miracles were among the charisms, and we can see them as providential given the historical and cultural milieu of the first century, where Gentiles expected these gifts as vital signs of religious life.

Paul recognizes and appreciates these genuine gifts. In these chapters, however, he demonstrates alarm at the abuses and forgeries that readily attach to such individualistic and emotional expressions. A detailed study of these charisms would be fascinating and would serve to alert us to the danger of reading Chapter 12 superficially. (It would also prove too complex for our purposes here.)

Paul stresses the need to distinguish the function from the person. He notes that, by definition, the charism is for the promotion of the Church. It does not place a divine seal of approval upon the individual.

Next, he rebukes the preference for the exotic gifts (pointedly, he mentions *glossolalia*, i.e., the gift of tongues, last). He reminds us that teaching, administration, and the offices of authority are more essential and truly of the same Spirit. We surely ought to recognize the problem he treats here. How often we separate "charismatic" from "institutional." How often we engage in personality cult—following a prolix, brash, innovative lecturer or writer like a herd of witless sheep. How often we prefer the exotic (not to mention the neurotic) to the routine. How often we criticize authority, as if the personality

---

excommunicate him and stripped him of his priestly faculties (however the Church recognized his marriage in 1993). He is still active in his reportedly effective charismatic healing ministry, which is based in Florida. At this writing, he is 81.

of a person in authority (the pope, let us say) were of more importance than his divinely constituted function (e.g., faithfully upholding and teaching revealed truth).

Here we see an application of the "testing of spirits" that the primitive Church universally stressed. The citations in my notes from Scripture and the Church Fathers are too numerous to list. Forms of the verb *dokimazein* ("test out and approve") are a technical index of this practice.[2] Elsewhere (e.g., Rom 1:29-32; Gal 5:16-26), Paul says if the Holy Spirit is genuinely operative, the proof-signs are charity, peace, joy, humility, patience, meekness, kindness, goodness, faith, modesty, and continence. But if on testing the spirit we discover immorality, enmities, contentions, pride, factions, parties, deceit, disobedience, plotting, irreverence, licentiousness, and "whisperings,"[iii] then the inspiration is Satanic.

We read in 1 Timothy 6:3-5, "If anyone teaches otherwise and does not agree with the instruction of our Lord Jesus Christ and that doctrine which is according to godliness, he is proud, knowing nothing, but doting about controversies and disputes of words. From these arise envies, quarrels, blasphemies, base suspicions, the wranglings of men corrupt in mind and bereft of truth, supposing godliness to be an increase in income."

What an inestimable boon it would be if we would consistently apply this apostolic testing of spirits today! When an initiative is taken, a charism claimed, or a "new" doctrine is proposed, what are the fruits? What is the source, the Holy Spirit—or the malignant deceiver? This "testing" is itself a charism, and the final judgment is in the hands of apostolic authority. Paul thus concludes his case by saying that he, as an apostle, is the final arbiter.[3]

Charisms caused factions, but there were numerous more earthly causes: crude ambition; lust for power; just plain lust; intellectual pride; sophistry; false teachers; and so on. Paul has noted that there are many functions but one and the same Spirit. As a living organism, the Body must thrive in a well-ordered, harmonized interdependence

---

iii   i.e., gossiping.

of its functions. Divisions and factionalism in the body cannot be tolerated. Each member must (in a good sense) "do his own thing"— only then will he find perfect fulfillment, and only then will the whole Body thrive. No organ must arrogate to itself the functions of another.

"For the body is not one member, but many... And if the ear says, 'Because I am not an eye, I am not of the body,' is it therefore not of the body? If the whole body were an eye, where would be the hearing? Now if they were all one member, where would the body be?"[4]

In modern terms, we would say that when cells group in rebellion against the bodily hierarchy and against the direction of the head, we have cancer.

Today, under the pretense of collegiality, we see an incredibly naïve attempt of laymen playing priest, priests playing laymen, priests playing bishop, bishops (and priests!) playing pope, Sisters playing airplane, Sisters playing guitar—well, you get the idea: Games People of God Play. Unlike the heresy of conciliarism,[iv] true collegiality cooperates, counsels, and collaborates; it does not usurp.

A third specific "life situation" of Chapter 12 follows from the text of Chapters 10-11, where liturgical abuses provoked a most detailed and precious discourse on the Mass, Holy Communion, and the Eucharist as sacrament and sacrifice. The eucharistic liturgy enables us to live the mysteries of Christ's life as members of His Body. The eucharistic Body (*soma*)[v] quite possibly suggested to Paul the image of the ecclesial body (*soma*). There is a need to see a co-extension between eucharistic unity and Church unity. We use the term "communion" in the sense of union with the sacramental Christ as well as of union with the Church community. This is no coincidence! Only a false ecumenism urges universal inter-Communion before Christianity has realized full ecclesial communion. The Eucharist is the stimulus

---

iv .   A heresy that taught final authority in spiritual matters resided not with the pope but with the Church as a corporation of Christians as embodied by a general Church council.

v   Greek for "body."

and magnetic goal for the labor and prayer of ecumenism. No magic bullet dispenses us from labor and love or from truth and fidelity to revelation.

These, then, are just three special lessons of First Corinthians 12. However poorly and however fleetingly, let us now back up to see the full range of the image of the Body of Christ.

The Church is a living organism, human and divine. It is not a merely societal organization of this world. It has one life, supernatural grace, which is the communication of the very life of Jesus the Lord. In a plurality of members, each with its own function, there is a unity of mind, heart, and purpose. The mind that is in the members is also in Christ Jesus.[5] There are an interdependence and hierarchy of members and organs that coordinate growth, promote progress, govern directions, and stimulate action. There is one faith, one Lord, one baptism, and, as Christ's Body, there is but one Father. Pain and joy, weakness and strength, defeat and triumph are shared by all, diffused through all, remedied by all.

In Ephesians, Paul adds that Christ is Head of His Body, which is the Church, the center of a common and united knowing and direction. The same Holy Spirit animates and "inspires" the Body. In Colossians, this vision is expanded to the dizzy limits of the cosmos, where Christ the King is Lord of all creation. "*All things* are recapitulated in Him."[6] The Greek text clearly brings home the truth: Christ brings all things under His "headship."

It is our glory and our loving labor to advance the growth of the Body, to make the kingdom come, to subject ourselves and all creation to the blessed Lordship of Jesus.

CHAPTER 10

"OF ALL THINGS ... INVISIBLE"[1]

"You know then how to read the face of the sky, but you cannot read the signs of the times" (Matt 16:3).

In 1968, Pope Paul issued *The Credo of the People of God*.[i] It is an updated expansion of the Nicene Creed in the light of the Second Vatican Council. It opens by confessing faith in God, the Creator of all things visible and invisible, "that is, the angels."

This is a reaffirmation of the constant belief of the Church in the existence of angelic spirits. Ecumenical Councils (e.g., Lateran IV), theological tradition (remember the "Angelic Doctor"?), and, even more constantly, the Mass have continuously and firmly upheld this belief.

With angels, as with so many other doctrines, it remained for the late 1960s to discover how wrong the Church has been since apostolic days and how poorly the Holy Spirit has been guiding the successors of the apostles. With regard to angels and spirits, a few men, usually having some liaison with Scripture studies, began to tell us that we have been honoring and fearing nothing! Rank superstition!

---

[i]   According to the July 11, 1968, issue of *L'Osservatore Romano*, Paul VI inaugurated the Year of Faith in 1967 "to mark the 1,900th anniversary of the martyrdom of Peter and Paul. He closed it in 1968 in St. Peter's Square, proclaiming *The Credo of the People of God*. This is a profession of faith, as he himself said, based on 'the creed of Nicaea, the creed of the immortal Tradition of the Holy Church of God,' but enriched by the fruits of the Council and prompted by the difficult problems of the new era."

Meanwhile, eminent scholars like Karl Rahner[ii] and Jean Daniélou[iii] (who last year was just great, but since then has been declared suspect without due process by the Holy Office of Greeley, Sheerin,[iv] et al.) ignored the fools who rushed in to tread on angels.

Rahner, for example, uses the traditional angelology for some fresh insights on life after death. Daniélou, a specialist on primitive Jewish Christian theology, devastates the specious arguments of the angel-killers. Teilhard,[v] after exhaustively sketching the *phyla* [vi] and species of corporeal life, asks this question: How can it be that this prodigious creativity ceases at man, the crown of material being, and that a lifeless vacuum gapes between man and God? His supposition is that, beyond man, whom God created "a little less than the angels," there exists an equally prolific variety of spiritual beings. We could greatly extend this list of theologians, Catholic and Protestant, liberal and conservative, who affirm angels.

A few years ago, an itinerant priest-lecturer stumped in a certain diocese "somewhere in the United States" and discovered there what he apparently hadn't found elsewhere: a fertile crop of itching ears. Along with volumes of speculative and practical propositions (many

---

ii   German Jesuit theologian who died in 1984 and was hugely influential in twentieth century Catholicism, especially at the Second Vatican Council.

iii Jean Cardinal Daniélou, SJ, another influential theologian whose work influenced the Council. He died in 1974.

iv   Fr. John Sheerin, CSP, Paulist priest and editor of the now defunct *Catholic World* magazine.

v   Fr. Pierre Teilhard de Chardin, SJ, French paleontologist and philosopher who denied the traditional Catholic understanding of original sin. This led the Holy See to condemn his writings, which were never published during his lifetime. Instead, they were mimeographed and otherwise copied and passed hand-to-hand around the world. Today, his books are widely available. On June 30, 1962, the Holy Office issued a monitum (i.e., warning) regarding the writings of Fr. Teilhard de Chardin. In 1981 the Holy See reiterated this warning against rumors that it no longer applied.

vi   Phyla is plural for phylum, a broad category of the animal or plant kingdom into which organisms are divided. Thus phylum is practically the same definition as genus.

of them harmless, but some of them both false and harmful), he reportedly declared that angels don't exist. This soon became a *cause célèbre*, eclipsing everything else he said. It forevermore became his trademark.

Overnight it became the fad—especially among priests and Sisters—to banish the angels. Angel hunts were popular, even in the grade schools. Enlightened by reflectors of the luminary, the children could now correct the stubborn superstitions of their parents. "No, mommy, I won't say 'Angel of God, my guardian dear!'" Wild-eyed curates rushed to the belfries twice daily to club the parish Quasimodos down from the Angelus rope.

The pathetic element in this and similar denials of Church doctrine (divorce, euthanasia, abortion, and so on) is that overnight some consecrated men and women, on the word of one lecturer and without further investigation, turned their backs on a lifetime of belief, prayer, liturgical confession, and two millennia of Catholic teaching! A priest who lived in that diocese said when he dared to question this development, some ridiculed him as a "damn fool!"

Some gullibly expressed that rejecting a "small doctrine like angels" would make little difference. But as Rahner cautions in his treatise *On Heresy*, truth is a living, organic whole. To attack any article causes immediate and profound distortions of the corpus of revealed truth in all its parts and in its totality. We might add that Jesus the Word, the existential, personal Object of our faith-act, declared, "I am the Truth." To attack any doctrine is to attack Christ, to blur our vision of His message, to begin to apostatize, and to withdraw our total act of faith. And we observe this phenomenon, which is an incubation of apostasy, in those who began by expelling the angels.

Those who seek an erudite pretense for denial say we got the angel concept from the Persian doctrine of *Amesha Spenta*.[vii] Mowinckel demolishes this by citing earlier Hebrew belief, though

---

[vii] A term of the Zoroastrian religion (originating and largely centered in Persia) meaning "Bounteous Immortal."

admitting that Persian influence was a stimulus and categorizer.[viii] But beyond that, there are a few other tenets of late Judaism that might be similarly credited to Persian influence—"little" things such as immortality of the soul, retribution and reward in an after-life, resurrection of the body, and so on. Now, logical consistency would demand that we also jettison these. After all, why stop at eliminating the angels?

The overwhelming fact is that while Jewish doctrine was an ongoing revelation, the fullness of truth is revealed in Christ. One of the fringe benefits of the disciplines of archeology and comparative religion is to behold how Christ fulfilled the aspirations and brought the gift of divine revelation to all the nations. Jesus canonized these concepts (angels included) regardless of their origin, and His Church has always confessed, prayed to, and revered some angels, while praying against and exorcising others.[ix]

Now, to deny angels is to deny devils. To deny devils is to do nothing to combat their wiles and snares. Is it a coincidence that, from the time we deny angels and devils, an incredibly infectious and malignant decadence sets in?

St. Paul often refers to the "Mystery of God," the divine plan unfolding in the history of mankind and signaled by His mighty saving acts—what is technically called *Heilsgeschichte*, salvation history.[x] But in Second Thessalonians, Paul outlines a parallel economy, the "Mystery of Iniquity." Satan, too, has a plan he wants to effect in man's history. He, too, has mighty acts. A seductive *Übels-Geschichte*[xi] counters the *Heilsgeschichte* in the arena of the world. Satan will, in the latter days, prepare for and propagate an anti-Christ. This person will establish among us what Bishop Sheen

---

viii Sigmund Mowinckel, prominent Swedish Old Testament scholar.

ix Editor's note: Recall that demons and Satan are fallen angels.

x According to Dr. Tim Bulkeley, who teaches Old Testament studies at Carey College in Auckland, New Zealand, this was "used in Old Testament studies in the '50s, as a theological principle, reading Scripture as the story of God's redeeming acts in history."

xi The literal translation is "evil history."

once called the "mystical body of Satan." Then will take place the definitive battle between good and evil.

We need to promote the touching little prayer to the "Angel of God" with zeal among all the children of God.[xii] And only of such—young and old—is the kingdom of heaven.

At a time when the power of Satan's angelic intellect is becoming more and more manifest to the eyes of pious and faithful Catholics, it is even more urgent that we renew in our daily private devotions the prayer to St. Michael the Archangel. Can you recall the words?[xiii] This prayer is timelier now than when Leo XIII initiated it.

In one of his epistles, St. Paul exhorts us, "Put on the armor of God, that you may be able to stand against the wiles of the devil. For our wrestling is not against flesh and blood, but ... against the spiritual forces of wickedness on high ... in all things taking up the shield of faith, with which you may be able to quench all the fiery missiles of the most wicked one."[2]

Oh, you're wondering what happened to that itinerant priest-lecturer?

He married an angel!

[xii]   Angel of God, my guardian dear, to whom God's love commits me here, ever this day be at my side to light, to guard, to rule, and guide. Amen.

[xiii]   Saint Michael the Archangel, defend us in battle. Be our protection against the wickedness and snares of the devil. May God rebuke him, we humbly pray; and do thou, O Prince of the heavenly host, by the power of God, cast into hell Satan and all the evil spirits who prowl about the world seeking the ruin of souls. Amen.

CHAPTER 11

THE FAMILY OF GOD[1]

"You know then how to read the face of the sky, but you cannot read the signs of the times" (Matt 16:3).

During an early session of the Second Vatican Council, a missionary bishop made an intervention asking that the Council's thematic concept be the "Family of God" rather than the "People of God."

The bishop remarked that in the vast missionary world, with its tribal orientation, "family" would be a much more comprehensible term. But in light of Scripture, it is abundantly clear that the People of God *are* the Family of God.

Now this is not a mere fuss about terms. The Council was inspired in retaining the profound biblical terminology of the "People of God." But the missionary bishop was also right. It makes every difference in the world (as we have so painfully learned) what kind of "people" is meant. In Scripture, the Holy People are a Holy Family.

When the "people" were constituted by covenant, we must remember something about those Israelites who escaped from Egyptian bondage: They were super-families retaining their familial stamp throughout all trials.

We see this at the outset by the family celebration of the Passover. In the covenant ceremony at Sinai, Moses sealed the creation of the one national People of God by sacrifice.[2] He then sprinkled the sacrificial blood upon the people saying, "This is the blood of the covenant."

Here we may observe the very special meaning attached to this sprinkling with blood.

In the desert pilgrim state, geo-political boundaries could not achieve anything approaching a national unity. The only unifying force, therefore, was the blood bond of family, and although the original family ties were largely legal fictions by this time, Moses ritually affected the unity of blood of this People that was also a Family. The prophets fortify this view of covenant with the bold image of Yahweh married to His people, who are bride and spouse.

Now when one turns to the New Testament, there echoes from beginning to end the intimate dialogue of Father and Son. This Child who was born to us is also a Son Who has been given to us. The Father so loved the world that He sent us His only Son.[3] The sustaining meat of this Son was to do perfectly and always the will of His beloved Father.[4] The Son was obedient unto death. In agony over the prospect of the cross, He emerged as a Son who in freedom and maturity could tell His Father, "Not My will but Your will be done."[5] And He prayed with His last breath, "Father, into Your hands I commend My spirit."[6]

Because of this love, the Father glorified His name and raised Him in glory from the dead.[7] So the golden thread of family, spun in the Old Testament, runs brilliantly through the perfected fabric of the New.

"When the fullness of time came... God sent His Son, born of a woman, that we might receive the adoption of Sons."[8] He has given us also the Spirit of adoption, Who enables us to cry out, "Abba!" the intimate child's word for Father. We are now co-heirs with Christ.[9] What He is by nature, God makes us by the adoption of grace. Brothers with Him, we are sons of the Father. "I am in My Father, and you in Me, and I in you... If anyone loves me ... My Father will love him, and we will come to him and abide in him."[10] "That all may be one, even as You Father in Me and I in You; that they also may be one in Us."[11]

Thus, the Son initiates us into the intimate life of the Trinity, and, taught by the Son, we dare to say, "Our Father."

In the Gospels, we discover the resolution of one of the most vexing problems of our times in the Person of Christ: the relation of freedom and obedience. Following the easy route, so many see freedom and obedience as exclusive contradictories. Yet on every page the Gospels show these two things are complementary. In relation to God the Father and God the Son, they present to us adopted sons a harmony that is perfect. Who was more perfectly obedient than Christ? Who could ever wish to be freer than Christ? This is the pattern of genuine authority in the Church, which only grows distorted when the spirit of family is smothered.

The human family, the Holy Family into which Jesus willed to be born and in which His saving Life unfolded, further illustrates the relation of the Father to the Son (which is the heartbeat of the Church). He was subject to Mary and Joseph through long, hidden years, and He grew in age, grace, and wisdom.[12] The Church asks us to meditate on this Family and make its spirit our own. It is no wonder that at a time when the family is disintegrating, the problem of freedom and obedience is exacerbated, and the love of the Church as a Holy Family declines.

At the Last Supper, along with the John 14-17 discourse (which is filled with constant and tender references to His Father), the Son of God initiated the new Covenant and established the new People of God. In solemn imitation of the words of Moses, He declared, "This is the new Covenant in My Blood."[13] Not satisfied with a mere sprinkling of the blood of a substitute, however, He gave us His own Blood—the Blood of the Son—as drink. So this new people in His Blood gather from all nations and tongues, and transcend all bounds of maps or politics. The only bond that can bind a Catholic people is blood. We are one with the Son, Who vivifies and unifies us. We are the universal "Family of God."

In a good Christian family, we experience an analogue of the Divine Community. The human family is seen in clearest focus as it gathers around the supper table. In the usual experience of families, the evening meal best teaches what life is all about. The father returns from his daily, routine, self-sacrificing work. The mother serves the food she has purchased and prepared. Sharing in the labor and life of their parents, sons and daughters gather around the table.

Here we see the true nature of human love—giving and receiving, productive and sacrificial. The food on the table represents the work of all and is the essential element for the life and growth of all. During the meal, there builds up an aura of love, unity, peace, and delight in labor's dignity. The family shares joys and triumphs, but also sorrows and failures.

The family thrives as a society that is the most rooted in nature, one that is both democratic and monarchic. The genuine freedom of sons, in perfect harmony with the father's fullest authority, is realized in this atmosphere. And when a child is blessed with a good and pious father (as is ideal), he will understand what it means to call God his Father. If the family fully shares in the supernatural life of grace, then the home becomes another Church, and the table becomes a reflection of the altar.

At this point, we can reassert that it makes every difference in the world that the People of God is a family. Since the Council (and contrary to its spirit), we have seen a corrosive attempt to interpret "People" in a way strictly equated to some transient form or purely human political society. Usually the attempt strikes out in the direction of modern democracy, and, in this country, we have naturally been tempted to twist and contort the transcendent Church into the form and image of American democracy.

The results have been disastrous. The heart has gone out of the institution, and in its place, would-be revolutionaries have introduced a compounded neurosis of bureaucracy and power politicking. We see Machiavellian maneuvering for positions, unionism of the clergy, slogans and platitudes to neutralize the masses, externalism in worship, and aping of the secular in a direction exactly counter to that of the Incarnation. But this new conciliarism is a subject all in itself. (And a hot subject it would be!)

What alternative do we have to this state of affairs? The alternative is to realize that although the Church is *sui generis*[i] (i.e., not susceptible of strict parallel with any one form of secular government), it is most approximate to the spirit of the family. Once more, the supernatural builds on the natural.

So much hinges on the family, and especially on the Gospel pattern of the Father-Son, which is the spirit of all authority in the Church. If a son's experience was wonderful in the family, he will know well how one can be truly free and yet obey. He will learn at home that the best kind of democracy is that of the monarchic family. He will never for a moment regard authority in the Church as mere paternalism, but rather will see and revere true spiritual paternity, whereby sons and daughters are begotten in the Gospel of Grace.[14]

This is precisely what the two Testaments teach us. From the warm hearth of a good and holy home filled by smiling children, security and reverence grow up to join the universal holy Family of God and to gather around that altar where the God of sacrificial love communicates eternal Life to them. For such blessed children of the Church, the "little ones," the home is another Church, and the Church is another home.[ii]

---

[i]   A Latin phrase that, in scholastic philosophy, indicates "an idea, an entity, or a reality that cannot be included in a wider concept;" unique, one of a kind, not repeatable.

[ii]   Editor's note: For an amplification of this, see *Lumen Gentium*, no. 11, and *The Priesthood of the Laity in the Domestic Church* by H. Lyman Stebbins (out-of-print but occasionally available online).

CHAPTER 12

WHO ARE OUR HEROES?[1]

"You know then how to read the face of the sky, but you cannot read the signs of the times" (Matt 16:3).

A friend once loaned me a book of incredible power and beauty. Titled *The Porter of St. Bonaventure,*[2] it concerns the Capuchin Fr. Solanus Casey, a native of Superior, Wisconsin.

It relates how, after various jobs and later than is customary, Barney Casey joined the Capuchins. He had insuperable problems with his studies. It was only because certain influential superiors recognized his virtues that he received Holy Orders. (His first Mass, incidentally, was celebrated on Sunday, July 31, 1904, at St. Joseph Church in nearby Appleton.)

There was a condition attached to this ordination, however. Fr. Solanus was to remain a "simplex" priest. In other words, he could never hear confessions, and his preaching was restricted.

Eventually, he became porter of busy St. Bonaventure Monastery in downtown Detroit. He also was in charge of the Seraphic Mass League. This was fitting because the power of the Holy Mass was something Fr. Solanus never doubted. Thus when people came with problems, he always signed their name to the register of Masses to be offered.

Gradually, whispers about this good priest passed through Detroit. At first timidly and with bewilderment, as if they were afraid of being laughed at, people would mention to intimate friends what had transpired at the doors of St. Bonaventure. The whispers gained voice and became common knowledge. As the years went by, the public became more and more aware of what appeared to be daily, astounding prodigies of grace.

In order not to anticipate the judgment of the Church in this or any of the cases mentioned in this chapter, let it simply be stated that thousands of people were convinced of what the mediation of the humble, jovial porter had wrought. The book lists many of the attested and recorded wonders: sight instantaneously restored to the blind; terminal cancer cured; gangrenous limbs healed; hopeless crippled people commanded to stand and walk. This happened day after day ... in Detroit ... not too long ago. If anyone tactlessly credited Fr. Solanus, his Irish would flare, and he would tell them in no uncertain terms, "It was the Holy Mass, not me! Don't you believe in the power of the Mass?!"

This holy priest died July 31, 1957, at the hour and on the anniversary of his first Mass.[i]

Near the end of this subdued but amazing and beautiful book, the author relates how, on his deathbed, Fr. Solanus kept calling the name of his favorite spiritual son, Fr. Gerald Walker, OFM Cap.

Tears welled in my eyes as I read this, for Fr. Gerald was rector at Mount Calvary when I began my studies for the priesthood, and words can never express what he means to me. And no one will ever convince me that this saintly man's vision of the priesthood that moved us in those splendid seminary days can be anything but true and valid for all times. Modified and deepened, yes. Contradicted or denied, never! When Fr. Gerald walked among us boys, we stood in awe, not quite knowing why; when he spoke to us of Christ, the words burned into our hearts, and God knows how we loved him.

This is one case, near home, almost yesterday of a saint in our midst. Yet God has lavished on our century exceptional, personal "signs of the times." One thinks of Bl. André of Montreal, again a saintly monastery porter, humble, physically weak, and incapable of

---

[i]   The Servant of God John Paul II declared Fr. Casey to be Venerable on July 11, 1995.

studying for the priesthood. He died about 20 years ago,[ii] yet this great promoter of devotion to St. Joseph similarly effected incredible cures, day after day, which touched the lives of thousands of souls, many of whom must be among us today.

There is also Theresa Neumann, who died a few years back,[iii] who bore the wounds of Christ for all to see, and who lived for much of her life on no other food or drink but the Sacred Host. There is Sr. Lucia, the only surviving witness of the visions of Fátima, carrying in her heart secrets which few men yet dream of, visited by Pope Paul at Fátima in 1967, living her days hidden in a convent, still mysteriously waiting to finish the mission given her by Mary.[iv] And there are many more, never publicly noticed by the Church, known only to a few—more than we realize.

Finally, let us recall the magnificent presence of Padre Pio, again a Capuchin priest, who died just a year and a half ago on September 24, 1968.[v] For most of our own century, he lived among us, bearing, like St. Francis, the wounds of Christ in his feet and hands and side. Many people in our own diocese have seen him. Many of our troops during the last World War had the chance to visit him. Always shying away from publicity, always perfectly obedient to the authority of his superiors and the Church, he spent most of his days in the confessional, where he read into the secrets of consciences, revealing the detailed states of the souls of his penitents.

He, too, is credited with thousands of wonders of healing. At times, he bilocated (i.e., was present simultaneously) in places as widely separated from his monastery as South America. During his daily Mass, the flower-scented blood flowed from his wounds, darkening the mitten-like bandages on his hands. But his life is so

---

[ii] Bl. André died in 1937 at age 90. His feast is January 6.
[iii] September 18, 1962. Her cause for beatification is pending.
[iv] Sr. Lucia went to her reward on February 13, 2005. On the third anniversary of her death, the Pope allowed her cause to be opened.
[v] John Paul II canonized him in 2002.

full of prodigies that it is best to leave the details to those who will feel moved to read one of the several excellent biographies about him.

However, it is worth noting how a week before he died, Padre Pio wrote—with a crucified hand—a letter to Pope Paul, part of which I will quote here:

> Holiness, I wish to take advantage of your meeting with the Capitulary Fathers to join spiritually with my fellow monks in laying at your feet my affectionate homage, all my devotion to your August Person in the act of faith, love and obedience to the dignity of Him whom you represent on earth. The Capuchin Order has always been foremost in love, faith, obedience, and devotion to the Apostolic See: I pray God that this may always be so and that it may continue in its tradition of religious seriousness and austerity, Evangelical poverty, faithful observance of the Rule and of the Constitutions, while renewing itself in vitality and internal spirit according to the decision of the Second Vatican Council in order to be more and more ready to run to the aid of Mother Church at a sign from our Holiness.
>
> I know that your heart is suffering greatly these days for the destiny of the Church, for peace in the world, for the many needs of the peoples of the world, but above all for the lack of obedience of some, even Catholics, to the great teaching that you, with the aid of the Holy Spirit and in the name of God, give us. I offer you my daily prayers and suffering as a small but sincere thought from the least of your children, that the Lord may comfort you with His Grace and help you to continue along the straight and difficult path in the defense of the eternal truth that does not change with the changing of the times. Also I wish to thank you for the clear and decisive words you pronounce, especially in the last Encyclical *Humanae Vitae* and I once more affirm my faith and unconditional obedience to your illuminated orders.

> May God grant the triumph of the truth and peace
> to His Church, tranquility to the peoples of the world,
> health and prosperity to Your Holiness so that these
> temporary clouds may be dissipated and the Kingdom
> of God triumph in all hearts through your apostolic
> work as Supreme Pastor of all Christianity. Prostrate at
> your feet, I implore your blessing... Your Holiness' most
> humble son. P. Pio, Capuchin."[3]

Now, scant as this survey has been, the impact is staggering. These are the heroes whose example we are invited to follow. God has wonderfully approved them, some by visibly sealing them in the flesh. It is not these people's extraordinary signs, but the virtues and attitudes to which these signs point that show us true interior renewal and reform. And it is this alone that will provide the external and structural renewal sought by the Council and for which we must all pray and work. By focusing on those individuals whom I have, I do not slight the canonized saints of the past. I only mention these because they lived in our very days. They were subject to our scrutiny.

And then there are those who were not subject to our scrutiny and yet who are no less heroes. Indeed, these men and women represent the most neglected mystery of our Lord's life. It is a mystery as profound as the Resurrection, the hidden life. For 30 years, God incarnate, in human flesh, omnipotent, omniscient, with a mission to save the world, stayed silently at home, unnoticed, in prayer and preparation.

Today, we rush out to action, take to the streets, and man the ideological barricades while neglecting and sometimes denying the need for preparation, for solitude, for prayer. The holy men and women who are hidden (the saintly nuns in our hospitals, for example) understand and love the mystery of the veiled life without neglecting God's work in the world. Many who have eyes and see never realize that these are the living, personal signs of the times: These are the movers and the eventual conquerors of human destiny.

All of these people, the hidden and the visible, God appoints as our heroes. He appoints them for all of us, but especially for our youth.

If I present these thoughts even more clumsily than usual for this column, it is because I write with emotion. Take only the words of Padre Pio cited above. When we consider who wrote this letter, how can we explain the fanatic eagerness of so many who still claim to be Catholic yet choose their idols from amongst the dissenters, the rebellious, and the anti-papal scholars (so many of whom have tragically and publicly become spiritual shipwrecks)? Why do we persistently call these men to our platforms, sit at their feet, listen to them with itching ears, pay them, applaud them, and credit them with "formation"?

If our times are to be redeemed, if peace, unity, and love are ever to be granted our world, the Council must succeed. But the Council will never be implemented unless our priests are holy, humble, and obedient. And this all depends on our seminaries, which must appreciate the mystery of Christ's first 30 years and introduce the young disciples of Christ to the holy heroes whom God has raised among us.

CHAPTER 13

THE ACT OF FAITH[1]

"You know then how to read the face of the sky, but you cannot read the signs of the times" (Matt 16:3).

So often we tend to think of our Faith as something very complicated and intricate. And in some ways, it is. ("Oh, the depths of the riches of the wisdom and the knowledge of God. How incomprehensible are His judgments, how unsearchable His ways."[2])

But it is urgent that we clearly and sharply see just how divinely simple our Catholic Faith also is. In a time of tangled sophistries and web-like confusion, nothing can be more comforting and confirming than to see the utter simplicity of what we mean by "religion" and "faith."

First, let us set our eyes on Jesus in the Gospels. John the Baptist introduced Him to the public. Our Lord next invites the Twelve and convinces them to follow Him. He moves among the people and makes astounding assertions about His Person and mission. As the crowds listen to Him, the sense of crisis heightens. Jesus demands each should confront Him, person to person, and make a final, absolute decision to "accept" or "reject" Him.[3]

It is nothing less than their total surrender that Jesus demands. They must love Him with their whole mind, their whole heart, and their whole soul. They must adhere to Him with their whole will. They must hold nothing back.

This initial act of faith fully engages the intellect, but seen in its totality, it also entails love, hope, and trust (i.e., emotions as well as the intellect). So considered, the act of faith encompasses the believer, who dies to self in order to enter into eternal life. It is a communication involving all the dynamics of personality, both human and divine. And since this involves connaturality, there must be, under the infusion of grace, an adoption of the creature into the Life of the Creator. "He came unto His own, and His own people received Him not. But as many as did receive Him, to these He gave the power to be the sons of God."[4] This initial act is, then, the "act of faith" in its core, its seed.

How simple! With the fullest freedom and love, a person surrenders unconditionally to the person of Jesus. Paradoxically, this radically free act of surrender that makes us servants also renders us fully free.

Faith is *seeing*. The disparity of natures—our visible human natures; His invisible divine nature—is overcome by faith, which empowers us beyond our nature to see God, "now in a dark way as in a mirror." Faith leads us to the perfection of "vision" when we see Him "face to face even as we are seen." Thus, we speak of the "eyes of faith."

But this initial act is an enduring act! From the simple seed of surrender (so complete that it is a death to self), there begins to grow a new life of interpersonal revelation, of complexity. So it is in every intimate friendship: The first encounter endures and must grow. It is not a matter of a single decision made once and never more pursued. Rather, it is a quest to know more and more the mind and will of the Beloved.

If the man of faith really loves Jesus, he must spend his whole life listening to every word, following every step, sharing every event and work, and straining toward the fullness of vision in eternity. The act of faith continues, deepens, expands, intensifies, describes, and formulates a creed, or it is not living, not genuine.

How hollow and fatuous are the claims of some who say, "I love Jesus." Because implicit behind that claim is this statement: "I love Jesus, but I have no desire to hear what He says or know what words He came to communicate to us for our salvation. I love Jesus, and I believe some of His words, but others just aren't relevant. Some of His teachings have no value for me. I just choose those I think are essential. I love Jesus, but, really? When it comes right down to it, I just couldn't care less what He wants me to do. Love is one thing, but law is quite another. He was surely wrong when He said, 'If you love Me, keep My commandments.'

"Honestly, since the Vatican II renewal, we know how medieval and outdated some of His commandments are. For instance, He formed a Church that He said we need to listen to or get treated as outcasts. But I don't want anything to do with an institution. He established a teaching authority to speak in His name, to bind and loose, but I just love Jesus, not the institution He created. I love Jesus, but I reject doctrine, creed, precept, and sacrament. I love Jesus, not His Body, the Church, and so on." (And this outrageous, irrational hypocrisy is commonplace these days.)

The experience of human love serves as an analogy of how we must approach our relationship with our Lord. The first tryst cannot be the last, and, unless it be a travesty, love dare not be a mere unformed expression. Once engaged, love is tested and proved every hour and day by deepening, by seeking, by anticipating, and by fulfilling no matter what the sacrifice. And so it is in the engagement of the believing soul with Jesus the Lord.

And the Catholic knows the Church is His Body, and that He continues to live and be encountered in her. All we believe and must observe in our Catholic Faith is implicit from the Church's first act, and Jesus continues to unfold and explicate these beliefs and observations through His Church. Christ is the Word made Flesh. His Person is the Word, but He condescends and adapts His divinity to the limits of our nature in order to communicate. He speaks words, human words with human lips to enlighten our human minds. Unlike angels, we creatures cannot know everything fully and immediately, so Jesus teaches us gradually, patiently, and piecemeal, thus allowing us to adjust to each new degree of understanding. The Word speaks His words, and if we love Him, we hunger for His doctrine and thrive on performing His precepts.

All of this will happen because through faith and the sacraments, we become a part of Him and He of us. C.H. Dodd[i] points out the unusual use of "believe into" (*pisteuein eis*) in the Gospel of St. John.[ii] Thus, the act of faith informed by love and hope allows us to enter "into" Jesus. Faith incorporates us *into* the living Christ and thereby *into* His Body. Faith is the door, the gate *into* the kingdom-Church that is the living body of the Lord. Faith can never be separated from this social, ecclesial context. It cannot exist in isolation or a vacuum.

Thus when we as individuals test, correct, and develop Christ's words, we can only do so *against* the Church, primarily the apostles and their successors to whom Christ said, "He who hears you, hears Me. He who despises you, despises Me. He who despises Me, despises Him who sent Me."[5]

When fully understood, faith in Christ is inseparable from faith in the living Church that continues Him. Faith is *fides quaerens intellectum*.[iii] Here we see the inescapable continuity of the "simple" act of believing *into* Jesus with the consequent "complexity" of the developing teaching of the Church.

The two are inseparable and indispensable aspects of one and the same act of faith. "There is but ... one Lord, one faith..."[6] There can be but one truth since there is but one teacher, and He is divine. This means He is not deceptive, is not contradictory, and cannot be deceived.

And because of our human condition, His truth must be expressed in doctrinal statements and in creeds. We cannot embrace

---

i   Influential Protestant theologian and Welsh New Testament scholar. He believed "Jesus' references to the kingdom of God meant a present reality rather than a future apocalypse."

ii   Cf. John 3:15, 16, 18. What Father refers to here is the more accurate translation of these verses. For instance, many sources normally quote John 3:15 along the lines of "that whoever believes in Him may have eternal life." However, according to Dodd and others, the more accurate translation here is "that whoever believes *into* Him may have eternal life."

iii "Faith seeks understanding."

this Teacher without embracing His doctrine. To the degree men discover the one Mind and Will of the one Person of Jesus, that is the degree we will have unity in the one living Body of Jesus, the Church. This unity depends on union in grace and in the communication of prayer, both private and liturgical, personal and communitarian.

"Now the multitude of the believers were all of one heart and one soul... And they continued steadfastly in the teaching of the apostles and in the communion of the breaking of the bread and in the prayers... And day by day the Lord added to their company such as were to be saved."[7]

CHAPTER 14

SIMON PETER[1]

*"You know then how to read the face of the sky, but you
cannot read the signs of the times" (Matt 16:3).*

You might remember how at Peter's calling, Christ changed his
name from Simon to "Rock" (*Kepha*, Peter).

Until the episode in Matthew 16, this must have been a real
brain-teaser and a likely source of amusement for the apostles.
Nonetheless, by some Semitic instinct, they knew this name change
would have a profound impact on their select group. They knew the
"Rock" was destined to some very special function. Indeed, whenever
God gives someone in the Bible a name change, He also gives them
a change in function.

Then came the highlight in all the Gospels. Jesus implicitly asks
for an act of faith from His disciples. As he does throughout the
Gospels, Peter, the "Rock," acts as spokesman in this most crucial
moment.

This happened one day near Caesarea Philippi, when the Lord
turned to the Twelve and asked, "Who do men say that the Son of
Man is?"

They replied, "Some say, John the Baptist; and others, Elijah; and
others, Jeremiah, or one of the prophets." He said to them, "But who
do *you* say that I am?"

"Simon Peter answered and said, 'Thou art the Christ, the Son
of the living God.'

"Then Jesus answered and said, 'Blessed art thou, Simon Bar-
Jona, for flesh and blood has not revealed this to thee, but My Father
in heaven.'

"'And I say to thee, thou art Peter (Rock) and upon this rock, I will build My Church, and the gates of hell shall not prevail against it. And I will give thee the keys of the kingdom of heaven; and whatsoever thou shalt bind on earth shall be bound in heaven, and whatsoever thou shalt loose on earth shall be loosed in heaven.'"[2]

This text has provoked volumes of controversy over the centuries. The literal sense of the promise, however, has been graphically fulfilled in historic fact by the enduring institution of the papacy.

Of course, the Reformation's primary task was to attack this obstacle and to devise arguments against the plain sense of this text. However, on the highest levels of Protestant scholarship, we have recently seen dramatic shifts in the usually rote polemics against Matthew 16.

Thus the dialogue (in its genuine sense) between Oscar Cullmann and Otto Karrer has revealed a willingness to accept the basic elements of the text very much in the Catholic sense.[i] Put simply, Peter was what we would call a Pope. But Cullmann maintains that Peter's function was not meant to be passed on to successors. This is what Karrer refutes.

Much more startling for me was the discovery of remarkable agreement by Rudolf Bultmann with specific points of Catholic exegesis (in the footnotes of his *History of the Synoptic Tradition*).

For one who denies the divinity of Christ, we naturally cannot expect Bultmann to promote the papacy.

Nevertheless—and this is of great impact—his exegetical and form-critical analysis of the text in several areas has shifted from the desperate polemics of Reformation interpretation to something

---

[i]   Cullmann (d. 1999) was a Lutheran theologian who was heavily involved in the ecumenical movement. He acknowledged Petrine primacy in the early Church, but said this only extended to the time that Peter was actually bishop of Jerusalem. Despite the apostolic evidence, Cullmann said this primacy somehow devolved to James upon Peter's leaving for Antioch. Karrer was a Swiss Roman Catholic theologian and a pioneer amongst Catholic ecumenists. He wrote a review of Cullmann's book, *Peter and the Church*. Hence Father's reference of a "dialogue."

very much like the traditional Catholic position. Again, however, the continuity of succession is rejected.

It is pathetic and ironic that at the moment of such an opening, some Catholics should discover the tired old acrobatic contortions quietly being scuttled by respected Protestants.[ii]

We should not let these people steer us on the wrong path. We should instead ecumenically disseminate a broadened and new appreciation of the papal function. We will never have a viable Christian unity that is not centered on the person of the pope.

It is agreed by Cullmann and Bultmann that the text must be a translation of a genuine Palestinian tradition of a saying of Jesus. The

---

[ii]   Editor's note: To get at least a sense what Father is getting at here, consider the following from the November 22, 1968, issue of *TIME* magazine: "Yet it is the firm view of Pope Paul—backed overwhelmingly by the bishops— that the church was founded by Jesus Christ as an absolute monarchy, and cannot be changed without doing violence to God's intentions. [Catholic writer] Michael Novak has defined this attitude toward church structure as 'nonhistorical orthodoxy.' It is not supported by an analysis of Christian origins. The papal claim to monarchic supremacy is based, in part, upon Jesus' words in Matthew 16:18: 'You are Peter, and upon this rock I will build my church.' Today, the majority of New Testament scholars agree with the view of Bishop Francis Simons of India, who notes in his new book, *Infallibility and the Evidence* (*TIME*, Nov. 1) that the sentence simply singles out Peter as first among the Apostles and says nothing at all about the rights and privileges of his successors. The first Christian cells—under ground churchlets in constant fear of persecution—were united by a common faith rather than any formal organization. Initially, there was no strong distinction between clergy and laymen; bishops were frequently chosen by the people at informal assemblies. In the post-Apostolic period, the special place of Rome came to be recognized by other churches—not as having any monarchical jurisdiction but as a symbol of Christian unity and court of appeals in doctrinal disputes. Even so, the epoch-making decisions on heresy that beset the early church were resolved by general councils in Asia Minor; the bishop of Rome usually ratified their decisions but otherwise had little to do with their formulation."

It should be evident to any well-formed, faithful Catholic that such opinions are not only untenable but unhistorical and unscriptural. This is especially true when one considers the parallels between Matt 16:19 and Is 22:22-24.

awkwardness and obscurities of the Greek text are bathed in clarity when re-translated into Aramaic.

I have before me several pages of notes on the key images of the text as understood by these scholars plus Jeremias,[iii] Dalman,[iv] and the rabbinic parallels given by Strack-Billerbeck.[v] But the technicalities and length of discussion prohibit anything more than a few remarks.

The concept of keys and of binding-loosing means a total religious authority. Thus Bultmann writes, "The church preserved a tradition of a saying by Jesus in which Peter is promised authority in matters of doctrine, or discipline: for I do not think *lysai* (to loose) and *desai* (to bind) can have any other meaning..."[3]

While there are Old Testament parallels, the most convincing factor is the use of these same terms by contemporary (*tannaite*) rabbis. The ratification by heaven fits this pattern also:

> It is not feasible to make too sharp a line of demarcation between doctrinal and disciplinary authority; both were in the hands of one individual in Judaism. It is also a Jewish idea that God (in heaven) recognizes the decisions of lawfully constituted authority in the church on earth.[4]

Though "gates of hell" is used by Homer for death,[5] the term is typically biblical in the Hebrew *she'arei she'ol*. The unusual Gospel use of *ekklesia* (Church) certainly must stand for the *qahal Yahweh*: the total assembly of the full People of God. In rabbinic usage, too, the *qahal Yahweh* stands firmly founded on a rock.[6]

[iii] Joachim Jeremias, twentieth century German Lutheran theologian and biblical scholar.

[iv] Gustaf Dalman, twentieth century Protestant professor for Old Testament and Jewish Studies at the University of Leipzig.

[v] i.e., Hermann L. Strack and Paul Billerbeck, twentieth century German theologians who wrote a highly influential commentary on the New Testament.

The parallelism, characteristic of Semitic syntax, has much to tell us in itself. Peter confesses, "You are the Christ (i.e., Messiah), Son of the living God." He declares the belief of the apostolic college in Jesus' function. Then Jesus confesses, "And you, Son of Jonah, are the Rock." He reveals at last the function of Simon, called the "Rock," to serve as the foundation upon which His Church will rest and to be the one who binds and loosens.

On Peter, our Lord assembles the New Israel, the new elect People of God (*qahal Yahweh*), in which the College of Twelve succeeds the leaders of the 12 tribes. And one of the twelve apostles is constituted as foundation Rock and key-bearer, ratified by heaven and guaranteed against hell's powers.

Those of us who believe in Peter's confession of Christ also believe in Christ's confession of Peter. We look down into the "confession" area before the main altar of St. Peter's Basilica (the area where St. Peter is buried), and then we look up into the dome that stands above this spot, where we read, "Thou art Peter and on this rock I will build My Church."

This is what disheartens us when we see—completely against the doctrine of Vatican II—some who, while claiming to be members of this same Church, pitifully play along with the powers of hell that hammer against the Rock.

Don't they know by now they will never prevail (though they may do much harm to souls)? But Satan must try in every age, mustn't he?

CHAPTER 15

FROM PETER TO PAUL[1]

"You know then how to read the face of the sky, but you cannot read the signs of the times" (Matt 16:3).

Today, in the "spirit of Vatican II," people openly question or even reject the Pope's authority. They wonder why they should take their cues from (much less obey) "some old white guy in Rome." "Why should I listen to the Pope?" they scornfully ask. Compounding this problematic situation are the often anti-papal sentiments preached from the pulpit, expressed in diocesan newspaper columns (to say nothing of those in the secular media), and taught in classrooms.

So why should we listen to "some old man in Rome"? To answer this, we could make an airtight case from Scripture alone, which would take up an entire column. However, in addition to the scriptural evidence, a number of beautiful and substantial writings by the apostolic Fathers corroborate and clarify the privileges not only of Peter but of his successors.

The apostolic Fathers are those writers in the first century after Christ's Ascension who are not included in the biblical canon but are highly regarded by the Church. Eucharistic Prayer I (also called the Roman Canon) mentions some of them, including the first popes to succeed Peter: Sts. Linus, Cletus, and Clement I.

While serving as bishop of Rome, Clement authoritatively intervened in an internal conflict in the Church at Corinth (and they listened to this old man in Rome). This intervention is recorded in a letter that presents many other points of testimony to Rome's primacy.[2]

Another apostolic Father was Ignatius of Antioch (died ca. AD 107). He succeeded St. Peter as bishop of Antioch, and he wrote seven letters on his way in chains to martyrdom in Rome. He was by then a very old man with memories of the apostles. When he finally addressed the Church of Rome, he concentrated on Rome's primacy in governing, teaching, and ecclesial communion.

We might mention Papias, the Shepherd of Hermas, and others in the same vein. But let's allow St. Irenaeus of Lyons to be our last primitive witness.[i]

In his celebrated passage on Rome, he explained the doctrine of papal primacy so clearly as to convincingly debunk the school of Tübingen's[ii] so-called "early Catholicism" theory. Indeed, from his time on, the literary record—Church Fathers, history, and so on—amply demonstrates the fullest claims of the papacy, claims never challenged from tradition.

---

[i] A native of Asia minor, Irenaeus was a convert who learned the faith from St. Polycarp. In turn, St. Polycarp had learned the faith from St. John the Apostle. Thus, Irenaeus was John's spiritual grandson (in a manner of speaking). He became bishop of Lyons, and his *Against Heresies* is considered a masterpiece of the early Patristic Age. It is widely available online. It shows the consistency of doctrine from the time of the early Christians to our own day.

[ii] Father here refers to the university of this town located in Baden-Württemberg state, southern Germany. Benedict XVI once held the chair in dogmatic theology at the University, and Walter Cardinal Kaspar taught there, as well. Dissident theologian Hans Küng still does. It is known as being an incubator of less-than-faithful thought. The "early Catholicism" thesis holds that hierarchy was a secondary consideration in the primitive Church and took a backseat to the workings of the Spirit, since the first Christians were thought to be too preoccupied with the coming *parousia* to care much about forming a Church as we know it today. As Jean Cardinal Daniélou has written, "This version of early Christianity is accurate in certain respects, but completely disregards the primitive character of the hierarchical structure established by Christ during His life on earth and also the existence of different currents of thought in early Christianity" (*Encyclopedia of Theology: A Concise Sacramentum Mundi*, p. 32, ed. Karl Rahner, New York: Seabury Press, 1975).

And how has our understanding of this unchanging Catholic doctrine developed? Let us jump from the apostolic age to the atomic age. What does Vatican II teach on the position of the pope as successor of Peter, Rock, key-bearer, and shepherd?

First of all, the Council fully accepts and repeats the infallibly defined teaching of Vatican I: "In order that the episcopate itself might be one and undivided, He placed Blessed Peter over the other apostles, and instituted in him a permanent and visible source and foundation of unity of faith and fellowship."[3]

"And all this teaching (of Vatican I) about the institution, the perpetuity, the force and reason for the sacred primacy of the Roman Pontiff and of his infallible teaching authority, this sacred Synod again proposes to be believed by all the faithful."[4]

For the bulk of this chapter, Vatican II will speak from its own words.

I have copied out 15 major sections from *Lumen Gentium*'s Chapter 3 alone. Unfortunately, they cannot all be recited here. They are overwhelming in their totality and context.

"Episcopal consecration, together with the office of sanctifying, also confers the offices of teaching and of governing. (These, however, of their very nature, can be exercised only in hierarchical communion with the head and members of the college.) ... The college or body of Bishops has no authority unless it is simultaneously conceived of in terms of its head, the Roman Pontiff, Peter's successor, and without any lessening of his power of primacy over all, pastors as well as the general faithful.

"For in virtue of his office, that is, as Vicar of Christ and pastor of the whole Church, the Roman Pontiff has full, supreme, and universal power over the Church. And he can always exercise this power freely.

"The order of bishops, which succeeds to the college of apostles and gives this apostolic body continued existence, is also the subject of supreme and full power over the universal Church, provided we understand this body together with its head the Roman Pontiff and never without this head.

"But this power can be exercised only with the consent of the Roman Pontiff. For Our Lord made Simon Peter alone the rock and key-bearer of the Church, and appointed him shepherd of the whole flock."[5]

"Among the principal duties of bishops, the preaching of the gospel occupies an eminent place. For bishops are preachers of the faith ... they are authentic teachers, that is, teachers endowed with the authority of Christ, who preach to the people committed to them the faith they must believe and put into practice. By the light of the Holy Spirit they make that faith clear ... vigilantly warding off any errors which threaten their flock.

"Bishops, teaching in communion with the Roman Pontiff, are to be respected by all as witnesses to divine and Catholic truth. In matters of faith and morals, the bishops speak in the name of Christ and the faithful are to accept their teaching and adhere to it with a religious assent of soul.

"This religious submission of will and of mind must be shown in a special way to the authentic teaching authority of the Roman Pontiff, even when he is not speaking *ex cathedra*. That is, it must be shown in such a way that his supreme Magisterium is acknowledged with reverence, the judgments made by him are sincerely adhered to, according to his manifest mind and will.

"His mind and will in the matter may be known chiefly either from the character of the documents, from his frequent repetition of the same doctrine, or from his manner of speaking..."[6]

May I succumb to temptation and add a word of comment? In respect to the popes' teaching on birth control and priestly celibacy and women's ordination and all the rest, do these words of the Council have no force?

No one with eyes and ears and a brain to coordinate their data could dare say we have had no dialogue on these matters. No one knowing the pensive, studious, and sensitive nature of recent popes can rationally suggest they have not read and listened more than any of us.

Yet after years of prayer and under incredible pressures, they have solemnly and repeatedly taught what the Church has always taught. Who can continue to reject this highest teaching authority and still say he possesses the "spirit of Vatican II"?

In any event, equally powerful passages follow the above quoted texts. Then there is the explanatory and prefatory note on Chapter 3 appended to the Constitution. It can be found in the easily available texts.

I confess that at the time (November 1964), these additional and highly cautious words seemed to be rather quixotic and superfluous. "Who would ever deny these long-defined essential truths?" I thought. Why then insist on stressing papal authority in such a way that might be interpreted unsympathetically?

Well, we now have the horrifying answer.

While pretending Catholic allegiance and even ministry, some have in theory and/or practice rejected these central Catholic tenets. This stress on papal primacy, so paradoxical at the time, is now for me one of the most convincing signs of the operation of the Holy Spirit.[iii]

[iii]   Father doesn't allude to the half of it. To read the truly alarming story about how and why this appendix to *Lumen Gentium* was inserted, read pages 231-33 of TAN Books' *The Rhine Flows Into the Tiber*, which is a journalist's account of what happened at the Second Vatican Council. The gist is that many Council Fathers and *periti* (experts) warned the Pope that the liberal forces were trying to craft *Lumen Gentium* in a way that would weaken papal authority. Paul VI would not believe it. As a liberal himself, he put great faith in the Commission that had formulated Chapter 3 of the document. But one of the liberals "made the mistake of referring, in writing, to some of these ambiguous passages, and indicated how they would be interpreted after the Council. This paper fell into the hands of the aforesaid group of cardinals ... whose representative took it to the Pope. Pope Paul, realizing ... he had been deceived, broke down and wept." Before promulgating this Constitution, therefore, the Holy Father had this appendix written, which affirmed the Church's perennial teaching on papal primacy. Some say Vatican II was the Council the Holy Spirit forgot to attend. Such a statement is hard to reconcile with the above account.

So the Council has said what Scripture and the apostolic Fathers said. It said, in fact, what true Catholics always have professed and always *must* profess concerning the vicar of Christ.

This is the mind and spirit of Vatican II—let us never be led astray. "Where Peter is, there is the Church." He who does not gather with him, scatters.

CHAPTER 16

THE SACRAMENT OF HEALING[1]

"You know then how to read the face of the sky, but you cannot read the signs of the times" (Matt 16:3).

Next to abuses of the Holy Eucharist, one of our times' most sinister signs is the increasingly successful propaganda campaign against the sacrament of penance. Even more alarming is the lack of resistance, the lack of defense against this campaign. Frequent confession is debunked and discouraged in lectures, in classrooms, in pulpits, and even in the confessional itself.

And more and more people are listening to the propaganda. "Aren't some scholarly priests and Sisters saying these things?" they ask. Coupled with the fact that confession was never intended to be easy, we understand the drastic drop in confessions, even in parishes where the sacrament is promoted.

An inseparable link exists between this campaign and the current defective and cancerous moral doctrine where guilt gets explained away and "sin" becomes simply an undefined failure to serve our fellow man, a cute, no-no type of selfishness. In the minds of many, objective moral norms no longer hold sway. The mills of subjectivism and relativism have crushed them.

With false doctrine like this rife even in many Catholic institutions, is there any wonder that many have made the sacrament of penance a primary target for elimination? For it is in this encounter with Christ the Judge and merciful Healer that a man is forced to examine himself and to confess the objective validity of God's law. This sacrament demands we accept responsibility, acknowledge guilt, and clearly see every sin—even against one's neighbor—as an offense against God.

In the confessional, an elemental component of conscience unfolds: It must be judged and guided externally. And after honest allowance for those subjective and external circumstances that might affect the objective norms (something the Church has always taught), sin, venial or mortal, is confessed, sorrow is generated, and interior renewal and reform are undertaken.

These actions help create saints, and that in turn brings ever more people to Christ. If the devil wanted to destroy the Church (and he does), if he wanted to undermine the healing power that comes from forgiveness (and he does), wouldn't this sacrament stand as the most crucial obstacle for him to overcome?

Recall how the Jews in our Lord's time believed an immediate and personal relationship existed between physical defects and moral guilt, sickness and sin. Sometimes this is true (as in the case of sclerosis of the liver from alcoholism), but more often it is not.

Nonetheless, while Christ did not come to reveal modern medical praxis, He did come as the divine Physician and Healer of souls. "Those who are well do not have need of a physician, but those who are ill."[2] Therefore He simply used the current notions to teach a powerful lesson. For He healed the blind, the deaf, the lame, the mute, the paralyzed, the leprous, and even the dead so "that you may know that the Son of Man has power on earth to forgive sins."[3]

Thus, the miracles of healing which constitute so large a part of the Gospels are commentaries and testimonies on the sacrament of penance. The Gospels are one long prelude to the institution of this sacrament, which embraces the core of the *kerygma*.[i]

It was on Easter night that Jesus breathed on His apostles, saying, "Peace be to you! Receive the Holy Spirit. Whose sins you shall forgive, they are forgiven; whose sins you shall retain, they are retained."[4] The gospel power of healing souls is passed on. Every well-

---

[i] This is the word most often used for "preaching" in the Greek New Testament.

disposed penitent experiences Holy Week in a few minutes' time. In union with Christ, he, too, dies to sin, buries the past, and rises to new life. He is bathed in the vivifying Blood of the Lamb, the Blood of Jesus our Passover. "By His wounds we are healed."[5]

Now here is the problem today: On the one hand, some proclaim we encounter Christ in the sacraments. Now this is a true and beautiful thought, and the Church has always taught this. But these same people tell us to stay away from the sacrament of confession! In confession, we meet Jesus the merciful Physician. Here He seeks to heal our souls. He reaches in with wounded hands to probe and touch and remedy the scars of sins past and present. He infuses us with the preventive medicine of His divine strength. If all this is true (and no one who claims to be Catholic can deny it), then how can anyone urge us not to go there to meet Jesus and to go there often?

The confessional is the seat of Christ's mercy. Here He allows us to accuse and judge ourselves prior to that day when He will come to judge the living and the dead. How self-damning are those who turn their backs on this means of Christ's mercy. Confession allows man to act with true courage (for it is not easy to look squarely at one's sins). In this sacrament of healing, a person must peer inward with honesty and examine himself unflinchingly in order to make progress in perfection and union with God. Even a pagan recognized that "the unexamined life is not worth living."[ii]

Now there was a time that many possibly examined themselves too much. This may be why, throughout much of Church history, few used to receive Communion. Starting with St. Pius X, however, modern popes sought to change that unhappy circumstance. They were successful, and today long lines approach what we used to call the Communion rail.

But this is not necessarily a good thing, for with a long Communion line has come a shorter line for the confessional. What if many of these people have not tested their souls in years? What

---

ii   Socrates said this after an Athens jury had found him guilty of sedition and heresy in 399 BC.

if they no longer believe in sin or guilt?[iii] Then they are "eating and drinking judgment to themselves, not discerning the Body of the Lord."[6]

To prevent this, Pius XII expressed at length the need for frequent confession in *Mediator Dei* (On the Sacred Liturgy), and he condemned certain abuses that have now become rampant. And what of good Pope John? What, in this matter, is the "spirit of Pope John?"

> Let those who are in charge of souls ... remember that Our predecessor of happy memory, Pius XII, expressed disapproval in the strongest terms of the opinion of those who have little use for frequent Confession, where it is a matter of venial sins; the Supreme Pontiff said: "We particularly recommend the pious practice of frequent Confession, which the Church has introduced, under the influence of the Holy Spirit, as a means of swifter daily progress along the road of virtue."[7]

Note the words cited by Pope John: "which the Church has introduced, under the influence of the Holy Spirit."

So, to those who say, "but Fr. Novigeneris, Sr. Renovata, and Dr. Omnisciens say not to go so often," the answer is that these teachers are forcing us to make a choice, in this case, between them and Pope John. Who possesses the best credentials and charisms? Who deserves to win our allegiance? Who best knows the "spirit of Vatican II?"

---

iii   On October 8, 2007, *TIME* magazine reported that, "In a 2005 survey by the Center for Applied Research on the Apostolate at Georgetown University, 42 percent [of Catholics surveyed] said they never went to confession, only 14 percent said they go once a year, and just 2 percent said they go regularly." As one letter writer to *Our Sunday Visitor* newspaper remarked, "If the survey is acceptable, it indicates 56 percent ... do not believe in damnable sin, which needs to be confessed and pledged 'to do penance and amend my life.'"

These people deplore the Middle Ages, yet rush blindly back another thousand years to the primitive Church as though no development since then had been good. They pick and choose (*hairesis*!)[iv] what they like. In the matter of confession, for example, they completely bypass the rigoristic discipline of penance that seemed necessary in the age of martyrs. Well, if we bypass this, why not the whole bag?

And finally, based simply on our own experiences, just how many of us really swallow this wicked nonsense that little children are corrupted and psychologically traumatized by confession? Who was ever traumatized by meeting Jesus, by learning in our tender years to discern right from wrong, and by always relating our deeds to a God who loves us? We may have been traumatized by bad confessors, but by confession?

Whom shall we believe on this matter? People who can't tolerate the words "Catholic" or "doctrine" or "sin," or the Lord Himself who says, "Allow the little children to come to Me and do not prevent them"?

We seldom hesitate, despite shame, pain, and the prospect of bitter remedies, to run to the doctor when illness hits us. The sign of one who really believes in the Life of the Spirit will be his eagerness to meet with the Physician of souls. But to do this that person must humbly confess that he suffers from blindness, deafness, muteness, lameness, leprosy, paralysis, and even death of the soul.

If we can see just how badly each of us needs the divine Healer, then we will see how the words of the propagandists hold no appeal, how they are hollow, void. And when we see this, and we start to form a line outside the confessionals again, as a result, we will see saints made and people drawn to Christ.

---

iv   *Hairesis* is a Greek word meaning, among other things, "to pick and choose," and is the word from which we get our own word "heresy."

PART III

COLUMNS FROM
NATIONAL PUBLICATIONS

CHAPTER 17

THE PIRATES OF PENANCE[1]

Since the mid-1960s, we have witnessed the collapse of the patiently built, longstanding practice in the United States of frequent confession, which had been the envy of the Catholic world.

We can easily see how this happened. By theological fiat, some declared there was no sin, a demonic idiocy. For those who would still allow that it could exist, sin became mere selfishness or a "hurting" of self, neighbor, and ecology with no reference to God.

In the process, the lethal line between venial and mortal sin was neatly rubbed out, an error justified by the theories of fundamental option[i] and situation ethics (with its denial of all objective moral standards and its declaration of independence for the subjective conscience).

---

i   According to Fr. Stephen Torraco, associate professor of Theology at Assumption College in Worcester, Massachusetts, this is "a theory of morals according to which each person gradually develops in a basic orientation of his or her life, either for or against God." As such, it reflects what St. Augustine wrote, that there are those who "love God even to the contempt of self, and [those who] love themselves even to the contempt of God." However, certain heretical variations on the fundamental option have arisen, so that the Holy See felt obliged to condemn these in the 1975 declaration *Persona Humana*. Fr. Torraco writes, "The Holy See admitted the description of a person's basic moral disposition as a 'fundamental option.' What is *not* admissible is to claim that *individual human actions* cannot radically change this fundamental option. '[It] is wrong to say that particular acts are not enough to constitute a mortal sin.' [This] heretical theory suggests *no mortal sin* is committed unless a person subjectively rejects God."

Fed on Piaget,[ii] the New Catechists insisted on delaying first reception of the sacrament of penance well into adolescence. For example, one "religion" course, the notorious Green Bay Plan, assigned it to the seventh grade![iii]

In the same spirit, frequent and devotional confessions were debunked. The only wonder was that anyone still went to confession. But, under Divine Providence, the difficult sacrament persisted, and where priests were orthodox and fervent, it even thrived.

Overseers turned onlookers

So now a final great assault is mounted, using as its pretext the genuine conciliar reform of the rite of penance. By latching onto a single phrase of the Roman text (*in loco et in sede*) and grossly mistranslating that phrase in their ICEL English version,[iv] the liturgy establishment, counting on sympathetic or apathetic bishops and confident of the mechanized ardor of most diocesan liturgical offices, now pushes (1) the reconciliation room and (2) face-to-face confessions.[v]

---

ii   Jean Piaget, Swiss developmental psychologist best known for his work with children.

iii   This series of lesson plans implemented by the Green Bay diocese was a type of experiential catechism written by Richard J. Reichert, who was a huge dissenter against *Humanae Vitae*. It was modeled on the Dutch Catechism, devoid of all doctrine, and filled with heresies.

iv   ICEL is the International Commission on English in the Liturgy. It is the body tasked with translating the Church's official Latin texts into English. For well over a generation, it had a bad reputation for the poor translations it produced. However, in recent years, it has done a much better job.

v   While Father's concerns are completely valid, it should be noted that this practice in some form has been around for a long time in places such as Italy, well before the "face-to-face" confession was made a universal option. According to a priest friend in Italy, "In fact, if you look at some older photos of Padre Pio, of course in the confessional—say, from the '50s—you'll notice that it was common for men (not women, though) to do this. On this last note, my guess is that the confessional grate was intended more for propriety

Already, after but a few months of experimentation, reports (which were easily predictable) flow in from all quarters of the nation:

1. Many people, long battered by changes, openly state that if they must confess face-to face, they will stop receiving the sacrament.

2. Despite supposedly having the screen option for penitents, many report that on entering the room there was no screen. Others tell of pressure exerted, especially on grade-school children, to confess "eyeball-to-eyeball," as one bishop rather inelegantly put it. Still others report that on entering what some of us priests have contemptuously labeled the "rec room," they are surveyed by the priest before they have a chance to see the shelter of the screen, which, in this case, no longer has any purpose. Most confessors will admit that any pressure to use the face-to-face procedure would result in many sacrilegious confessions. This may be a special problem for women, but certainly also for adolescents. While young children may not be inhibited, what will happen when these same children reach the upper grades and high school?

3. There is an ominous increase in the unauthorized and invalid practice of general absolution with permissive bishops saying nothing to counter it. In this, the Overseers have become Overlookers.

To illustrate this pernicious practice an eyewitness told me that in a large city parish only two penance periods were scheduled in preparation for Holy Week and Easter. Vast crowds (about 1,000 at each session) assembled.

One of the parish priests came out, delivered a bland sermon, and then gave general absolution to all. He gave no justification for

---

between the sexes (i.e. confessor and woman penitent) in such close and private contact, than for anything else."

this procedure, which the people generally presumed to be valid and sacramental. He made no qualifications or stipulations. When the people did not move to disband, no doubt confused by the ease of it all, he had to inform them, "That's all there is to it."

Fifteen minutes per session for 1,000 lambs at a clip ... voilà!

Priests dedicated to the sacrament know the thorny cases of conscience that arise when the people so "absolved" later come to their senses. I have also seen a letter from a bishop to his priests in which he tells them they may not use "Form III" (general absolution) until next Lent when the bishops of the province will issue guidelines for its implementation. That sounds good on quick reading, but think of the possible implications. Are not the strict limits of the Roman text more than sufficient ... unless, that is, a liberalizing reinterpretation is in the works?

The option beast

From these observations alone, it is safe to forecast that unless our bishops rouse themselves to defend the integrity and validity of the sacrament, the previous slump will look splendid in comparison.

Two recent articles have appeared like beacons on this blackened horizon, one by Fr. Bruce A. Williams, OP,[vi] (*Homiletic & Pastoral Review*, October 1975, reprints available) from a theological and canonical viewpoint, and another by Msgr. Schuler.[vii] They argue that, within a few limits, the law must fully preserve the confessor's given discretionary powers to adapt the overall rite to his concrete pastoral situation. With the due deference to the directives, we observe that the reform offers some built-in and possibly unforeseen problems.

[vi] Whatever the merits of Fr. William's arguments in the article to which Father refers, he has since become something of an apologist for those who think homosexual sexual acts are compatible with Christian morality. He teaches at the Angelicum in Rome.

[vii] This is Msgr. Richard J. Schuler, who was pastor of the famed St. Agnes Church in Minneapolis and an authority on sacred music. He died April 20, 2007.

Chief of these is the encroaching "option-beast." As the process of renewing the sacramental rites evolved, the adoption of options grew apace. It is most notable in the marriage rite where it stimulates in the couples an appetite for novelties that drive even portly pastors up a tree; in the rite of the anointing of the sick, where any priest can recount having had to thumb through pages of options, sometimes in emergencies; and now, in full bloom, in the penance rite.

It does seem, *salva reverentia*, that this prolixity is the brainchild of theorists rather than practitioners. Furthermore, it contributes more to the deplorable situation of rare confessions than the healthy, frequent use of the sacrament we once had.

One lady recently told me her last confession took nearly 40 minutes, with the priest unctuously reading into her face huge tracts of Scripture with ample commentaries on each pericope. This is not pastoral realism. The option could well open the door to deadening verbosity and even to cheapened secular-humanist psychological counseling. Needless to say, this pleases publishers, because they can market books three or four times the size actually required for any one administration of the sacrament.

The options, too, are uneven in content and allow mavericks to hunt and pick for the formulas that are least doctrinally expressive or to quite simply make up "options" of their own.

But the biggest problem of the options is this: In our mobile society, one no longer finds a reassuring uniform practice from one parish (or even from one confessor) to the next. All of this simply presents one more barrier for timid and sensitive penitents seeking only to confess and receive encouragement and absolution.

Sincere, sorrowful, integral confession

Of course, the essential complaints we have stem not from the Roman ritual but from the innovative directives issued by national and diocesan liturgical bureaucrats. Perhaps because they are theorists and not practitioners, they seem to never know these penitents whom they seek to manipulate. A good, experienced confessor knows all too well that the average penitent is neither an exhibitionist nor a masochist. The average penitent is just a good Catholic, burdened by a need to submit his sins to a priest whom he recognizes as a personal agent of Christ, to express contrition and amendment, however awkwardly, and to receive the sacramental grace of absolution. The simpler and more routine the ritual framework, the better. For him, the concentration should be on the sincere, sorrowful, and integral confession, and on the Christly words and absolution of the priest.

How often has a confessor delivered a masterful little homily (known as the *ferverino*), only to be interrupted by, "O, Father, I forgot to mention ..." showing that the penitent had not heard a word and was still deeply absorbed in purgation of conscience? Even in the past, we have sensed the genuine strain placed on souls in their most vulnerable situation to recall even the most rudimentary forms. Are we now to imitate the Pharisees by placing burdens on these humble souls heavier than we ourselves could bear?

Consider, too, the frequent cases of the hard-of-hearing, the stammerers, the poorly educated, the scrupulous, the chronically nervous, or those ill-at-ease in self-expression. Where do the innovations leave them? Were these people (or even those who simply liked the old way of doing things) ever considered? Whatever happened to the highly-touted need to consult the faithful?

A March 28, 1976, article in the German Catholic newspaper *Bildpost* describes a survey taken among West German Catholics of all ages and conditions in which 92 percent strongly asked that the anonymity of confession be kept. In fact, they wanted no changes in regard to the confessional. Accordingly, Auxiliary Bishop Ernst Tewes of Munich has insisted the confessionals will remain.

Now what prompted this poll? There are reports in the daily press that certain American dioceses have abolished the confessional, though *Bildpost* thinks the reports are confused in fact. Earlier, similar reports had caused Pope Paul to insist emphatically on three occasions that priests preserve anonymity by means of the confessional and protective screen.

Some who have seen the latest schemata of the new *Code of Canon Law*[viii] have told me that the text speaks of the screen as before and does not mention exceptions.[ix] In consideration of these and many other factors, we feel justified in asking—urgently and from whatever authority can most competently answer or is willing to answer—several straightforward questions:

1. Did Rome concede to our American bishops the permission to allow the face-to-face confessions of women? In Fr. Williams' article, he mentions the "advisory" note sent by the United States Catholic Conference (USCC)[x] to the bishops. Although he cites the Roman ritual's insistence on preserving the previous norms of canon law, he "assumes" that a grant to allow this may have been given. Considering the dire consequences of such a concession and its radical departure from past praxis, I think he may be too charitable in his assumption. It is crucial to demand a direct reply: In point of fact, has Rome explicitly granted such an abrogation of previous canon law? If so, for conscience sake, do priests not have the right to see the Roman re-script and study its wording and intent?

2. Does Rome really feel that "reconciliation rooms" are desirable? The experience of the Church seems to militate against this subtle evasion of the physical separation of confessor from penitent. Have we forgotten the all-too-

---

[viii] The *Code of Canon Law* was released in 1983, but at this writing, canon lawyers were still preparing its texts. The preliminary drafts were known as *schemas* or *schemata*.

[ix] Canon 964 says, "The proper place for hearing sacramental confessions is a church or oratory. As far as the confessional is concerned, norms are to be issued by the Episcopal Conference, with the proviso however that confessionals, which the faithful who so wish may freely use, are located in an open place, and fitted with a fixed grille between the penitent and the confessor. Except for a just reason, confessions are not to be heard elsewhere than in a confessional."

[x] Now called the United States Conference of Catholic Bishops.

human history that prompted the confession box and screen? In the best of times, hostile tongues wagged about mostly imagined intimacies between confessor and penitent. Canon law sought to plug up even the remaining avenues of verbal improprieties. Need we mention that ours is not the best of times, and that we shouldn't necessarily presume as imaginary such allegations? In an age of clerical laxity unparalleled for its brazenness in Church history (pace Abelard, who at least admitted sin was sin[xi]), is this the propitious moment to dismantle the safeguards? Once the "rec room" door is closed, speculation can run rampant.[xii]

3. Msgr. Schuler is absolutely correct in his fears for the reputation of even the most innocent priest. And unless the priest has completely lost his sacred respect for the seal of confession, only the penitent emerges from the room free to talk. The priest may not even speak in his defense. What does Rome really think about this procedure of face-to-face confessions (now officially mandated in some dioceses), even aside from the abuses of refusing the screen or frustrating its purpose of anonymity? Let's not even comment on the rubric of "imposing hands." One lady recently reported that she entered a "rec room" expecting to kneel at a screen, when, to her torment, a young priest looked at her from across a

---

[xi]   This refers to Peter Abelard, a French scholastic philosopher and professor, and a hugely successful one at that. At the time he lived (the twelfth century), professors were considered clerics and were supposed to act in a like fashion (i.e., remain celibate). However, he fell in love with a pupil, the beautiful Héloïse, and she with him. They had a child out of wedlock (although they eventually married). This produced a scandal and many woes for both of them. Their story is easily accessible online or in most encyclopedias.

[xii]   Regardless of the veracity of individual claims, several victims in the priest-sex abuse scandal have claimed they were molested while they were in the confessional. Since it is impossible for abuse to happen in a conventional confession stall, this must have happened in a "rec room" setting.

table, held out his hands, and said, "Come, Doris, put your hands in mine..."

4. We also need preemptive help in the area of possible expansion of general absolutions. The case was stated above, but Rome should also know of another approach that militates against "integral" confession. In a number of instances of which I am aware, the people at a penance service were invited to approach priests at various confession stations but were specifically advised to confess "only one sin." This seems to be not a one-shot experiment but a new practice. In one case, the priests involved included very responsible diocesan officials.

Look to heroic confessors

As Msgr. Schuler so justly asks, how would St. John Vianney, patron of parish priests, have reacted to these novel directions in the practice of penance? His example would be one of a thousand reasons why modernists must strive to eclipse the galaxy of saints. Typical of their propaganda is a new catechetical program where, in addition to complete silence on the saints, it is deemed necessary to canonize a host of more relevant heroes such as John Kennedy, Martin Luther King, and—please fetch the basin—the Brothers Berrigan,[xiii] Angela Davis,[xiv] et al.

[xiii] This refers to Daniel and Philip Berrigan, two brothers who became priests (although Philip later left the priesthood to marry). Because of their anti-Vietnam War activities (which included spilling blood and napalm on draft records and damaging and pouring blood over the cones for nuclear warheads), they were for a time on the FBI's Ten Most Wanted List. In his lifetime, Philip spent a cumulative total of 11 years in jail for crimes committed in the name of his anti-war activities (he died in 2002). Daniel Berrigan is still a priest and teaches at Fordham University, where he is also poet-in-residence. While he is involved in the pro-life movement, he also promotes the homosexual rights agenda.

[xiv] During the 1960s, few names were more associated with the age's radical politics than that of Angela Davis. A communist and former member of

We priests need to fix our eyes even more intently on the Curé d'Ars, and we might add, on our own contemporaries who were heroic confessors, the newly beatified Fr. Leopoldo[xv] and his illustrious brother Capuchin, Padre Pio.

Padre Pio lived well beyond the Council and even beyond *Humanae Vitae*. Unlike many priests today, he believed in the soul, its immortality, grace, the supernatural order, salvation, redemption, and the transcendence of God. He was no social worker, no amateur psychologist. He had no identity crisis, and, let us note, he was rigid on the canonical regulations for hearing women's confessions. We should all get ourselves a photo of this man of miracles, taken where he was most often to be found, sitting in his confessional with his crucified hand raised to absolve.

---

the Black Panthers who sees Cuba as the world's model society, she was implicated in the murder of Judge Harold Haley, which was committed during a prison break of Panther members in which she participated. She was acquitted. She currently directs the Feminist Studies department at the University of California, Santa Cruz, and works for abolition of the death penalty and prisons.

[xv] St. Leopold Mandić, Capuchin friar, 1866-1942. An ethnic Croat, he lived his priestly life in the Veneto region of Italy. Although wracked with speech problems, physical ailments and deformities, and stunted height, he was a spiritual giant and is known as the apostle of confession and the apostle of unity (the latter for his efforts to reunite Catholicism and Orthodoxy). Concerning confession, he spent most of the last 34 years of his life in the confessional and some criticized him for being "too" compassionate and merciful. His feast is May 12.

CHAPTER 18

AN OPEN LETTER TO OUR BELOVED BISHOPS

Agony in the Vineyard

I want first to stress that this "letter" is written with the deepest respect for the office and person of the bishop. Second, the priest who writes this knows his situation is shared with thousands of other priests. He represents the one group no one has ever listened to, a group that has not agitated or protested, and a group that never even organized and which now finds itself in some dioceses without a voice or avenue of communication.

In much of this letter, I will use the first person plural, for I know I speak for many priests. No doubt all of us might express ourselves somewhat divergently, and if we all pooled our data, we could enrich the letter by many cogent and stunning examples beyond the few included here. But make no mistake: What I have written here is based on real experiences, not chimeras. I have deliberately drawn the following examples from several geographically distinct dioceses.

The very fact that I do not dare approach my own bishop with these concerns for fear of reprisal is one indication of the depth of the problem. This letter is the only way I can find of communicating indirectly with my bishop without jeopardizing my freedom to serve the Church and without scandalizing the public by open and direct criticism of him.

I also fully realize that the picture adjusts dramatically from diocese to diocese. In many places, some of these problems are nonexistent, or a priest can at least live in the full confidence that, whatever the problems, his bishop is one heart with him and in union with the Holy See.

But even in these happier cases, the burden of this letter must deeply concern all bishops. Due to the collegial nature of the national conference, when critical situations exist in neighboring sections of the Church, all the bishops are obliged to exert brotherly admonition.

A meteor in a dark sky

Dear bishops, how grateful we are for some of your recent collegial exercises of the Magisterium. To name the two most outstanding: the *Basic Teachings*[i] and the pastoral letter *Behold Your Mother*.[ii] We priests who are determined to remain in union with Rome thrill when a bishop here or there, *motu proprio*,[iii] like a meteor in a dark sky, reaffirms faith, discipline, and devotion.

But how often have we trembled to see our bishops, the successors of the apostles, immobilized by the parliamentary threads of the USCC's Lilliputians.

Why, we wonder, does the cult of liberal acclaim mesmerize so many of you?

---

[i] *Basic Teachings for Catholic Religious Education*, issued by the National Conference of Catholic Bishops on January 11, 1973. It listed the "major doctrinal truths that had to be included in all Catholic religious education." According to the respected Catholic scholar Kenneth Whitehead, however, there was never any effective follow-up by the bishops' conference.

[ii] According to the resource page on the University of Dayton's website, "*Behold Your Mother* is a pastoral letter addressed to the dearly beloved of the Church in the United States. The bishops promulgated the document on November 21, 1973, the ninth anniversary of *Lumen Gentium*, The Vatican II Dogmatic Constitution of the Church. As the document states, the bishops wished to share with the American people their 'faith in the truths concerning her' (BYM 1). At the same time, the bishops wished 'together with you to express publicly our filial love for her'" (BYM 2).

[iii] Latin for "of his own accord."

Why do bishops routinely give key positions to men of dubious loyalty?

Have we no experts in this vast land who are of unquestionable orthodoxy and, dare it be mentioned, piety?

We know we have. We see them all around us, men of credentials and devotion, but we see them silenced. We wonder why no one has called on these men to serve the Church in a time of utmost crisis, and why you seemingly do not *want* them to stand by you in defense of the Faith. Meanwhile, we are jostled by wave after wave of deleterious fads, poorly considered suggestions, stubborn precedents, and innovations with corrosive effects, all of which emanate from "experts" who do their damage and then, all too frequently, decamp.

When we "unorganized" and "unhyphenated" priests share our problems amongst one another, we speculate on the incredible lack of priorities evident on the agendas of National Conference of Catholic Bishops (NCCB) meetings. Time after time, we look in vain for even a hint of recognition that the Church is in crisis and that someone is assessing that crisis' dimensions. Instead, topics of lesser urgency are repeatedly debated and highly publicized. And again, we find dangerous recommendations that would further confound or debilitate the faithful repeatedly resurrected, only to see defeat at the hands of a rearguard defense that clearly betrays polarization amongst the bishops themselves.

When we turn to the diocesan level, we find precisely the same pattern. In those dioceses where the ordinary is weak, silent, or openly allied with progressivism, we see him, whether by capitulation or connivance, caught between two paralyzing bureaucracies, national and local. It is in dioceses like these that we suffer. It is to the bishops of such dioceses that we primarily address our plea.

Sometimes we have strong indications that our bishops themselves are in accord with the destructive directions, but here we will void any final judgment on motives, since whether a bishop is victim or director, the results are the same.

And we know that if a bishop would be fearless and firm, the era of reconstruction and true reform could begin. Loyal priests could rally to you and stand proudly by your side without compromising their conscience. The distraught faithful would breathe a sigh of relief, regain their spiritual bearings, and give you full support. The vast gray area of those who easily shift allegiance to the "winning" forces would gravitate to your side, and frankly, we can number many of the priests and Sisters among these theological chameleons.

Needed: A lifeline with Rome

Dear bishops, your silence is ominous. Your failure to teach, to correct, and to admonish paralyzes and bewilders us. Your unwillingness to welcome, transmit, and enforce papal teachings and directives—even of the most essential nature—isolates us from the lifeline of Rome.

Instead of being a channel of Catholic communion with Christ's vicar, you become a clog at best. And yet we know our ultimate loyalty and obedience must be to Rome.

Thus, in order to authenticate our Catholic teaching, we often have to ignore you and appeal over your head and your officialdom to Rome or to other, more courageous bishops. All around us, voices contradict the orthodox Catholic position, and often enough, these voices come from nuns, priests, and diocesan officials. Since you are the one who has either chosen or kept these people, we obviously cannot appeal to you, successors of the apostles, living silently and ambiguously in our midst.

What a joy it would be to have your authority and to appeal to that! But we dare not even come to you for support or encouragement. You would chide us for our presumption, caution us for our lack of prudence, our "inflexibility," our lack of openness to change. You find it hard to stomach a priest or layman who has the courage to defend and profess what, in your conscience, you surely know it is your sworn duty to assert, even at the cost of blood. You are supposed to be the arteries that bring life to the limbs, yes, but we find those arteries so clogged, they fail to do their jobs.

When bishops fail to rally to the Holy Father, when they fail to insist on loyalty to his supreme authority, it immobilizes the entire hierarchical structure. If the bishops do not uphold the authority of the pope, who will respect the authority of the bishops? Indeed, the authority of these others depends on the authority of the one. And if the bishops subsequently have no effective authority, how much does the authority of a pastor count? And if the pastor on the front line cannot exercise the authority inherent in his office, what simple curate can ever teach the Faith or insist on elementary discipline?

Often we see bishops insist on loyalty and obedience to themselves, while they in practice, if not in deeds, show no visible loyalty and obedience to the Holy Father. Pity the genuinely sincere young priest assigned to a pastor who has no respect for doctrine or discipline! And, yes, there are young men in this impossible situation, torn in conscience.

In many cases today, a truly Catholic priest, loyal to Rome and the Catholic Faith, determined to be as liberal as the Pope and as conservative as the Pope, finds his life a daily torment and even his nights are interrupted by hours of sleepless anxiety. What, then, are some of the items that we should enter in this diary of our agony in the vineyard?

Not a kingdom, but a commune

The priest today lives in a divided priesthood. It is not a "polarized" priesthood (although in the beginning, it may have seemed so). Rather, it is a division of faith. Many priests are completely alienated from the Pope and, indeed, from the supernatural. They are ordained social workers who insist that the kingdom is of this world, and that it is not a kingdom but a commune.[iv] Yet there are times

---

iv   Keep in mind that at the time Father wrote this—1974—it was fashionable for hippies to form together in communes (today the favored term is "intentional communities"). These were voluntary associations of people on a farm, for example, where work and other responsibilities were shared and where there was little or no personal property. "Sounds like a monastery,"

when faithful priests and the social workers are expected to act out the myth that our priesthood is united under our bishop and that our bishop is united to the Pope.

It is excruciating for the loyal priest, who knows these others are in *de facto* schism. Chasms divide them from the true Church that pretense cannot span. With some fellow priests, one can discuss only weather or sports and must carefully avoid any mention of religion. This becomes most palpably evident, for instance, when priests gather for the funeral of a confrère. Often the bishop presides, and one watches the group assembling to concelebrate. The polychrome sports clothes and business suits mingle with clerical black. The hirsute stand next to the clean-shaven. But the diversity is far from being only external. An elderly priest once whispered to me, "*Tot capita, tot sententiae.*"[v]

Now the scruple: Ought we to concelebrate when we know there is no unity of faith? Doesn't this obliterate the very purpose of concelebration? If we manage to silence the scruple, however, we may stand next to a colleague who repeatedly denies the authority of the pope in his pulpit and his lectures, or another who, at priests' meetings, persistently attacks essential Catholic doctrine, or a priest who, as a thousand good sources report, is living in concubinage. No one dares whisper the diagnostic verdict "schism," but what else is this? And how can we ever begin the restoration and cure without acknowledging the diagnosis?

One of the major divisive elements in the priesthood is the once virulent and now malingering shadow hierarchy of the National Federation of Priests' Councils (NFPC), dissident and corrosive in root, stalk, and branch. In some dioceses, the Priests' Senate or

---

some might think. However, given the hippie ethos, these places were often founded on a New Age spirituality, endemic use of narcotics, and "free love." Father probably is not getting so much at that aspect, but rather at the "Kumbaya," "let's focus on a quasi-communistic way of living" that many of the people he's referring to espoused.

[v]   Again, this Latin proverb means, "There are as many opinions as there are heads."

Council is identified with a unit of the NFPC in such a way that to have presbyteral union with one's fellow-priests, one has to belong to and financially abet an organization that, on the record, is notoriously and consistently anti-papal.

I have heard that in one diocese at least, a priest cannot vote in the priests' council unless he has paid his dues—most of which goes to support the NFPC. This poses the following dilemma: A priest who refuses to support an anti-papal group cannot vote as a priest in his own diocese! Moreover, this arrangement neatly guarantees that only NFPC-oriented men will occupy those key consultative and policy-making positions that are elective.

Strategic ignorance

An offshoot of this is that mainly dissidents staff the elected personnel boards. Tooth and mane, these men strive to gather and feed into their computers every conceivable datum except "religious affiliation." There is, then, no concern to match Catholic priests with Catholic parishes (and, even more critically, with Catholic nuns) nor to send secularized and dissident priests to already disaffected parishes.

The result is constant clash and ferment. But perhaps to the more sophisticated members of the new politicized and radicalized personnel boards, this is a calculated oversight, a strategic ignorance. The unrealizable promise of giving every priest exactly what he craves leads to a constant shuffling from one green pastorate to another. The spiritual value of obedience in assignment is consigned to oblivion.

For a priest who loves the Church and the clerical life, his morale also suffers keenly from the continuing abandonment of the priestly vocation by those seeking marriage, more fulfillment, and so on. In some dioceses, the number is staggering, and the circumstances are, at times, sources of severe shock and scandal to the faithful.

Added to this is the large number of retirements when the powers-that-be exert pressure on the older men to leave the field open to younger and more "flexible" men. One cannot but notice how often new, radical policies are advocated and won by younger priests who, a year or two after their victories, leave the priesthood having saddled those they leave behind with their painful innovations.

Compounding all of this is that the once flourishing major and minor seminaries are in shambles. And despite the dire lack of vocations, we simply could never recommend that young men with faith and ideals go for training to seminaries with unorthodox professors and a country-club reputation.

In his parish, a priest often finds himself a mere pawn of middle management. He has a parish council, which sometimes acts as if it has dictatorial powers (even in the areas of doctrine and liturgy). These organs, through all the varied committees (education, liturgy, etc.), are often manipulated by diocesan sand traps through use of regional workshops, lectures, study days, and so forth. Add to this the proliferation of lay "ministries," and the priest in many places has become a helpless figurehead. His only purpose is to consecrate, absolve (when people actually seek absolution), and provide legal, administrative signatures.

When an orthodox priest attempts to maintain the purity of Catholic doctrine (and note that we are not talking about the priest who is out of consonance with the Council), he runs into the power, prestige, and financial clout of the diocesan religious education establishment. It is amazing to note how much "old church curial despotism" the liberal subordinate official can exercise when the bishop does not dare exercise his own proper authority. Solid religious education texts, even the superlative and methodologically faultless new *Christ Our Life Series* (Sisters of Notre Dame of Chardon)[vi] are banned *nominatim*[vii] and by curial fiat, while they push and promote every humanistic and doctrinally defective text.

[vi]   Still in print and in conformity with the *Catechism of the Catholic Church.*
[vii]   Latin for "by name," "in particular."

No rare situation

If the teaching nuns or a few vocal radicals in a parish insist on a faulty text, all they need to do is relate their "problem" to the education office (and perhaps hint that the nuns will withdraw), and the conscientious priest is in for the struggle of his life. This is not a rare situation, and it has led to the unwillingness of orthodox priests to take parishes with schools. Hence, the largest parishes pass into the hands of radical priests.

Sometimes, the defective catechetical series comes provided with the warmest endorsement of a bishop from whose local offices the texts emanate. This is the case with a series that is demonstrably contrary to Catholic Faith and that some 40 dioceses use. It is horrible to speculate how difficult it must be for a priest in that diocese to condemn what his bishop explicitly endorses (since it is hard enough for those in other dioceses to reject such a series) or to convince the faithful that even a bishop can be in error.

And beyond the *officially* sanctioned heterodoxy, there is the continuing barrage of false teaching given by neighboring priests, assaulting the very essentials of Catholic doctrine. (Are they essentials? Indeed they are, for you bishops have given us the *Basic Teachings*, and these are the doctrines that those in pulpits and seminars openly attack in whole or part.) Parishes are not hermetically sealed. The counterfeit currency passes the boundaries, confounding and alienating the people from orthodoxy.

Besides this homegrown variety of false teachers, numerous dioceses regularly call in and pay for dissident lecturers, stellar names with stellar stipends, from every corner of the nation and the world. Rarely does a moderate, let alone an unblushing Catholic loyalist gain the podium.

The diocesan press is also in lock-tight liberal control, so the faithful who subscribe get a regular diet of the progressive pabulum.[viii]

[viii] This is still true today. Witness how many diocesan editors still feature dissenters such as Fr. Richard McBrien and Fr. Ronald Rolheiser, OMI, as

Fortunately, many refuse to pay for poison, but then the pressure for total parish coverage enters the scene.

But what does a priest do with the neighboring pastors:

1. Who surround his parish and routinely give Communion to Protestants and divorced persons?
2. Who encourage Communion in the hand?[ix]
3. Who permit or even advocate birth control?
4. Who use "pastoral solutions" to obviate matrimonial obstacles?
5. Who allow rock-and-roll combos, pop love songs, and other secular (sometimes even blasphemous and suggestive) music during what we can only call pagan weddings?
6. Who nonchalantly give Communion to women dressed (or rather undressed) in hot pants and halters?
7. Who in some few but well-known cases hold "simultaneous celebrations" of the Eucharist in which priest and Protestant minister each have a table or share corners of an altar with

---

columnists. Meanwhile, legitimate news is often suppressed when it presents an orthodox side.

[ix] This was written before Communion in the hand was a valid option. Communion in the hand started illicitly in Holland and soon spread to the neighboring countries, becoming so endemic that the Holy See eventually gave in and allowed the use of this practice by indult (i.e., the Holy See allowed bishops and others to do something not permitted by the common law). Hence, it released *Memoriale Domini* in 1969, which gave limited permission to do this. This practice soon hopped the Atlantic in much the same way. With no permission to do so, pastors started encouraging Communion in the hand until the American bishops petitioned the Vatican for authorization as a *fait accompli*. Nonetheless, Communion in the hand is only allowed as an indult, and so the practice could be outlawed again, as it is in most of the world's countries. An excellent article on the subject ("Rethinking Communion in the Hand") can be found at www.catholic-pages.com/mass/inhand.asp. Catholics United for the Faith also has a Faith Fact on the subject available at www.cuf.org (click on Faith Facts).

the option for all to receive "under the Catholic or Protestant form"?

8. Who renovate or build new churches without kneelers and see this as only an architectural, not a theological innovation?

9. Who give general absolution, or instruct the people to tell "just one sin," or hold such vague and misleading penance services that people feel their sins, even mortal sins (Mortal sin? What is that?) have been sacramentally absolved?

10. Who exclude all devotions yet fanatically promote Pentecostal cells, well-attended by nuns and clergy, often meeting at the Assemblies of God, and who are not at all distressed when participating individuals abandon the Catholic Faith and one-by-one join other religions?

11. Who deny the serious obligation of Sunday Mass attendance?

12. Who postpone first confession years beyond First Communion?

13. Who set up and support "ecumenical" summer Bible schools?

The list could go on indefinitely! And when a priest loyal to authentic Catholic tenets refuses to give his own people such "changes," they look at him with scornful disbelief and say, "How dare you refuse us. Fr. So-and-So does it and the bishop surely knows. In fact, Fr. So-and-So is a close collaborator of the bishop."

Worse yet are the Monday morning religion classes where the innocent children who attended Mass elsewhere over the weekend ask, "How come you don't do neat things like Fr. So-and-So?"

Yes, we could expand this list (and do so with voluminous documentation), but that would risk identifying a specific area.

In conscience and orthodoxy

And in the face of all this, what do we get from bishops? Silence, or at most an ambiguous, benign, private remark that has absolutely no effect. It seems Their Excellencies reserve the stern caveats only for those priests who dare to question or protest. Many who could speak powerfully and cogently must remain in painfully discreet silence to avoid disrespect toward their bishops. When you bishops, the chief teachers, are silent, we priests must mute our own preaching, speak in generalities, and straddle the fence. We dare not alienate the people from you, even in those rare cases when we clearly see that you are hirelings and not shepherds.[1] "If the trumpet gives an uncertain sound, who shall prepare for battle?"[2]

Please, dear bishops (and especially you good bishops, who are the vast majority), at least stretch out your hands to us, open your hearts to us. Allow us the freedom to exercise our priesthood among the People of God in conscience and orthodoxy. Allow us to remain fully in union of mind and affection with the vicar of Jesus Christ. We look ahead, and, humanly speaking, we know that unless you take firm and general action or unless God intervenes in a direct way—the possibility of which we do not for a moment discount—we may wake up some dawn and realize we can no longer exercise our priesthood in conscience. Whither, then, can we run? Where can we appeal for faculties to minister to our people if our local bishop will not protect us or even tolerate us?

With the Gospel pericope of the storm at sea in mind, we do not wish to have little faith, screaming hopelessly, "Lord, save us, we perish!"[3] We know somehow and at some time, Jesus will stand up and calm the destructive elements. We know Christ, the apostles, and all the faithful are in the same boat, a boat that is battered but unsinkable.

But this does not mean that we should not pray and act. Nor perhaps does it forbid us to look beyond you to Peter and make a final, tearful query, "Will there be some way to continue to function as faithful priests if our bishops discard us or consign us to the wolves?"

CHAPTER 19

THE PLIGHT OF THE PAPIST PRIEST[1]

The basic question is: What do papist priests do when they experience a conflict between the authority of the Pope and that of the local bishop?

Webster's Collegiate Dictionary: "Papist: A Roman Catholic regarded as a partisan of the Pope; —used disparagingly."

The tag "papist priest" came about in post-Reformation England, and it has always been a divisive term. The division it represents grew out of King Henry VIII of England's lustful demand for an annulment. Two powers opposed one another: King versus Pope; State versus Church; temporal versus spiritual. We all know, at least schematically, that the historical drama resulted in the abject capitulation of the English bishops to the royal power, which was, in contrast to Rome, uncomfortably proximate and potent.

In 1534, Henry formally issued the Act of Supremacy via a rubber stamp Parliament. It read, "Be it enacted by the authority of this present Parliament, that the King, our sovereign lord, his heirs and successors, kings of this realm, shall be taken, accepted and reputed the only supreme head on earth of the Church of England called *Anglicana Ecclesia.*"

In 1535, Henry underscored this by formally renouncing the Pope. Henry then demanded of the clergy that they fully submit to the Act of Supremacy.

Years passed, as did the sovereigns, and England even saw a brief Catholic restoration. Eventually, however, bishops, priests, religious, and laity abandoned the papal communion. There were some splendid exceptions, lone stars in the night sky all the more brilliant against the darkness: Fisher, More, Franciscan and Carthusian martyrs, some abbots, Margaret Pole, and many simple faithful, peasants and gentlemen alike, in the wake of the Pilgrimage of Grace.[i] These obstinate few, then, along with their spiritual successors, constituted the disgraced cohort of the "papists."

However cursory our review of the *Anglicana Ecclesia*, the phenomenon provokes serious meditation, if not the sense of *déjà vu*, in these days when in some quarters disarming code words such as "the American Church" are evolving into the semantics of schism.

---

[i] Fisher is St. John Fisher, the only one of the roughly 20 English bishops to resist King Henry. More is St. Thomas More, Henry's good friend and chancellor (the equivalent today of a Prime Minister), who refused to agree with Henry's divorce of Catherine of Aragon and subsequent marriage to Anne Boleyn. For this, the king had him beheaded. The Franciscan and Carthusians mentioned here refer to the Carthusian monks, Brigittine nuns, and Observant Franciscans who imitated More and Fisher's stand for Catholic orthodoxy and loyalty to the Pope. They were all hung, drawn, and quartered. Bl. Margaret Pole was the mother of Reginald Cardinal Pole. His Eminence wrote a book, *De Unitate Ecclesiae*, in which he proved how all of Henry's recent declarations on the Church were false. He made such an effective case that a cry of condemnation arose throughout Europe. Henry ordered his agents to assassinate the prelate, but he was under heavy guard as papal nuncio to the Low Countries (what we now call Holland and Belgium) and because he was attempting to organize the opening of the Council of Trent. As such, Henry had Pole's friends and relatives executed.

Not content to stop there, he had Pole's 65-year-old mother arrested and eventually thrown in the Tower of London. After three years of incredibly harsh treatment, he had her beheaded. The regular executioner was away, and his accomplice was apparently inexperienced so it took several painful attempts for him to complete the job. The Pilgrimage of Grace refers to a revolt in the staunchly Catholic north in 1536. The revolt was so successful that Henry authorized several nobles to enter into negotiations with the rebels, who were led by a London barrister named Robert Aske. Henry made promises that led Aske to disperse his 40,000 rebels. Not only did Henry not keep his promises, he had Aske and other revolt leaders executed and Aske's body hung from the walls of York as a warning to other would-be revolutionaries.

Some 15 years ago, there was much talk of "polarization" on the American Catholic scene.[ii] Even back then, some reflective observers sensed it was more than that. Those were the heady days of the newly hatched NFPC and the fledgling *National Catholic Reporter.* A spirit of alienation from Rome wafted through clergy, religious, academe, and an elitist "mature" laity. Fr. Thomas Dubay, SM, wrote prophetically about the "A" and "B" strains in religious communities, and he left no doubt that a true division in faith was entailed.

Now, in the dawning '80s, the complex evolution of the revolution is neatly defined and well advanced. Msgr. George A. Kelly's *Battle for the American Church* abundantly musters the basic documented facts, however resented. Through these long years, subjected to a paced but relentless drift-shock-drift-shock syndrome, the Church in many places has become desensitized to what is an unholy amalgam of authentic reform with schismatic rebellion.

Camps are demarcated

Raymond Brown's 1981 National Catholic Education Association (NCEA) Convention address neatly outlined the extent to which this has developed. In essence, he suggests that it is now lawful for divided Catholics to recite the same *words* of the Creed with different *meanings.* He sees two basic camps: one, the "rightist," is rigid and literalist; the other, the "centrist," is liberated and laid-back.

Now a Catholic instinct should suggest that the "centrist" position must somehow be that of the Pope, foundation rock of the Church. Not so! The Pope (who clearly shows he takes the Creed as the literal, divinely revealed truth and thus as something not subject to ongoing reinterpretation, undivided by a false pluralism) has

---

slipped to the right of true "center," which is, of course, the hallowed turf of exegete Brown and his co-religionists.

What Brown's revealing speech calls "rightist" and "centrist," this article will call "papist" and "modernist." Harsher terms, yes, but any careful reading of *Pascendi Dominici Gregis* and *Lamentabile Sane* alongside the positions of Brown's centrists will establish our identification of centrist with modernist.[iii]

Do sieges exist?

As I write this, I have six United States dioceses in mind. What I describe in a very abridged way here is typical of these six, although you may not find some elements present in one or the other. These dioceses are the only ones of which this writer has sufficient first-hand information to speak. How many others are in similar straits? Cursory reading and occasional conversations with priests and laity suggest there are many more.

At the outset, I must stress that I do not relate anything here in bitterness, but in sadness, not in despair, but, ultimately, in urgency. Here are *facts*, from personal experience in most cases. Given these facts, we need moral guidance from the Holy See, the only source on earth to whom we papist priests can turn.

To whom else can we go?

For all practical purposes, these "control dioceses" are dominated by theological modernism.[iv] I would judge that at least two of the

---

[iii]   *Pascendi* and *Lamentabile* were the names of two 1907 documents from Pope St. Pius X. The first was an encyclical condemning the heresy of modernism (which he called "the synthesis of all heresies"), and the second was a "syllabus of errors," which listed 65 propositions of modernism. Both can be found at www.papalencyclicals.net.

[iv]   Modernism is the heresy that the Church and her teachings are of merely human design, and as such, they may radically change over time. It is characterized by a belief that the miracles of Jesus didn't really happen,

ordinaries are themselves willingly modernists. The true leanings of the other four are harder to discern. However, suffice it to say they have appointed modernists to all or most of the key positions. They have voiced public praise and support for these officials. They have never attempted to correct these men's errors (at least publicly). Are they, then, "neutral" victims, or does a clerical *coup de siège* perhaps unwillingly paralyze them?

Is there a new Index?

In these control dioceses, at least three-eighths of the clergy stand in a posture of radical alienation from the papacy. Whatever other issues there may be, papal authority is the cutting edge. About half the clergy comprise the swing area, a vast, mushy no-man's-land where priests will flip-flop wherever and whenever convenience dictates. At present, this means conforming to the radical modernist leadership. For some of these men, nostalgia for Rome surfaces now and then, but it quickly becomes submerged. Theirs is the tired refrain: "But this is what the bishop wants, and we took a vow of obedience to our bishop." Here one might well flash back to the nascent *Anglicana Ecclesia*.

Only about an eighth of the priests teach and act in full accord with the Pope. These openly promote and defend papal teaching among their people and in their schools. They are proud of their despised allegiance to the Holy Father. They do not look for fights, but they do not dodge issues when raised. They are not Lefebvrists.[v]

---

that His death did not atone for sins, that there was no virgin birth, no Resurrection, and even holds in the most virulent of cases that God does not exist. At its most benign (and this is using the word loosely), it says the Church should adapt her teachings to the times, particularly those of a moral nature. Thus if people in general come to accept that homosexual genital acts are no problem, then the Church should agree. If the general consensus holds that birth control is okay, who is the Church to say differently?

[v]   After the Council, Archbishop Marcel Lefebvre became the unofficial spokesman for those who saw Vatican II (as opposed to its interpretation

They are, like the Pope, in harmony with the Council and all it entails when authentically interpreted. They are as liberal as the Pope is; they are as conservative as the Pope is. These, then, are the "papist priests."

In his diocesan context, the papist priest is a pariah, the butt of infamy and condescending pity. He is barred from any positions of influence and quarantined to small enclaves, usually isolated rural places where he can do the least "damage."[vi] For all that, we must emphasize that what we here call the "papist priest" is, in any healthy Catholic diocese, just another priest in good standing.

To get some grasp of the jeopardy in which he exists, let us, sketchily, survey some conditions in the control dioceses in which modernism has all but smothered Roman Catholicism. In all six, the Priests' Senate is affiliated with the NFPC. It is true that in recent years a few have worked out compromises that allow "conscientious objectors" to withhold that portion of the dues that are allocated to

---

or implementation) as a break from sacred Tradition. Of particular concern to those for whom he spoke were the changes in the liturgy and the Council's decrees on religious liberty and ecumenism (despite whatever objections he had at the time or later developed, the record shows he voted for both). He was asked to serve as their spiritual head, and he later formed the Society of St. Pius X. In 1988, he definitively broke with the Church and incurred *latae sententiae* excommunication when he consecrated four bishops against the Holy See's express prohibition. John Paul II then released *Ecclesia Dei*, a *motu proprio* that encouraged bishops to generously allow the celebration of the Mass according to the extraordinary form of the Latin rite (aka, the Tridentine Mass). He also set up a Vatican office whose purpose was to minister to those attached to the old Mass and called it the Pontifical Commission "Ecclesia Dei." Nearly 20 years later, his successor Benedict XVI issued another *motu proprio* titled *Summorum Pontificum*, which allows priests to celebrate the extraordinary form without the local ordinary's permission. As you will see later in the book, Father's argument for supporting those attached to the pre-conciliar Mass mirrors that used by Benedict.

vi   For the last 23 years of his priesthood, Father was pastor at Holy Trinity in Casco, Wisconsin, a town of 550+ souls. Thus, he wrote from personal experience.

the NFPC. But in these dioceses, the animus of the Priests' Senate has been dominantly that of the NFPC.[vii]

Now the history of this dissident organization is open for all to see: It is simply anti-papal, and whenever any bishops attempt an exercise of authority in union with the Pope, the rebellion is extended to them.

Each Senate has its panoply of committees and sub-committees. The senators are almost entirely NFPC enthusiasts, with a few token "semi-papists," usually retired priests, allowed in to refute claims of exclusivism. Among the manifold commissions are "ministry to priests," "continuing education," "justice and peace," and so on. These front groups are Senate-appointed and stacked with NFPC types.

Hence, invited outside speakers, the itinerant gurus for priestly indoctrination, are consistently dissidents and more or less openly anti-papal. Priests are urged (at times ordered) to attend these harangues at which the bishop sits listening to sundry heresies, only to rise at the end to thank and praise the heretic. There are also permanent, ongoing structures for intensive "re-education" of the clergy, e.g. Fr. Vincent Dwyer, OCSO's *Genesis II*.[viii]

Modernists also control the most sensitive diocesan offices. They exert, as was boasted publicly a decade ago, "lock-tight control" of the religious education establishment. All the staff must be in harmony with the director's philosophy. The chancery staff rigidly excludes any papist catechetical books, aids, lectures, etc., and places them

---

[vii] Animus refers to what our personality really is after we strip off the "mask" we use in public, but which isn't our true self. So in other words, Father is contending here that the Priests' Senate is a puppet of the NFPC.

[viii] Ostensibly, Dwyer's program grew out of a need to help priests develop positive self-images. (Such programs were trendy at the time.) The Trappist monk added behavioral techniques to spirituality, and he encouraged the formation of priest support groups. Many were enthusiastic about him and his theories. However, one former seminarian who went through his program claims "one (if not the main) objective of the Dwyer Program was to welcome gay students into seminary formation with open arms, and by doing so, begin to acknowledge and legitimize the gay priesthood; or in other words, bring it out of the closet."

on a *de facto* Index of Forbidden Books.[ix] Only modernist texts get a favorable nod. Thus, they have revived the Index ... to destroy the Faith! Diocesan education conventions are brainwashing spectacles whose roster of speakers and topics are completely predictable.

The wine is modernism

The desacralizing change-agents also head and staff the various liturgical commissions. Gradually over the years, liturgical abuses became a seamless part of regular worship, and, with rationalizing doubletalk, of pontifical services as well.[x]

One would clearly see the malice involved if one attended the official lecture circuits on baptism, reconciliation, and so on. At these regional meetings, the assertions are vintage modernism. It is noteworthy that the Religious Education department and the liturgical commission work in tandem to pressure pastors into delaying first confession until later grades. Furthermore, they insist on Communion in the hand for small children.

The deconstructing forces subtly attain these official objectives. Often word goes to the nuns, who then take the matter out of the pastor's hands. In fact, on many fronts, the role of the teaching Sisters is that of commandos. The nuns can essentially legislate catechesis and liturgy in all its aspects; they evidently know well how to reduce the pastor to impotence.

In these dioceses, the veiled (?) threat of the Sisters pulling out of the parish school had only to occur in a few instances before every

---

[ix] For centuries, until the early 1960s, the Holy See maintained an "Index of Forbidden Books." This was a list of books that Catholics were discouraged from reading because they contained material that was damaging to faith and morals.

[x] A pontifical Mass is not the same as a papal Mass. According to the online 1913 *Catholic Encyclopedia*, the "Pontifical Mass is the solemn Mass celebrated by a bishop."

pastor learned that what Sister wants, Sister gets.[xi] (I would quickly add that there are some noble exceptions, and I have found myself blessed in this way.) Where there are no nuns, religious education coordinators perform this ministry of the barricades. Furthermore, most of these control dioceses insist that all religion teachers, including volunteer CCD teachers, receive certification by attending modernist courses sponsored by the diocese. At this late stage of the takeover, there is no adversarial relationship in most parishes. The exception exists in those few remaining bastions where the pastor is a papist.

The diocesan press is also firmly in the progressive camp with columnists such as McBrien, Greeley, Bosler, Curran, *et al.*[xii] Features such as "Know Your Faith"[xiii] (whose slant is showing) even filter the diurnal flow of news. We can see that Rome knows the problem by the remarkable message of Archbishop Pio Laghi to the American episcopal publishers.[xiv] In any event, the parishes are under enormous

---

xi According to the National Catholic Education Association, there were 57,407 Sisters teaching in US Catholic parochial primary schools during the 1969-70 academic year. In the 1980-81 year, around the time Father wrote this piece, that number had dropped to 24,454. In 2006-07, there were 3,746.

xii McBrien is Fr. Richard McBrien, a widely read newspaper columnist, dissenting theologian, and theology professor at University of Notre Dame. Bosler was most likely Msgr. Raymond Bosler, a priest from the archdiocese of Indianapolis and a *peritus* at the Council who had a question-and-answer column that featured misleading and questionable answers. As an example, he gave an anemic answer on purgatory that some fundamentalists have used to "prove" that this doctrine has no biblical basis and the Catholic Church "invented" it. Greeley and Curran are discussed elsewhere in this book.

xiii This was a syndicated column featured in diocesan newspapers that attempted to teach the faith but did so in a dubious fashion.

xiv On April 27, 1981, papal delegate Archbishop Laghi wrote the American episcopacy, "With increasing frequency, the Holy See receives letters from the United States complaining about articles appearing in Catholic newspapers, including diocesan publications, which cause harm to the faith of the people because of lack of respect for the teaching and decisions of the Magisterium. As you know, it is not unusual for such articles to contain criticisms and attacks even on the teaching authority and the person of

pressure to take "full coverage."[xv] A papist priest has the choice to disobey his bishop or feed poison to his flock.

The Offices of Family Life also bear the mark of Cain. From these busy-busy people there is nary a word about abortion, no support of pro-life activities, not even the meekest hint of a prophetic critique of Planned Parenthood. On the contrary, the immoral theology of Kosnik & Co. infects their official marriage preparation courses.[xvi] The papist priest cannot send his young couples to these required courses in good conscience.

Irregularities teem

The modernists use diocesan structures (pastoral councils, deanery councils, parish councils, boards of education at all

---

the Holy Father. The impact of such criticism is heightened when columns are syndicated and widely circulated. A letter from the Secretariat of State (March 31, 1981; Protocol N. 63408) expressed concern over this problem, and ordinaries are encouraged to consider their responsibilities in governing the policies of those publications over which they have control. To this I would add a word of encouragement for the promotion of a sound and vital Catholic press, so useful an instrument for evangelization and so vibrant in the life of the Church in the United States."

[xv] Full coverage means every parish family would have a paid subscription.

[xvi] Kosnik is Fr. Anthony Kosnik, a dissident theologian who spoke at Call to Action meetings, promoted abortion, and was chairman of a CTSA committee during the late '70s and early '80s that produced the book, *Human Sexuality: New Directions in American Catholic Thought*. This widely used seminary textbook denied that anything—even bestiality, according to one source—was intrinsically evil. The book's authors also opined, "We think it appropriate therefore to broaden the traditional formulation of the purpose of sexuality from procreative and unitive to creative and integrative." This would, of course, have obliterated the Church's understanding on the truth about sexuality and, along with it, her claim to be led into all truth by the Holy Spirit. At that point, she would have simply become another human institution.

Fr. Kosnik most recently made news in 2002, when he and three other Detroit priests publicly endorsed the candidacy of Michigan Governor Jennifer Granholm precisely because of her pro-abortion position.

levels, parish committees, especially on the liturgy, as well as that ominous enforcement arm, the personnel board) to throttle the non-conformists with polypodal tentacles, ever sucking, sapping, squeezing. In turn, these people must extract huge sums from their parishioners to feed the monster that does this to them.

To add to this dismaying set of circumstances, we realize that the seminaries utilized by our dioceses are now hot beds of modernism. We send bright-eyed idealist, Catholic youth into these dens of revolution only to have them come back on vacations and, rarely, for ordination as programmed anti-papal, un-Catholic activists. The few ordained thus build up the youthful base of dissidence far beyond the wildest dreams of those who got drunk on the spirit of the '60s.

The only salvation for seminary candidates, unless they can master the art of dissembling, is for the pastor to dissuade them from going. (In the control dioceses, there is no chance for a candidate to attend the few well-known orthodox seminaries.) Most of us then urge the young men to postpone entrance, hoping for eventual reconstruction of the system. Here is a peak of priestly suffering: Dissuading a candidate from the seminary in order to save his soul!

Pastoral life is a new ball game. There is a general collapse of discipline and doctrine in the six dioceses. Each parish is a brave new world, teeming with its own flora and fauna. *Tot capita, quot sententiae. Cujus regio, ejus religio.*[xvii] Even we papists are honestly confounded by the claims and counterclaims of what Rome has or has not allowed. Edicts emanating from diocesan or national sources give all the pretense of bearing Vatican authority. An egregious example: Just what is Rome's will concerning the communal use of a chalice at weekend Masses?[xviii]

[xvii] "There are as many opinions as there are heads." "Whose region, his religion." In other words, whoever rules the region gets to choose the religion.

[xviii] While this is allowed, as Prefect of the Congregation for Divine Worship and the Discipline of the Sacrament Francis Cardinal Arinze wrote Bishop of Spokane William Skylstad on October 16, 2006, "Christ is fully present under each of the species... Communion under the species of the bread alone, as a consequence, makes it possible to receive all the fruit of eucharistic grace."

What has transposed this from being a nightmare into a wide-awake scream in the dark are the activities of the matrimonial tribunals. For years, we priests have suspected that something was rotten with their praxis. The powers that be constantly assured us that all was beyond reproach, that the soaring numbers of annulments simply grew out of new norms, expanded staffs, greater efficiency, and so on.

Meanwhile, in our (typically) small country parishes, there were disproportionate volumes of annulments. Folks at the bars began to gossip and make bitter, accusatory jokes. They knew people on the next farm who had been married for years and had five children, and suddenly their union was "rent asunder."

We pastors closed our eyes, swallowed hard, told God that we couldn't overrule the bishop's own experts, and we married the new annulees to new spouses, who were usually annulees themselves. Thank God, we were not made privy to the grounds, much less to the *acta*.[xix]

But then came cracks of thunder.

In November 1979, Pope John Paul II spoke of "*divortio sub alio nomine tecto*"[xx] in reference to unjustified annulments.[2] The full storm broke loose publicly at the Fall 1980 Synod on the Family. Cardinal Felici told us what we had long suspected, and the Holy Father seconded the complaint in equally firm, if less inflammatory terms.[xxi]

Communion takes its most complete form as a sign when administered under both species. But as Cardinal Arinze said, whoever receives the Host alone fully receives Jesus Christ, and in receiving under both species, one receives neither more of Jesus Christ, nor less of Him. It is only the way of receiving Him that is different.

[xix] This is the Latin word from which we get "Acts" (as in Acts of the Apostles). It means a recording of events or things that took place. Father uses the word to mean the details from an annulment case.

[xx] Loosely translated, this means, "divorce by another name" or "divorce under the cover of another thing."

[xxi] A summary of Cardinal Felici's report on Church annulments presented to the Synod on October 6 is in *Origins*, v. 10 (October 1980), 314-15. One

It was this crisis more than anything else that drove me to write this chapter. Once more, the papists may be constrained to stand up for the Pope on the matter of annulments—this time by the hundreds of thousands. Poor Henry! Why the fuss in 1534?

It is now *imperative* to pose hard, excruciating questions that we cannot leave unanswered. There is now sufficient doubt about US annulments that pastors cannot drift along without a final decision. It is the opinion of this writer that the annulment debacle has for a decade rooted and institutionalized the potential and dynamics of an American schism. How can we reverse thousands of these cases, affecting new families and affecting all those related to them? How do you annul an annulment? On the other hand, how can the Church close her eyes to these invalid unions, for that is precisely what the Roman comments suggest is happening.

Mobility allows a seeping effect

By the grace of God, we papist priests find ourselves entrenched here and there in these arenas of apocalyptic anarchy. Usually we are in the "boondocks"—small, rural communities. It has become nearly impossible to serve larger parishes except where two papists have contrived to be assigned together and have been in place for some time.

Also, these priests must have found good religious who will satisfy their "scruples." Once a parish has been converted to the "new

can find the full Felici intervention in *Le famiglie al Sinodo: interventi, relazioni, testimonianze alla V Assemblea generale del Sinodo dei vescovi*, 26 settembre-25 ottobre 1980/Catholic Church: *Synodus Episcoporum* (1980); (*Consilium de Familia. Città del Vaticana: Libreria editrice Vaticana*; [Torino]: Marietti, 1981), as well as *The 1980 Synod of Bishops "On the role of the family:" an exposition of the event and an analysis of its texts*, by Jan Grootaers and Joseph A. Selling (Leuven: University Press, 1983). For John Paul II's "less inflammatory" take, see the apostolic exhortation that flowed from this, the Fifth Ordinary General Assembly of the Synod of Bishops. It is called *Familiaris Consortio*, available at www.papalencyclicals.net under "John Paul II."

Church," it becomes interdict to papists.[xxii] I have seen a brilliant, devout, vigorous priest attempt to assume control of a modernist parish. Within six months, he had been ground to powder by the parish council and the nuns. He left for the hinterlands, broken and disillusioned.

In our foxholes, we must compromise as far as we can, for, as we are well aware, there are few places left to take us in. These "priest holes," to allude again to the past, are far from hermetically sealed.[xxiii] Our parishioners are very mobile. They often visit modernist parishes as they travel or attend weddings and funerals. Their children bring the stories to school on Monday mornings. "Father, guess what they do in that other church?" Do we then tell innocent children that the other priests are disobedient? The confusion mounts as the months go by. Less stable parishioners apply pressures for outdoor polka Masses, for scandalously secularized weddings, for intercommunion, for general absolution, and so on.

Many papist priests are despised

In modernist dioceses, the papist priest has no chance of attaining an effective [i.e., influential] position. This is the least of his problems, though it dooms the whole diocese to a regime totally alienated from the Holy See. What is pathetic, however, is that given the current practice of prior consultation, no chance exists that modernist priests and religious will vote on episcopal candidacy for a papist. Recent appointments, e.g., Archbishop Szoka of Detroit, offer some hope

---

[xxii]   An ecclesiastical penalty that nowadays is the equivalent of excommunication. However, it used to be that whole countries could be placed under interdict, which meant that the only sacraments that could be performed were baptism, extreme unction, and the celebration of Mass and hearing confessions only on Christian holidays. Countries that have been placed under interdict include England under King John and Mexico during the 1920s.

[xxiii]   Priest holes are concealed places in homes to hide priests during times of persecution (such as those used in Elizabethan and Jacobin England, as well as the 1920s in Mexico).

that we can bypass this barrier.[xxiv] It is exasperating to think that loyalty to the pope has become a diriment impediment[xxv] to the episcopacy in some dioceses.

If Rome seeks methods to restore the Church, surely the clearest way seems to be the appointment of bishops who are truly Roman Catholic. We cannot correct the disorders discussed here unless the *bishop* is sound and courageous. Even the seminaries, the crucial next priority, cannot be reconstituted without heroic, good shepherds. Heroic, because they will have to purge the present faculties and begin all over again.

Words of exhortation from Rome will not effect changes so long as the present bishops control these control dioceses. There is simply no way to reform seminaries, religious education offices, marriage tribunals, the diocesan press, or liturgical and other abuses until tough, papally-oriented bishops are in charge.[xxvi] Such a bishop

---

[xxiv]   After he resigned as Cardinal Archbishop of Detroit, Edmund Szoka was called to Rome in 1997 to run the Holy See's finances. He was then named governor of the Vatican City State. In this position, he helped run the 2005 conclave that elected Benedict XVI. He is now retired.

[xxv]   This is an official canonical term that means "an impediment that nullifies marriage."

[xxvi]   This was not possible before 1981 (the year Father wrote this piece). It could be argued that the key person in appointing bishops in a nation is the pope's diplomatic representative there, either the apostolic nuncio or, in countries having no formal relation with the Holy See, the apostolic delegate. From 1973-80, the apostolic delegate was Archbishop Jean Jadot, a Belgian. According to numerous sources, Jadot was "bent on reshaping the American hierarchy" in the modernist image, and a look at his appointments shows he largely succeeded. Since he left, the situation in one sense has become demonstrably better. There are many more orthodox, "papist" bishops in place now than at any time since the Council. However, many of the older active priests and curial bureaucracies are modernist. This makes it difficult for good bishops to make any substantive changes. As the priests and curial officials from the era Father writes of retire, more orthodox individuals are slowly replacing them.

would immediately rally the *pusillus grex* of papists,[xxvii] and soon the fence sitters would slither over to him. The losses will be heavy and battles bloody. But what is the alternative? To betray the Church? To abandon souls? To play the hireling?

I have not seen the need to rehash the now copious documentation on the state of the Church. The horror stories hardly generate a chill anymore. One thing is certain in the six dioceses considered here: The priests with full allegiance to the Pope are a despised minority, and the faith of most of their fellow priests and, yes, God help us, the faith of their bishops is simply and plainly *not* their faith. They often hear the Holy Father exhorting priests to unity with their bishops. These words sear into their consciences. They have always wanted this. But as we end this article it is time speak the unspeakable, to raise the ultimate, explosive, historic questions that no one thus far seems willing to broach in public.

Whom do we obey?

The basic question is, what do we papist priests do when we experience a conflict between the authority of the Holy Father and the authority of our local bishop? What are we to do when the bishop directly (or indirectly through his officials) orders us to disregard (and in fact, disobey) repeated and insistent papal directives? Do we obey the bishop or the pope? To state the question seems to answer it, but to know the answer in theory is not to solve it in practice.

We need guidance from the highest authority since problems such as time of first confession, general absolution, inter-communion, to name only a few common conflicts are well known to Rome, but the Holy See has permitted these bishops to remain in authority and, to all appearances, in full communion. We appreciate that remedial

---

[xxvii] *Pusillus grex* comes from Luke 12:32, and translates to "little flock." See also *Nos es muy conocida*, no. 10, an encyclical by Pius XI available at www.papalencyclicals.net.

action takes time, but meanwhile, we need moral direction for our consciences and pragmatically clear pastoral guidance.

The questions become specific: Must we attend lectures given by heretics when the bishop so insists? Should we concelebrate with priests who openly deny essentials of the Faith, including the doctrine of the Real Presence, or when glaring abuses take place, since our participation seems to endorse them?

Very specifically:

1. If the diocese has directed us to put the leftover Precious Blood down the *sacrarium*, should we do so in peaceful conscience?
2. When priests, notoriously radical in doctrine and in liturgical discipline come to our parishes (say for weddings or funerals), what should be our response?
3. Are we to continue to suspend judgment, stifle our fears, and routinely cooperate with our tribunals in areas of suspect annulments?
4. Is it tolerable that the now public disagreement between Rome and US canonists simply drift for years without a resolution?
5. What should be our stance in regard to the people committed to our pastoral care?
6. Must we remain forever silent about the errors and abuses that inundate them?
7. Dare we risk causing scandal by warning our faithful people about this virtual poison when they know that specific priests and perhaps the bishop himself are prescribing it?
8. We have been prudential for years; is this a virtue or a vice?

These are momentous, historical questions. They are of utmost urgency. If they are not answered soon, or if remedy is not otherwise given by corrective action, the papist priest will have no recourse but to meekly and silently retire and live out his life (be it years or decades) without public exercise of his priestly ministry. And why? Simply because in these sorry times, he must, in conscience, remain loyal to the vicar of Christ. He demands the right to believe what the Pope teaches and to obey freely his directives. In his address at the Catholic University of America in Washington, DC, on October 7, 1979, Pope John Paul reminded the bishops of the "greatest right" of the faithful: To receive the Catholic doctrine purely and entirely. In April 1980, he issued *Inaestimabile Donum*, in which he added to this "bill of rights of the faithful" the "right to true liturgy, which means the liturgy desired and laid down by the Church…"

Surely faithful priests, *a fortiori*, since they shepherd the flock, must have these same rights:

1. the right to openly profess and teach and defend the Faith as it is taught by the pope;
2. the right to adhere to the liturgical law as authorized by Rome;
3. the right to defend the Holy Eucharist from profanation;
4. the right to keep inviolate the Profession of Faith and the Oath Against Modernism, which we solemnly swore on the eve of our ordination.[xxviii]

Were we not imbued with a sense of deference and reverence toward ecclesiastical office, we would be sorely tempted to call for

---

[xxviii] The Oath was in effect from September 1, 1910, until July 1967, when the Congregation for the Doctrine of the Faith repealed it. Every ordained cleric and anyone who taught theology had to swear it. Today, in large part because of the issues Father has discussed in this chapter, any who teach theology or philosophy at a Catholic college or university must take the "Oath of Fidelity" in accord with Canon 833. Canon law also requires that a theologian teaching in a Catholic university receive something called a *mandatum* from the local bishop, which says they are fit to teach this subject at these institutions. Most of these places, however, have ignored this. Of the roughly 220 Catholic colleges and universities in the United States, only 26 require the Oath.

a "priests' liberation movement" in order to demand these rights without which we cannot survive.

We beg the Pope's guidance

History now affords us a vantage point of centuries to look back on the gestation period of *Anglicana Ecclesia*. From it, we learn to our great comfort that the epithet "papist," intended as a brand of shame, has emerged as a badge of honor. We think of the wounds on the Cross that shone in glory on Easter night. The papists of old are on the pages of Church history; they are the nobility of Catholicism. We are confident that some day the Church will recognize that the papist priests now trapped here and there in a specious *Americana Ecclesia* will become respected movers in a yearned for era of reconstruction. What a blessing for those laity and those parishes that shelter these scorned but faithful priests!

Meanwhile, we pray that our beloved Holy Father will somehow find a way to enable us to survive and to illuminate us as to precisely what he wants us to do.

Not least of all, we beg his guidance to make it possible for us to full-heartedly obey and revere our bishops without the impossible dilemma of thereby weakening our loyalty to the vicar of Jesus Christ.

CHAPTER 20

THE AGENDA OF THE NFPC[1]

*Is it possible to embrace the agenda of the NFPC without thereby
rejecting the "agenda" and authority of the papal Magisterium?*

Even the most detached observers have sensed an epochal and
imminent turning point in the bimillennial history of the Roman
Catholic Church. In a recent issue,[2] *TIME* magazine devoted three
cover stories to this topic, perceptively portraying a crisis that, while
universal, has somehow become uniquely engaged in the arena of
US Catholicism.

The past months of escalating Roman intervention have confirmed
the prophetic socio-theological analyses of Kelly, Hitchcock, and
others.[i] What they surveyed on the full national scene, an unnamed
author sketched on a modest scale for the narrower sector of the
priesthood. The response to that *HPR* article ("Plight of the Papist
Priest," December 1981) disclosed a vast reservoir of fidelity to Rome
among American priests who sensed that somehow they were being
manipulated into a stance of confrontation with papal authority.
The "Papist Priest" saw as a central problem the encroachment of the
National Federation of Priests' Councils (NFPC)[ii] into a plurality of
diocesan presbyteral structures.

I wish to zoom in on this organization and its agenda in order
to ask in an objective and fraternal way whether one can possibly
embrace the agenda of the NFPC without thereby rejecting the

---

[i] Msgr. George Kelly, previously mentioned, and James Hitchcock, PhD, who
teaches history at Saint Louis University.
[ii] A group founded in 1968, and still in existence today.

papal Magisterium. I submit that in some essential respects the two are incompatible. Hopefully, the following will convince priests who know well they cannot serve two masters to work toward disaffiliation.

The NFPC does not allow individual memberships. Although it will permit independent "associations," its main thrust is to affiliate the diocesan presbyteral councils. The reason for this is obvious. The NFPC knows these apparatuses will deliver power, structural control, and inflated numbers. The presbyterium of a diocese is a sacramental, ecclesial, and canonical organism. The NFPC is none of these. It is an independent and autonomous, spontaneously-formed organization. When queried about this point, the Sacred Congregation for the Clergy responded in a decree of October 10, 1969: "That document (Vatican II, Presb. Ord. Ch. II, 7) contemplates diocesan senates; it does not contemplate a national federation of senates."[3]

Non-canonical superstructure

The NFPC claims some 30,000 priests. Every priest in every affiliated diocese is tallied. The NFPC uses this count in its publicity press releases to support its agenda. Thus, when it agitates for the abolition of mandatory celibacy, the ordination of women priests, and the like, it counts every priest, regardless of personal protest, to advance its causes. This is patently dishonest and is unjust to those who conscientiously object. There are over 58,000 priests in the United States. Thus, the NFPC claims the allegiance of slightly more than half the American priesthood.

Past surveys, however, have shown large proportions of disagreement among the automatically affiliated priests. At one point in one large archdiocese, two-thirds of the priests reportedly withheld dues. The NFPC now prefers to have the dioceses fund the dues. The flux of affiliation and disaffiliation makes an interesting history of its own.

The NFPC has insisted that affiliation must be a decision of the presbyteral council alone, without a poll of the priests. This from an organization that constantly calls for democratic processes in the Church! A priest sent a letter to the newsletter of the NFPC precisely challenging this contradiction. The official response came in an editorial:

> ... thus it is very possible that the rank-and-file priests of the US, who make up the bulk of the US Catholic clergy, are not knowledgeable on theological and other crucial developments, and that as a consequence, could, without sufficient reason, view NFPC as a threat to them or even to the Church. We do not believe that Fr. Munzing's call for democracy in this area of the Church would serve the best interest of the Church any more than if all adult US citizens were to participate in a vote on an issue that rightly belongs in the halls of Congress... (*PRIESTS/ USA*, September 1972)

It is imperative that every priest become informed of the specific agenda of this non-canonical superstructure, and that he demand the right to vote for or against affiliation on the grounds of priestly conscience. For all purposes, affiliation endorses and ratifies the NFPC agenda that, to a large extent, becomes the agenda of the diocese concerned.

What is this NFPC agenda? I found the most objective answer in the official resolutions passed at the annual meetings of the "House of Delegates." After all, these feature carefully crafted language on which the delegates had debated, amended, and voted. These gussied up public policy statements understate, never overstate the controversial aspects involved. They are the statements of the NFPC itself, not of its critics.

I am indebted to Fr. Richard Hynes, president of the NFPC, for graciously lending me the large volume containing literally hundreds of resolutions from 1969-1984.

It would be impossible to reproduce all this data (over 100 pages) in this article. Here I can only summarize what is already a summary. I highly recommend that others read this record in its entirety. In what follows, the numbers indicate the year. Repetition indicates distinct resolutions on the same issue in the same year. In later years, they numbered the resolutions in sequence. Thus, 84:6 indicates the sixth resolution passed in 1984.

Some core items

CELIBACY. One of the perennial crusades. The 1971 Synod of Bishops on the priesthood fanned the controversy. NFPC issued its "Moment of Truth" manifesto. Officers lobbied at the Synod in Rome and deplored the "bad choices" of US episcopal representatives. President Fr. Frank Bonnike (subsequently married) warned that if the Synod didn't overturn mandatory celibacy, "Any prohibitive pronouncements about the matter are going to be counterproductive... Priests are going to socialize more frequently and openly with women than before..." 69, 69, 70, 70, 70, 70, 70 Further resolutions: 71, 71, 72, 73, 73. (There was a parallel drive to ordain married men on a routine basis.)

LAICIZATION. Repeated resolutions chide Rome for the strictness of its procedures. This concern has reached explosive proportions since the accession of John Paul II and the implementation of his new norms.[iii] Also repeated calls that "resigned" priests be restored to positions despite the prohibition by Rome: 69, 69, 69,

---

[iii] From early in his pontificate, John Paul II sought to reestablish control of an otherwise out-of-control situation. First, in April 1979, he issued the first of what would become his traditional Holy Thursday letters to priests, *Novo incipiente nostro*, which, among other topics, addressed the laicization of priests. Then on October 14, 1980, the Congregation for the Doctrine of the Faith issued norms for the laicization of priests, *Per litteras ad universas*. Both are available in Flannery's *Vatican Council II: More Post Conciliar Documents*, available at most Catholic bookstores.

71 ("free ministry"), 71, 71, 71, 72, 73, 73, 74, 75, 77, 77, 79, 80, 80, 82, 83, 84.

WOMEN PRIESTS. This cause emerged more recently. The NFPC began with a call for women deacons, 72. The following year saw the first call for ordaining women priests, 73. In 1975, the delegates voted for collaboration with the Women's Ordination Conference. Similar resolutions: 77, 77, 77, 77 (one calling for opening the permanent diaconate to women), 82, 84. (We might recall how the Holy Father ordered United States bishops to have no relationship with any group promoting the ordination of women.)

SELECTION OF BISHOPS. In 1973, Fr. Jerome Fraser, chairman of the Detroit Convention, stated:

> The third area in which we should direct our efforts this year is the realignment of the authority of the Church. Each council should set up the committee called for in the CLSA's[iv] proposed plan for the selection of bishops. We should recognize that there is already going on a selective ecclesiastical disobedience, e.g. in giving communion [sic] in the hand, in providing a pastoral solution to giving advice on birth control and marriage after divorce. This disobedience is likely to expand unless authority and decision-making are more representatively structured.

The selection of bishops is, then, another recurring theme at House of Delegates convocations. The excerpt above is transparent in its motives for championing this cause. As Fr. Bonnike said in his State of the Federation speech, 1972:

> We need a derby or a race to see which ... diocese can first claim to have elected its own bishop. Not to have people sharing in the decisions which closely affect their lives constitutes the greatest danger that society and the Church face today. It breeds violence and revolt.

---

iv   Canon Law Society of America.

(Yet as we have seen, when pressed for a democratic vote of all priests on the pivotal matter of affiliation, the NFPC reaction can be quite autocratic.) Resolutions on this subject: 69, 69, 69, 69, 70, 70, 72, 74, 84.

INTERFERENCE IN LOCAL BISHOP'S AUTHORITY. We see evidence of what some call a "theology of pressure" in the NFPC's thrust to control the local agenda, thereby usurping the bishop's initiative. Cf. 69 (RS-10) and 78 (Vision Statement VII):

> We emphasize the necessary autonomy of the council and the need for the council to set its own agenda. Confrontation with the bishop may be a component of this approach, but that is accepted as a healthy sign of a viable process...

In addition, the NFPC has not hesitated to use its collective national clout to intervene in the exercise of individual bishops' disciplinary authority within their own dioceses, e.g., Cardinal O'Boyle and the "Washington 19" (issue of contraception); Archbishop Robert Lucey in San Antonio;[v] and Bishop Paul Tanner in St. Augustine.[vi] Many cases never reached the status of official resolutions.

---

[v]   One biography of His Excellency states, "His [July 4, 1969] retirement stemmed [from] disagreements between himself and local priests within the Archdiocese over [whether] priests should become involved in politics. As a result, the Vatican instructed Lucey to retire. He served as bishop for twenty-eight years."

[vi]   One can only surmise to what Father refers here. One retired priest in the diocese said there are two possibilities. The first concerns a Fr. Jules Keating, who, when asked to perform a wedding on a Sunday, refused. The couple appealed to the bishop, who then directed Keating to accede to their request. Father held his ground, and His Excellency removed him from the cathedral parish to one in Niceville, Florida. Fr. Keating appealed to the Congregation for the Clergy, who directed Tanner to reinstate his priest, stating that priests should not be moved for disciplinary reasons. However, the NFPC had nothing to do with this.

    The other more likely possibility concerns the local priests' senate's desire to affiliate with the NFPC, for which Tanner apparently had no use (this event

Akin to this is the feverish action for "due process" where the concern was to protect dissident priests: 69, 69, 69, 78. The increasingly successful drive for liaison with the NCCB/USCC and their committees is another avenue by which dissidents can circumvent the local bishops, cf. 69, 70, 70, 70, 70, 74, 74, 79, 80, 81, 81, 82. The periodic desire to move national offices to Washington is expressly geared toward facilitating an umbrella coalition with like-minded organizations.[vii] This entire field of action surely raises a question of ecclesiology, since the local bishop should be the liaison between his own priests and the episcopal conference.

CORPORATE RESPONSIBILITY. Under this title, the NFPC seeks supervision and effective control by procedural pressure over the fiscal policies in general and the investments in particular of affiliated dioceses. Directives are spelled out with specificity, targeting offending businesses and banks—all this dictated by the social and political goals of the NFPC. The code word is "accountability." (NFPC helped found the Catholic Coalition for Responsible Investment in 1973.) Resolutions: 69, 71, 72, 73, 73, 74, 74, 74, 75, 77, 78, 81, 83.

Various objectives

"BIG BROTHER." The NFPC seeks an influence also over continuing education, formation programs, invited lecturers,

---

was confirmed by another priest with whom the editors spoke). Tanner said if they voted to affiliate, he would abolish the group. During a meeting, a vote was taken on the matter, and a very strong majority voted in favor. Not wanting this outcome, Tanner immediately said words to the effect of, "This body is disbanded. Let's go get dinner." This created a huge amount of publicity, but this did not cause the bishop to relent. However, during a subsequent *ad limina* visit to Rome, His Excellency was asked whether he had a priests' council. When he said, "No, I don't," Vatican officials told him to form one, and so he did. Until his successor took office, however, it did not affiliate with the NFPC. But the NFPC had nothing to do with the situation, other than probably contributing to whatever negative publicity occurred.

[vii]   The group's headquarters is in Chicago.

agendas, and texts. It also spearheads the movement to impose analysis, evaluation, and assessment—not only on councils—but also on individual priests, cf. 71, 72, 72, 74, 79:5 (detailed investigatory methods), 82.

The NFPC offers the evaluative guideline for ordained ministers and provides models to help councils implement the programs (Comment: In whose image and likeness are we forming priests? Who ever evaluates the evaluators, and by what criteria and on whose authority? There are numerous and prestigious clerical and lay defenders of the positions proposed by the paper Magisterium. How often do they receive invitations to speak in our dioceses?)

SUPPORT OF ERA. All councils summoned to support passage, 81. (Action steps given.)[viii]

CLERICALISM. The August 1971 issue of the NFPC organ (then PRIESTS/USA) quotes ex-Jesuit Bernard Cook as saying, "What we're saying in effect, and I'll say it quite explicitly, is, the clergy must go. There's no room in the Church for the clerical-lay distinction as we've known it."

See also the working paper, "Serving in a Ministerial Church": "For too long the Church has given the clergy the primary role in ministry..." In 1984, resolution 84:13 ordered that a "clericalism" study by CMSM[ix] be sent to each council, which, in turn, is urged to "make copies available to their constituents." We recall the trend to emphasize the "professionalism" of the priest, including a resolution on "Freedom of Residence," 72.

[viii] ERA stands for Equal Rights Amendment. This was a proposed amendment to the United States Constitution that would have enshrined equal protection under the law regardless of gender. While it is reintroduced in every Congress (and has been since 1982), it effectively is a dead letter. Court decisions and the legal codes of the federal and state governments have evolved in such a way that the need for such a constitutional amendment has been mitigated.

[ix] According to its website, the Conference of Major Superiors of Men (CMSM) "... serves the leadership of the Catholic orders and congregations of the more than 20,000 vowed religious priests and brothers of the United States."

Relations with Rome

We can discern an aura of nationalism and anti-Romanism in Fr. Neil McCaulley's "American Church" keynote in 1981:

> We need to become aware of the American Catholic experience and the American Catholic identity as real and positive. Until the bishops, priests, religious women and men, laity, and all segments come to a consensus on what is this positive American Catholic identity and stand up for it and articulate it, we are not in a position to dialogue with Rome very effectively ... our national identity and self-respect as the American Church is presently so weak that the new code will take away the American procedural norms—and who will speak for the people?[x] Do we want uniformity for senates? Is all the experience of the last 13 years going to be swept aside in favor of a model from a code into which we, as the American Church, had little input? ... [It is] a failure of vision and demeaning for a senate to deal only with matters pertaining to priests and to allow themselves to be relegated to a limited clerical agenda.

One senses here that he considers Rome an alien antagonist. This animus contrasts sharply with the true spirit of Vatican II in the words of *Presbyterorum Ordinis*, no. 15:

> Since the priestly ministry is the ministry of the Church herself, it can be discharged only by hierarchical communion with the whole body. Therefore, pastoral love demands that, acting in this communion, priests dedicate their own wills through obedience to the service of God and their brothers. This love requires that they accept and carry out in a spirit of faith whatever the

---

[x]   The new *Code of Canon Law* came out in 1983.

Sovereign Pontiff, their own bishop, or other superiors *command or recommend.*

APOSTOLIC DELEGATE. A resolution urged that Rome drop this office and name an American to a similar post.

WASHINGTON 19. This resolution defends those who dissented against *Humane Vitae.* A threatening tone is used in two resolutions of grave consequences if the Pope does not support the dissident priests, 69, 70—the stick, and then the carrot: "NFPC commends the very few courageous bishops who spoke on behalf of the Washington 19," 69.[xi]

LAICIZATION NORMS. (See separate treatment above, esp. 69.) The NFPC believes the local bishop, not Rome, should decide every appeal, 71. Concerning John Paul II, the language is that of an indictment making an invidious contrast with the *modus operandi* of Paul VI (whom the NFPC had also previously criticized!). In 1981, the NFPC urged United States bishops to "voice their opposition" to the Pope's norms.

[xi] Near the end of the Council, Paul VI formed a commission to study whether the Church should change her teaching on contraception. In June 1966, the majority of the commission's members said she should. On October 29 of that same year, His Holiness made a tactical mistake, in a certain sense, by announcing that he found some of the reasoning in the commission's arguments flawed. Between that time and July 25, 1968, the date he released *Humanae Vitae*, proponents of doctrinal change developed a stunningly effective PR campaign that featured not only arguments against the Church's unchanging teaching, but also the means of rapidly disseminating those arguments. So it was that two days after *HV*'s release, Fr. Charles Curran of the Catholic University of America in Washington, DC, and 18 other dissident theologians released a declaration at the University saying conscience should trump Church teaching in deeply personal and private issues such as birth control. They ignored another constant Church teaching that said while conscience should be followed, that conscience had to be formed to the mind of the Church and not our own whims, because otherwise conscience would invariably lead us astray.

GENERAL ABSOLUTION. The NFPC backed Bishop Dozier's Memphis rites despite Vatican condemnation and urged that these general absolution rites be spread everywhere, 77:3.[xii]

DIVORCE AND REMARRIAGE. Resolutions call for use of internal forum and pastoral solution methods, "... new insights and understandings into [sic] the Church's teachings on marriage, divorce and annulment ... urgent need of bishops, priests and laity for instruction re-education, etc." 74, 75, 81. The NFPC calls for the divorced and remarried to receive the sacraments despite Rome's prohibition, 80, 81.

WOMEN'S ORDINATION. In addition to the earlier reference above, the NFPC (Action Step X, 77) scornfully rejects the arguments from theology and history presented in the Vatican's *Inter Insigniores*.[4]

NATIONAL PASTORAL COUNCIL. Despite Rome's repeated ban on the creation of NPCs, the NFPC continued its drive for such a body in the US, promoted the Call to Action as a move in

---

[xii]   During the mid-1970s, Memphis Bishop Carroll Dozier (1970-82) hosted "Homecoming Celebrations," which thrice filled the Memphis Coliseum, and which prominently featured general absolution. (In 1984, John Paul II issued an apostolic letter that clarified and discouraged common use of this form of the sacrament of penance.) Bishop Dozier also encouraged people who had divorced and remarried without benefit of an annulment to come up and receive Communion at these events. At the end of an article in *The Wanderer* ("Memphis on the Rubicon," January 20, 1977), Fr. Gilsdorf wrote, "... if episcopal collegiality fails to exercise fraternal correction and if Rome decides to use private diplomatic channels to smooth over what is a pandemic *public* scandal, as seems to have been the approach in Holland, what lies ahead? ... if absurd silence persists much longer after Memphis, the vacuum of authority will suffocate Catholic unity and life. As Abbot McCaffrey said recently in another context, 'Silence is golden, but sometimes it is just plain yellow.'"

   Fortunately, Rome did respond. On January 14, 1977, the Congregation for the Doctrine of the Faith sent a letter occasioned by the Memphis event and a similar one that took place in Newark. The CDF also issued a reply to a query on January 20, 1978, against this use of general absolution.

this direction, and sought to develop rationale and methodology for this type of structure, 70, 70, 70, 70, 70, 70, 70, 70, 77, 79.

MEETING WITH THE POPE is called for in order "to express the views of American Presbyteral Councils regarding pastoral issues of the American Church," 80.

INTERCOMMUNION. With non-Catholics on "special occasions," uniformly and strongly rejected by Rome, is urged in 84:4.

ABORTION. In several resolutions throughout the years, the NFPC has stood on solid ground in condemning abortion. In the last month before the 1984 elections, however, the executive committee issued a statement on behalf of the federation rebuking the first NCCB letter and certain easily-identifiable bishops for the support of a single-issue focus on abortion, urging an all-inclusive stance. Many understandably interpreted this move as stroking the conscience of Catholics who wanted to vote for pro-abortion candidates.[xiii] It will be a genuine "moment of truth" if and when the NFPC debates support for the religious who signed the *Times* "pro-choice" ad.[xiv] We recall how the NFPC backed dissenters against *Humanae Vitae* with

---

[xiii]   Which it did. This effort was aided by Joseph Cardinal Bernadin's "seamless garment" philosophy, which said "that issues such as abortion, capital punishment, militarism, euthanasia, social injustice and economic injustice all [equally] demand a consistent application of moral principles that value the sacredness of human life." Many took this as a pass to be soft on abortion. The problem with this philosophy is that the Church allows prudential disagreement on issues such as "militarism," the death penalty, and even which policies constitute social injustice. But its ethic on abortion has always been consistent. And as the bishops later stated in their 1998 document "Living the Gospel of Life," if one does not have the right to be born, all other rights are pointless.

[xiv]   On October 7, 1984, a month before that year's presidential election, the *New York Times* ran an ad titled, "Catholic Statement on Pluralism and Abortion." Sponsored by Catholics for a Free Choice and placed by Planned Parenthood, it opined that that there were many "legitimate Catholic positions" on abortion. Ninety-four Catholic priests, religious, and laymen signed this.

the disclaimer that it was not making a judgment on the theological issue. Will the NFPC hold fast to its anti-abortion tradition or will it follow its tradition of defending dissenters—or will it do both and thereby do neither?

Has the NFPC matured?

In 1984: 1) Rome is called on to drop its norms for selection of bishops, 84:5; 2) Rome is caustically rebuffed on the matter of the revoked imprimaturs,[xv] 84:17; 3) women's ordination is again demanded 84:16; 4) intercommunion with non-Catholics is called for, 84:4; 5) a lecture is delivered to the Holy See for creating a "climate of distrust," 84:15.

Lately, many have repeatedly asserted that the NFPC has greatly "matured" and has shed its previously strident anti-papal tone. I invite the reader to study the resolutions of the past few years. The year 1984 is a particular case. The NFPC sharply challenges the Holy See's basic positions, and the language of its resolutions has become more acerbic than ever before.

It is impossible to reproduce all these 1984 resolutions here, thus one will have to stand for all:

> WHEREAS recent and present practices of the Curial congregations, although intended and described as "pastoral services, studies, and visitations," are being perceived and experienced by many American Catholics as one-sided investigations, without open dialogue and broad consultation, without closure, and causing the fear of unknown penalties;
>
> and WHEREAS the NFPC recognizes the legitimate role of the Holy See;

[xv]   The CDF under Joseph Cardinal Ratzinger apparently did this in the early 1980s after bishops gave imprimaturs to books that should not have received them. An imprimatur says a work is free from error in terms of faith and morals.

BE IT RESOLVED THAT THE NFPC, so that a climate of suspicion and distrust develop no further, urge that all such Vatican services be conducted collegially and openly, with due process and respect for all persons, as well as with allowance for valid dissent, and with genuine affirmation of the legitimate diversity and plurality in the Church.

BE IT FURTHER RESOLVED that the NFPC continue to collaborate with and support the NCCB in its pastoral service of deepening and authenticating the renewal of the Church in the United States, while stressing our belief that such leadership service should continue to be based upon the principles and practice of collegiality and subsidiarity, which have successfully created a positive environment of dialogue and development... (84:15).

In other words, "dialogue" must continue and never be deemed "fruitful" until Rome capitulates to the NFPC's demands. Recall what issues are involved here.

Social and political agenda

The bulk of NFPC resolutions consist in detailed action steps that reach into every area of political, economic, and military life, confronting civil and ecclesiastical authorities on all levels. These ringing challenges range from calling all councils to enforce boycotts (grapes, 69; lettuce, 69, 73—also all Safeway and A&P stores—all Gallo wines, 79; Farah and J.P. Stevens, 77; tourism in Guatemala, 81; Nestlé and all subsidiaries, 81; to the impeachment of President Nixon, 74:4).

Some of the many other causes:

1. advising the Republic of Ireland to "revamp [its] present Constitution" to appease Protestants in the north;
2. homosexual rights, 74, 74, 78;

3. moratorium on nuclear power plants, 80;
4. condemnation of death penalty as a "teaching of our church;"
5. unconditional amnesty for draft dodgers and deserters;
6. repeated condemnation of the "immoral" Vietnam war;
7. opposition to the Trident submarine, the B-1 bomber, and cruise missiles;
8. for global disarmament and against deterrence, for cutting the military budget, arms watch panel, involving schools and education offices in Peace Programs crafted by the NFPC Justice and Peace director (already in 1972!);
9. collaboration with "such groups as Witness of Peace in Nicaragua;"[xvi]
10. and a blanket indictment asserting the "Catholic Church as an institution [is] affected by institutional racism."

Regardless of how priests would choose to stand on such issues, the fact remains that these are *not "in se"* moral principles that can claim to bind the conscience. They are highly specific conclusions as to *means*, and in this area, Catholics are free to disagree conscientiously. Yet NFPC acts as a parallel moral Magisterium whose supposed authority goes far beyond any papal claims. It would be hard to distinguish the NFPC social action agenda from that of the National Council of Churches.

In September 1984, the NFPC sent invitations to national episcopal conferences of 26 English-speaking countries to send representative priests to an international gathering. Co-sponsors with NFPC were the National Conference of Priests of England and Wales; National Council of Priests of Australia, and National Federation of Senates of Priests/Canada. At this event, Fr. Richard

---

[xvi] This group describes itself as "a politically independent, nationwide grassroots organization of people committed to nonviolence," but in the 1980s, it essentially was a front group for Nicaragua's Marxist Sandinista regime.

McBrien offered two presentations on the post-conciliar development and future of the priesthood. Fr. Donald Bargen, OMI, served as the process person helping prepare the representatives (five from each nation) before and during the gathering.[xvii]

Nations invited included Bangladesh, Bermuda, Fiji, Ghana, India, Ireland, Kenya, Malawi, Malaysia, New Zealand, Nigeria, Northern Ireland, Pakistan, Papua New Guinea, Philippines, Scotland, Sierra Leone, Singapore, South Africa, Sri Lanka, Tanzania, Tonga, Trinidad, Uganda, Zambia, and Zimbabwe. I mention this meeting, held in Chicago, August 12-16, 1985, simply to show that what were national federations are now reaching out on the international level.

This brief but crammed survey gives some idea of the agenda of the NFPC. Consider what we have just reviewed: no supernatural dimension, no concern for transmitting the content of divine revelation, no commitment to "holding fast" to the deposit of faith; no fragrance of traditional devotion; no attitude of reverence (let alone affection) for the Holy Father. In summary, one might say it bespeaks no memory of the spirit of saints and martyrs. A total reading of all the resolutions would, I believe, confirm my contention that this agenda is in serious and essential conflict with the "agenda" of the universal Roman Catholic Church.

We should note there are other national priestly associations. For example, the Confraternity of Catholic Clergy has quietly served priests in a spiritual and fraternal way for a decade. It is nonpolitical and, on ecclesiological principle, does not seek affiliation with presbyteral councils. It is open to individuals or (purely voluntary) chapter membership. As a rallying point of assent to the Magisterium, it strives to foster allegiance to the Holy Father. Hours of eucharistic

---

[xvii] Ordained in 1964, Fr. Bargen served as director of the Social Action-Social Welfare Department of the Minnesota Catholic Conference and was a member of the provincial council of the Oblates of Mary central province. He left the priesthood in 1987, married in 1991, and died in 2004 at age 65 after a successful career as a meeting facilitator.

prayer and systematic study of Catholic doctrine from orthodox sources are central features of monthly chapter meetings. Interested seminarians and priests (whether diocesan or religious) may write to the Confraternity of Catholic Clergy, 21-72 43rd Street, Astoria, New York 11105.[xviii]

In my judgment, the American priesthood is about to be tested. As we survey the scene, the Gospel imagery of the winnowing fork, the clearing of the threshing floor, and the sifting of wheat from chaff (Matt 3:12) seems *à propos*. At this dramatic juncture, to whom should we priests give our allegiance? Whose agenda should we adopt? Whose claim to authority should receive our adherence? For beyond the agenda there are crucial doctrinal issues at play: orthodox ecclesiology, the limits of lawful dissent, and communion with magisterial authority.

Whatever latitude one might allow for dissent, dissent cannot be the usual, public, and orchestrated response to the supreme and universal pastor of the Church. I am convinced that no priestly community can exist that is genuinely Catholic unless it is centers itself on doctrinal, disciplinary, and affective communion with the vicar of Jesus Christ.

Some of the most crucial pages of American Church history are about to be written. The script is being pondered and prepared in our own days within the sanctum of the conscience of every American priest.

[xviii]   Today the address is 121 William St., Marysville, PA 17053-1434. The website is www.catholic-clergy.org.

CHAPTER 21

OPTIONAL CATHOLICISM[1]

Several years ago on a dark and blustery late fall afternoon, I was called to the side of a man stricken by a heart attack in a small crossroads village some 10 miles from my rectory.

I found the victim lying on the ground outside a small cheese factory where he had been installing a cement platform. By the time I arrived, his wife and son, several fellow workers, and some neighboring farmers had gathered and watched in silence while rescue squad personnel attempted in vain to resuscitate him. The wife was in a nigh hysterical state.

Enter the priest, holy oil, and current ritual in hand. I immediately recited the conditional absolution from memory. Next, I recall frantically paging for the essentials of the rite, which I located at long last near the center of the book. Then, after the anointing *in extremis*, I hunted for the apostolic blessing. Having awkwardly thumbed back and forth through the book, I found it obscurely tucked near the index with the numerous other "meaningful" options. Finally, for the consolation of family and friends, I fumbled through options A, B, C, D, and E at every stage of the rite, the wind tearing at the pages of my standard ICEL ritual book, hoping (and struggling) to discover some suitable prayers.

That event was traumatic. It "raised my consciousness" as to the madness of the unpastoral aspects of optionalism.

What follows here is *not* a call to eliminate all options. It is the plea of a pastor to the bishops for a critical review of the current state of liturgical "optionitis" that, after a decade of accretions, is rampantly chaotic (when it is not worse). Some options are useless, some senseless, some bombastic, some banal or downright suspect, some few are noble. Some are even helpful and inspiring.

Here, note, we are speaking of legitimate, approved options. But as anyone must confess who compares our new rituals with what we observe in the flesh (well, at least in leotards), there now exist myriads of practices in the Mass and sacraments that are *not* lawful. They are the *ex nihilo* creations of an anarchical clergy. Since they are illegitimate brainchildren, they are, by definition, bastards.

This plea, then, begins with a call to the bishops to extirpate the bastards, but to also seriously consider applying a machete to the tangled jungle of authorized options. Are *all* of these pastorally helpful? More to the point, are they the fruit of front-line pastoral experience or are they, after all, only the busy theorizing of office bureaucrats?

Our liturgical blight began with options in the *novus ordo Missae*:[i] salutations, penitential rites, orations, canons, and so on. This was in the earliest, most restrained stages of renewal, when Pandora's box was first cracked open. But as the revision of liturgical rites progresses apace, these sober beginnings look almost restrictive. The benefit (read: profit) to publishers is evidenced by the thicker and thicker books we are compelled to purchase. And now that the "sexism" so long enchained in Pandora's box has finally fluttered out on gossamer wings and (in her liberated zeal) has bitten our bishops with its inclusive language, more and more volumes are in the offing.

To return to the case of anointing of the sick, many of us priests have learned to cope with the ritual by:

1. cutting and pasting (helped in this by the example of high school CCD coordinators skilled in making collages);
2. by using crayons to edit out whole pages with big Xs;

---

[i]   This is what many call the new Mass (i.e., the Mass instituted by Paul VI in 1969), although the Church has never officially used this name. It translates to "new order of the Mass."

3. by using paper clips to isolate the essentials;
4. or by simply printing out the essentials on a very small pasteboard.

Matrimony

During wedding rehearsals, what otherwise sane priest has not gone insane (almost irretrievably)? Here "local customs" run berserk. Because of this, most priests (even some liberals) would rather have a hundred funerals than one wedding. At least the departed don't talk back, and the survivors are somewhat subdued. I say somewhat, for even funerals are no longer embalmed against rampant optionitis.

The case with weddings, however, is pathological. This sacrament should be a powerful occasion for impressing on the young couple the sanctity, the mature commitment of their covenant, set as it usually is within the Sacrifice of the Mass and including the sacramental reception of Christ, the Cana Guest.

But what is the common scene? It is a demonic caricaturizing, a desacralizing of this major religious event. We witness contests among local couples to outdo the last big show: tasteless juvenile theatricals, elaborate choreographies (which often enough, in the tension of the moment, end up in a foot tangling pandemonium). Creation has reverted to *tohu w'bohu*.[ii] There are literally thousands of options leading to unproductive hours of discussing and agonizing over optional processions, positions, prayers, readings, entrance rites, exit rites, not to mention candle lightings, kissing, etc., etc. And these are (mainly) rubrical options! Now let the endemic abuses be heard! Let legitimate rites yield to puberty rites! Madness reigns. "Well, Fr. So-and-So and even Bishop So-and-So allow it!"

Then we must add the final *coup de grâce* aimed at the reeling head of the pastor: the music. The use of profane music has deformed the sacred sealing of sacramental love into a pagan bacchanal set to the strains of erotic epithalamia. (I could cite here even obscene

---

[ii]   Hebrew for "without form and void."

music: "Help Me Make It Through the Night,"[iii] sung during Communion—an actual case!)

Reconciliation

Let us now survey the present state of the sacrament of reconciliation. In the wake of a decade of errors in moral theology,[iv] the liturgists have sponsored their own *aggiornamento* which (insofar as it goes beyond the Roman directives and tacitly tolerates the innovative abuses that are now legion) has left us a pale parody of the confession.

Even in the most legitimate expression, the options of this sacrament are prolix. And each option itself embraces a welter of further options. Add to this the special American concession of "face-to-face," the gross abuse of the rarely justified general absolution, the contumacious refusal of some diocesan officials to obey the popes on the time of first confession, and, as any sincere priest can attest, the bottom line is this: The people are bewildered to the point of abandoning the purifying, salutary, and often enough necessary use of this sacrament. Hell seems to have come close to eliminating its greatest threat.

The people ask, "How do I confess in any given church to any given priest?" Even in the same parish, each priest may opt for a vastly different format. In numerous places, "face-to-face" is mandated, or the "rec room" is so arranged that anonymity is thwarted. The more reserved person, when burdened by serious sin or overwhelmed

---

iii   This is a song written by Kris Kristofferson and performed by Elvis Presley among others. Sample lyric: "I don't care what's right or wrong, I won't try to understand. Let the devil take tomorrow. Lord, tonight I need a friend."

iv   Father's original footnote: "These errors were disseminated by experts in religious education congresses, thence infiltrated into catechetics, propagated from pulpits, published in the raw for the CTSA-sponsored 'human sexuality' study, canonized in 'Catholic' sex education courses à l'Imbiorski, a 'renewal' during which the Catholic doctrine on sin was all but extinguished."

with shame, must conjure up heroism to confess in this way. Another problem is that the tribunal of mercy has often become the couch of amateur psychology or the stool of ham sociology. School children, when their being in a state of grace is still cared about at all, are forced into face-to-face. In their early years, this may have been fun and games, but in adolescence, it gravely tempts the youth to omit, for example, sexual matters of conscience (which were often enough never the object of instruction).

Have the options run amok? Just glance at the list even in the prescribed rituals. To show the extent of confusion in this matter, we end with a sad symptomatic fact. Even fully orthodox priests who come to assist similarly sincere priest friends cannot begin to help without a lengthy briefing, which begins typically with the question, "How do you do it here?"

We cannot *pastorally* call the present orgiastic state of the method of confession a true, healthy reform. It is an unmitigated disaster, which has nearly eradicated the magnificent American tradition of frequent, devotional confession. Today, the people bypass even the most obligatory reception of the sacrament. Granted, we needed reforms, and we can find these in the Roman directives. But we did not need the demolition of the present scene (however dramatic or titillating the revolutionary experiments may have seemed at first blush).

Holy Eucharist

In these sacraments, we get an impression of what one might call "sandbox liturgists," wizened gnomes squatting in their USCC sandboxes. They erect elaborate dream castles, giving free vent to their fantasies to endlessly alter the features, and then, when bored with the game, they petulantly smash their creations. This insensitive approach to the sacred institutions of Christ reaches satanic dimensions when we come to the sacrament of the Eucharist, the most excellent of the seven, because it not only conveys the grace of the Lord, but makes Christ Himself present.

We just mentioned the visiting priest needing a briefing to hear confessions for a neighbor. How it tears at the heart when good priests must carefully probe, "How do you say Mass here?" Even among the most faithful priests, the optionalism requires learning quite a few variations, almost like deacons preparing for their first Mass. It sinks much lower than this when a priest is called to assist or feels obliged to concelebrate Masses with fellow priests who care nothing about "what Rome says." Either the good priest acts like a "gentleman" and, for "the common good," proceeds to compromise his deepest priestly convictions, or he simply excuses himself and refuses to take part.

It is horrifying but true that this can even be the problem when the bishop is concelebrating with his priests a Mass where the diocesan liturgist has planned to incorporate commonplace abuses. Here the beast of optionalism emerges to attack the person of Christ, the eternal Priest-Victim, and seeks to tear asunder the seamless robe of His priesthood. It is at this point that the leadership of the Church must act. To fail to do so would be to accept complicity in the auto-demolition of the Church.

Some years back, the *National Catholic Register* printed a letter to the editor. The writer listed the options for Communion at that time: on the tongue, standing; on the tongue, kneeling; in the hand, standing; in the hand, kneeling, and so on. He ends with a note of profound pity for the priest who must do this over time for many people of all heights from babes to basketball centers. He concludes that only acrobats can henceforth be ordained priests.

Ah, but that was some years ago. Add to the scenario receiving the common cup or refusing the cup or asking for intinction of the Host for sanitation's sake, self-intinction, "self-service" of one or both species, and so on.

We can all see this with our own eyes. This is what we have done to the most solemn sign of ecclesial unity. The *vinculum unitatis*[v] has been deliberately unraveled. At Communion time, optionalism creates a division of the house. It has divided the parish church

---

[v] Latin for "the bond of unity."

against itself.[vi] In this matter, however, options are for everyone to do almost anything, except the priest, who is the ordinary minister of the sacrament. He must function as a mindless, neutral, and automatic dispenser of absolution and Communion. Here I mean, specifically, the conscientious priest who believes in Church law. The liberal priest who gave Communion in the hand years before it was lawful now forces the practice on his people, while hypocritically denouncing priests who are not happy with the option and try to restrain its use. The scene at Communion is chaotic: the casual mishandling of the Host, the fumbling with the Host down the aisles, the one-handed receptions, the popping of the Host in the mouth, and worse.

What truthful person watching in our parishes has not seen this?

The option of receiving in the hand has become the norm in many parishes. What was to be the fruit of a prayerful, instructed, and fully matured judgment is now forced on small children. This new and "more perfect, more mature" way is dictated to First Communion classes, and if the pastor prefers the children to receive on the tongue while the Sisters are convinced of the perfection of hand-Communion, who wins? Most of the time, the pastor will concede.

After all, in reality, the liturgists did not seek an option but rather a universal change. They are wise enough to know that in this type of situation, priests will face a pressure to conform, to make the practice uniform. Here we come, at the heart of sacramental life, to an "option" that was never intended to remain an option. For all practical purposes, the reception of Communion on the tongue is now the "option," if it is even tolerated—a far cry from the intent of *Memoriale Domini*.[vii]

[vi]   Note: To combat this, the United States bishops now say we should receive standing and that we may bow before doing so (but should not genuflect). If one does choose to genuflect or kneel to receive, however, no priest may refuse Communion on this basis alone.

[vii]   "On the Manner of Distributing Holy Communion," instruction, Sacred Congregation for Divine Worship, May 19, 1969. It allowed Communion in

And we should not fail to mention how commonplace it has become for all the priests and bishops to sit down and allow the nuns and lay people to distribute Communion. The extended use of the cup at weekend Masses (let our bishops answer as to its legitimacy) has doubled the number of ministers and ministresses needed. The reports of routine spilling of the Precious Blood are constant and verified. Several years back we all were subjected to the propaganda of how unsanitary was the reception of Communion on the tongue, how uncouth we had been for a millennium plus. But now the same hypocritical liturgists have the faithful drinking by the hundreds from a common cup, which even some liberal priests refuse to purify because "it makes them gag."

A terrifying truth is involved: When a precious gift is abused, the gift will be withdrawn. Rome has repeatedly intervened in the matter of the validity of the material to be consecrated. The rulings are specific and directed to American abuses. It becomes clear that many "eucharistic celebrations" were not Masses at all and any present (who still might adore the Sacred Species) were worshiping mere earthly bread. Every Catholic has a right in justice to demand that these directives receive full and effective compliance everywhere. Without the Eucharist, there is no Catholicism. The sheep have an urgent hunger and need for the true Bread come down from heaven. The bishops must show us whether they are good shepherds or mere hirelings.

But to return to the truth stated above. People in many places have flagrantly abused the divine gift, which is Christ in Person. In the case of invalid matter, we see the predictable result: The gift is being withdrawn! If priests, beguiled by liturgists, now consider the Sacred Species a plaything for their sandboxes, let them play with earthly bread—for too long they have repeated the mauling of Jesus

---

the hand only in limited areas and under special circumstances. Of course, priests (and many bishops) ignored these conditions, so the Church released *Immensae Caritatis* in 1973, which gave wider permission for this "option" in response to the growing number of episcopal conferences asking for it.

by the roughnecks in the pretorium! How cold this fallen world will become if the sanctuary lamps die in our churches, one by one.

Doctrinal optionalism

Finally, optional Catholicism in the liturgy is symptomatic of optionalism (read pluralism) in creed. *Lex orandi, lex credendi*[viii] has never been more verified, but in such a reversed and negative sense. Behind the mania for options in liturgical practice, there lies the far more ominous reality of optional faith and morals. Our creed, our deposit of faith, and the whole fabric of authentic moral teaching are said to be "up for grabs," wide open to any and all options. One may raise the cause-effect dilemma of the chicken-egg syndrome. In my opinion, the "*lex negandi*" has provoked the "*lex optandi*," which is but its external symptom, though for nearly 15 years the two have been concomitant and mutually supportive. We have barely skimmed the surface. Optional Catholicism raises battle cries on all fronts: optional celibacy, optional habit, fundamental options.

This little excursus is, I repeat, not a call to eliminate some reasonable, faithful options where they are not divisive. It is, however, a plea to our bishops to heed the unequivocal trumpet resounding from Rome to stop the evident abuses of unlawful optionalism. It is also a plea that they seriously consider some revision of current liturgical practices in order to prune our most sacred actions of those accretions that obfuscate the essence of the visible signs instituted by Jesus Christ to give grace. May these divinely instituted signs once more shine forth as effective, clear, visible marks, not of division characterized by pandemonium, but of unalloyed Catholic unity.

What a glorious day of renewal it will be when all our options have run out!

---

viii   Latin for "The law of prayer (i.e., worship) is the law of belief."

CHAPTER 22

OF SHEPHERDS AND HIRELINGS[1]

When a Christian today hears Jesus declare, "I am the Good Shepherd," his mind is flooded with the serene and comforting artistic imagery from the ages. On hearing or reading John 10:11-15, the mention of the hireling "whose own the sheep are not," whose voice is unknown to them, whose only concern is his wage, and who takes craven flight when he sees the wolf stalk near—all this seems muted. At most, it is regarded as a literary foil to enhance the idyllic figure of the *Pastor Bonus*.

But in the original context (*Sitz im Leben*), when our Lord delivered this self-designation, the Jews gave immediate and knowing attention to the hireling. They were well aware of the tragic drama of the "bad shepherds," the apostate hirelings of the past who the great prophets excoriated. What must have shaken them to the core was the implied anathema against the hirelings of their own day, the blind guides, the brood of vipers, the whitewashed sepulchers, those faithless, venal, hand-washing religious leaders who always spoke of the Messiah but never recognized Him when He stood before their biased eyes.

To capture the explosive impact of the hireling theme, one should read the graphic and instructive passages (e.g. Ezek 34; Jer 23:1-4; Isa 56:11) at the climax of which comes the astounding prophetic promise, "Behold I, myself, will search for my sheep, and will seek them out... I will rescue them from all places where they have been scattered on a day of clouds and thick darkness... I will feed them... I, myself, will be the shepherd of my sheep... "[2]

So Jesus referred to the past and the present, but just as certainly, He addressed the future, the historic lot of His flock of the New Covenant. In His Church, the spiritual leaders (the apostles, their successors, and every rank of the priesthood) were to be patterned upon Himself, the Good Shepherd. From the beginning, they are named bishops ("overseers" of the flock to be entrusted to the supreme pastorate of Peter) and pastors, that is, shepherds.[i] And, yes, there was even then a hireling lurking in the apostolic college: Iscariot—"one of you is a devil."[3] Beware, then. For in the earthly migration of this flock there will be those, sometimes more, sometimes fewer, who become renegades after the pattern of the bad shepherds.

Over a decade ago, orthodox priests were shocked into the realization that the fraternity of the priesthood was split. Only gradually did they plumb the depth of that fissure. It was not, as the euphemism wistfully suggested, a "polarization." By now, most of us know that it involved a genuine apostasy. Until now, we spoke of this in private for fear of scandalizing the laity. Now perhaps, it is time to share this with solid laymen who can stand by us in our grief and assist in ways not open to us.

The modernist priests no longer believe in the supernatural. They reject the order of grace and divine revelation. They dismiss the whole spiritual realm, including the soul and its immortality. Theirs is a cruel and sterile parody of the Church, an anti-Church, limited to this world and caged in dialectic materialism.[ii] Though they still speak of God, it is not the God of Tabor, nor is it the God of the burning bush. By rejecting transcendence, they have also apostatized from the true God. Their dread, dark, unspeakable secret is that they do not believe in the God of the Creed. And in many areas, they are legion.[4] In not a few dioceses, the orthodox priests know well they are

---

[i] The Greek word for overseers is *episkopoi*, from which we get our words "bishop" and "episcopal," as in "episcopal conference."

[ii] This is "the Marxian interpretation of reality that views matter as the sole subject of change and all change as the product of a constant conflict between opposites arising from the internal contradictions inherent in all events, ideas, and movements."

a dispossessed and despised minority. The hirelings are the majority, and they are in control.

We could suffer through this coexistence with wolves in shepherd's clothing and even their appointment to positions of control over us. But this is not yet the most horrifying disclosure.

In the past few years, we have come to the crushing realization—and we have fought with all our hearts to deny it—that what has happened among the priests has also happened among the bishops. This is a worldwide phenomenon, but for our purposes, we will limit our consideration to the episcopate of our own country. I state nothing here with glee or contempt, but rather with reluctance, fear, unspeakable pain, and hopeful love.

So even though it sticks in the throat, we must say the body of American bishops is in much the same state as the body of priests. In public view, the successors of the apostles stand divided in allegiance and in faith. The completely sound and orthodox bishops may possibly be in a minority—the voting pattern on sensitive issues seems to suggest it—but it is hopefully a substantial, if frustrated, minority. It seems the modernist and "drifting" bishops may indeed constitute a majority, and through their energetic allies in the USCC, they are in control. The good shepherds are beleaguered, to say the least, but they are all the more worthy of love and honor.[iii]

We mention the "drifting" bishops, and this is a key concept. (We also see this phenomenon in the priesthood.) There is, between orthodox and apostate, papal and anti-papal, a considerable number of bishops who fall into a mushy mid-position. They will follow convenience and self-interest, and will predictably swing to the element in control. In many a disaffected diocese, if Rome appointed a strong bishop who would fill his curia with orthodox priests, this segment would move back to conformity, "for they have no concern for the sheep, but work for their own advantage." Incidentally, this

---

[iii]   It should be noted that while much of what Father writes here is true, things have gotten incrementally better. Obviously, however, there is still a ways to go.

is a good reason to encourage Rome to appoint bishops who are not compromise candidates. One should reckon with this large segment, not just with the small number of committed "papal" priests.

And so with the American bishops, many seem to be switch-hitters. If only the bishops would purge the USCC bureaucracy of the entrenched radicals, and if Rome would gradually replace bishops who openly aid and abet their modernism or Marxism, the considerable number of drifters, the "wandering stars" of Scripture,[5] would doubtlessly swing back to Catholic orthodoxy.

There is a fateful question mark hovering over the Catholic Church in our nation. We need to have answered an unheeded question. In concert, we should shout this question over and over again until we get it answered: "How can orthodox, papal priests survive in the modernist dioceses? They ask only to be good shepherds. Yet how can they continue to serve their flocks when modernist bishops pressure (or allow their officials to pressure) them to convert to modernism and abjure their Catholic conscience?"

I recently conversed with a priest in such a diocese. At my request, he put in writing the gist of what he told me:

> The most terrifying experience of my priestly life can be summed up in a few words: My bishop and I are not of the same faith. I do not say this lightly. For a decade now, I have listened to what he has said and noticed what he has not said. I have watched what he has done and what he has left undone. I have seen him sit in placid silence at lectures where speakers expounded heresy and rebellion, lectures he himself endorsed. While the most numerous sins were of omission, moments came in casual conversation, in larger groups, even in writing, when people directly though cautiously contradicted the Faith. I see a diocese I love slowly but ever more surely alienated from the Faith. The supernatural is already extinguished in many (very likely in most) of the large parishes. Secular humanism with a thin veneer of Christian vocabulary reigns.

Just the other morning at Mass, the responsorial psalm read, "How shall we sing the Lord's songs in a foreign land?"

Tears came to my eyes. Am I not living in a Babylonian captivity? I am forced to live in an alien and hostile land under the sway of a bishop who apparently has lost the Faith but still exercises authority over me. I know that my faith is in full harmony with that of the Holy Father, but it is not with that of my bishop. I am trapped. To stay with my good people, I must more and more ignore my bishop and his officials. I must cut myself off from many diocesan activities. Lately, there have been times with fearful but clear conscience I have had to refuse to obey him. *"Quomodo cantabimus cantica Domini in terra aliena?"*[iv]

I have raised the same questions before. Only reverence and some comprehension of the immense problems keeps one from calling out, "Holy Father, please listen to us. What do you want us to do? Surely you do not want us to compromise on the essentials of the Faith or to disobey your serious orders. But the time is already here when in a number of dioceses we are on a collision course with our own bishops. Do we, then, abandon our little flocks and seek out compatible bishops or other apostolates? For we cannot minister as pastors to our people without the approval of these bishops. All we want to do is remain loyal to you and the Faith. We are not 'traditionalists.' We are priests of Vatican II. We only seek to be obedient to you, to profess the same faith that you profess, to move ahead with you. Tell us, in this dilemma, what do you want us to do?"

Do I exaggerate the crisis? I know from personal contacts with priests from a number of modernist dioceses that I do not. I omit some exceptional cases that would identify the priests involved and only add to their torment. Yet it is not hard to grasp that the

---

iv   Ps 137 [136]:4, which translates to, "How shall we sing the song of the Lord in a strange [foreign] land?"

conditions revealed to the nation last year in Memphis are not unknown elsewhere. Only a "papist" priest fighting the odds in a modernist diocese could know all the existential details of the daily struggle. To get a glimpse, however, let us try cataloguing some of the problems, a veritable jeremiad gleaned from various dioceses:

1. Growing casual use of general absolution, especially near major feasts.

2. Decline of confessions in modernist parishes, where the "new rite" has morphed into a lengthy face-to-face amateur psychiatric interview.

3. "Thunder on the Right," the siren magnetism of Lefebvrism. It captivates sincere but confused laity who hear his *mainly* justified indictment of current heresy and abuse. We see fellow priests grow so discouraged and dismayed with the current state of affairs that they are sucked into this anti-papal stream. Then this faction scorns us for "apostasy" because we remain within the present system.

4. The exquisite pressures that modernist chancery bureaucracies put on priests to attend seminars, continuing education courses, off-beat retreats, study days and study weeks, twisted catechesis for liturgical innovations, with the featured speakers always bearing an anti-Magisterium stamp. Meanwhile, we watch the rejection of orthodox *periti*,[v] who have to be smuggled in by lay people and are heard only at small discredited meetings.

5. Concerted pressure to force total subscription coverage of the diocesan paper on one's parishioners, who are thereby guaranteed a weekly dose of heresy.

6. Our desperate efforts to protect unsuspecting laity from exposure to numerous mind-altering conferences endorsed by the diocese.

---

[v]   *Periti* is the plural of the Italian word for "expert," *perito*.

7. The constant coercion by petty officials of the deanery to "conform."

8. Trusteeism with a vengeance, fostered by mandated councils and boards which often ignore the canonical safeguards. The pastor is reduced to one-man, one-vote status. Not surprisingly, this new trusteeism encroaches on doctrine and worship.

9. Diocesan marriage courses conspicuously evasive or permissive on matters of marital morality.

10. Dead silence on contraception and sterilization.

11. Whole parishes that surround us are alienated from orthodox Catholicism, their members continually affecting our own people, who are their friends and relatives.

12. Watching good priests with impeccable credentials (aside from their orthodoxy) volunteer for city parishes, get ground up and spit out by liberal parish machinery and then scramble ignominiously to find a remote hamlet that will still tolerate their kind. The number of such refuges decreases yearly.

13. The incredible hammerlock on pastors with parish schools, squeezed ever tighter by diocesan religious education offices and/or liberal convents.

14. The decay of sound catechetics and the pressure to control the training of volunteer parish catechists, effectively cutting off the pastor from teachers and children alike.

15. Strangulating and blood-sucking financial demands by a burgeoning diocesan bureaucracy.

16. The mind-boggling proliferation of tainted pietistic movements favored by the diocese (why?): *Genesis II*, support groups, Marriage Encounter, Cursillo, the charismatics with their itinerant healers and "slayers-in-the-Spirit" who succeed in dazzling even the elect.

17. Deliberate and quasi-official muffling of Roman decrees and papal teaching.

Msgr. Nelson Logal more masterfully described the whole sick syndrome in an address last year to the Confraternity of Catholic Clergy national forum in New York. I received copy of the text titled, "The Pastor: An Endangered Species." A year later, we could title the talk, "The Pastor: An Entrapped Species."

The web has become all but ineluctable: The agenda of Call to Action[vi] has been discreetly implemented (along with many of its rejected outrages), and the bishops' only response is a wrist slap. Random sampling polls are being sent to thousands across the country, replete with questions on doctrinal and moral issues. The questions elicit multiple-choice answers, many of which are in complete opposition to the Magisterium.

Diocesan offices are also busy holding conferences with the open or disguised goal of softening up the faithful on the ordination of women and new positions on divorce. The CTSA-sponsored study on human sexuality is inspiring even greater boldness in the already polluted atmosphere of the New Morality.[vii] The courageous and quick reaction of a number of individual bishops was a cause for rejoicing. It will be a further acid test of the NCCB to see whether it will produce the promised Conference rebuttal. If it fails or misfires, we urge good bishops to bypass the establishment and form an ad

---

[vi]   In 1971, Paul VI urged Catholic laity to play their part in "the renewal of the temporal order," addressing "to all Christians ... a fresh and insistent call to action." Because of this, the United States bishops held a Call to Action Conference in Detroit in 1976. At this event, the delegates effectively voted in favor of the Church changing her teachings on priestly celibacy, the male-only priesthood, homosexuality, and birth control. A year after Fr. Gilsdorf wrote this piece, the Call to Action organization was born. It exists to this day as the principle organ of dissent and umbrella group for other dissenting organizations.

[vii]   The Catholic Theological Society of America. Here Father refers to *Human Sexuality: New Directions in American Catholic Thought: A study*, New York: Paulist Press, 1977. CTSA Committee on the Study of Human Sexuality: Anthony Kosnik, Chairperson; William Carroll, Agness Cunningham, Ronald Modras, James Schulte, members. The book was officially repudiated by the Holy See.

hoc coalition and issue an independent statement. This would be a refreshing example of what genuine collegiality is all about.

The role of the pastor in the Church has received short shrift. Thus, the recent Synod of Bishops seems to have missed a golden opportunity to fortify the pastor as canonical catechist in the parish.[viii] In practice, he is one of a team of experts, the rest of whom officialdom strongly backs, which progressively whittles away at his rights in this crucial area. Hopefully, the new Canon Law will come to our rescue by clearly defining the responsibilities and rights of the pastor.

Notice, again, in the absurd but legally binding imposition of the "Communion in the hand" option, that the bishop has freedom and the people supposedly have their option (who is kidding whom?), only the pastor has no discretionary option.[ix] Yet he is the man who must exercise this maneuver and, if conscientious, strains to see whether the next communicant, even his seven-year-olds, will maturely decide to be a "hand-Catholic" or a "tongue-Catholic." We feel the confusion and social pressure placed by this option on the already harried conscience of devout Catholics, now to be divided as they receive the very sacrament of unity.

And this is still not an exhaustive list. Just a few more disparate but symptomatic items:

[viii]   This is a reference to the Fourth Ordinary Assembly of the Synod of Bishops, Vatican City, September 30-October 29, 1977, on catechesis.

[ix]   Editor's note: While the practical realities may be different, it is not legally binding to receive Communion only in the hand. The Congregation for Divine Worship and the Discipline of the Sacraments stated in the April 1999 issue of its official publication *Notitiae* that "the right to receive the Eucharistic bread on the tongue still remains intact to the faithful. Therefore, those who restrict communicants to receive Holy Communion only in the hands are acting against the norms, as are those who refuse to Christ's faithful [the right] to receive Communion in the hand in dioceses that enjoy this indult... [Let] all remember that the time-honored tradition is to receive the host on the tongue. The celebrant priest, if there is a present danger of sacrilege, should not give the faithful communion in the hand, and he should make them aware of the reason for [this] way of proceeding."

1. Priests in the Midwest have told me of the contagious spread of "polka Masses," sometimes staged as an outdoor come-on adjunct to the parish picnic, with the same whoopee band hired to play at Mass and at picnic. We hear of polka Masses celebrated in the local dance hall for wedding anniversaries, no doubt because the tubas were too cumbersome to haul to the church and back to the beer hall.

2. A well-informed priest confided that in one parish, a priest scattered the consecrated Hosts from the ciborium over the floor and instructed the congregation, "This is your manna from heaven. Come and pick it up." Elsewhere, people came to Communion with a container and requested "a few to take home."

3. And last, but not least: the inexorable flow of annulments to the grievous scandal of the faithful. This, of course, is at the root of the Canon Law Society's revolt against the proposed draft of the Law. It is a bitter root that each year strikes deeper and ramifies its poisonous system into more families and communities.[x]

No doubt this constitutes the final and all but irreversible thrust toward a schismatic American Church. The appointment of the canon law architect Pericle Cardinal Felici to head the Supreme Tribunal of the Apostolic Signatura heartens us.[xi] Felici is alert to

---

[x] According to the reputable canonist Edward Peters (author of *Annulments and the Catholic Church: Straight Answers to Tough Questions*), the annulment situation has improved in the United States. He agrees with the opinion of John Paul II that there are still too many annulments granted in this country (indeed, in the West in general). Nonetheless, while his book is worth reading, it is especially worth noting his argument here vis-à-vis Father's contention. You can find his argument on pgs. 159-178.

[xi] Paul VI named Felici to this position in 1977, which he held until his death in 1982. Since he was senior cardinal deacon in 1978, the Year of Three Popes, he "had the rare honor of twice giving the *Habemus Papam* announcement" ("We have a Pope!"). The closest equivalent to the Apostolic Signatura in

the problem and his dual role may solidify the defense. The present writer has also read a lengthy manuscript on the subject by William Marshner.[xii] Herewith goes an appeal for its speedy publication, preferably in monograph form. It is brilliant, thorough, and relentless in its logic.

Meanwhile, we pastors must permit these humanly pitiable cases to receive sacraments and must proceed to marry them to new partners on demand. We, however, are mercifully blindfolded. We never see the acts of the cases, and the grounds are not communicated to us. We can and do suspect, but the laity feel much less restrained. They bitterly complain, and who can blame them if they reach the conclusion in local taverns that divorce is now permitted in the Church of Thomas More?

When young men see their pastor reduced to such straits of impotence, is it any wonder why vocations do not thrive? What can the priest do that everyone cannot do, for people may overlook the act of consecration and seldom see him absolving from sin. They see every man, woman, and child doing what used to be his ministry, directing his every step, while he, it is true, is allowed to care for vigil lights (if there are any) and to tidy up the sacristy.

Having considered these representative but hardly comprehensive cameos, the heart of the matter is this: In modernist dioceses the orthodox priest, who is precisely the most convinced of the dignity and authority of a bishop, knows he is no longer of the same faith as the bishop, who nevertheless remains his canonical superior. The priest no longer "knows the voice" of his bishop. He can remain faithful to the pope and Church only by ignoring, circumventing, and occasionally disobeying his bishop.

---

our system is the US Supreme Court. It is the highest legal organism in the Church besides the pope.

[xii]   Convert to Catholicism from Lutheranism and professor of theology at Christendom College. The manuscript was indeed published under the title, *Annulment or Divorce? A critique of current tribunal practice and the proposed revision of canon law* (New York: Crossroads, 1978).

The situation is desperate and explosive. It must not continue much longer. Such a priest recalls that when Thomas More was chided, "All the bishops in England are against you," the saint retorted, "Yes, but all the bishops in heaven are for me." But this is not Henry's England, and we well know there are many heroic and faithful bishops in our land. We know their suffering. We share it.

Let us conclude on a positive note of trust and faith: We know Christ the Good Shepherd has not abandoned us. Daily, we look at the Host and chalice before our Communion and pray with intensity, "Keep me faithful to Your teaching and never let me be separated from You." The Confraternity of Catholic Clergy and the Marian Movement of Priests comfort us with their messages coming like arrows to the target of our trouble. We fully expect divine help through the intercession of the Mother of the Clergy. Yes, and we expect a miracle, for only a miracle can now save us.

Until that blessed relief, it remains necessary (as this article has attempted) to reveal our tortured conscience to our good shepherds in the apostolic college, as well as to that supreme Good Shepherd, who, with limitless love and courage, tends all the lambs and sheep on our planet.

CHAPTER 23

THE DOCTRINE OF THE FRAGMENTS[1]

How large must a fragment of the Eucharist be before we can make the spiritually crucial judgment: Here is the Real Presence of Jesus Christ?

Before answering this question, let us ask one that is different but ultimately related: What is the proper response of man to God? From looking in Scripture, the answer is clear: Awe is the proper response to theophany, man's perception of the divine Presence. But as we will see, awe is not enough.

Consider Exodus 3, the episode of the burning bush. Moses is drawn to a bizarre phenomenon on the slopes of Horeb, a bush that burns intensely but is not consumed.

For our purposes, we shall consider mainly what God commands as a response to His Presence and what, in fact, are the subjective psychological and spiritual reactions of Moses:

1. ... and lo, the bush was burning, yet it was not consumed (Moses "looked," God "appeared") (v.2).
2. God said, "Do not come near; put off your shoes from your feet, for the place on which you are standing is holy ground" (v. 5).
3. ... and Moses hid his face for he was afraid to look at God" (v.6).
4. Moses requests to hear the name of God (v. 13).
5. God said to Moses, "I AM WHO AM" (v.14).
6. "This is My name forever, and thus am I to be remembered throughout all generations" (v. 15).

So God appeared and declared, "I AM," here and now, "WHO AM" (i.e., He is the transcendent eternal One whose Being is Existence itself). God indicated an external sign that all should observe on approaching His Presence, a sign that would manifest faith, the recognition of the truth of His words, and a manifestation of the awe that is the proper response of worship on the part of a creature before his Creator.

How did Moses respond? On his own initiative, he hid his face "for he was afraid to look at God." But for all that, he still was under compulsion to probe, to contemplate, to discover more. He sought the very core of God's being: His name. The "fear" of Moses, then, is not craven terror or dread. Yet it is still more than "fear of the Lord" in the proper sense of *pietas*. In a word, it is the ecstasy of awe.

We could easily draw from the Old Testament numerous similar accounts of awe on the part of poor mortals when God chose to manifest His Presence—the vocation-theophanies of the major prophets, for instance—but our attention races ahead to the fullness of time when God manifested Himself in His Son.

Awe is the natural response

When the Word became flesh and dwelt among us, He mercifully "emptied Himself," restraining His "glory" so that men could tolerate the light. The Gospels, however, recount how on occasion Christ manifested His divinity to some degree, and when He did, the response was awe. Think of the Transfiguration. "They fell on their faces, and they were filled with awe."[2] Peter vocalized their sentiments, saying, "Lord, it is good for us to be here. Let us put up tents..."

At times, this awe also overwhelmed the disciples and the crowds. The Gospels often note it explicitly with a rich vocabulary in recording miracles of exorcism and healing. "And amazement seized them all, and they glorified God and were filled with awe."[3] How much greater when the dead were raised to life? "They were overcome with amazement."[4]

We should not omit the pivotal interlude in John 6. This episode is not an intrusion. It is an interpretative nexus between the multiplication of the loaves and the eucharistic discourse. I refer to Christ walking on the water. This is what only Yahweh does in the Old Testament.[5] It signifies creative power over the elements, vanquishing heels poised upon watery chaos. And Christ, Who soon will promise to change the very elements, pronounces "*ego eimi, me phobeisthe*—I AM (or, it is I), fear not."[6]

There can be no doubt from Johannine usage that here the name of Yahweh is on the lips of Jesus. Very soon He will take it up again: "I AM the living bread come down from heaven." In Matthew 14:25 ff., the walking on water prepares for the ecclesial Petrine promise. Here, Peter is called to do what Jesus does and, to this extent, to share in the divine prerogatives of conquering chaos, of establishing judgment and harmony. Here also note the human response of Peter to this manifestation of the transcendent God: fear, hesitation, awe.

In the similar passage where Jesus stills the storm, we learn of the reaction of the apostles: "And they were filled with awe, and said to one another, 'Who then is this, that even wind and sea obey Him?'"[7]

I develop this admittedly long answer to my second question only to underscore the fact that when a person who has faith senses the presence of his God, awe is the spontaneous response. This plays into our primary concern here, which is the Real Presence of Christ in the eucharistic fragments and how we should respond to that. We wish to address this primarily to fellow priests, but, of course, it applies to all who truly believe. And we will stress that the more the Lord condescends to us, the "smaller" He makes Himself, the more incumbent it is on us to sense holy awe in His Presence.

Surely we need not elaborate the doctrine of the Real Presence. We find perhaps the most readily available treatment in Pope Paul's *Mysterium Fidei*. Here we shall assume the basic truths of altar and tabernacle, fully aware, however, of the devastating erosion of faith, even on the part of priests, which evoked the encyclical in the first place.

We marvel at His descent

When a believing priest contemplates the Eucharist, there is disclosed to the inner eyes of faith the real, divine Presence and, with that awareness, a vista of the mystery of "transcendence and condescension" that lies at the heart of the Incarnation. We priests should often dwell on that mystery as we stand or kneel before the Sacred Species: true God and true man, king and servant, priest and victim, shepherd and lamb—the paradox of the Incarnation; transcendence and condescension. And our genuine response must be a holy and inebriating awe whenever God gives us the grace to perceive it to some degree in contemplative prayer. From time to time, we priests surely do experience such a heightening of our consciousness. Like Moses on Hebron, we face the temptation to hide our face, but we cannot resist the urge to penetrate the mystery.

Like Peter on Tabor, we stammer, "It is good for us to be here... Let us put up tents, let us stay here forever." How desperately we need this sense of awe, this tasting of the sacred in the Church today, but how will the people experience it if their priests have not?

On the other hand, it should never discourage or depress us when the time comes to descend back to the plain, to the level dusty road of our apostolic labor and, often enough, to climb the priestly mountains of Olivet or Calvary. Once we have seen the glory of the Lord, we can never erase its memory, never deny it. The gentle aura lingers, follows us in our daily pastoral work, haunts us, and summons our return. The flame burns fiercely at times, moderately or weakly at others, but the pilot light of faith never goes out.

It is the ordinary approach to eucharistic devotion to emphasize the truth of the transcendence, the infinite splendor and glory of Christ the divine Person, real, living, omniscient, and omnipotent before us. And this truth must never escape our mind. Yet in our prayers, we must also thrill to the heart-rending spectacle of the divine condescension. As we have seen, this is a complementary truth based on the mystery of the Incarnation, and it is one that is crucial for priests in our times.

He is King and Victim

Blaise Pascal has a breathtaking passage in his *Pensées* in which he portrays this complementarity from a different aspect.[i] He guides his reader to move his gaze outward to the grandeur of external creation, to the unfathomable sizes, distances, and powers of the macrocosm, only to stop halfway and lead in the other direction to the smallest, infinitesimal atomic depths of the microcosm—"*l'extreme petitesse.*"[ii] Here we share in the intoxication of the mathematician-mystic as he beholds man situated at the crossroads of creation: "*Un néant à l'égard de l'infini, un tout à l'égard du néant, un milieu entre rien et tout...*"[iii]

Though applied to a different perspective of the divine, namely the external, material works of the Creator, where infinity is only apparent, this essay by Pascal can give us an insight into something far more awe-inspiring: the transcendence and the condescension of Christ, the *anabasis* and *katabasis* of the creative Word made Flesh.[iv] We must not be satisfied with the sense of the transcendent. We must also consider the complementary pole of this mystery, which is how truly God has stooped to conquer our hearts.

In the Incarnation, the Word became Flesh, emptied Himself, and took on the form of slave. We shall see that at each degree of

---

[i]   Cf. Section II, 72. Pascal was a brilliant French mathematician, scientist, and philosopher, who is best known for the book Father refers to here. You may have heard of Pascal's Wager, which says God exists or He doesn't. Which alternative will you wager on? You can't avoid choosing one or the other; you have embarked on the wager already. A refusal to choose carries the same result as choosing that God does not exist. What if you choose to bet that God exists? If you win, you win everything; if you lose, you lose nothing.

[ii]   French for "the extreme smallness."

[iii] French for "Nothing with regard to the infinite one, all with regard to nothing, a medium between nothing and all..."

[iv]   *Anabasis* and *katabasis* are Greek terms that respectively mean a journey, the first from the coast up into the interior, and the second term representing a trip from the interior to the coast. In other words, the former means a going up and the latter a coming down.

condescension there is a deepening and corresponding "risk." Here note the risk: Christ put Himself at the mercy of men, and see what we did to Him in the Passion.

Still, this was not enough. Christ took a second step. He gave us His flesh in the Eucharist. Note the greater concomitant risk of love: Under the species of bread and wine, He is even more "helplessly" vulnerable to the perversion and negligence of men. (How many, even Catholics, believe His Presence in the Eucharist is simply symbolic?) In these times of eucharistic outrage, we should often reflect that the word "host" derives from *hostia*, "victim."

The Fathers repeat the fact

But there is still more to this epic, an even deeper descent of love, and for this, all I have written so far was but a preamble: He remains present in the fragments, the ultimate in the divine condescension! A crumb, a drop ("*Cujus una stilla salvum facere/ Totum mundum quit ab omni scelere*").ᵛ Why write of this? Consider how often priests today heedlessly neglect or casually abuse these fragments, and you have your answer.

What one might call the "doctrine of the fragments" is a corollary of the doctrine of Transubstantiation. It is a crucial subject, because it is a matter that lies at the heart of many of our present eucharistic problems. This will be, then, the final and major consideration in this chapter on awe.

St. Thomas expressed the position of earlier centuries in this limited stanza of his eucharistic hymn *Lauda Sion*: "*Fracto demum Sacramento/ Ne Vacilles, sed memento/ Tantum esse sub fragmento/*

ᵛ   From the Latin hymn *Adoro Te Devote*, the full verse of which is, "Deign, O Jesus, pelican of heaven, me, a sinner, in Thy Blood to lave, to a single drop of which is given all the world from all its sin to save." The pelican reference comes from when, in times of famine, a pelican mother will pluck at its breast to bleed so that her young will have at least that on which to feed.

Quantum toto tegitur.[vi] Consistent with this, liturgical practice has allowed the minister to break hosts if necessary to accommodate a number of communicants greater than foreseen.

Long before Aquinas, there is the patristic witness, of which the following is a sampling:

7. St. Ephrem: "Do not now regard as bread that which I have given you; but take, eat this Bread, and do not tread upon (or crush, grind—*conteratis*) its crumbs (*micas*); for what I have called My Body, that it is indeed. One particle from its crumbs (*e micis ejus*) is able to sanctify thousands of thousands, and is sufficient to afford life to those who eat of it."[8]

8. St. Caesarius of Nazianzus: "The divine Body is divided without partition (*sine sectione*) and is shared in without deficiency."[9]

9. St. Cyril of Jerusalem: "Partake of it, but be sure not to lose any of it. For if you lose any of it, you would clearly suffer a loss, as it were of your own limbs. Tell me, if anyone gave you gold dust, would you not take hold of it with every possible care, ensuring that you would not drop any of it or suffer any loss? So will you not be much more cautious to ensure that not a crumb falls away from that which is more precious than gold or precious stones?..."[10]

After Thomas, we have conciliar doctrines:

10. The Council of Florence's *Decretum ad Armenos*: "Also in every part of the consecrated host or the consecrated wine, when separated, the whole Christ is there."

11. Council of Trent: "For Christ is whole and entire under the form of bread and under any part of that form; likewise the

---

vi   "Nor a single doubt retain when they break the Host in twain, but that in each part remain what was in the whole before."

whole Christ is present under the form of wine and under all its parts."[11]

12. Related Canon 3: "If anyone should deny that in the venerable sacrament of the Eucharist, the whole Christ is contained under each form and under every part of each form when separated—*anathema sit*."

And precisely in our own days, the Magisterium categorically reconfirms this very timely doctrine:

13. Paul VI: "In fact the faithful thought themselves guilty, and rightly so, if after they received the Body of the Lord in order to preserve it with all care and reverence, a small fragment of it fell off through negligence."[12]

14. In *Memoriale Domini*, the CDF states:

> As a person takes (the Blessed Sacrament) he is warned, ... "receive it: be careful lest you lose any of it" (citing the passage from Cyril). Further, the practice which must be considered traditional ensures, more effectively, that holy communion is distributed with the proper respect, decorum and dignity. It removes the danger of profanation of the sacred species, in which "in a unique way, Christ, God and man, is present whole and entire, substantially and continually" (cf. *Eucharisticum Mysterium*, no. 9). Lastly, it ensures that diligent carefulness about the fragments of consecrated bread which the Church has always recommended: "What you have allowed to drop, think of it as though you had lost one of your own members" (again citing St. Cyril).[vii]

[vii] Father's own footnote here stated, "The doctrine of the fragments has obvious implication in the matter of Communion in the hand. To discuss this would require a lengthy treatment in itself. This writer is in total agreement with the position expressed by Paul VI in *Memoriale Domini*. In that mysteriously neglected document, concern for the fragments is only

15. The Congregation for Divine Worship, in letters to episcopal conferences who had asked for the option of Communion in the hand, admonished, "Whatever be the form [of distribution] adopted, care must be taken not to let fall or scatter fragments of the Eucharistic Bread... "

16. In a declaration of May 2, 1972, the Congregation for the Doctrine of the Faith stated, "After Holy Communion, not only should the remaining Hosts and the particles that have fallen from them that retain the appearance of bread be reverently preserved or consumed, as the reverence due to Christ's eucharistic Presence, but even for the other fragments of Hosts the directions for purifying the patens and chalice should be observed as they are found in the General Direction of the Roman Missal."[13]

17. In the Congregation for Divine Worship's *Immensae Caritatis*, dated January 25, 1973, we read, "Especially in the manner of receiving Holy Communion (in the hand) some points indicated from experience should be most carefully observed. Let the greatest diligence and care be taken particularly with regard to fragments, which perhaps break off the hosts. This applies to the minister and to the recipient whenever the Sacred Host is placed in the hands of the communicant..."

A word about vocabulary: Some occasionally use the word "particles" to describe the smaller hosts distributed to the faithful. This doubtlessly derives from the earliest times when full loaves were broken at Mass, and the term persisted even after individual small hosts were consecrated. We also frequently apply "particles" to pieces broken off from the integral hosts. When we find this term in our sources, the context readily alerts us to the precise sense. In this article, aside from citations, we will use the term "fragments,"

one of many reasons the Holy Father gave for his 'preference' (too mild a word!) that the traditional usage be maintained."

i.e., "broken pieces" to refer to those pieces broken off, deliberately or not, from the original host.

He is present in a crumb

Let us once more examine these texts. What precisely is the object under discussion?

Cyril used the word *micae* (i.e., "crumbs," "dust," "fragments"), which most certainly designates pieces smaller than an integral host. Now even if Cyril speaks metaphorically, "crumbs" and "dust" are clearly minute fragments. Yet he clearly exhorts the greatest concern for these.

In *Mysterium Fidei*, Pope Paul speaks of "small fragments." In the May 2, 1972, CDF instruction, a special distinction is included that seems to be a reference to a thesis by Karl Rahner (which we shall soon discuss). Rome orders that the priest follow the missal directives and purify even the smallest fragments (which some may argue do not retain the "appearance of bread"). Note here that even the first mentioned "fragments which fall from them" are already plainly quite small, and the priest must consume or preserve these with "the reverence due to Christ's Eucharistic Presence."

Now any priest can understand the obvious sense of these texts. We know what we see on the paten and Communion plates. All these pieces are tiny. Some are slivers. Others are minute, white specks, "crumbs" if you will.

Care must be taken

This brings us back to our original (and pivotal) question: How small can a fragment be and still retain the Real Presence? Shortly we shall reverse this question to the discomfort of the maximalists.

First consider that St. Thomas says the Real Presence ceases for two reasons: 1) the quality of the species (i.e., the accidents are corrupted) and, what mainly concerns us here, 2) the quantity of the species.

We refer the inquirer to all the clarifying questions 74-77 in part three of the *Summa Theologica*. We will limit our citation to III, 77, 4, the response:

> If, indeed, there occurs such a change that the substance of bread or wine would be corrupted, the Body and Blood of Christ do not remain under this sacrament. And this as much on the part of qualities, if, for example, the color and taste and other qualities of bread and wine be so changed that in no way could they be compatible with the nature of bread or wine; or also on the part of the quantity, if, for example, the bread be pulverized (*puta si pulverizetur panis*), or the wine be divided into the smallest parts with the result that the species of bread or wine no longer remain.

Presumably, Aquinas would at least assert that in any fragment of the host larger than this elementary "powder," the Real Presence perdures. As for the Precious Blood, we have already seen his phrase from the *Adoro Te* in which he speaks of *"una stilla,"* a single drop. What he considers here, then, is smaller than a "drop" of that Blood that can save the whole world from its guilt. In these cases, St. Thomas regards the species as catalyzed into their constituent prior elements. He is not speaking of anything we can see on the paten. *Si pulverizetur* surely indicates a direct, deliberate action exerted on the species to grind it down to powder or dust, not the ordinary attrition from handling. We must discuss this text again.

Having considered these sources, I researched the standard manuals in use up to the time of Vatican II. Aside from affirming this consensus, the main considerations were scattered but clear when taken in the ensemble. Probably the most concise and helpful summary is in Noldin-Schmitt[viii] (Note: Here "particles" is used in the sense of fragments):

[viii]   *Summa Theologiae Moralis Iuxta Codicem Iuris Canonici*, by the Jesuit theologians H. Noldin and Albertus Schmitt, was a popular theology reference prior to the current age (and is still used by some).

> Since Christ remains present when separation is made under each and every part of each species (cf. Council of Trent, Sess. XIII, Can.3), all particles, even the smallest, which are perceived by the senses, must be treated as consecrated.
>
> It is certain that even the minutest particles that we can see remain consecrated, but it is not certain that those particles that are so small we cannot see them would remain consecrated. But even if they are consecrated, one must still acknowledge that Christ the Lord does not demand that the ministers be solicitous about these all but perceivable particles.[14]

This is the genuine Catholic sense. Fragments that are discernible *in se* retain the Real Presence. As for praxis, if the priest cannot discern them, and assuming he has taken all due care, he is in no way obliged to be concerned.

Even in this case, some hold that these sub-sensible fragme:nts retain the Real Presence as long as we could prove they are genuine "bread" upon examination. Others say not.

I would hold the former opinion, but for this discussion I will point out that this is not what we are considering. We are concerned with small pieces, however small, as long as they are *objectively discernible in themselves*.

Let us state the case as simply as possible. After Communion—almost always—there are small but plainly visible flakes on the burnished background of the paten and Communion plates (and even more copiously at the bottom of an emptied ciborium). An unbeliever will say those are breadcrumbs. A believer will say, "This is the eucharistic Body of Christ."

On the interior of the chalice after the first consumption, there are flowing drops that gather in a small but clearly visible pool at the bottom of the cup. An unbeliever will say those are drops of wine. I maintain a believer *must* say, "This is the eucharistic Blood of Christ."

I would also hold that these same fragments, if they for any reason fall elsewhere and are not empirically observed, do not on that account cease to be the Real Presence of Christ. The priest and recipient must take reasonable care not to lose these fragments. If through no one's fault they are nonetheless lost, the Lord will not hold it to the account of minister or recipient. He Who has taken this "risk" will provide.

This was the undisturbed consensus in the matter until recent post-conciliar days. Now, seemingly without a ripple, this sense of custody of the fragments has nearly faded into oblivion. Witness the insouciance of celebrants and the casual attitude of recipients, even those otherwise very solid in their doctrinal positions. We will not even attempt to mention the numerous grotesque abuses we hear of from all corners of the nation.

It is precisely when faith and devotion have diminished or vanished that priests and people are unimpressed, even unconcerned about the fragments. Our next question, therefore, must be, how did this silent overthrow of the traditional attitude occur?

How large is a fragment?

First came the assault of the condemned but highly publicized theories of transignification[ix] and transfinalization.[x] The inroads

---

[ix] Transignification comes from the modernist attempts of Roman Catholic theologians such as Edward Schillebeeckx to better understand Christ's Real Presence in the Eucharist in light of contemporary physics. According to this theory, "although Christ's body and blood are not physically present in the Eucharist, they are really and objectively so, as the elements take on at the consecration the real significance of this body and blood, which thus become sacramentally present. It is thus contrasted not only to belief in a physical or chemical change in the elements, but also to the doctrine of Transubstantiation." For obvious reasons, the Church ultimately rejected this idea, but it gained a foothold amongst Anglican and other Protestants.

[x] According to the late Fr. John Hardon, SJ, this "is a view of Christ's presence in the Eucharist as the purpose or finality of the bread and wine is changed ... by the words of consecration. [However,] what remains after the consecration

these errors made by way of the *Dutch Catechism* and allied theologians were not minimal.[xi] Pope Paul's *Mysterium Fidei* did much to stem the tide, but the residual concepts lingered, even in priests of good will. Pope Paul condemned these errors insofar as they diverged from Transubstantiation.

Mysterium Fidei, then, corrected these errors for those who sincerely wished to be orthodox. But the more telling, even if

---

is still bread and wine, in other words, the bread and wine are now serving a new function as sacred elements that arouse the faith of the people in Christ's redemptive love. We might say that transfinalization is another name for transignification. In both cases the substance of bread and wine, I repeat and I wish to emphasize, remain. There is no change in their being bread and wine — [they] merely take on a new meaning."

[xi] *De Nieuwe Katechismus* was produced by radical Dutch theologians and released in 1966, and though it carried the imprimatur, it rejected the doctrine of original sin and was purposefully vague on Christ's being born of a virgin. It also cast doubt on the Church's teachings regarding the Eucharist, birth control, the soul, and the existence of angels (to name a few). As of the summer of 1968, it had sold 400,000 copies in Holland, and its first printing of 75,000 copies in America sold out in three weeks. Many Catholic colleges used it in their religion courses. Some argue it laid the groundwork for the rejection of *Humanae Vitae* and thus the flowering of cafeteria Catholicism (whereby people pick and choose which elements of the Faith they want to hold) that has afflicted the Church since the late 1960s.

Here is how this happened: When the *Dutch Catechism*, with its soft-pedaling and/or veiled rejections of the Church's teachings, was released with the imprimatur of the Dutch bishops' conference, people wondered what Rome would do. To its credit, the Holy See issued a series of clarifications it wanted made, but the Dutch bishops responded by essentially ignoring the Vatican. There was an appendix that pretended to address Rome's concerns, but it was buried in a sea of words that essentially said, "We don't see why this is a problem, but to get the Vatican off our backs, here you go." Coupled with Rome's muted reaction to a similarly problematic 1964 French catechism for children and another Dutch book, *The Grave of God*, the modernists realized the game had changed. They grew more emboldened. They realized they could engage in either blatant heresy or at least dissent and then ignore the Vatican's inevitable remonstrations at no cost. This set the stage for what happened in the wake of *Humanae Vitae*, which is discussed elsewhere in this book.

unintended, impetus has arisen from the thought of Karl Rahner, and this has swayed many priests and scholars who otherwise would not have been convinced.

In Rahner's eucharistic theology, the leitmotif is "food" or "meal." He makes repeated assertions at every step of complete adherence to the magisterial teaching of Transubstantiation. Having professed this, he stresses the sign value of the Eucharist as food. In the case we are considering, then, he says the Real Presence ceases once we can no longer deem the fragments before us as adequate signs of food to be eaten. This position of his has been tremendously influential.

It is disconcerting that he never gives us a canon of judgment as to what size the portion must be. It is clear, though, that he would not accept the norm of mere visibility given by Noldin.

Rahner states:

> One recognizes today that bread is a typically anthropological entity. Physically and chemically bread is no real substantial unity, but an accidental agglomeration of many combinations of atoms and molecules, united physically only by a very extrinsic, accidental, and almost local concentration. Humanly speaking, however, and hence sacramentally, this formation is a unity, an intelligible unit, created by man, and possessing such unity only in relation to him, within the sphere of his life and action. Hence, it is clear that the real presence of Christ lasts as long as this humanly intelligible unity of "bread" exists. No theologian can question this in principle...[15]

One senses here a shift to the subjective. While affirming the change of substance, Rahner, with Germanic precision, distinguishes *to death*. After the discussion of atoms and molecules, it is refreshing to see him fasten on the humanly intelligible estimation of what "bread" is. But this subjective judgment must not prescind from the objective reality. The average man and woman speak of breadcrumbs. Do these crumbs—if consecrated—constitute the sacramental Real Presence?

What does Rahner say?

> Hence St. Thomas quite correctly sees that a purely quantitative reduction of the species of wine can prevent one from calling it wine any longer, though chemically it remains "the same" as before for a long time—and thus the presence of Christ ceases...[16] St. Thomas was therefore quite correct... when he said that the presence of Christ ceases if the bread is ground down: dust is, in fact, not bread in the human sense of the term. St. Thomas looked on such pulverization as a sort of substantial change even in the physical world, which it is not. But St. Thomas recognized correctly that dust is not bread, even though in chemistry or physics it is still exactly the same as bread. Hence, the presence of Christ also ceases. (This, incidentally, ought to be noted by priests with scruples, who are so over-anxious that they can never purify the paten well enough.) Hence, the principle remains: only where the species of bread is present and remains present can we speak of the real presence of Christ... [17]

Now these perceptions raise some pertinent questions. If one re-reads the Roman instruction of May 2, 1972, it seems the relative curial officials wrote it with Rahner's position in mind. It distinguishes between larger fragments that retain the appearance of bread, but also pointedly calls for careful purification of even the very minuscule albeit visible fragments. It maintains the discipline of Noldin, but prescinds from a declaration on Rahner's hypothesis.

From the above texts (and the full contexts) of Rahner, this writer cannot find the eminent theologian stating precisely how small the fragment must be to "lose" the Real Presence. He cites the "dust" of the Thomistic text, he presumes that purification of the sacred vessels is to be done, but he never tells us what may safely be classified as "dust." To my knowledge, he cannot be explicitly cited beyond this. Yet when the Noldin position is stated, many today instinctively appeal to Rahner.

It is time then to transpose that initial question: "How large must a fragment be before we can make that spiritually crucial judgment: Here is the Real Presence of Jesus Christ?" Note also the *illatio* in reference to Thomas' judgment on "dust" or "powder." Rahner claims Thomas was deciding on the basis of medieval concepts of substance, which all modern theologians reject. But he says Thomas was nonetheless correct!

He is correct for Rahner's reasons, however, not for his own. I think the logic of the case would demand saying: If Thomas had known what science now knows, he would have held that even this "dust" retained the accidents of bread, not the prior component elements he supposed. It smacks of defamation to suggest that had *Angelicus* begun with completely opposite premises, he would have reached the same conclusion! Thomas rigorously held that as long as the accidents of bread and wine remain, the Real Presence remains.

The allusion to scrupulosity is also ill considered. It implies that a pathological problem of some priests can be germane to our question. And, we may add, scrupulosity is hardly the dominant fault of the modern clergy. What is advocated here is what most normal pious priests can relate to: A duly careful, reverent purification of the vessels. As convinced as I am that the Real Presence remains even in very small fragments, I have never felt compulsive or worried once I have made a duly careful purification and see no visible residue.

In a word, the norms given by Noldin are sane norms that call for fidelity, not scrupulosity. As we have seen, the May 2, 1972, instruction confirms these norms. And here let us turn the specter of scrupulosity in the exact opposite direction. Even perfectly normal priests who take Transubstantiation seriously (but who nonetheless choose to follow Rahner's lead) will find themselves driven into a dilemma that would easily induce scrupulosity. For Rahner has not told us how large a fragment must be before the Real Presence is there. When can we safely disregard what we see on the paten as mere "dust"?

Disciples neglect subtlety

From hundreds of similar reports, I cannot resist to mention this one, repeated to me twice by a priest of intelligence and balance.

At a Mass last year in a western state, the celebrant distributed Communion using consecrated loaves, breaking off morsels which he placed in the hands of recipients who, in turn, walked away consuming them en route. Some of those present were dismayed to notice that a clearly visible accumulation of fragments, some larger than crumbs, had amassed at the celebrant's feet. These people refrained from going to Communion at the time. After the church had emptied, they knelt before this abandoned pile and tried to consume the fragments with their mouths.

Now using this actual example, and without malice, we must address these questions to Fr. Rahner: Were those people fanatics? Were they deluded in seeing in this heap of copious, relatively large crumbs the adorable Real Presence? Did they, in fact, receive Holy Communion? Or should we, as doubtless did the celebrant, follow the "common estimation" that crumbs on the floor are not "food to be eaten?" If these same crumbs had fallen on a paten, would there be any doubt of the Real Presence? And what of the pieces of considerable size that had dropped on the carpets, most likely by some of the more heedless communicants? Once they fell into the piling of the carpet and one could not observe them, were they or were they not the eucharistic presence? In effect, does this Real Presence depend on phenomenal subjective observation of an "adequate" sign, or does it depend on the reality *in se* of the species? Here we adduce a further and crucial text of Paul VI from his *Credo of the People of God*:

> Every theological explanation which seeks some understanding of this mystery [Transubstantiation] must, in order to be in accord with Catholic faith, maintain that in the reality itself, *independently of our mind*, the bread and wine have ceased to exist after the

Consecration, so that it is the adorable Body and Blood
of the Lord Jesus that from then on are really before us
under the sacramental species of bread and of wine, as
the Lord willed it, in order to give Himself to us as food
and to associate us with the unity of His Mystical Body.[18]
(emphasis added)

The use of loaves (and typically the liturgists press the bishops to
ratify as universal what they now widely and illicitly practice) is a spin-
off of the food-meal centrality of Rahner and shows its influence over
large sectors of the clergy. It would be unjust, however, to presume
his endorsement of what may well be unintended applications of
his germinal principles. Where the master carefully sews into his
chiaroscuro[xii] theses repeated asseverations of the orthodox doctrine,
some of his less subtle disciples may implement his insights without
the saving *cautelae*.[xiii]

Digested food flourishes

The above-cited texts from Rahner came from one of his essays in
defense of a position he admits goes counter to the nearly unanimous
consensus, namely, that upon consumption of the host, presumably
in the act of swallowing, the Real Presence ceases. He certainly holds
that it ceases as soon as the digestive process commences. This is true,
he says, since the Church does not regard food once consumed as
"food to be eaten."

Here, too, we sense an inconsistency. Surely in common human
estimation we speak of food until it is digested. We all have heard
our mother's refrain, "Put some food in your stomach. It will make
you feel better."

And how can we speak of *food* if we exclude its essential function
beyond the act of swallowing? Will we omit these aspects of the

---

xii   A contraction of the Italian words for "clear" and "dark." It also refers to the
      technique of using light and shade in pictorial representation.
xiii Latin for "methods of getting round legal enactments."

Bread of Life? For an indefinite time these species *in se*, though no longer observed, do exist. It is hard to avoid the sense of lapsing into symbolism if we deny it.

Where does he stand?

And what of adoration of this food? Rahner is disturbed by the fact that the theology manuals generally treat first of the Real Presence and only afterwards of the Eucharist as sacrifice and sacrament. As an exegete, I think Rahner has so isolated the essential but not total aspect of food (bread from heaven, bread of life) that he has failed to consider sufficiently further revelation. This is the living bread, syntactically stressed: *ho artos ho zon*.[xiv] And Christ makes an identification of His divine Person with this heavenly living bread: *Ego eimi*... I am...[19] When it comes to adoration of the reserved Presence, Rahner reminds us that the Eucharist was originally reserved as *viaticum*, food for those unable to attend the celebration.[xv] He recalls that adoration was a later aspect since embellished by medieval piety. We can feel the strong repercussions of this thinking in the "primitivism" current today.

Perhaps it is an injudicious application of Rahner's thought that has fed the current emphasis of the Eucharist as a meal, the demotion of the tabernacle, and the decline in eucharistic devotions. But the master again states firmly the Church's position.

[xiv]   This is the transliteration of the Greek from John 6:51, where Jesus says, "I am the living bread come down from heaven ..." The literal sense of the phrase is akin to, "I Myself (My being, My essence) am the bread (namely) the life which out of the heaven came down."

[xv]   Here Father cites Rahner's book, *The Eucharist: The Mystery of Our Christ* (Denville, NJ: Dimension Books, 1970), p. 20. However, we would note that viaticum usually refers to the Eucharist given to those receiving last rites (or extreme unction), and translates to "food for the journey." The online *Catholic Encyclopedia* has a good discussion of this matter.

Consider, however, the following excerpts (and the nuance of the wording), and ask what results they may stimulate in the less doctrinally anchored reader:

> The silent adoration of the Lord by the single believer who kneels in front of the holy shrine on our altars, the presentation of the sacrament in the monstrance by which the mystery is "exposed" to our eyes, rightly understood, need not necessarily lead away from the significance of the sacrament.
>
> On the contrary, in this way, too, the food proclaims the eternal life of our dying Lord; and venerated precisely in this way, it calls us to partake of it. When the mystery of Christ always and everywhere encompasses our being (whether or not we heed it), why should this secret of our being not be allowed to become visible so that our eye may fall on the food of the Church, in which one eats life or judgment?... It would be pitiful if we were to reconcile ourselves forever to the inadequate and perhaps half-magical misconceptions of this sacrament that we drag along with us from early religious instruction and from the practices of our childhood...[20]

There *has* been a need to highlight the eucharistic sign of food. For doing this, we must thank Rahner. But I leave it to careful readers of the texts just quoted to decide whether these may not, laced by the professorial sneer, do grave damage to the legitimate development of piety. Guided by the saints and the Magisterium, the faithful have long cherished this piety. They have *first* been drawn to the transcendent personal presence of our Lord and then, reflecting on His words, have further grasped the sacramental sign and so understood that He is our living Bread, the object of spiritual hunger.

From these few remarks, which cannot claim to do full justice to the elaborate work of Rahner, we can see how the incautious application of his thinking has largely influenced modern attitudes toward the Eucharist. Our intention, of course, was mainly to discuss his influence on the doctrine of the fragments. I hope that someone will do a comprehensive critique on the whole spectrum of his eucharistic teaching.

And we would welcome something else at this juncture: A Vatican declaration on the fragments, perhaps clarifying the May 2, 1972, instruction, which broaches but does not adjudicate the precise problem discussed here.

This writer, then, adheres to the common consensus as capsulated in the Noldin-Schmitt text, which is fully consistent with perennial Catholic tradition, and which, to my knowledge, has never been abrogated. In fact, the post-conciliar statements only fortify this "doctrine of the fragments."

So we come to the end of an essay on awe, gazing once more at the paten and the chalice at the time of purification. And surely, if awe were ever the proper response, it must be here at this ultimate condescension where the Creator of the universe, of all things big and small, visible and invisible, risks to lie before us as a crumb, as a drop.

Fragments are a key issue

As custodians of the Eucharist, the adoration we priests exhibit while purifying the remnants should demonstrate our priestly solicitude. It would also edify the faithful. How much reparation would we provide to Christ for the cavalier carelessness of our times if we priests *slowly* and *adoringly* purify the sacred vessels with awe.

The Benedictine who prepared our deacon class at St. Meinrad Seminary to celebrate Mass admonished us several times, "You can tell a good priest by how he cares for the fragments."

That was in 1956. I believed it then; I believe it now. Our crisis today in the priesthood and in the Church is precisely a crisis of faith. This crisis is largely reflected in a failure to respond to this eucharistic condescension and to defend, as courageous custodians, our "vulnerable" Lord with all our energies. For, as this admittedly long discussion hopefully shows, on these fragments stands or falls the doctrine of Transubstantiation, and with it, the mystery of faith.

CHAPTER 24

THE TOUCH OF FAITH[1]

The all-embracing consciousness of a transcendent divine Person, true God and true man, is the vital breath that animates all Catholic spiritual life.

Each morning before every working session during the Second Vatican Council, there took place a brief but impressive ritual action. A precious book of Gospels was borne in solemn procession down the aisle between the tiers of Council Fathers and was enthroned and incensed near the papal altar.

Thus venerated by the Fathers, it remained there, a visible, silently eloquent witness—*scrutator rerum et cordium*—of every thought, act, and emotion of the assembly.[i]

In solemn papal Masses and in less elaborate liturgical actions televised to the world since the Council, we have seen this veneration of the Gospel book: flanked by candles, kissed, elevated, honored with incense. Eastern rite people are even more accustomed to this scenario.

For all that, the image of the daily procession in the context of the Council seemed to charge the act with a new meaning. One might almost draw a comparison of these ancient "baptized" imperial rites granted to the book with those given the celebrant of the Mass (who acts *in persona Christi*, i.e., in the place or person of Christ) and, indeed, to the eucharistic species. From this, we intuit a deeper connection between the Liturgy of the Word and that of

---

[i]   *scrutator renum et cordium*—"Searcher (or examiner) of hearts and reins." The Jews thought the rein—or kidneys (*kilyah* in Hebrew)—was the seat of passion and the innermost being. This phrase, then, is an allusion to Scripture. One example would be Ps 7:9 (v. 10 in the Douay-Rheims).

the Eucharist. The mind grows fascinated by the parallel: It is almost as though this book were somehow a living person, as though this impressed word of God were somehow the Presence of the Incarnate Word of God.

How far is such an intuition valid? How far is a whimsical observation like this grounded in fact? May we not see in these traditional ceremonies surrounding the scriptures an invitation to regard them, not only as a science to study, but also as a *mystery* to contemplate?

Our musing is spurred on by Paul VI who, in the eucharistic encyclical *Mysterium Fidei*, distinguished the various "presences" of Christ in the Church, among which he numbers, "The Gospel which She [the Church] proclaims is the Word of God, which is not preached except in the name of Christ, by the authority of Christ, and with the assistance of Christ, the Incarnate Word of God."[2]

Let us begin on the intellectual ground of the scholar's approach to the scriptures as a scientific discipline. The exegete regards the canon of Scripture as a historical literary datum that challenges his mastery of antiquities, philology, literary genres, historical and cultural context, the biography and even the psychology of the authors and personages treated, etc. (We speak here of the biblical scholar in general, leaving aside, for the moment, the essential duty of the Catholic exegete to utilize the analogy of faith.[ii]) The far horizons of this critical study (pioneered by the Protestants, often of a liberal stamp) have been pointed to in *Divino Afflante Spiritu* and have been pursued assiduously, if sometimes recklessly, since that papal signal.[iii]

This labor is a search for interpretation, for meaning, for the true sense (or senses) of what Catholic scholars must confess to be

---

[ii] For a fuller discussion of what "analogy of faith" means, see Chapter 25, "Samoa and Sacred Scripture." In the original article, Father included a footnote here: *Dei Verbum* (Dogmatic Constitution on Divine Revelation), nos. 9, 10, Second Vatican Council, November 18, 1965.

[iii] Issued on September 30, 1943, this encyclical of Pius XII encouraged Catholic biblical studies.

the revealed and inspired word. This deepening and broadening penetration of the text is of utmost importance. Yet it remains an examination of the word on its own horizontal plane, which is a "horizontal" rather than a "vertical" or existential plane. Such is also the usual approach of the layman, even when he reads the text with devotion. In the Gospels, the Christian reader finds the historical Jesus as He was, as He existed, spoke, acted and reacted *in illis diebus*.[iv] Both scholar and layman, of course, *apply* these historical events to their present, existential condition, yet this hermeneutical application is effected solely by moral influence, by reflex, by drawing a lesson, all the while regarding these events as simply past and disconnected from the *present*. While this common approach is certainly a true and valid vision of the gospel, is it the complete vision?

Was the original intention wrong?

Recently, we have seen efforts by scholars, mainly Protestant, to make the "Gospel Jesus" present to modern man as a vital, communicating force. Rudolf Bultmann, for example, maintains that we must look at our Lord more through the Scripture than by detached historical study. He notes the "I AM" declarations of Jesus in the Gospel of St. John, where the Word is linked to His word.

But by his historicist demythologizing premises, Bultmann vitiates this seemingly inspirational superstructure. He shrugs off the question of the historicity and facticity of the mysteries of the Gospel, artificially opposing *Historie* to *Geschichte*.[v] All that counts, he believes, is how these events affect man subjectively here and now.

---

iv   Latin for "in those days." See Mark 13:17, 24.

v   On their face, these are simply two German words for "history." However, the deeper sense is that *historie* alludes to ancient history and *geschichte* to modern history. They also allude in some sense to the synthetic tension between the so-called Jesus of History and the Christ of Faith (which will be discussed in greater depth in a later chapter). Some scholars such as Bultmann have wanted to look at Jesus only from a modern, historical-critical perspective. For this reason, they reject our Lord's miracles and so

Thus, the master "demythologizer" makes them myths. He fails to see that once we reduce the gospel to naked naturalist symbolism, no possibility exists for the existential contact he seeks.

Warned repeatedly by Rome against this anti-supernatural methodology, the Catholic scholar sadly discovers he cannot accept Bultmann's conclusions at word value. This is because Bultmann seeks to stimulate life in the tips of the branches, having severed them from the historical and divine taproots of the vine.

Despite the basic errors of Bultmann's premises (and even in the corrective advances of the so-called post-Bultmannian school of the "New Hermeneutics," the same errors are not remedied), one can nevertheless be goaded to seek for a sound basis and true premises which yet may salvage the stated goal of this quest. For this, the historicity of the Gospels and the supernatural reality of the mysteries must be the firm foundation. It grieves the reader to see that Bultmannian hermeneutics, which on the surface conjure up an existential efficiency, are—for the lack of an historical criterion— reduced, in fact, to mere moral causality and to what is liable to be a causality by deception or myth!

This is a fatal error, but was the original intention wrong? Is it possible that a conclusion such as this, even though the stated premises are unacceptable, may yet contain intuitively valid perceptions?

Here are two aspects

I offer what follows more as a battery of questions, a probe, rather than a systematic attempt to elaborate an answer. The value will hopefully be that these questions need positing and consideration. One can only wonder whether the promise of an existential encounter might not be fraught with authentic potentials if only Bultmann made the supporting premises orthodox. A preliminary move in this direction can be discerned in an article (1960) by Padre Juan

---

on, not to mention the analogy of faith, which takes into account Scripture, Tradition, and Magisterium.

Leal in which he discusses the technological distinction of *kairos* (transcendent Messianic era) and *chronos* (purely historical order) in the Gospel of St. John.[3]

To begin our "probe," let us posit two steps toward contemplation of this mystery.

1. Christ is simultaneously and perfectly *conscious* of every human act, internal as well as external, of every human being, past, present, and future. Therefore, Christ's recorded words, emotional responses, internal and external acts from the moment of His conception in Mary's womb, throughout His entire public ministry, and indeed, forever are conditioned by this all-embracing consciousness. For the magisterial texts supporting this premise, we need only refer to the precious collection found in Fr. William Most's *The Consciousness of Christ*.[4]

For our purpose here we fasten on one of the texts by Pius XII:

> Now the only begotten Son of God embraced us in His infinite knowledge and undying love even before the world began. And that He might give a visible and exceedingly beautiful expression to His love, He assumed our nature in hypostatic union: hence—as Maximus of Turin with a certain unaffected simplicity remarks—"in Christ our own flesh loves us." But the knowledge and love of our Divine Redeemer, of which we were the object from the first moment of His Incarnation, exceed all that the human intellect can hope to grasp. For hardly was He conceived in the womb of the Mother of God when He began to enjoy the beatific vision, and in that vision all the members of His Mystical Body were continually and unceasingly present to Him, and He embraced them with His redeeming love. O marvelous condescension of divine love for us! O inestimable dispensation of boundless charity! In the crib, on the Cross, in the

> unending glory of the Father, Christ has all the members
> of the Church present before Him and united to Him
> in a much clearer and more loving manner than that of
> a mother who clasps her child to her breast, or than that
> with which a man knows and loves himself."[5]

We are involved here with the complex discussion of the *communicatio idiomatum*.[vi] We are well aware of the controversies over whether Jesus knew He was God, and so forth. Because of the Magisterium's perennial authoritative witness, we are obliged to affirm the *fact* of Christ's comprehensive consciousness. We leave the reader to study the tangled disputations and refinements, and you would do well to begin with the data given by Most.

From this first Christological assertion, I realize that when I read or hear the Gospel, all the words and deeds and affections of *Christ* are "conditioned" and "influenced" by all of *my own* needs and *my own* human personal response. The Gospel is, indeed, an historical record of the past, but in this manner, a similar encounter is effected *here and now*.

For example, Christ, in His historical agony, is affected by *me*, me as an individual and me as a member of His Body. He is moved either toward consolation by my sympathy (com-passion), my conversion, and my adherence, or toward a sharpening of His agony by my indifference (a-pathy), my sin.[vii]

His agony in the Garden of Gethsemane may well illustrate what is meant. In His consciousness, Jesus' mental agony simultaneously registered the love and hatred, the fidelity and apostasy, the salvation and damnation of every soul from Adam to the *parousia*.

The same dimension of awareness enters into every word and act of Jesus the Gospel records (for an act is also dramatically

---

vi   "The communication of attributes," i.e., how one sees the attributes of Christ applied to His divine and human natures.

vii   Compassion comes from the Latin *com-pati*, "to suffer together" (i.e., that we suffer with Christ). Apathy comes from the Greek *a-pathos*, "without emotion." Father broke up the words to emphasize the root meaning.

and efficiently a "word"). My whole existence and being share in prompting and formulating this word of Christ in its final Gospel expression. Therefore, I can read my personal "situation" into the Gospel, not merely by detached application, but by a dynamic involvement.

I am, thus, actively involved in this "word" that never passes away. I live in and act upon the pages of Scripture. And what has been labeled "I" here embraces every "I" of every human soul, created or yet to be created, however ignored or unappreciated by history that soul may be.

2. Christ transcends time. In the divine hypostasis of Christ, there exists no past or future, only an eternal all-comprehensive *now*. The mysteries of Christ (i.e., Incarnation, birth, preaching, miracles, Transfiguration, Passion, death, Resurrection, and Ascension) are *present* to Christ who lives them *now*. The mysteries are now and forever. Our incorporation into His Body lifts us above and beyond the life of nature and outside time reference. We shall see how the sacramental liturgical life effects this and actualizes the events recorded in the Gospels for those who enjoy the connaturality of grace. As members of His Body, we also live these same mysteries now in timeless solidarity with Christ our Head.

A series of questions looms

From these two briefly sketched premises, there emerges a vision of the Gospel as a relevant, living, ever-present "epiphany" of the Lord. One may object that this is merely a mystique. Insofar as it leads one to contemplate a mystery, it may be so regarded. But one must not overlook that insights so gained are also theological and practical. The statement of the principles and the indication of what they open to us comprise something beyond a mystique. Are they not the often unspoken principles of perennial Catholic mystical theology?

There looms on the horizon of our probe a series of questions: In what sense may we identify the Word made Flesh, the Incarnate Second Person of the Trinity, with His recorded word? In what sense do the Johannine "I AM" statements suggest such an identification?

For the sake of focusing on the person of Jesus, we speak here of the Gospels.

3. In what sense can we extend this insight to the whole canon of inspired Scripture that prepares for, typifies, and explicates the unique fulfillment of revelation in Jesus Christ in post-Ascension accounts?

4. In what sense can we accommodate "the Word was made Flesh and dwelt among us" to the written, recorded "word of the Word"?

5. In what sense is this word also made flesh, i.e., incarnated in human language, and in what sense is this impressed word living among us?

6. Is not this linguistic "incarnation" somehow an extension of the Incarnation of the divine Person of the Word?

7. Was it not for the purpose of pronouncing this Gospel word (and to preserve and broadcast this word) that the Son of God, Himself the expressed image of the Father, has taken on human flesh so as to speak in the fullest sense in the human vocabulary with human lips to human minds?

Obviously, we in no way imply a strict and substantial identification of Christ with the material scroll of Scripture. There is, however, a parallelism by analogy. Somehow, we do *encounter* Christ Himself in the Scriptures, and this is an engagement with the living Person of the Word—*semper vivens ad interpellandum pro nobis.*[viii] We should not say, perhaps, that the Gospel is Christ, but rather that in the Gospel we meet Christ. The Gospel record effects an epiphany of Christ as was the historic epiphany of the Word made Flesh, as is the epiphany of Christ in His Body the Church, as is the epiphany of Christ in private prayer, in the liturgy, in the *septenarium* [sevenfold] of sacraments converging on His supreme, real and substantial Presence in the Eucharist.

The existential dimension we have considered helps us to focus these manifold epiphanies into a unity, a constellation that is susceptible of our personal experience at this moment. It brings the eternal transcendent communicability of the *nunc stans* to the *nunc fluens.*[ix] For the Christ living in the Gospel account is the living Christ manifested in the Scripture, is the living Christ of the Church, is the living Christ encountered and communicated in the sacraments.

For the sake of relevance to man today, one must clearly engage the Christ of the Gospel. One must be aware that He exists and acts efficiently *in* the Gospel. And one must experience the transcendence of the Lord of Scripture, realizing that this indeed is "Jesus the Christ, *heri et hodie, ipse et in saecula.*"[x]

These principles do not solve what remains an ineffable mystery, but they help us contemplate and probe it. In turn, this helps us find in this treasury of truth ever-new facets reflecting still further insights and intuitions. From Christ's empty tomb resounds the haunting rebuke of the angel, "Why seek you the living among the dead?"[6] This angelic rebuke should be posed universally and relentlessly. Is this not the quintessence of the everlasting life of divine grace, which is the dynamic core of Catholicism?

---

viii   "He always lives to make intercession for them" (Heb 7:25).

ix   i.e., the "abiding (or eternal) now" to the "moving present."

x   "Jesus Christ, yesterday and today, and the same for ever" (Heb 13:8).

Denial extinguishes devotion

Full belief in the consciousness and transcendence of Christ bears extensive positive implications. The earliest Christians learned the gospel through oral preaching. For the majority of Christians two millennia later, the case is the same. The gospel is learned in oral preaching. More people learn the gospel through preaching and catechesis than by personal reading. It is the same gospel with the same effects.

While our main concern here has been the written Gospels, we must insist that the oral paradosis is truly the "gospel." In the first centuries and for most of mankind, evangelists spread the gospel from mouth to ear.

An example suffices to bring home this fact. An old man in an empty church slowly makes his way around the Stations of the Cross. He knows the Gospel background to some degree, probably more from hearing than from reading. With sure instinct of faith, he knows the truths we have so ponderously explained. He knows that his love, his compassion, his resolve *somehow* affect Jesus at the moment of His Passion. He knows His love alleviates the Lord's agony. Every faithful devout soul knows this. Is not Jesus true God and true man, and therefore did He not know back then what love is proffered now?

Again, the consciousness of Christ is the linchpin of all devotion in the Church. When people deny or obscure this doctrine, we annihilate devotion.

Unfortunately, this denial of the "consciousness" and the divinity of Christ have spread like contagion through the post-conciliar Church. This two-fold denial is, of course, a benchmark of classical modernism. The errors of our days are precisely the same as those diagnosed and condemned by St. Pius X in *Lamentabile Sane* (Syllabus Condemning the Errors of the Modernists),[xi] though they have spread more virulently through the immediacy of today's media.

[xi]   Decree, Congregation of the Holy Office, July 3, 1907.

The average Catholic senses something is amiss, but, being unable to identify the disease, can't adequately treat what will be, unless God intervenes, a terminal case.

Bad catechesis, theological speculation, popular lectures, preaching, a whole library of writings by our modernist scribes and Pharisees, all of these have infected the faithful with the incubus of these Christological errors: Jesus was just a man; Jesus didn't know who He was, etc. We must state here in the strongest possible terms that denial of either (or both) of these interdependent doctrines of the Church extinguishes liturgical and devotional life in any genuine Catholic sense. The all-embracing consciousness of a transcendent divine Person, true God as well as true Man, is the vital breath that animates all Catholic spiritual life. To choke off that breath is to asphyxiate the life of devotion and liturgy.

Given the relentless spread of these errors, we should not be surprised at the devastated state of the liturgy, at the ruthless, iconoclastic purge of sound popular devotion, at the neutering of genuine Catholic spiritual life that has made a wasteland of so many religious communities and has mass-produced cloned social workers from some of our seminaries.

In these and other areas only graceless, ersatz shells remain. The liturgy has been progressively desacralized. Its core (i.e., the vertical, existential encounter with Christ to live with Him and His mysteries here and now) is all but obliterated. Deprived of this essential upward thrust, the horizontal arms have been stretched out in a frenzied search for relevance, falling off the deep ends in polka, hula, and clown Masses.

In their place, people have invented new forms of piety and prayer to fill the void, and these have proven alien to the mystical discipline of the Church. On one extreme, an emotional binge, uncontrolled by ecclesial and traditional norms; on the other, prayer "experiences" which are but cerebral exercises of the imagination, leaving the depths of heart and soul unmoved by divine grace.

This has smothered the true mysticism of the saints. In its place, a natural mysticism of political and social activism, a "renewal" centered on nature rather than on supernatural grace, or even a fascination for the demonic pagan mystic cults of the Orient. In some convents, they have packed the libraries and prie-dieus with writings on Yoga, Zen Buddhism, and the Hindu faith. Why these counterfeits when we have the real thing?

The writings of mystics such as John of the Cross and Teresa of Avila have long since fed the flames of a new breed of book burners. The genuine mystical encounter with Christ and, in Him, the Trinity *cannot* be experienced without pure orthodox faith concerning the consciousness of a transcendent Lord. How else could we contact Him? How else could we communicate with Him? If He is merely Jesus, the man from Galilee separated from us by 2,000 years of history, no liturgical anamnesis, no devotional experience of the divine Presence can exist.

The liturgy centers on the re-presentation of the mystery of Calvary in the Mass. Day by day, week after week, the liturgical cycle, like the annual rings of a tree trunk, leads us progressively through the life, words, and mysteries of Christ's life. The relation of Scripture to liturgy is obvious. If we regard the Gospel as just another historical (albeit inspired) book that *only* records past events that, in turn, have no connection to the present, then we doom our understanding and living of the Mass (and the liturgical cycle that enshrines it) to be a mere routine memory of the past, a lingering at the tomb. We thus lose the true anamnesis, the here-and-now commemoration and re-presentation that the context of Scripture and the *paradosis* of the Church demand. Our grafting into the life of Christ as members of His indivisible Body involves our living these once-for-all mysteries together with Him now.

St. Paul uses a profusion of verbal compounds with the prefix *syn*, meaning "together with" to describe how the Christian lives Christ's mysteries together with Him. This Pauline realism demands far more than a merely moral causality. The Eucharist must be the central action in which we realize this sacred symbiosis. The Eucharist proclaims the death of the Lord until He comes. We must be born, suffer, work, and die "with" and "in" Christ our Head every "now" of our lives, so as to rise and be glorified "with" Him.

At Mass, we break out of space-time reference and enter the eternal *now* of Christ. The acclamation reminds us of this timelessness of the Eucharist: Christ has died (past); Christ is risen (present); Christ will come again (future). In the Eucharist, the whole life of Christ is made present. Not only do we die with Him, we simultaneously experience His risen glory in heaven, and we anticipate the future coming and judgment. For Christ (in whose life we share by grace and in Communion), there is only *now*.

To grasp the connaturality of the Eucharist, we need a deepened sense of Christ truly living and present in His Gospel. This will not happen if we regard the Gospel as a disconnected memoir of events long past, with but a lingering moral or suasive influence here and now. To view Scripture in this way is to relegate the liturgy (suffused and pregnant as it is with the word of God) to a flat, horizontal, remote, historicist review unable to "engage" us, unable to touch us. In a sense, the liturgy *is* the existential aspect of the Gospel. As we stated concerning private devotion, when we deny the consciousness and transcendence of Christ, the liturgy too becomes an empty husk, a secularized spectacle.

In a word, it ceases to be.

Baptism incorporates us into Christ. It regenerates us into a new and supernatural life, that of the Most Holy Trinity, a life that is everlasting, that was, is, and ever shall be. Once gained, this life of grace is caused to increase and, if necessary, be restored by the other sacraments, which are the signs of life and channels of grace. The sacraments effect connaturality, which in turn enables us to live the mysteries of Christ to the fullest degree. We shall cite but two.

In the sacrament of penance, the same Jesus of the Gospel continues His assault against the kingdom of darkness and works His miracles of healing. The diseases of sin—blindness, paralysis, deafness, mutism, leprosy of the soul—the Blood of the Savior washes all of these away. Indeed, even those for whom mortal sin has extinguished the life of grace are raised to life again.

As we have noted, the eucharistic sacrifice fully actualizes the Gospel. The Liturgy of the Word becomes alive in the Liturgy of the Eucharist. Here and now, we live those mysteries in and with Christ. In sacramental Communion, we are nurtured in everlasting life. We receive the *pharmakon me apothanein* (i.e., "the medicine of deathlessness"), as Ignatius of Antioch named it. In the Eucharist, Christ is with us all days, really and substantially. He has not left us orphans. We can come to His feet at the tabernacle at all hours through all centuries.

And when we go out from His Presence, He remains with us in other ways. In our mental prayer, in our scriptural reading, in our study of the Faith, in our daily work, in sufferings and temptations, in our encounters with all our brothers and sisters, the Gospel becomes alive as we become more and more aware of our union in and with Christ. It is the eucharistic Real Presence, the encounter *par excellence*, that animates the liturgical cycle in such a way that we truly live the pages of the Gospels.

Christ is touched through faith

We have stated that our comparison of the personal Word to the recorded word is by way of analogy. Yet, granting this caveat and using the above-mentioned principles, one does somehow encounter in and through the Gospel the living, personal epiphany of the source of revelation. This source, the revealed Word Incarnate, is the *same* Christ encountered in the Church. Thus, one discerns a unity of the *fontes* (i.e., sources) of revelation, for the transcendent Christ Who delivered the oral Tradition is the transcendent Christ Who established and maintains the hierarchical Magisterium and is also the transcendent Christ of Sacred Scripture.

The standard Protestant view regards the Bible as a closed letter with no recognition of the oral Tradition. It holds Holy Writ to be radically immune from any teaching authority that would give an authentic interpretation of its contents.

Our considerations here, however, show that the Bible is rather a living letter, animated as Christ by the Spirit who quickens, the Spirit who, through apostolic authority, teaches all truth.

Such a view of Tradition, Scripture, and Magisterium is brought to unity in the Person of Christ seated at the right hand of the Father, though each *fons* (i.e., spring, fountain) remains logically distinct and constitutes the analogy of faith insisted on by *Dei Verbum*. Once the unity is made clear, a way of envisioning the two *fontes* as interpreted by the Magisterium becomes possible.

Moreover, the idea of embracing the self-communicating Person of the Word, encountered in His word, the Gospel, offers us a fresh new notion of the unity we must seek. Suffused with love and faith, such an "embrace" will never tolerate a selection, an *hairesis* of the truth personified in the Lord. Christ is Himself the truth, indivisible, complete, and unconfused, whatever the cruces the critics may stumble on in the biblical pages. One who embraces the Person of Christ in His Gospel may not indulge in selectivity, accepting some words and rejecting others. We must embrace the entire Word in His personal totality, in His *individuum*, not mere blocks of words.

Such a perception spells the demise of "indifferentism" and with it the very concept of heresy. The expression of the Word in the Trinity is simple, unique, eternal, personal, and filled with the fullness of life. Not to belabor the point, but we must similarly accept as the expression of the same Person the words of the Word made Flesh. In our human reason, we distinguish these, laboriously digesting piecemeal the several doctrines that the Church catalogues in her creeds. But in the act of faith, we embrace Jesus, Word Incarnate, in His fullness (i.e., in His *pleroma*).

Jesus alone could say, "I *am* the truth." This is why we cannot pick and choose, for we know the truth is an organism: individuable, inseparable. By faith, we cause "that mind to be in us which is also in Christ Jesus,"[7] and in the embrace of the unity of His transcendent Person, we embrace Him in all His "epiphanies." We embrace His Body, the teaching Church. We are born into and live His life in the sacraments, in the liturgy, and in prayer.

This leads us to a final note, one that also has ecumenical value. In the Gospel, the woman suffering from a chronic issue of blood touches the hem of Christ's garment.

In the pressing crowd, Jesus is being shoved and jostled on all sides. Yet this gentle, shy touch of the lowest fringe of His robe causes Him to exclaim, "Someone has touched Me, for I have felt power go out from Me!"[8]

His saying this dumbfounds the apostles. *Everyone* is touching Him! But this contact releases virtue and power, and by her timid touch, the woman is healed.

What touch, what contact is this that triggers the awareness and response of Christ and causes power to go forth from Him? It is the touch of faith. "Woman, great is your faith!"

Many read, hear, and even proclaim the Gospel, therefore placing themselves in contact with Christ. Blessed are those humble believers who have discovered that this *same* all powerful and all-knowing Christ can ever be touched by this *same* act of faith, *here and now*, in His Gospel, in His Church, in the liturgy, in prayer, and in His sacramental signs, especially that of His Real and substantial eucharistic Presence.

CHAPTER 25

SAMOA AND SACRED SCRIPTURE[1]

Recently, Mrs. Stebbins[i] sent me a fascinating clipping from the *New York Times* describing a new book that explodes the basic theses of Margaret Mead's "maiden" anthropological study *Coming of Age in Samoa*. Published in 1928, that book sold millions of copies in 16 languages, turning the tide for cultural determinists.[ii] Margaret Mead reigned supreme for 55 years.

Even now, Professor Derek Freeman, the brassy colleague who made bold to challenge her, is branded by many of his peers as an iconoclast. Most of them do not bother to contest the content of his critique but are satisfied with caricaturing him as "troublemaker," "envious," even "sacrilegious." However, Professor S.L. Washburn, a past president of the American Anthropological Association, now says, "The entire academic establishment accepted the conclusions in Margaret Mead's book, and those conclusions are fundamentally in self-deception in the history of the behavioral sciences."

---

[i]   Father wrote this for *Lay Witness*, the magazine of Catholics United for the Faith. "Mrs. Stebbins" is Madeleine Stebbins, wife of CUF's founder, H. Lyman Stebbins. For information on CUF, go to www.cuf.org.

[ii]   Cultural determinists believe the culture in which we are reared determines who we are emotionally and behaviorally. It holds that environmental influences dominate who we are instead of biologically inherited traits. Another example of a cultural determinist would be someone who says sexual morality is not based on any objective truths but on the culture in which one is raised. The same could be said of religious truths, philosophical truths, etc.

We can say to Professor Washburn, "Let us show you one other example (albeit in another science). It is in Scripture scholarship." There is, in fact, a striking parallel.

Parallel in Scripture scholarship

Today's clergy, religious, and faceless hordes of "mature" lay people fawn over and parrot "establishment" biblical scholars. These have a nefarious influence on the whole of catechesis, as Cardinal Ratzinger testified when he dropped that bombshell at a conference in France in January 1983.[iii] Even some bishops patronize them and rush to protect them from critics. God help the adventurous soul who would challenge the premises of such scholars. No one would give the truth or merit of his criticism any attention. The critic would simply be tarred with obloquy. Mrs. Stebbins suggested I write something about the present state of biblical scholarship with this in mind.

To range over this vast field would not be possible in a short article. However, the prolific Msgr. George A. Kelly has just accomplished the task in his latest work *The New Biblical Theorists: Raymond E. Brown and Beyond*.[2] I urge all CUF members to get this book. The first chapters offer an excellent overview of the modern scene in exegesis. It is readable and written for the non-specialist.

The bulk of the book illustrates those elements in the form criticism approach to biblical studies that are destructive of Catholic Faith. That said, we should note that Monsignor does not say we should reject all aspects of form criticism and of its spin-off

---

iii   "Handing on the Faith Today," Joseph Cardinal Ratzinger. Excerpts from an address to a Paris symposium on January 16, 1983. The full text of this profound talk was originally published in *La Documentation Catholique*, March 6, 1983. It was then excerpted in English in the *Fellowship of Catholic Scholars Newsletter*, Vol. 6, No. 3, June 1983, which is still available online. The closest thing to a "bombshell" the editors could find was his acknowledgment that catechesis had gone awry and had become marked by a "tendency to subordinate truth to praxis" (i.e., experience).

disciplines, such as redaction criticism. Some, in fact, can be useful and represent true progress.

However, the basic underlying premises of most practitioners of form criticism have been contrary to and destructive of Catholic Faith. These, of course, must be condemned. As a result, they cast a dark cloud of suspicion on the entire methodology. Catholics must exercise the greatest caution in this matter. To guide us, the Pontifical Biblical Commission issued a *Declaration on the Historicity of the Gospels* in 1964.[3] This document sifts the chaff from the wheat.

Fr. Raymond Brown, SS

Fr. Raymond Brown, SS, is, s*alva reverentia*, the Margaret Mead of the United States' Catholic biblical "establishment." CUF members know well the multiple assaults on orthodoxy introduced under his aegis. It is *important* to take time to study this man and his major works and to be cognizant of his major accomplishments, as well as his fatal errors. Msgr. Kelly helps us to do this, richly documenting his case with magisterial statements. But like the iconoclastic questioner of Ms. Mead, he will no doubt be awarded many seething epithets with no attention to the merits of his criticism. Yes, there is indeed a parallel!

Litmus test for judging Scripture scholarship: The analogy of faith

I cannot offer here a survey of good modern criticism. However, I can offer a guide to discernment for anyone who wishes to explore the tangled jungle of literature on biblical subjects.

Whenever an editor asks me to review a current book written by one who chooses to identify himself as a Catholic biblical scholar, I hammer at the point of the "analogy of faith," without usually having enough space to discuss the term. But it is imperative for Catholics to know the analogy, to grasp its meaning, and to apply it rigorously as the litmus test of a scholar's orthodoxy.

First coined by Pope Leo XIII, the term expresses indispensable norms required by the Church through all the centuries of her biblical scholars in the service of the Faith. Perhaps we find the clearest source of understanding the analogy in *Dei Verbum*:[iv]

> Having explained Revelation in general and the distinction and unity of the two sources (*fontes*) of sacred Tradition and Sacred Scripture, and having explained that the authentic interpretation of them has been entrusted to the living teaching office of the Church alone, the Council teaches:
>
>> It is clear, therefore, that Sacred Tradition, Sacred Scripture, and the teaching authority of the Church (Magisterium), in accord with God's most wise design, are so linked and joined together that one cannot stand without the others, and that all together and each in its own way under the action of the one Holy Spirit contribute effectively to the salvation of souls.[4]

Later, having treated divine inspiration, inerrancy, the need to expose the literal sense intended by the sacred author, the use of literary forms and other legitimate tools of modern exegesis, the Council Fathers remark:

> But since Holy Scripture must be read and interpreted according to the same Spirit by whom it was written, no less serious attention must be given to the content and unity of the whole of Scripture, if the meaning of the sacred texts is to be correctly brought to light. The living Tradition of the whole Church must be taken into account along with the harmony which exists between

---

[iv] Vatican II's Dogmatic Constitution on Divine Revelation (*DV*). The Council's emphasis on the "analogy of faith" is a major feature of the document and was developed by Paul Yoshigoro Cardinal Taguchi. Taguchi was cardinal archbishop of Osaka, Japan, and died in 1978.

elements of the faith. It is the task of exegetes to work according to these rules toward a better understanding and explanation of the meaning of Sacred Scripture, so that through preparatory study the judgment of the Church may mature. For all of what has been said about the way of interpreting Scripture is subject finally to the judgment of the Church, which carries out the divine commission and ministry of guarding and interpreting the Word of God.[5]

Tradition, Scripture, Magisterium

The analogy of faith, then, is the concomitant and harmonious use of the inseparable triad: Tradition, Scripture, and Magisterium. No scholar can claim to be Catholic whose whole labor does not proceed within this divinely ordered methodology.

The most common and obvious objections against the analogy are:

1. It imposes an outside bias upon the scholar, forcing him to approach his studies with presuppositions that cloud that antiseptic objectivity required of rigorous scientific investigation.
2. It inhibits freedom of speculation, closing off in advance many avenues deemed contrary to the Catholic Faith by Tradition and Magisterium.

These arguments have a specious cogency and strongly appeal to the liberated modern with his shibboleth of academic freedom. But they are groundless, as a few comments will serve to show.

Belief in divine revelation a necessary basis

1) No exegete approaches the biblical data without presuppositions. The Bible is unlike any other book. It is alive! "For the word of God is living and active, sharper than any two-edged

sword, piercing to the division of souls and spirit, of joints and marrow, and discerning the thoughts and intentions of the heart."[6] It makes staggering claims about itself. It claims to transmit divine revelation with the consequent qualities of inspiration and inerrancy. The scholar who approaches this unique literature must first resolve his response to its claims.

Many a believing Protestant biblicist accepts these claims. By his faith commitment, the authentically Catholic exegete does likewise but, beyond that, sets the biblical data in the overall framework of the word of God as taught by the Church in her doctrine on divine revelation and the precise place and function of Holy Scripture within that doctrine (cf. *DV*).

The exegete who believes in the supernatural order but rejects the analogy of faith approaches his study with his own prejudgments. His faith commitments are those of some variety of Protestantism. Even more arbitrary and preconceived biases shackle the liberal or "modernist" exegete. He rejects those special transcendent claims of the Bible, treating it as he would any other classical literary corpus.

Moreover, he excludes, again in advance, any and all of the Bible's persistent assertions of the supernatural, the miraculous genuine prophecy, and often, because of these biases and not for scientific reasons, rejects the historicity of the text involved.

What about the modernist "Catholic" exegete?

Some modernist "Catholic" exegetes, like the believing non-Catholics, follow the specifically Protestant principles of "Scripture alone" and "private interpretation." In other words, they reject the role of Tradition and Magisterium. For an exegete to act in this way is to forfeit the integrity of Catholic doctrine, not to mention the mission incumbent on him to illuminate and defend the Faith in collaboration with the Magisterium. But—and this needs to be absorbed by the Catholic faithful—many of the self-styled "Catholic" exegetes are, like the liberal critics, nonbelievers.

In addition to the Protestant errors, they reject transcendence, the supernatural order, and the very possibility of the miraculous. Fired with a liberal demythologizing passion, they reject the historical literal value of passage after passage because of their biases. Since they still arrogate to themselves the title "Catholic," we can properly label them modernists, carriers and spreaders of a heretical cancer that erodes the Church from within. Their premises, more or less openly stated, are almost verbatim those of the classical modernists condemned by St. Pius X at the dawn of the twentieth century.

The analogy of faith does not inhibit, it liberates!

2) The believing Catholic exegete enjoys two magnificent advantages. First, sensitized by faith, he discerns and shuns unfruitful hypotheses. He does not squander time and energy aimlessly probing down blind alleys. I have watched students begin one major project after another only to end up frustrated and disgusted because they had selected random, trendy theses that the instinct of faith should have precluded. It is obvious they had already lost the *sensus fidei*, a tragedy they lacked the courage to confess.

Secondly (and very positively), the analogy of faith guides the believing scholar into the richest lodes of the biblical mine. His faith is rewarded by having his labors crowned with success and discovery to his personal profit and that of the whole Church. Notice that this aspect in no way keeps him from full use of scientific method. It merely guides him to where the genuine deposits lie. It liberates him for productive scientific work.

I discovered the clearest example of the difference the analogy makes by first reading *Priest and Bishop* by the Sulpician Raymond Brown, and then reading *Church Ministries in the New Testament* by the Franciscan Manuel Miguens. The first ignores the analogy, the second embraces it. The believing Catholic will be thunderstruck by the contrast between the two priest-scholars working on the same subject. Miguens candidly admits the limitations and ambiguities of the New Testament evidence on certain specific questions, but he never distorts this into a source of doubts and insinuated denials as Brown does. Miguens, an impeccable scientist, never forces the text, but, as an "analogist" who knows the true place of Scripture in the totality of revelation, he fortifies the faithful by clearly noting interpretative arguments from Tradition and Magisterium.

By way of summary and conclusion, I offer a schema for discerning of biblical spirits (i.e., the varieties of the species "exegete").

Non-supernaturalists

A disbelief in the supernatural characterizes perhaps the majority of contemporary movers in the field. Many are indistinguishable from their rationalist colleagues.

1. They do not acknowledge the special claims of the Bible to be divine revelation.
2. They treat the documents before them as they would any other literary data.
3. They reject the methodology of the analogy of faith.
4. They do not recognize the superior competence of the Magisterium.
5. They do not feel bound to a continuity or harmony with Tradition.
6. They demythologize, dismissing in advance any assertions of a supernatural character.
7. They indulge in shocking, debunking, sensationalizing, insinuating doubt.

Supernaturalists

Two subdivisions believe in the supernatural:

Non-Catholic Christians

1. They hold a faith commitment to the supernatural order and a transcendent revealing God.

2. They accept the special claims of Scripture to be divinely revealed, inspired, and inerrant.
3. But they also reject the analogy of faith, holding to the Protestant principles of *sola scriptura* and private interpretation.
4. Consequently, their confessional tendencies often depart from the integrity of Catholic interpretation, and the external norms of ecclesiastical authority do not protect them.

Authentic Catholic exegetes

1. They fully accept the supernatural order and a transcendent revealing God.
2. They uphold the authentic Catholic positions on inspiration, inerrancy, and historicity.
3. They interpret both Old and New Testaments in the total unitary biblical context.
4. They willingly follow the analogy of faith and allow Tradition and Magisterium to guide them.
5. They eagerly assist and support the Magisterium.
6. They use their skills to defend and illuminate the doctrines of faith, never to undermine that faith, to systematically insinuate doubt, or to unsettle the faithful by reckless hypotheses.
7. They are scientific professionals in every respect. With humility and pious reserve, they test their advanced theories among their peers and seek the judgment of the Church.
8. They are men of faith and prayer, knowing that holiness is their first and essential requirement.

Let us pray for the conversion of our biblical Margaret Meads and the rehabilitation of their perverted Samoas.

CHAPTER 26

ADDRESS TO THE CONFRATERNITY OF CATHOLIC CLERGY[1]

Until the end of time, the Church lives the mysteries of Christ. Not only in the sense that each individual member lives these, but that the Church, as the Body of Christ, actualizes these mysteries of our salvation. Can we not discern that the Church is now experiencing the Christ's Passion? It experiences this from "within," by betrayal, denials, abandonment, and what the French once called *"trahison des clercs."*[i]

And also from "without, the verdict of abject failure, of impotence in the face of hostile declared enemies." Once more one can almost perceive the massive stone being rolled astride the entrance to the tomb... The Light has shone among us, but darkness seems to have overcome it.

But just as surely, and precisely *because* of these ominous trials, the Body of Christ is about to experience a Resurrection, a dawning of triumph, a third day. So many prophetic voices—literally from heaven—circulate among us. Now is the time for hope. St. Leo the Great once declared in similar times: *"Appareant nunc quoque in civitate sancta, id est in Ecclesia Dei, futurae resurrectionis indicia."*[ii] Now, if ever, is the hour for the Confraternity of Catholic Clergy to experience a second spring.

---

i   French for "treason of the clerks" (i.e., clerics).

ii   "And let them show themselves in the Holy City, i.e., the Church of God, as signs of the Resurrection to come." This quote comes Sermon 66, on the Passion of the Lord by St. Leo the Great (*Sermo LXVI De Passione Domini XV*, Synopsis I, Cap. III).

Yet we are still standing in the darkness of Friday and Saturday. Therefore, until we reach Sunday, there is a need for realism, a need to see what is transpiring and conspiring around us, a need to see the truth of the present condition of the Church here in the United States and in the world. To date, the most salutary and courageously honest source is *The Ratzinger Report*.[2]

Everyone not in a coma has the word crisis on his lips. We should recall that this comes from the Greek work *krisis*: A time for decision, a time to judge and choose, a time to take sides, a time to know and make known where we stand on Calvary—for us it must be *juxta crucem*.[iii]

Name the crisis

A tantalizing problem arises: How shall we name this crisis? I recall two years ago our discussions at this forum on this very point. Is it heresy? Schism? Or is it, as I suspect, apostasy (which implicitly is atheism)?

Canon 751 comes to our aid. Heresy is "the obstinate denial or doubt, after Baptism, of a truth that must be believed by divine and catholic faith." Who can deny this malignancy among us, as modernism, the "synthesis of all heresies," gnaws at the vitals of the Church?

Schism is "the withdrawal of submission to the Supreme Pontiff or from communion with the members of the Church subject to him." Who can deny an extensive *de facto* schism exists? What we term (by ambiguous nomenclature) "the American Church" daily edges itself toward a *de jure* status.[iv] In the western Church's new epidemic of ecclesiastical brinksmanship, we witness a legal game of poker. The bluffs are called, the ante is relentlessly raised, and the stakes are infinitely high.

[iii] "Near (close to) the Cross."
[iv] *De facto* means "in fact," *de jure* means "based on law."

Apostasy is the "total repudiation of the Christian faith." Despite the semantic camouflage and the hypocritical, cynical retention of external forms, I believe we can make a case that much of the nominally "Catholic" membership is already in this category.

At Fátima, Mary said Russia would spread her errors throughout the world. The errors of Russia are labeled "dialectic materialism." Materialism is the denial of the supernatural order, of transcendence, while "dialectic" derives from the same root as "dialogue."

But whatever the diagnosis, one or all of these, we turn to Canon 1364: "An apostate from the faith, a heretic or a schismatic incurs a *latae sententiae* excommunication..."[v]

Are we really capable of absorbing the horrifying implications of this fact? In the eyes of God, what is the actual Catholic population of the USA? Of a given diocese? Of a given parish? On April 12, Pope John Paul said to the bishops of Rome and Lazio that he sees in the world "*de facto* apostasy from the faith with a broad diffusion of historical and practical atheism and a loss of fundamental values."

The two organizations

As we strive to regenerate the CCC, to stir up the embers, as it were, let us begin by using the other national priests' organization as a study in contrast. Here we can take only a sampling, a "culture," to put under the microscope. (Rather fitting imagery: It's usually a pathological specimen that is examined in such a culture!)

Why the drastic divergence between these two groups? There was a fatal fork in the road after Vatican II, two diametrically opposed

---

[v]   This is an excommunication that occurs automatically as a penalty for various violations of canon law. For instance, if one formally participates in an abortion (performs the abortion, has the abortion, drives the mother to the abortuary, pays for the abortion, etc.), one incurs excommunication *latae sententiae*, i.e., automatically. Because it is automatic, it requires no formal trial or announcement, for the offender has brought such a penalty upon himself. This is in contrast to a *ferendae sententiae* excommunication. This only happens with a formal (and often public) canonical trial.

interpretations of the Council. After 20 years, we see how dramatic the contrast has become.

We might have examined other areas of the Church. Thus: "A Tale of Two Nations"—Holland and Poland. Or "A Tale of Two Sororities"—LCWR and *Consortium Perfectae Caritatis*.[vi] The list could go on and on. What was once called "polarization" is now clearly "divorce."

"A Tale of Two US Priests' Organizations"—NFPC and CCC. The following exercise will isolate for us the "culture" we mentioned. This culture eulogizes the disease that is called the "American Church." A disease triggers fever, confusion, discomfort, distress, dysfunction, often severe pain. Have we priests not felt this? Gatherings of priests now often feel like ecumenical gatherings or ministerial associations. Aside from each group consisting of ordained priests, there is hardly any communality between us. We have traveled on separate roads since the Council.

The NFPC

For details and specifics, I refer to my article on the agenda of the NFPC that appeared last year in the *HPR*. There I reviewed some 16 years of their annual official resolutions. For our purposes, we will summarize in a few descriptions.

The vast majority concentrated on political (even strategic military) policies and on social action concerns, all in a radical liberal platform. Others were "self-service," the material betterment of priests: salaries, housing, "liberation," optional celibacy, rights, and privileges, with an especially heavy emphasis on the "grievance" machinery.

[vi] According to its website, "The Leadership Conference of Women Religious (LCWR) is the association of the leaders of congregations of Catholic women religious in the United States." The CPC is a group that broke off from the LCWR out of a conviction that the mother group was not faithful to Church teaching.

It is true that a considerable number of these resolutions concerned doctrine, sacraments, and clerical discipline, but only to stridently dissent from Vatican positions. In the long parade of 16 years, there is a total lack of assent to Church teaching. The record shows the adversarial stance of the NFPC.

There is likewise no interest shown for the promotion of piety and devotion or for the traditional spirituality of the saints. In fact, one could indict the NFPC for a total lack of a supernatural dimension, which brings us back to the diagnosis of dialectic materialism. The NFPC ethos is a branch of the condemned species of Liberation Theology, which we must never suppose is found only in Latin America![vii]

Dissent? Among many other matters, the NFPC dissents vis-à-vis the Church's teachings on contraception, divorce, celibacy, homosexuality, women priests, and intercommunion with non-Catholics. Indeed, we see it just in the support given the signers of the *Times*' advertisements and condemnation of the Vatican for its reaction. By the way, the NFPC just gave its award for hero of the year to Archbishop Hunthausen. There was no mention of his auxiliary, Bishop Wuerl, as would have been expected.[viii]

[vii]   While this is simplistic, for the sake of space, Liberation Theology essentially is Marxism with a Christian veneer. It sees Christ not so much as Savior but Liberator of the oppressed masses, and sees Christianity's most important work in the field of political activism, even when this included revolution and violence. Indeed, it focuses on this world practically to the exclusion of the next. The Church's strongest argument against it was written by then Joseph Cardinal Ratzinger in the Congregation for the Doctrine of the Faith document, "Instruction on Certain Aspects of Theology of Liberation," August 6, 1984. It is available at the Vatican website.

[viii]   Archbishop Raymound Hunthausen, a Jadot appointment, was one of the most liberal and controversial ordinaries ever to hold episcopal office in the United States. He served as archbishop of Seattle from 1975-1991. In 1985, the Vatican appointed Donald Wuerl as auxiliary bishop of Seattle, and gave him power over administration of the archdiocese with respect to areas such as sexual morality and marriage. (Wuerl currently serves as archbishop of Washington, DC.) This incident plays a somewhat pivotal role in the

Even this brief survey indicates the problem is not a minor "slippage" in discipline, but a consistent evidence of the NFPC having the apocalyptic mark, the character of alienation from Rome and the Magisterium. One need only stress the language in which the resolutions address or discuss Rome. The language always stresses the "American Church." Let us take time for just one sample of the Gallican or Febronian theme.[ix]

In 1981, Fr. Neil McCaulley gave the keynote address at the NFPC assembly:[x]

> We need to become aware of the American Catholic experience and the American Catholic identity as real and positive. Until the bishops, priests and religious women and men, laity and all segments come to a consensus on what is this positive American Catholic identity and stand up for it and articulate it, we are not in a position to dialogue [!] with Rome very effectively... Our national identity and self-respect as the American Church is presently so weak that the new code will take away the procedural norms ... and who will speak for the people? Do we want uniformity for senates? Is all the experience of the last 18 years going to be swept aside in favor of a model from a code in which we, as the American Church, had little input? ... [It is a] failure of vision and demeaning for a senate to deal only with matters pertaining to priests and to allow themselves to be relegated to a limited clerical agenda.

recent history of the Church in America. As such, it is illuminating to read the letter Cardinal Ratzinger sent Hunthausen after an apostolic visitation to his diocese. The Seattle archdiocesan newspaper has the full text on its website.

ix   Febronianism and Gallicanism are two names for the same idea, that the local Church and its episcopal conferences should have more say in doctrine than the Holy See. Both would make the pope a figurehead with no real power, much like a constitutional monarch. Much of the work of the modernists has been to achieve the Gallican or Febronian vision.

x   Fr. McAulley served as NFPC president from 1980-82.

There is, finally, but most tellingly, as this quote suggests, a quintessential difference in the structures of the two organizations, theirs and ours: The NFPC accepts exclusively corporate affiliation with diocesan presbyteral councils (hence its name). Its politicizing and, yes, unionizing goals aim at control of these councils to remake them in its own image and likeness.

It is, in effect, a national union of priests with local chapters. All priests of an affiliated diocese are counted in order to give NFPC's radical positions the clout of inflated numbers. But, they insist, there should be no polling of all the priests on critical issues, even on affiliation. Success? The NFPC is thus able to claim 50 percent of all United States priests, though they are showing growing signs of morbidity. But Christ warned that a branch closed off from communion with the vine withers and eventually dies. It can bear no fruit—unless it is bitter fruit, poison fruit.

Contrast with the CCC

By contrast, the CCC, on doctrinal principle, never has and never will seek an alliance with the presbyteral councils. We seek individual membership. Our chapters are independent, voluntary, and autonomous. We are a Confraternity, not a Federation. A sacramental bond between a bishop and his priests constitutes the presbyterate of a diocese.

In addition, its organism is now canonically sanctioned. Catholic ecclesiology and canon law do not envisage a national federation of priests' councils, let alone one which strives in every way to instill an ideology hostile to Rome into the priests of a nation and to initiate and direct policies that are often the source of controversy rather than germane to the diocese itself. A diocesan presbyteral council is meant to be consultative to the bishop ordinary, who, himself, is to be the bond of priestly communion with the bishops and thus, with the pope.[xi]

[xi]   The 1983 *Code of Canon Law* made bishops chairmen of the priests' councils. This greatly changed the character of councils, and thus the NFPC, not only

The NFPC, therefore, acts as an alien and alienating incubus that arrogates to itself by use of pressure tactics, lobbying, and manipulation the role of central command center of priestly communication, a shadow/ersatz hierarchical office that often sets priests at odds with their ordinaries and consistently, on the record, foments alienation from the vicar of Christ. So, at the heart of the divergence between the two organizations, NFPC and CCC, there lies an irreconcilable cleft in ecclesiology.

Our CCC acts as a pious confraternity. It promotes Catholic orthodoxy, stresses universal priestly virtues, and strengthens bonds of effective and affective communion with the bishops and the supreme pastor of the Church, the head of the episcopal college. To the degree that the local bishop has a union of heart and mind with the pope, to that degree the CCC will be a powerful support for him. The CCC is a reverse image of the NFPC, a counter-sign. The NFPC fosters alienation, the CCC fosters Catholic allegiance, *Roman Catholic allegiance.* It promotes communion at all levels and in every way.

If Fr. Jean Marie Vianney faced these alternatives in his day, would he have favored NFPC or CCC?[xii]

Rome's response: The Relatio Finalis

This excursus on the NFPC in no way distracts us from our main topic, the recent Extraordinary Synod. To the challenge of Holland, the Pope called the Particular Synod of 1980. To solve the problem, the central theological theme he offered was that of "communion." Since that time, this theme has been increasingly dominant in the discourse of Pope John Paul.

Now, with a universal crisis reaching a feverish climax in a Church more and more infected by the virus of Hollandization, Rome responded with the Extraordinary Synod of late 1985.

---

in regard to its influence, but to the positions it championed.

[xii] St. Jean (aka, John) Marie Vianney is patron saint of parish priests.

To date, the clearest summary of its orientation is the *Relatio Finalis*, or final report (it is, in fact, a manifesto).[xiii] In its restricted compass, it does not lay out detailed strategies, but it clearly sketches the lines of action.

It was by no means an "uncertain trumpet" that sounded last December. And it should surprise no one that the biblical doctrine of communion again emerges as the key ecclesiological motif. Our firmest resolve should be that every CCC member (and ideally every chapter where they exist) should study and master the *Relatio Finalis*.

Here lies our immediate mission for the Church. It gives us a program of Catholic renewal, reform, and restoration. In short, it gives us a major correction of courses.

Synod themes

Let us now list some of the prominent programmatic themes of the Synod and mentally compare them to the agenda of the CCC:

It affirms the genuine interpretation of Vatican II, not as a break with all that had come before but in light of Church Tradition and the constant teaching of the Magisterium (echoing my own reaction of seven years ago). The *RF* offers a frank and refreshing admission of "shadows."

The *RF* even says "we" (i.e., we bishops!) are responsible for them! One could not expect a complete catalog of the horrors we have recently lived through, but the document sufficiently analyzes underlying causes. The unequivocal admission of sidetracks on the road to conciliar implementation clearly allows the more extensive

---

[xiii] Among other things, it spoke about "the false opposition between pastoral and doctrinal duties," since "true pastoral intention consists in rendering real and concrete the truth of salvation which, of itself, is valid for all times" (*Relatio Finalis* B, a, 1). It also criticized modern biblical criticism and lack of attention (read: submission) to *Dei Verbum*, Vatican II's document on divine revelation. Fr. Richard John Neuhaus has written that "*The Ratzinger Report* ... is an indispensable aid to understanding the [*Relatio*]."

Ratzinger Report to shine. Ratzinger's influence is obvious as the listing of false interpretations and "shadows" are discussed—that fatal "fork in the road"!

There is a dramatic ecclesiological shift. "Mystery" and "communion" are the key words. They are all complementary, not isolated. They are like the multiple facets of an inexhaustibly beautiful jewel. But even here, *koinonia* (or "communion") is the major key to restoration of a sound ecclesiology. The isolated and misinterpreted image of "People of God" is, in a sense, relegated to a back burner.

I cannot begin to explain the potency of the doctrine of communion to remedy our dangerous situation. I urge that we take time to understand as much as possible what this scriptural concept entails. It is the very spirit of the CCC. Among the false interpretations of "People of God" are the secularized political and sociological "models" of the Church. (cf. the NFPC, also the influential *Models of the Church* by Avery Cardinal Dulles).

Yet I hasten to stress that "People of God" is perfectly valid and illuminating if correctly understood in its genuine biblical sense and context. In a phrase, the People of God is the Family of God.

The *Relatio Finalis* also insists that the Church recover the consciousness of her "primary mission." This, too, can be recapped in a phrase: "To save souls." How this phrase has become an object of scorn and obloquy! It is almost eradicated, even among otherwise orthodox Catholics. Many priests feel inhibited from using the term in public.

On all sides, even from NFPC groupies, the term "evangelization" is the "in-word." This too, describes the primary mission of the Church, but has often been denatured. "Evangelize" means to disseminate the good news of revelation. But what is the content of evangelization?

What precisely is the good news? Paul VI in his exhortation on evangelization pointed out:

"The content of the Faith is either Catholic or it is not."[xiv]

The *RF* singles out *Dei Verbum* among the major conciliar constitutions for new and intensive study. It explicitly deplores that *Dei Verbum* has been neglected. At the core of this document is the insistence on the analogy of faith. The *RF* speaks of this litmus test of Catholic orthodoxy at several points, though not using the term. If we diligently applied this perennial rule of faith, it would correct all the modernist errors not only in exegesis but also in all other disciplines of doctrine and in every aspect of dogmatic and moral theology.

"Orthodoxy" is once again a respectable word, according to the *RF*. It indicates that the Church will no longer tolerate the explosive spread of dissent we have seen in recent years. The valid parameters of legitimate dissent must be established. Thus, the Synod opted for the term "pluriformity" [i.e., uncountable] to convey the true sense of the note of Catholicity. "Pluralism," usually usurped for two decades in the sense of contradictory pluralism (the toleration of heterodoxy), is no longer a polite word in ecclesiology. It is no fluke that Charles Curran's impeachment surfaced so shortly after the Synod.[xv] While

---

[xiv] The Holy Father actually said this at the close of the 1974 Synod of Bishops. According to *TIME* magazine, he said it was "dangerous to speak of diversified theologies according to continents and cultures. The content of the Faith is either Catholic or it is not." See also *Evangelii Nuntiandi* (apostolic exhortation, Paul VI, December 8, 1975).

[xv] In August 1986, Joseph Cardinal Ratzinger with the CDF sent Curran a letter stating, "You will no longer be considered suitable or eligible to exercise the function of a professor of Catholic theology." At that point, Curran could no longer able to teach theology at the Catholic University of America. Of course, the so-called progressive crowd complained he had been denied due process and claimed he should never have been censured (despite nearly 20 years of vocal opposition to the Church's teachings and a seven-year, meticulous process leading up to his censure). His supporters call him the "bravest," "most consequential" moral theologian and ethicist "over the past forty years." Southern Methodist University later hired him, and he still teaches there.

the process long anteceded the Synod, this action clearly signals that the defense of orthodoxy in the Church in no way contradicts the mind of the Synod.

One of the most debilitating slogans bandied about in the backwash of Vatican II has been that bishops must be "pastoral." The Pope has often blown the cover of those who exploited it to excuse the lack of episcopal correction of errors. In fact, he did so pointedly during his visit to the United States.

Now the Synod states, "It is not licit to separate the pastoral character from the doctrinal vigor of the documents. In the same way, it is not legitimate to separate the spirit and the letter of the Council, which must be understood in continuity with the great tradition of the Church, and at the same time must receive light from the Council's own doctrine... The Church is one and the same throughout all the councils..."

The *RF* repeatedly insists on reverence for the sacred. The program of the future calls for holiness, a true sense of divine grace, an internal (not merely structural) renewal of the liturgy, a recovery of the sense of transcendence, which is a correlative of mystery. To coin a phrase, in the face of massive desacralization, the Synod calls for a "re-sacralization." The graceless *Secular City* of Harvey Cox is scheduled to become a ghost town.

Catechesis received an unexpected but precious boon: A call for a universal catechism or compendium of all truths Catholics must hold. The earliest and most credited voice was that of Boston's Bernard Cardinal Law.[xvi] The surge of support that this generated at the Synod surely bore the signs of inspiration. The CCC must embrace this catechism, insist on its directive authority, and purge

---

[xvi]   Apparently, His Eminence gave an intervention in which he said something to the effect that kids from New York to St. Petersburg, Russia, and Santiago, Chile, had a common cultural language, that blue jeans and rock 'n' roll meant the same to each and formed a shared point of reference. So why, he asked, should we in the Church be without a common language? This in turn built off of speeches given by Joseph Cardinal Ratzinger in 1983. The *Catechism of the Catholic Church* finally appeared in 1992.

out the defective and often heretical texts now so long choking the Faith out of the minds and hearts of our children and youth.

The *RF* also clarifies the strict sense of "collegiality," which in *Lumen Gentium* concerns only the college of bishops in union with its head. In this area, the analogous relation of the presbyterium in union with its head the bishop is recognized but not confused with episcopal collegiality. Here the Synod Fathers state, "Between a bishop and his presbyterate there exists a relationship founded on the Sacrament of Orders..." As we said earlier, the bishop is the nexus (or artery) of communion with the Universal Church. (The sad reality today is that some of these arteries have become occluded, clogged up. We dare pray for some bypass surgery ... soon.)

The last but very significant item of the Synod we shall mention is its strong proclamation of the mystery of the Cross. This again strikes at the heart of our crisis, which can be called precisely a "crisis of the Cross." The Cross compels decision and judgment; no one can ultimately escape its scrutiny.

The Cross, the essential school of the saints, offers two immediate lessons. First, it teaches us the stark reality of sin. The Cross is a clear indictment of the personal reality of objective and subjective sin. One cannot blame the existence of sin on the "structures." And the second, co-equal lesson is the infinite love and mercy of God. These lessons are critical for a world on the path to self-destruction. The denial of sin and the refusal to seek the Christ's mercy in the sacrament of reconciliation are obvious symptoms of the past 20 years.

The Cross (and, to be more specific, the crucifix) has been suppressed by those whom it silently indicts. What does the Cross demand of the Church? Sacrifice, victimhood (cf. Archbishop Fulton J. Sheen), humility, obedience, penance, mortification, self-denial, and discipline. However, whole sectors of the Church—seminaries, convents, colleges, and universities, among others—have rejected these "values" of the Cross. The Cross calls us to hope against all odds, to have absolute confidence that the Crucified has conquered the world and its prince. On Calvary, before the Cross, the sign of contradiction, the crowd was divided into two groups: those who love, who assent and embrace, and those who vociferously hate, who dissent and reject: "Come down from the Cross and we will believe." There can be no neutrality under the Cross. In today's crisis of the Cross, each priest must decide.

The CCC and all true Catholics belong "*juxta crucem*" with Mary our mother and St. John the Evangelist, with the minority, the *pusillus grex*: Magdalene, the holy women, Nicodemus, Joseph of Arimathea. We find the *summa* of the *Theologia Crucis* in the first chapters of First Corinthians. How well St. Paul expresses the two camps that are found almost everywhere today in the western Church... Those who seem to be powerful and pride themselves on their wisdom will be revealed as defeated by those who, in the eyes of the world, seem weak and foolish.

Later, Paul says to the Philippians, "I say it with tears: they are enemies of the Cross of Christ."[3]

Today too, the Synod elevates the criteria of the Cross to lay bare the truth. Those who are anti-Cross are also anti-Church and hence anti-Christ. They have branded themselves with the mark of the beast. On the other hand, revelation teaches the elect have the sign of the Cross sealed on their foreheads.

The CCC's role

We are now ready to discuss the CCC agenda. We do so in two parts.

First, what can the CCC do to promote the *RF*?

1. Study the *Relatio Finalis* with conciliar and post-conciliar documents. (Flannery I and II are handy texts.) This means personal study, but also study in our chapters, and then in parish and school study groups. Added to the above basic materials should be all post-synodal exhortations. These should be prime resources for homiletic topics.

2. Fan the embers of devotion and revive genuine popular piety, because the fire has gone out in the furnace of the Church.

3. Blessed Virgin Mary—Mother of the Church, woman of assent (cf. *Marialis Cultus*).[4]

4. Cautiously and prudently discuss apparitions and help people discern the genuine from the spurious.

5. Recognize the astounding prolific evidence of the supernatural and miraculous in our very days.

6. Franz Werfel said it well: "For those who believe in God, no explanation is necessary: for those who do not believe in God, no explanation is possible." Here we have a powerful refutation of the secularism and immanentism of the modernists. At Fátima, Mary's first words were "I come from heaven." This shatters the pretensions of the "American Church."

7. There should be much talk about the saints. In the saints, we have the living witness to the fullness of Catholic faith and morals.

8. Sacred Heart of Jesus: We need to grasp how this devotion is deeply rooted in Sacred Scripture and therefore is not a luxury or a sentimental froth. It is at the very core of Christianity and is as strong, virile, and sacrificial as the Cross. To squelch the spirit of rebellion, we are bid to "learn of Jesus, for He is meek and humble of Heart ... obedient unto death."[5]

9. Eucharistic devotion: We are nurtured in this by the holy hours at our chapter meetings. Priests must again make themselves conscious of being not only confectors of the Eucharist but custodians as well. We should be convinced that the Eucharist is the source of vocations, holiness, zeal for God's House (i.e., for awe and reverence).

10. We should promote holy hours, "eucharistic days" (the vestige of St. John Neumann's 40 hours devotion, Benediction, perpetual adoration if possible, the First Fridays).

11. Symbolic of what we have to fight against and what is at stake: the ruthless elimination of kneelers from our churches ... by what authority? (*Environment and Art in Catholic Worship*?)[xvii] This action alone effectively forestalls all future adoration of the Blessed Sacrament. Meanwhile, abuses inundate the faithful in a billowing sea of blasphemy, sacrilege, doubt, denial, and neglect.

12. Sacred music is on the front line of the battle between the sacred and the secular. To be convinced of this, read Cardinal Ratzinger's address on the subject earlier this year.[6] Only sacred music has any right to be used at any time in a temple of the eucharistic Presence. What is your experience at weddings, for instance?

13. Respect in church at all times. If we believe that the Real Presence perdures outside of the "liturgy," there should be insistence on the discipline of silence, on behavior based on faith in that divine Presence, and on decent dress. CCC members must insist on implementation of *Dominicae Cenae* and *Inaestimabile Donum*. Among other matters, we should, as the Pope orders us, correct irreverence in the now chaotic method of receiving the sacrament and sign of unity: one-handed, snatching, walk-aways, et al. Here we might want to re-read *Memoriale Domini* for ourselves, not to mention for those shocked people who probably have never heard a hint of its message.

[xvii] As Duane L.C.M. Galles with the St. Joseph Foundation explains, "*Environment and Art in Catholic Worship*, published in 1978 by the National Conference of Catholic Bishops, Bishops' Committee on the Liturgy (NCCB/BCL) is cited as the authority for the sometimes drastic changes such as destruction of communion rails, ripping out of high altars and replacing them with 'tables' in the center of the church building, moving the reserved Blessed Sacrament out of the sanctuary, etc." However, in the same article, he explains quite clearly that *EACW* has no authority, and thus those who appeal to it do so illegitimately.

14. As an important aside: By any standard of Catholic pietas, assent to the pope should mean obedience to his desires, not just to his commands. It is just such eager and ready obedience that is the benchmark of the CCC spirit. This is what we mean by adding the term "affective" to that of "effective" communion.

15. Seminaries: The CCC came to the aid of priestly vocations by opening and recruiting membership to seminarians. We need them; they need us. Beyond this, how can we pick up the bruised and battered candidates ruthlessly expelled, usually on the grounds of "rigidness" (translation: They are papists)? Can we instigate the creation of a haven, a "safe house" for battered vocations? This could be done on a very modest, unpretentious scale, without public fanfare. We would need a friendly bishop, an old house, a few professors, and they are out there—in CCC and [Fellowship of Catholic Scholars] ranks. Msgr. Schuler's plan will work effectively in some circumstances, notably under his personal aegis, but will not succeed in others. I suggest both approaches be undertaken. They will complement each other.

Agenda II

The second part of our agenda must begin with the confession that we have been floundering in the doldrums. It is time to move or be buried.

The questions for our second phase of the agenda: What methods are at hand to revive and restore the CCC?

16. Advertisement, publicity, and aggressive recruitment of "papist" priests and seminarians. Many have proposed this year after year with no action. It is a task we need to assign (perhaps to a part-time professional PR man). Our major efforts to hold national forums have had scant attention—

even in the friendly Catholic press. Our resolutions, worked at for hours, are consigned to the archives of oblivion.

17. Will this forum be reported in the media? Will our resolutions be flashed to the public? Will recruitment ads be placed in *HPR*, *National Catholic Register*, *The Wanderer*, etc.? Will we use the mailings of CUF, Wanderer Forum, Institute for Religious Life, St. Joseph Foundation, Keep the Faith, etc., to add notes to priests urging they join us? KTF volunteered to do so. Now we face the moment of truth: Do we have the faith and the zeal to help heal the wounded Church and priesthood in our nation? The CCC can be a powerful vehicle for priests to stand together and publicly express the assent and allegiance ... to pull us back from the brink ... now or never!

18. Regional organization. We need to stretch out beyond the Mississippi and even beyond the Continental Divide. We need to be truly national, from sea to shining sea. We could effect this by restructuring our directorate. We should map out regional areas, and we should have at least one director for each region. This person would answer to the national office, stimulate growth, organize chapters, and attend annual directorate meetings. In turn, each region should hold its own local annual forum. Whenever possible, an officer of the national CCC should attend these meetings. This is the pattern used by CUF.

19. We should solicit new episcopal advisory board members. We have some promising new bishops who we could contact. Our stationery should feature their names. If a bishop is ashamed of us, we should look elsewhere.

20. Position statements: We need a mechanism that allows us to react to the periodic controversies that flare up in the life of the US Church. The CCC should be able to give testimony to a priestly voice that assents to the Magisterium and adheres to the vicar of Christ.

21. How can we implement this? Will the CCC authorize its officers to speak on behalf of the membership when time is of the essence? Issues can rage for some time and then be forgotten. This results in missed opportunities for us to give voice to the faithful clergy and laity. Such statements might be circulated among the directors with a time limit set. The membership will surely make its displeasure known if their trust is violated.

22. And precisely now at this meeting, we should send a pledge of support to the Holy Father, to Cardinal Ratzinger, and to Cardinal Baum[xviii] in regard to the Curran case and the underlying broader issue of the draft statement seeking to implement *Sapientia Christiana* and the related canons in institutions of higher learning.[7]

Conclusion

At this historic juncture of extreme crisis, when the allegiance of American priests to the vicar of Christ is being ultimately tested, when we sense a threat of *de jura* schism—one more desiccated national Church in the annals of history—when the future of Catholicism in the United States hangs in the balance, the CCC is a providential and potentially decisive response to the Catholic restoration signaled by the 1985 Extraordinary Synod as capsulated in its *Relatio Finalis*. The CCC is and should be a collective voice for United States priests who are truly American and proud of their patriotism, but are also truly Catholic and proud of their universality and their Romanism. We are indeed American priests who thrill to call ourselves Roman Catholics.

[xviii] William Cardinal Baum, former Cardinal Archbishop of Washington, DC, from 1973-80, and later Cardinal Major Penitentiary of the Apostolic Penitentiary, an office in the Vatican. He was the oldest cardinal elector in the 2005 conclave, and is on track to be the longest serving American Catholic cardinal of all time.

Recently, Msgr. George Kelly reported an American who met the Holy Father and heard from him a pained comment: "All I ever hear these days from the United States is dissent."

Holy Father, to your tearful lament, we priests of the Confraternity of Catholic Clergy respond to you with vigor and love, "Holy Father, we assent!"

RESOLUTIONS OF THE 1986 NATIONAL CCC FORUM

1. The members support the Holy See in its correction of the doctrinal errors of Fr. Charles E. Curran, and it supports the draft declarations of the Sacred Congregation of Catholic Education on the implementation of *Sapientia Christiana* and the related canons on the reform of Catholic education in colleges and universities.

2. The Confraternity rejoices in the *Relatio Finalis* published by the bishops of the Extraordinary Synod of 1985 and pledges its cooperation in making that outstanding document better known.

3. It urges the Holy See to conclude its studies on seminaries and religious life in the United States with a determined program of action to restore the integrity and communion of these institutions that are so vital for the life of the Church in this nation.

4. It petitions the Sacred Congregation for the Doctrine of Faith to clarify the parameters of legitimate dissent in the Church and to reaffirm the binding nature of the ordinary Magisterium in its teaching office.

5. It seeks from the Sacred Congregation of the Clergy a clarification of the competence of diocesan presbyteral councils and the propriety of their affiliation with national federations of priests' councils.

6. That concern is entertained relative to the growing practice of appointing pastors to parishes with only limited tenure in

view of the provisions of Canon 522 and in the light of the morale problem it has on the affected priests.

7. The members of the CCC will labor to restore integral faith in the Most Holy Eucharist, promote adoration of the Real Presence of Jesus Christ in the Blessed Sacrament, and in collaboration with the Holy See, require our bishops to pass judgment on the practice of eliminating the traditional kneelers in our churches.

8. With heartfelt filial devotion, we renew our consecration to the Immaculate Heart of Mary, and we shall assist in spreading her message delivered at Fátima for the peace of the world.

CHAPTER 27

THE CHURCH AS COMMUNIO[1]

In January 1980, Pope John Paul II summoned the Dutch bishops to Rome for a "particular Synod."[2] The crisis of the Church in Holland had long since gone beyond the limits which could be corrected by merely private, *sub rosa* interventions on the part of Rome.[i] The breach was public. Many construed silence as consent. What, then, was to be the theological initiative that Rome would advance at the Synod as the key to resolving the crisis?

This question takes on an added impact when we realize that since 1980 (and despite the new "Roman" configuration of her hierarchy), Holland still stands as the showcase of a universal ecclesial crisis, a microcosm of alienation and dissent, both in doctrine and in practice. Moreover, since the Council, Holland has exported more than tulips.[ii]

Thus, in 1985, the Holy Father summoned an extraordinary Synod in order to confront what has become a worldwide crisis. In symbolic captions, the present crisis might be called "A Tale of Two

---

i   Meaning "under confidentiality."

ii   John Paul II called the Dutch Synod to address endemic dissent and possible schism. At this event, held in January 1980 at the Vatican, he sided with the minority of new bishops appointed by Paul VI (namely Johannes Gijsen and Adrianus Simonis). He further ordered all the bishops to sign the final declaration, which supported orthodoxy and in effect silenced the heretical and censured Dutch theologian Edward Schillebeekx. According to various sources, the Dutch Church still has major problems (witness the country's Dominicans recent call for priestless Masses). The Synod did succeed, however, in ending the quarrels and the sort of rabid dissent that had plagued the Netherlands since the mid-1960s.

nations: Holland and Poland," and subtitled, "Will the real Vatican II please stand up?"

The key theological concept offered in 1980 was *koinonia*, the inspired biblical word for "communion." It comes, then, as no surprise that one of the repeated themes at the 1985 Synod was "communion."

In this discussion, we shall probe this theme in its biblical roots and suggest that it is crucial at this fateful juncture in her history for the whole Church—and religious communities in a special sense—to study and assimilate the doctrine of "communion." This doctrinal treasure has always been among the *nova et vetera* of theology.[iii] Following the Dutch Synod, however, one notices that the wise and prudent householder John Paul II draws upon this theology with increasing frequency, clarity, and urgency.[3]

Furthermore, as recorded in the interventions of so many Fathers, the emphasis of the 1985 Synod on ecclesial communion shows the Pope's prompting has had its desired influence.

I urge you to make the Synod's "final report" the central theme of a community-wide study.[iv]

The key vocabulary

One cannot dispense with the admittedly tedious chore of etymology [i.e., the study of words and their development]. The New Testament word *koinonia*, "sharing something with someone," has a cognate adjective, *koinos*, meaning "possessed or used in common," or "to share in."

In turn, this conveys the Old Testament root *habar*, "to bind, to unite, to join together." The rabbinic noun derived from this root is *haburah*, the primary religious use of which is the "company" that is joined together to celebrate the Passover Seder.

---

iii   "New things and old," cf., Matt 13:52.
iv   This document is available at http://www.ewtn.com/library/CURIA/ SYNFINAL.HTM.

Significantly, in the Old Testament this complex of Semitic words also relates to the matrimonial covenant or bond (i.e., the communion of the spouses). In popular usage, the *haburah* denoted any group banded together in common enterprise, among which, let us note, is "co-op" (which in the Palestine of apostolic days was often a fishing co-op).

We must also face a final and very practical philological problem. In current English translations (which are, for better or worse, enshrined in liturgical texts) *koinonia* and its cognates are not consistently represented by the same English words. Thus we easily overlook the semantic force of repetition and cognate relationship.

This is especially a problem when the word "fellowship" is heard, but *koinonia* is what the inspired Greek text reads. It is my sense that this word fellowship, so cherished, especially in the Protestant tradition, greatly weakens the potent interior sense of "communion" (*koinonia*).

"Fellowship" has a connotation in English that renders an impression of an external, *juxtaposed* assemblage, of superficial conviviality, of *Gemütlichkeit*.[v] "Fellowship" stresses one aspect of *societas* but does not usually convey the full inner force of *communion*.

While the Greek and Semitic words bear the sense both of "communion" and "community," we usually do distinguish the two words in English. "Community" is the corporation or entity that is the external effect of communion. "Communion," on the other hand, is the interior living essence of that "union together." A major theological conclusion must be that there can be no genuine Christian community without *communion*. In our garrulous modern Church, use of the word "community" as a quasi-theological term has become a ubiquitous buzzword. It wafts up in the air whenever two or more Christians gather in their *own* name. By any Catholic definition, this

---

[v]   Literally, "cosiness," denoting cosiness between persons, a certain sense of belonging and cheerful society amongst people, in whose company the cares and hectic woes of the world are cast aside.

term has absolutely no meaning unless it is constituted and sealed by *communion* in the authentic sense, which we must now consider.

Trinitarian communion

The source and supreme paradigm (or model) of communion subsists in the Most Holy Trinity. We cannot offer here a treatise on this central mystery of Christian faith. All we can do is to beg your indulgence to accept a few "shorthand" propositions, knowing we do not presume to display the treasury of theological subtleties.

From all eternity, in the unchanging Now (*nunc stans*) of the Godhead, the Father knows His divine essence and expresses it in a Word. This Word, limitless and infinitely perfect, is the second Person of the Trinity. The Father begets the Word, His Son, in an eternally simultaneous act. The Word is the only-begotten, co-eternal act; the Father and Son breathe forth Their mutual love. This mutual Breathing (*Pneuma, Spiritus*) in its infinite perfection is the third Person, the Holy Spirit.

Even this awkward and schematic recital shows us that the relational acts of knowing and willing with their objects, truth and love constitute the essence of this divine communion, which thereby constitutes a community of three Persons. This is the Trinity, a community of three co-equal, co-eternal Persons, possessing one undivided, limitless life, one essence, one existence, related together in the bonds of infinite truth and love. We also observe that communion entails communication,[vi] the active commerce of intellect and will, whose objects are truth and love, which in the divine relations of the Trinity are synonyms for the Godhead. God is truth; God is love.

[vi]   Father's original footnote reads, "In the first option for greeting the faithful at Mass, taken from 2 Cor 13:13, the Trinitarian formula ends with 'the fellowship of the Holy Spirit.' The Latin translates *communicatio* for the original Greek *koinonia*. Communion is imparted and received by 'communication.'"

Whenever we discuss the theology of communion, the mystery of the Trinity must always serve as the foundational image. Again, we insist: The Trinity is the supreme source and paradigm of all Christian communion. No further application of the term is valid in any Christian sense unless it conforms to and communicates in the communion of this community, which is the Trinity. The triune God has freely willed to send forth, to communicate this interior communion into temporal contingent creation, which is for that very reason crowned with men, rational creatures, themselves made in the image and likeness of the Creator, and capable, therefore, of knowing and loving and, when elevated by grace, sharing in the life of the Trinity.

Thus, the goal of communicating the Trinitarian communion motivates the temporal mission *ad extra* of Son and Holy Spirit. The uncreated persons of the Trinity bring communion to the human and angelic persons They created.[vii] Communion can only exist between persons. Even at this first stage of our study, in the light of the Trinity, we raise some eminently practical questions: Can we, dare we imagine dissent, contestation, alienation, division, antinomianism, anarchy among the Persons of the Holy Trinity? Can we, dare we suggest that these phenomena are healthy, desirable signs of *any* Christian community? Such was the challenge to Holland in 1980; such is the challenge that the 1985 Synod sets before the universal Church today. Such is the challenge for every religious community.

We repeat: In the Trinity, there exists a perfect communion of life, truth, and love. Therefore, every genuine Catholic community must have these marks or self-destruct.

Lumen Gentium describes the Church as "a communion of life, charity and truth."[4]

1. Sanctifying grace is the life of the Trinity communicated to us. A religious community (which must mirror the

---

vii   Father notes here, "The role of the angelic communion is also germane to our understanding of *koinonia*, but can here be mentioned only in passing."

Church in its purest essence) must fully know and appreciate "grace" and must preserve it in her members by sacramental practice.

2. Love: The persons of the Trinity are united in affective, not merely effective, love. Charity, not just cold and calculating efficiency; hearts, not just brains; devotion, not just programs ... the Holy Spirit must continue His breathing of divine love into the Church.

3. And truth. Just a few bad ideas, even one doctrinal error, can destroy a community, a parish, a diocese, and the Church in a nation. Multi-million dollar empty buildings—convents, seminaries—ecclesiastical white elephants, strew the landscape of our nation. Monsignor Logal calls it "the Rubble of Renewal."[5] They are the proof of what doctrinal error can do. In the Church, nothing can succeed without truth and grace.

Therefore, discernment is urgent and necessary. The Church in the United States is suffering from spiritual AIDS. It caught this disease through a perversion of doctrine. It has altered the immune system (i.e., the normal healthy instinct of Faith) and has proved highly contagious. Sadly, those afflicted with this malady will likely never admit they have caught it (i.e., have sinned).

The cure? First and foremost, the superiors must exercise discernment. Discernment, however, is also incumbent on all members of the community. Prayer and charity are indispensable, but dissidents must be quarantined. Their books, periodicals and journals, lectures, summer courses and seminars, and retreats ... their every presence must be banned like the plague they are. Mennonites have a term for what we must do with these people: "shunning."[viii]

In the epistles of charity, listen to the Beloved Disciple speak to us:

[viii] The Amish also practice shunning, as did the Church in limited circumstances until the revision of the *Code of Canon Law* in 1983.

4. 1 John 2:19: "They came forth from among us, but they were not of us...."
5. 2 John 8-11: "Look to yourselves, that you do not lose what you have worked for, but that you may receive a full reward. Anyone who advances and does not abide in the doctrine of Christ, has not God; he who abides in the doctrine, he has both the doctrine and the Son. If anyone comes to you and does not bring this doctrine, do not receive him into the house or say to him 'welcome.' For he who says to him, 'welcome,' is sharer in his evil way."

This is charity.

The cure has two parts, however. Its second part is the reverse side of the first: Seek out the despised "papists," those faithful to the pope and the Magisterium. Welcome them, profit from them, promote them, and harbor them.

The Last Supper discourse (John 13-17)

In His priestly discourse to the Twelve at the Last Supper, Jesus precisely revealed His mission, speaking words that came burning from His heart. He would extend the eternal communion of Trinity to those who believe and thereby "abide," "dwell," "remain," and "live" in Him.[ix] Jesus describes the divine indwelling of grace by saying, "Abide (live) in Me... As the Father lives in Me, and I live in the Father, so also you must live in Me..."

Beginning with the organic analogy of the vine and branches through the whole high priestly prayer, Christ's pleas for interior union and exterior unity take on a pathos, a crescendo rising from the very heart of the Word made Flesh. We see this most especially in His prayer: "That they all may be one, even as You, Father, in Me and I in You ... that they may be perfectly one in Us that the world

---

[ix] All these verbs are variously used to translate the single operative Greek verb *menein*.

may know that You have sent Me."[6] In the discourse, note also the refrain of "mission" and "consecration" and the communication of truth and love. These words emanate from the eternal "council" of the Trinity. Religious and priests should thrill to this dimension of their special mission and consecration.

This communion described by Christ is nothing less than admission into the life of the Trinity by filiation. This admirable *commercium*, this wondrous exchange, is effected by grace, which, as 2 Peter 1:4 capitulates, makes us *theias koinonoi physeos*, that is, communicants (*koinonoi*!) in the divine nature.

Here, then, is the *koinonia* we are discussing. The branch must adhere closely and open fully to the life of the vine: no "hanging loose," no occlusion, no separation.

Eucharistic communion

And it is in the context of the Last Supper that we discover that this *koinonia* is also eucharistic. The words of Jesus in John 6 ("He who eats My Flesh and drinks My Blood lives/abides in Me and I in Him") are echoed later in the discourse at the Last Supper. Paul, in 1 Corinthians 10:17, uses the technical words in reference to the Eucharist: "All we who eat the one Bread are one Body...We are *koinonoi* (communicants) in His Body and Blood."

The Eucharist, we read in John 6, gives us life everlasting. Unless we consume it, we have no life in us. It is in eucharistic communion that the mutual indwelling is nurtured, sustained, and consummated. And the more complete our communion with Christ, the more complete our communion with each other in His body. No wonder we call this sacrament simply "Holy Communion."

As we shall see, the central simile of the vine and branches in the Last Supper discourse is also ecclesial. One need but compare it to all the other specifically ecclesial images in the New Testament. The Eucharist is the sign of unity and the bond of charity. It is the life and center of the Church. It effects the solidarity of the People of God. "No Christian community can be built up unless it has its basis and center in the celebration of the most Holy Eucharist,"[x] so the implications already begin to accumulate. Thus, Christian communion (*koinonia*) is Trinitarian, ecclesial, eucharistic, and our duty becomes clear: We need to defend the Eucharist.

The Pentecost experience (Acts 2:41-42)

Standing with the college of the apostles on Pentecost and speaking in their name, Peter delivered the inaugural sermon of the Church. Luke records the results:

> So those who received his word were baptized, and there were added that day about 3,000 souls. And they devoted themselves to the apostles' teaching (*didache*) and the communion (*koinonia*), to the breaking of bread and the prayers. [7]

The *koinonia* mentioned here has now reached a complete, unqualified sense. Thus, Luke uses the word with the article and with no further need for explanation. It is the communion. It is ecclesial, the "calling together" (i.e., *ekklesia*) of those who receive the word in faith and lovingly bond themselves in the New Covenant. This bonding in life has the biblical background of the marriage covenant between husband and wife (*berith* and *haburah*). For the New Testament, Paul makes it explicit in Ephesians 5 that the communion of Jesus with His Church is the intimate communion of groom with bride: It forms one flesh. The ecclesial communion is nuptial.

---

x   *Presbyterorum Ordinis*, no. 6. Father notes here, "See also *Lumen Gentium*, no. 9: *Itaque populus ille messianicus ... A Christo in communionem vitae, caritatis et veritatis constitutus...*'" (So it is that that messianic people ... Established by Christ as a communion of life, charity and truth ... [are] also used by Him as an instrument for the redemption of all, and [are] sent forth into the whole world as the light of the world and the salt of the earth).

The text cited above highlights other facets: the communion is eucharistic (the "breaking of bread," *fractio, klasis*); it is apostolic and hierarchical (the Magisterium is cited); it is also a doctrinal faith-communion (devoted to the apostolic teaching). In the summary of Acts 4, we see the communion as possessing "one mind and one heart." One cannot bypass the apostolic service of authority and still live in this communion. The college of the Twelve has just received the endowments of the Holy Spirit, whose proper mission *ad extra* has now begun. As the Father has sent the Son, so now Father and Son have breathed forth the Holy Spirit of love, unity, truth, and life *ad extra* into our world via the Church. Peter is the head and spokesman of the Twelve and preaches in full collegial communion with them. In the Gospels, Jesus designated Peter as the visible center and guarantor of the *koinonia*.

Now in Acts, he assumes this function: The *koinonia* is Petrine. We cannot knowingly bypass Peter and pretend to be living in this communion with the Trinity. The "teaching of the apostles" is normative in the Church. What Peter, keeper of the keys, and the apostolic college bind on earth will be bound in heaven. "As the Father has sent Me, so I also send you" (John 20:21). Reception of and obedience to the authentic doctrine, laws, and discipline of the Church are requisites for inclusion in the *koinonia*.[xi]

Koinonia and paradosis (1 John 1:1-8)

The opening chapter of First John displays one of the most developed and prolific uses of *koinonia*. It serves as an exegetical meditation on the Johannine Last Supper discourse and underscores

---

[xi]   Father notes here, "Canon law is at the service of *koinonia* (e.g., no. 209). For the pope, see Canon 333, § 2. For bishops, see canons 375, 381, 391, et al. For parochial pastors, see Canon 519ff. Note the use of 'hierarchical communion' in the *Code*. It is the function of the bishop to maintain hierarchical communion in his particular Church. He is the artery between the flock and the universal communion in and with the supreme and universal pastor."

the plenary sense of *koinonia* expressed there in the words of Jesus, though without using the specific term on that occasion.

6. That which was from the beginning, which we have heard, which we have seen with our eyes, which we have looked upon and touched with our hands, concerning the word of life.
7. The life was made manifest, and we saw it and testify to it and proclaim to you the eternal life which was with the Father and was made manifest to us.
8. That which we have seen and heard, we proclaim also to you so that you may have *koinonia* with us, and our *koinonia* is with the Father and with His Son, Jesus Christ.
9. And we are writing this that your joy may be complete.
10. This is the message we have heard from Him and proclaim to you, that God is light. In Him, there is no darkness at all.
11. If we say we have *koinonia* with Him while we walk in darkness, we lie and do not live according to the truth.
12. But if we walk in the light, as He is in the light, we have *koinonia* with one another, and the Blood of Jesus, His Son, cleanses us from all sin.

The rest of First John fleshes out the meaning of this *koinonia*. It is a grand summation of what has already been considered. The *koinonia* derives from and subsists in the Trinity. The Incarnation is its projection *ad extra* into the arena of this world. Jesus Christ is the "Eternal Word ... from the beginning." He brings the interior of life of the Trinity to us creatures, elevating us by grace to a connaturality with God.

This enables us to become His children and communicants (*koinonoi*) of His divine nature (*theias physeos*). The invitation and means to enter the *koinonia* is transmitted by the perfect apostolic eye, ear, and finger witness to the flesh and blood historical manifestation of the Word. This transmission (communication)—

the Sacred Tradition (technically, the *paradosis*),[xii] the integral and authoritative handing down of what Jesus revealed in words and deeds—is the vehicle by which access and ingress into communion is offered to all mankind.

Corollaries

In this brief survey, we have looked at the New Testament's more explicit *koinonia* texts. In addition to the few explicit texts cited above, the Pauline theology is rife with implicit correspondences: indwelling, filiation, mystical body, ecclesial unity, mystical nuptials, prerequisites of doctrine and morals for Christian communion, and so on.

Nor should we overlook the extraordinary use of "*syn*" verbs, showing that the Christian must "suffer together with," "die together with," "rise together with" Christ. Many look upon the famous "collection" passages as being pragmatic, but they are deeply ecclesiological and express a dimension of communion that we must not neglect.

Summary

So how is this brief schematic review of the incidence of the New Testament concept *koinonia* relevant to our own historical moment?

In a time of pandemic dissent and chronic alienation from within and fearsome assault from without, we must recover and experience anew the essential biblical understanding of Catholic communion. The *haburah/koinonia*/communion is at once Trinitarian, ecclesial, Petrine, magisterial, eucharistic, Marian, familial, and nuptial. We

---

[xii]   Father notes here, "The term *paradosis* is explicit in St. Paul (especially 1 Cor 2 and 1 Cor 15). The rabbinic background is instructive. The term became commonplace in early patristic and ecclesiastical sources.

could add as many modifiers as there are aspects of the genuine life of the Mystical Body of Christ.

Without this communion, there can be no community. Without this communion, we cannot be *heias koinonoi physeos* (i.e., "communicants in the divine nature"). Without this communion, the Church (which, like Mary, must be "full of grace") would become "graceless," secularized—and some sectors already lie earthbound like severed branches.

This is the communion that is the life of the one, holy, Catholic, and apostolic Church. It requires assent. It is dissolved by dissent. With it, there is community, without it, alienation and a house divided.

What the Church needs today is that remedy offered by the Holy Father at the Dutch Synod and echoed by so many Fathers at the 1985 Extraordinary Synod: A recapturing in mind and heart and soul of that communion which by divine grace derives from and returns to the Most Holy Trinity.

CHAPTER 28

A LITTLE CORNER OF HEAVEN[1]

By worldly standards, our little parish church may seem to be quite small and simple, but those with faith know better. Those with faith judge by heaven's standards.

In the Bible, there is a passage concerning the ancient Temple of Jerusalem: "How awesome is this place! It is the very House of God and Gate of Heaven!"

Now, if this was true concerning the shadowy Temple of the Old Testament, how much more wondrous is the Temple of the New Testament, where Jesus Christ, the Son of God, is present in our tabernacle day and night, dwelling among us, enthroned as King of Kings. Here He is always eager and ready to receive us, to hear us, to heal us, to strengthen us.

Dedicated to the Most Holy Trinity, our church is in the fullest sense the very House of God and a little corner of heaven. When we enter the church, our faith tells us we have left the world behind and have come into the divine Presence. Any Catholic who believes in the Real Presence of Christ in the Eucharist can feel this holy atmosphere. It is a sense of peace, of security, of the deepest joy, of reverent awe.

Our good people deserve congratulations for maintaining this reverence in a time when bad example and even scandal might lead them astray. Our people dress decently when entering God's house. They genuflect to salute our Lord. They preserve a holy silence and keep in mind where they are. They reverently receive the Body and Blood of Christ. These are the surest signs of true faith. They also draw enormous blessings from the heart of Christ.

In October, we will celebrate 84 years of continuing worship of God in our parish Church. For 84 years, Jesus has lived and been present among us in the tabernacle of the altar. Think of the daily Masses, the baptisms, the First Holy Communions, the confessions, the quiet visits of the faithful when no one else was around to see, the funerals, the weddings, the devotions, the missions, the blessings, the confirmations, and so on. What an accumulation of grace and glory! In every church, the angels of God abide in loving custody of the Eucharist.

In some churches today, however, the angels also may well weep. They have become centers of entertainment rather than of divine worship. One hears the loud and boisterous chatter of people visiting each other, oblivious of *Who* is present. One hears the worldly strains of pop music and secular love songs. One even sees people in immodest dress daring to defile God's holy temple. These actions surely speak to us as signs of *lost* faith.

Join me in prayer to St. Thérèse, the Little Flower of Jesus (to whom I make a monthly novena just for this purpose), that all of us will love and respect this house of the Holy Trinity, our "little corner of heaven."

CHAPTER 29

THE PASCHAL MYSTERY: FOUNT OF MISSION OF THE CHURCH AND CHRISTIAN CULTURE[1]

With desire have I desired to eat this Passover with you..."[i]

Desiderio desideravi... "With desire have I desired." This Semitic superlative captures the ardor, let us say the "passion" of Christ's Sacred Heart when at last His *hour* had come, commencing with the institution of the Eucharist.

In Exodus 12, establishing the Passover of the Israelites, we read, "This day shall be unto you *le zikkaron* (for remembrance)." From the outset, the Jews called the Passover "the Night of Memories." At the Last Supper, Jesus commands, "Do this in memory of Me."[ii] Anamnesis, the process of calling into memory, was a word already freighted with centuries of meaning. Our word "memory" is but a pale shadow of its dynamism. For the Jews it bore a vivid sense of liturgical actualization (i.e., making it actually present in the here and now). Hence, the key ordinance of Pesahim 10:5: "Each generation must so regard itself as if it had been led out of Egypt."[iii] St. Paul echoes this in 1 Corinthians 10.

But on the lips of Christ! Through His omnipotent will, He empowers the word "anamnesis" to reach a fulfillment beyond man's highest expectations. In this new and everlasting covenant, through

---

[i]   Luke 22:15, the first words of Christ in Luke's account of the Last Supper.

[ii]   *Eis anamnesin emou.*

[iii] The reference here, *Pesahim* (the Hebrew word for "Passovers"), is the third tractate for the Passover Seder "Order of Festivals."

the transcendence of grace, the frame of time-reference dissolves. Jesus, Son of God made man, the new and perfect Mediator, embraces in His consciousness each individual person of all ages and all nations, past, present, and future, as Pius XII insists in a crucial passage of *Mystici Corporis Christi*.[2] For Christ, as a divine Person, all is *now*. The acclamation, "Christ has died! (past) Christ is risen! (present), Christ will come again! (future)" expresses the infinite depths of this mystery. In the Eucharist, we confront and penetrate the *nunc stans*, the eternal *now*.

What, then, flooded the mind and heart of the Savior at this Pasch? Let's find out by exploring a few of the factors in this anamnesis of the Lord's Supper.

Seder

On the fourteenth of Nisan, the "Preparation Day," between the hours of 12:00 p.m. and 3:00 p.m., the father of the family brought an unblemished lamb for sacrifice to the Temple court. There were thousands of these lambs, and as the priests were killing them, basins caught their blood. The priests passed these down a line so that someone could gently pour them out at the base of the altar of sacrifice.

In readiness for this sacrifice, the Jews kept huge flocks of the required lambs in a staging area in the hills near Bethlehem, and a number of Gospel passages infer that the Baby born at Bethlehem was—like these victim lambs—born to die a sacrificial death. After the Temple sacrifice, the father of the family brought the slain lamb home for preparation of the Passover meal by the mother.

The Passover Seder begins with a blessing by the father as the leader of the assembly. Jewish law recommended that 10 or 12 persons gather for the meal, which was essentially a family meal. Jesus, therefore, makes the Twelve His brothers by associating them with Himself in this Passover of the New Israel, forever after the Family of God. In Aramaic, the name for this assembly is *haburah*, which underlies the New Testament word *koinonia*, the doctrine of communion. Peter's fishing co-op was also called a *haburah*, as was the bond or communion of marriage. Therefore, ecclesial communion is at once eucharistic, Petrine, and nuptial.

The unchanged Passover ritual proceeds with a cup of wine in remembrance of the deliverance of Israel from bondage in Egypt. On the table are three squares of *matzah* (unleavened bread). The leader elevates the *matzoth* and declares, "This is the bread of affliction," and expresses the hope of the pilgrim Israelites that they may celebrate the Passover "next year" as free men in the land of Israel.

The youngest son then asks, "Why is this night different from all other nights?" At the Last Supper, the beloved disciple John (the one who would remain with his Master through the entire Passion) would have asked the question, since he was the youngest. The true import of John's question was, "Why is this Passover night different from all other Passover nights?"

In response, the leader recites the *Haggadah*, the narrative proclamation-discourse proclaiming God's liberation of His people in the Exodus. The *Haggadah* finds its fulfillment in the Eucharist Prayer of the Mass, in which the priest proclaims the redeeming death of the Lord "until He comes." It is St. John who precisely records Christ's long and intimate discourse at the Last Supper. He stressed in this account the need for unity, just as God had called the Jews to enter the community of the Passover as a united people.

Then follows the second of the four cups of wine prescribed by the Passover ritual (or Seder), and the leader takes the bottom *matzah* and distributes it to those present. This is the point at which Jesus took the bread, spoke the words that transubstantiated it into His Body, and distributed it to the apostles.

The Passover meal proper then followed, and "after they had eaten," He took the third cup of wine—the *cos berakah*, the "cup of blessing"—pronounced it the Blood of the New Covenant, and gave it to the Twelve to drink.

The Passover concludes with the singing of the *Hallel* psalms.... "and singing hymns, they went forth."[3]

There is no question that Christ followed the general pattern of the Seder. However, as rabbinic scholars observe, He did so with a sovereign freedom that allowed for significant moderations. That the meal was anticipated causes little discussion since such a practice was known among some groups, especially Hasidic. Also of importance for comments we will make later, the Jews reckoned their day from 4:00 p.m. to 4:00 p.m. Hence, all the events of the Passion, from Seder to burial, took place on Good Friday. Some calendar experts have conjectured that the first Good Friday corresponded to a first Friday of the month by our calculation.

Praeperatio evangelica

The world created by God "in the beginning" and the whole awesome experience of human history under His Providence have set the stage for this *hour*. In the Discourse, as He begins the "Priestly Prayer," Jesus raises His eyes to heaven and proclaims, "Father, the *hour* has come!"[4] This is the *hour* of fulfillment, of *redemption*. "Having loved His own in this world, He loved them unto the end."[5]

In retrospect, we can trace God's great design, this *praeparatio evangelica*, most evidently in the history of Israel. But we can especially do so in the decades before that night Jesus reclined at the table with the Twelve. There is a remarkable phenomenon of convergence that focused on the "night of Memories" that Passover and its Seder. The four main motifs of sacrifice were the *'holah* (i.e., holocaust) in adoration; the *shelamim* (the "peace" offering), with the goals of thanksgiving, praise, and communion; the *hattath* (the sin or atonement sacrifice); and the *'assam* (the "guilt" or restitution offering).

All these sacrifices assumed a predominant motif of atonement, and the *pesah*, the Passover sacrifice, became the focus of this convergence and was seen as atonement *par excellence*. It was also the center of all these sacrificial motifs, which we recognize as those of the Mass.

Moreover, the Jews saw all the festal and liturgical institutions as resumed in the feast of Passover: *Shebuoth* ("weeks" or Pentecost); *Rosh ha-shannah* (the New Year); *Succoth* ("booths," at harvest-time).

Meanwhile, the intertestamental Judaica,[iv] with its liturgical hymns and tractates, developed the theme of the "Four Nights," which Roger Le Déaut, CSSp, masterfully treated in his *La Nuit Pascale*.[v] These events—creation, Passover-redemption, exodus-liberation, Sinai, the *eschaton*, the "day of the Messiah," the inauguration of the *'olam ha-bah*—all will occur on the night of Passover.[vi]

Indeed, the Messiah Himself will appear on that night. All those institutions that we now see as types of Messianic fulfillment have their realization on this night: the kingship, the series of covenants, the fullness of prophecy, and the priesthood. All the personages of the Old Testament, "our fathers in faith," are connected with this most holy night: the patriarchs, Abraham, Isaac, Jacob/Israel and his twelve sons, as well as Moses and the prophets, are present on this night, which, as the Jews say, "is light and not darkness."

Can we ever begin to assess the mind of Jesus as He celebrated this supper with His Twelve and heard young John ask, "Why is this night different from all other nights?" We find ourselves transported into this vortex of convergence. We are here limited by time and can only sketch the phenomenon. However, after all efforts to explicate are exhausted, no one could ever conceive that vision of universal fulfillment that was enshrined in the mystery in the mind of Jesus, the Messiah. But following the admonition of St. Paul, "Let this

---

iv   i.e., the period of time that overlapped the writing of the last book of the Old Testament with the writing of the first book of the New.

v   Professor of ancient languages at the Pontifical Biblical Institute. *La Nuit Pascale: Essai sur la signification de la Pâque juive a partir du Targum d'Exode XII 42* (Rome: Biblical Institute Press, 1980).

vi   *'olam ha-bah* is Hebrew for "the world to come."

mind be in you that was also in Christ Jesus," we must try to bring to our own minds some of this splendor of the "Night of Memories."

Truly, everything centers on the Mass. "It is the Mass that matters!"[vii] As the Council teaches, "the Eucharist is the source and summit of all Christian life."[6]

Catechetical aberrations

It is painful, but necessary, to interrupt the flow of our appreciation by noting some destructive elements of the catechetical chaos of the past quarter-century.

First, we advert to the grievous, lethal error of the "ignorant Jesus," by now insinuated into the minds of our contemporary Catholics. This error clashes with the Magisterium, and I have shown elsewhere how it eradicates all genuine spiritual and devotional life and with it, the Catholic culture of the ages. All liturgical efficacy, all valid scriptural hermeneutics depend on the Catholic doctrine of the "consciousness" of Christ.[7] For documentation on the Magisterium and full development, see William Most's *The Consciousness of Christ.*

While we cannot pursue this here, let us savor the words of Pius XII alluded to earlier:

[vii] For roughly 200 years, the English tried everything in their power to stamp out the Catholic religion in Ireland. They failed. In 1907, Augustine Birrell, chief secretary of Ireland, wrote, "Our children ... will have to make up their minds what happened at the Reformation. My suggestion is that they will do so in a majority of cases by concentrating their attention upon what will seem to them most important. And especially will they bend their minds upon the Mass. Nobody nowadays, except for a handful of vulgar fanatics, speaks irreverently of the Mass. *It is the Mass that matters.* It is the Mass that makes the difference; so hard to define, so subtle it is yet so perceptible between a Catholic country and a Protestant one, between Dublin and Edinburgh. Here I believe is one of the battlefields of the future" (*Ireland's Loyalty to the Mass*, Fr. Augustine, OFM Cap, London: Sands, 1933, reprinted by The Neumann Press).

Now the only-begotten Son of God embraced us in His infinite and undying love even before the world began. And that He might give a visible and exceedingly beautiful expression to this love, He assumed our nature in hypostatic union: hence—as Maximus of Turin with a certain unaffected simplicity remarks—"In Christ our own flesh loves us." But the knowledge and love of the Divine Redeemer, of which we were the object from the first moment of the Incarnation, exceed all that the human intellect can hope to grasp. For hardly was He conceived in the womb of the Mother of God when He began to enjoy the beatific vision, and in that vision all the members of His mystical Body were continually and unceasingly present to Him, and He embraced them with His redeeming love. O marvelous condescension of divine love for us! O inestimable dispensation of boundless charity! In the crib, on the Cross, in the unending glory of the Father, Christ has all the members of the Church present before Him and united to Him in a much clearer and more loving manner than that of a mother who clasps her child to her breast, or than that with which a man knows and loves himself.[8]

A second grave wound inflicted on our generation by a Christ-less catechesis (as Sheen once called it) is that of the unqualified "meal." The Mass is just a "meal," some have told us. We have seen what forms some have imposed on this mercurial meal in the liturgical sandboxes. Yes, of course, the Mass is a meal, a *sacrum convivium*. But it is not only a meal. Our discussions so far allow us to assert that the Mass is:

1. a sacrificial meal, at once cenacle and Cross
2. a sacred meal, *sacrum convivium*, the messianic banquet
3. a Passover meal
4. a family meal, an ecclesial *communio* of the Family of God
5. a memorial meal

6. a communion meal reflecting the *koinonia* of the Church
7. a Covenant sacrifice, one that is new and everlasting and embraces all previous pacts between God and His people
8. a Last Supper imbued, therefore, with solemnity and bittersweet farewell

The Christian Passover: The Christian Exodus

We find the earliest written source we have of the institution of the Blessed Eucharist in St. Paul's 1 Corinthians 11. It follows in the context of Chapter 10, where we note that the Passover dominates the mind of Paul. He recalls the passage of the Israelites though the sea, led by the bright cloud, and their eating the manna God provided them in the desert. St. Paul twice tells us that these things happened as "types" for foreshadowing. A few lines later, he speaks of the Eucharist, the true manna from heaven, received at the table of the Lord, by which we become "one bread, one body." He calls us *koinonoi*, communicants, "sharing in the Body and sharing in the Blood of the Lord."

Then, in Chapter 11, he explains what our Lord did at the Last Supper, prefacing his account with the testimony that he received this teaching "from the Lord" (v. 23). These then are the true actions and words of Jesus. In turn, Paul handed this doctrine on to the community in Corinth. "Receiving" and "handing on" constitute the technical concept of *paradosis*, what we call "Tradition" in English (i.e., the Catholic Faith) "received from the Lord" and "handed down to us from the apostles."

After each consecration in Paul's text, Jesus commands, "Do this in memory of Me!" With these words, our Lord empowers His apostles to do as He has done. He has instituted the priesthood. The full impact of these words of commission on this night of memories evades us in the English. The Greek is *touto poiete*, which we translate as "Do this," but the Greek verb indicates "Keep on doing this," followed by *eis ten emen anamnesin*, which literally means, "into memory of Me," suggesting incorporation, full communion *into* His Life.

We consider again the sacrificial binomial *"flesh and blood"* in distinct formulas and actions. The sacramental sign shows forth a Body drained of its Blood, "shed for us," again the precise sacrificial act of Passover. St. Paul tells us in 1 Corinthians 11:26 that as often as we eat the Body and drink the Blood of this sacrifice, "We proclaim the death of the Lord until He comes." This "proclaiming" recalls the *haggadah* (or proclamation) recited at the Seder of God's deliverance of His people from bondage, but now actualized in the reality of the Mass, where all stands still around the Cross at the center of time.

Now we proclaim the Christian redemption, our genuine liberation from sin and death. Our Lord's death then shows forth sacramentally in the separate consecrations of the bread and wine. It is the essence of sacrifice that the blood be separated (drained, poured out) from the body. Of course, in His risen state, our Lord's Body and Blood can no longer be physiologically separated as in His once-for-all sacrifice on the Cross, and we receive Him in His risen life, Body and Blood, Soul and Divinity, under each species. However, by the power of the words of the priest, the unique sacrifice becomes present sacramentally on the altar "until He comes again."

Recessional ... Passion ... Cross

Let us now return to the closing element in the Passover Seder, the singing of the Great Hallel, the recessional, which, in the unique case of the Last Supper, took the form of a liturgical procession of Jesus with the 11—the number is ominous. The goal was, as on previous nights of this Holy Week, the Mount of Olives. The events that transpired there are forever etched in our minds. We cannot here rehearse all the details that Scripture affords us. We must move beyond the betrayal and the trials and the pain, the blood and the blasphemy of this Friday, which had already begun by the time of the Supper. We simply advert to the paradoxical fact that these are all royal emblems of Christ's kingship.

We must hurry to the Cross and join the few believers and friends of Jesus, surrounded as they are by the hostile enemies and the morbid curious. This Friday was the "preparation day" for the Passover feast yet to be celebrated by the majority of Jews after 4:00 p.m. on the "great Sabbath," as the Gospels name it.

Exodus 12 gives the ancient rubrics, which called for the sacrifice of a lamb, one for each household. The lamb had to be an unblemished male, and its blood was to be drained in sacrifice during the twilight hours.

I found a touching directive in the rabbinic corpus. It dictates that the mother of the household must break the heart of the lamb to drain the last drops of blood before she roasts the kosher victim with no breaking of its bones.

At the time of Jesus, the priests performed the sacrificial rites at the great altar of sacrifice that stood in front of the Temple in the open court. They sacrificed countless lambs between the hours of noon and 3:00 p.m., and the blood of these animals filled bowls, which rapidly passed from priest to priest to be poured out at the base of the altar.

Entailed here is the rich "blood theology" of the rabbis. I have written a lengthy study from which I can only highlight a few concepts. The blood that has atoning properties must be *dam ha-nephesh*, "blood of the soul." The purest, most atoning blood of all is the blood of the heart. With the last breath of the victim, this blood is thought to be forced into the chambers of the heart. The virtues of this blood are especially enhanced if the victim is violently slain.

The application to Jesus is evident. The true Lamb of God was bleeding for us on the Cross during the same hours when Old Testament priests performed the now superseded rites of the Old Law down below Calvary at the Temple. After "He breathed forth His Spirit" (cf. John 19), St. Longinus pierced His Heart with his lance, and the last drops of Blood were shed for us, followed by the water serum.

Indeed, as the rabbinic adage states, "Without the shedding of blood, there is no forgiveness of sin."

Let us see what is happening through the eyes of John, theologian of the Sacred Heart, in his densely allusive chapter 19. The Fathers have copiously recognized the evocation of Genesis. Here is a new Creation, with a new Adam and a new Eve. Here, too, is the new Temple, which, once destroyed, He will raise in three days. (John earlier said Jesus referred to "the temple of His body.") Now there flows from His Sacred Heart the trickling of water that becomes the great river of Messianic salvation. For John, the full background is Ezekiel 47. This river flows to all the waters of the earth, turning salt into fresh, nurturing trees along its banks with healing and vivifying powers. Here again, the rivers of Eden and the Tree of Life are identified, a theme John resumes in the last pages of his Apocalypse.

On the cross, the new Adam is overcome by the sleep of death. The Church, the new Eve, is derived from His open side. He rests now on the Sabbath, and on Sunday, the Jewish *'omer*, He rises as "first fruits from the dead," a new creation.

The Blood of the Lamb fulfills all the insights and aspirations of mankind, from the most primitive to the theologized and purified doctrine of the Old Testament where "life is in the blood."

But in the New Testament, there is a quantum leap in the development of the theology of blood. Here blood is focused uniquely on the blood of one Person, no longer on the endless slaughter of animal victims. And this Blood of the Lamb of God has multiple and awesome properties: It purifies, atones, redeems, expels evil, nullifies sin and death, renews, liberates and vivifies, restores the order of creation, effects peace, constitutes and ratifies a *New Covenant*, and generates a unified family of adopted sons who are at once blood brothers.

All these concepts crystallize around the Blood of the Cross, which is one with the Blood of the eucharistic cup and one hypostatically with the divine Person of Jesus, in whom are fulfilled all the previous instincts and speculations of mankind.

Our time is so limited. We have been able merely to sketch and suggest. Let us, however, be convinced that behind these summaries there open awesome depths. When Christ pronounces His *teletelai*, "It is consummated," we have reached the *telos*, the "end." All the scriptures have been fulfilled. We take refuge in the *Adoro Te*, a hymn of Thomas Aquinas referring to the precious Blood, where we sing, "*cujus una stilla salvum facere, totum mundum quit ab omne scelere*" ("one drop of which is able to save the whole world from every sin").

For me, this comes to mind at every Mass at the purification of the chalice when I look into the cup and see a few drops of the Precious Blood trickling down the golden sides into a small pool at its bottom.

Cult and culture

This forum is devoted to the theme of culture.[viii] To be sure, we are concerned mainly with Christian culture, but it is necessary to remember the polyvalence of the term. It is not univocal. Yet the supreme goal of genuine culture in the design of the Creator, in the will of the One who fashioned the universe, earth, and men is expressed and effected in the Mass. As Vatican II states, the Eucharist is the source and summit of all Christian life. As we conclude these reflections on the Eucharist (and before we approach the altar), let us be convinced of the inseparable bond of cult and culture. That bond is not merely one of etymology; it lies in the divine will, the economy of salvation.

One should also remember the prophetic warning of Cardinal Newman, who cautioned that tampering with liturgical cults would surely result in incalculable upheaval. We, in these days, surveying what the great Msgr. Nelson Logal dubbed "the rubble of renewal," have tasted the bitter denouement. We live in the age of "optional Catholicism." If the faithful, a royal priesthood consecrated by

---

[viii] Every so often, *The Wanderer* convokes "Forums" on various topics where Catholics of note speak on a particular theme. This chapter is adapted from one such event that took place in Washington, DC.

baptism to worship, are to be the leaven of grace in the resistant dough of human culture, we must first and foremost defend liturgical laws and the often-scorned rubrics.

The anarchic body blows against liturgical discipline constitute at once the most grievous assault against Christian culture. On all sides, we suffer wounds—as a Body—with open denials of the eucharistic mystery. Among many, even those nominally our own, the taunt of the "hard saying" is voiced again. The blatant and uncorrected desacralizations and trivializations sting us.

Obvious neglect is the least of the sins—the Americanists have moved from abuse to profanation, sacrilege, and blasphemy. Meanwhile, the denial of sin, the contempt for the sacrament of confession, and the effects of perversion in moral theology have produced a flood of unworthy receptions.[ix] Paul, in his *paradosis* of the Lord's Supper, sternly rebuked the Corinthians for their abuses of the Eucharist. His *dokimazeto* ("let a man examine himself") has fallen on the hardened hearts and deaf ears of self-proclaimed "mature Catholics." Once more, "the Son of Man is betrayed into the hands of sinners."[9] Their relentless purging of the kneelers in our churches is one of the purest signs of demonic influence in our days. We see the Passion of Christ relived today in His eucharistic presence. "When the Lord comes, do you think He will find any faith left on the earth?" The *cri-du-coeur*[x] of Catholic culture in every age of persecution remains, "It is the Mass that matters!"

History recalls the poignant "Pilgrimage of Grace," the heroic procession of some 35,000 despised peasant papists who defied the English Reformation, marching behind the Holy Eucharist carried at the head of their line. A remnant of the faithful had realized that the source and center of their culture was the Eucharist, that indeed Christ had not left them orphans.

I recall reading that, in our own times, on a Feast of Corpus Christi in Kraków, the communist militia tried to stop the eucharistic

---

[ix]   For what Father is getting at here, read 1 Cor 11:27-29.

[x]   French for "cry of the heart."

procession by barring Christ's entrance into the central city square. Then-Archbishop Karol Wojtyła moved quickly, monstrance in hands, to the front of his faithful. The confused police made way for a triumphant procession that the people will never forget.

We have suffered through a "Call to Action." I dream of a great national gathering of all orthodox Catholics, the despised and disenfranchised papists of America, closing ranks behind the Eucharist and the Mother whose womb was the first tabernacle. We need at some point—soon—to convoke a "Call to Faith."[xi]

As we celebrate the Holy Eucharist this evening in the nation's capital, let us pledge ourselves in every way we can to restore adoration, awe, and reverence, a bending of mind and heart and knees before the eucharistic Christ. As John Paul II declares, "Christ is the light of culture." Who can doubt the power of His light, the Light of the World, and its ability through us to pierce the dark night of apostasy and to repossess the brilliance of Catholic Faith and culture?

We recall again the night of the Passover, which the ancients said was "light and not darkness." The Christian Pasch is indeed a new creation: "Let there be Light!" The Light of Christ shines in the darkness "and the darkness will not overcome it."[xii]

Christus vincit! Christus regnat! Christus imperat![xiii]

[xi]   Father partly got his wish when the first Call to Holiness conference convened in 1996. It has taken place every year since.

[xii]   This comes from John 1:5. Until 1969, the first part of the Gospel of John was read at the end of every Mass, and so these words would have been familiar to many in Father's audience.

[xiii]   Christ conquers! Christ reigns! Christ is Lord of all!

In the late 1940s, Father left high school in his junior year to enter the Norbertines, taking the name Brother Herman. After two years, he left the Order and continued his studies for the Diocese of Green Bay, for which he was ordained a priest in 1956.

Fr. Gilsdorf with his sister Shirley (aka Sr. Ricardo, OSF) shortly after she took final vows as a Franciscan Sister of Christian Charity. This photo was taken in the late '50s in front of the family residence on 12th St. in Green Bay.

Father's ordination ceremony at St. Francis Xavier Cathedral Church in Green Bay, with Bishop Stanislaus V. Bona serving as celebrant. A native of Chicago, Bishop Bona served the Green Bay diocese from 1945 until his death in 1967. He started the famous Bishop's Charity Game, an annual preseason football match-up featuring the hometown Green Bay Packers.

Another shot from the ordination ceremony at St. Francis Xavier Cathedral, 1956. Fr. Gilsdorf is third from right.

The ordinands washing their hands after the ordination ceremony. Fr. Gilsdorf is on the right.

Fr. Gilsdorf's ordination class picture after the ordination Mass. The picture was taken at the building adjacent to the cathedral rectory. Bishop Bona is in the middle of the picture. Fr. Gilsdorf is third from left.

Official composite picture of the 1956 ordination class for the Diocese of Green Bay.

Fr. Gilsdorf in his later years.

PART IV

BOOK REVIEWS BY FR. GILSDORF

Chapter 30

The Final Confrontation

The Antichrist, by Vincent P. Miceli, SJ (Hanover, MA:
The Christopher Publishing House, 1981)[i]

A few years ago, Fr. Miceli stayed overnight at my rectory. As we talked into the wee hours of a new day, he told me he was writing a book on the Antichrist. I recall how all the technical and theological pitfalls of that challenging but timely subject registered in my mind. I had done graduate school research on eschatology and the *parousia,* so I knew the literature. My own impression is that almost every study fell into one of two excesses:

1. the rationalist, demythologizing scholarly analyses (e.g., Lambrecht, Marxsen, Beasley-Murray, Pesch), which are valuable for data and observation of text but never once take their subject as real or even possible.
2. the fundamentalist fanatics who will not concede any room for symbolism even in the apocalyptic genre, who brush off any requirements of scholarship, and have either deciphered the "day and the hour" or at least can give photographically detailed scenarios of the day or two before.

It was a privilege, then, to review Fr. Miceli's latest work, which succeeds in its purpose. Having the reading of this book interrupted is painful. It is indeed valuable for chapter collections of the most essential witnesses (i.e., Old Testament and New Testament, Eastern

---

[i]   TAN Books, Rockford, Illinois, currently publishes this title.

Church and Western Church patristics). Miceli demonstrates expertise in the texts he selects to study and even more so in the numerous ones he excluded. The Greek text in some passages is not exegetically "milked," but the result would only have been to intensify, not to diminish the points he makes. Indeed, it is refreshing to see the words of Scripture taken seriously.

Miceli avoids the shoals of the two schools described above. He allows for the obviously "coded" symbolism of the apocalyptic genre, but he insists that the message, once "decoded," is literal, real, and prophetic in the strictly futurist sense.

The author repeatedly asserts that the Antichrist is not "theology fiction." Moreover, he insists that this parody of the Messiah is personal and individual, not (as many Catholic commentators hold today) a "moral person" and, hence, a political system or ideology. Miceli is backed on this score by patristic consensus and by sound scriptural exegesis.

Theory and event are matched in the final heart-pounding chapters, which are the logical sequel to the author's own *The Gods of Atheism* and, in a way, Msgr. George Kelly's *Battle for the American Church*. Msgr. Kelly's monumental contribution is a blow-by-blow, thoroughly documented historical review of post-conciliar America.

When a genuine, honest-to-God Catholic finishes Kelly's book, he asks in bewilderment, "How could this have happened? Is there a mastermind lurking and leering behind this intricately orchestrated apostasy? How fares the rest of the Catholic world? What does the future hold? Can and will there be a reconstruction of the Church among us, a happy ending to the battle?"

Miceli's book answers these questions. He offers a prophetic framework in which we can "organize" the data of dissidence around us into meaningful patterns. In a word, we are reassured about what the hell is going on.

I stress again that Miceli has not fallen into the superficial sensationalism of the spate of fundamentalist tracts on this subject.

He will not tell you whether the Antichrist is already among us or exactly where and when to meet him or the precise plot of the final act.

But Father apprises us of the inexorable setting of the historical stage of the entrance of Satan's greatest protagonist. This ardently orthodox scholar leaves us with an alarm of urgency, but with no claim as to "the day or the hour." Instead, he makes clear "the stage is being set for the Coming of the Antichrist. Is this person waiting in the wings? Will he soon receive his cue from Divine Providence to make his entrance? Will he play out in our time of history the tragedy of the abomination of desolation and the consummation of the universe? True, his name and time are known only to God. But the portents of his nearness are evident everywhere in the general desertion of the Faith" (p. 219).

In desperate conversations during this past decade, many of us priests have whispered over and over, "It has to be diabolical." One of the dramatic quotes given by Miceli is that of Cardinal Wojtyła after a tour of the United States in 1976:

> I do not think the wide circles of American society or the wide circles of the Christian community realize... We now face the final confrontation between the Church and the Anti-Church (p. 11).

In light of the last chapters (with their comprehensive panorama of mass apostasy), one finishes this particular review with an eerie sense of pressure: Will these words of recommendation be published "in time" so that many good people will read the book "in time"?

CHAPTER 31

THE REMEDY[1]

What the Catholic Faithful Can Do, by Gerard Morrissey
(Front Royal, VA: Christendom College Press, 1986)

The Church is infected by the disease of dissent. Some may complain about the use of the word "disease," but it aptly clarifies our current ecclesiastical malaise.

The symptoms are discomfort, distress, confusion, and dysfunction. Disease in the Church is peculiarly psychosomatic because it afflicts soul and body. To seek remedy, one must first *recognize* the symptoms, which serve as a salutary alarm that prompts a confession of the truth and the humility to approach a physician. The doctor can then provide an honest examination and diagnosis, followed by the patient's courage to undergo the indicated treatment, however bitter the medicine, however penitential the regimen, however excruciating the surgery.

"Gerard Morrissey," the *nom de plume* of a pastor, is a special grace to the Church in her current throes of disorder in that, like a good doctor, he has the ability to examine the symptoms, identify the disease, and recommend a cure. With this book, he fulfills his promise of a trilogy, which has revealed him to be a most providential physician.

In the first book, *Defending the Papacy*, Morrissey exhorted the Church to recognize the illness and seek remedy. In his clear and cogent expounding of the principles of ecclesial health, he contrasted this normalcy with the confusion and dysfunction that now torment us. His deft handling of the binding authority of the ordinary Magisterium was most timely.

The second book was a masterpiece of diagnosis. The title tells our malady: *The Crisis of Dissent*. The text is a classic of psychological analysis tempered by pastoral virtue, wherein hard truth and tender charity embrace. His section discussing the bishops is a *sine qua non* for all concerned Catholics, but not least of all for the bishops themselves. Here, too, reverence for the episcopal office suffuses Morrissey's tough, cerebral exposition of the failure of so many shepherds.

And now, the crowning work of the trilogy, *What the Catholic Faithful Can Do*. Here our physician begins the redeeming process of strengthening and purging, those preparatory phases to any cure in which the laity and lower clergy and Religious can and must engage.

This book is a "how to" manual of action. It features rare pastoral sense; controlled prudence; compassion for the errant, weak, confused, and angry; and love for the Church in its wholeness. All characterize this practical, readily understood program. There must be prophylaxis (i.e., disease prevention). What remains healthy and sound, we must immunize and fortify. What is infected, we must isolate and, hopefully, restore. It is quite possible that, in the end, the patient will require some (perhaps even radical) surgery—but only the apostolic hierarchy can do this.

Fr. Morrisey begins by inspiring confidence in the loyal but quiet Catholic lay person who, in the face of the crisis, may feel inadequate to the task. However impotent he may feel, anyone who reads these pages is bound to take heart. As urged by Pope John Paul II in *Catechesi Tradendae*, family catechesis receives thorough attention. And he reminds us that in all that is undertaken, perseverance is the key. While we well may expect persecution, a joyful willingness to suffer and bear insult must nonetheless characterize the faithful.

In Chapter 2, the author begins tapping the resources of another great pastor, Fr. Robert J. Fox, the remarkable priest-journalist whose pioneer defense of the Faith will fill a glorious page in American Church history. Fr. Fox's "spiritual program" is presented, along with excellent variations and commentary by Fr. Morrisey. This is the soul of the restoration, without which further treatment would be ineffective. Only holy people can heal the wounds of the Church.

Chapter 3 describes how the willing reader can build up an ideal Catholic home life that will counter the contaminated general environment and the often inadequate (or positively erroneous) instructions labeled as "Catholic" religious education. Numerous examples of actual cases prove most beneficial. This chapter is a "sermon" that should be preached from orthodox pulpits everywhere.

In Chapter 4, very crucial cautions are laid to channel action in the Church community only where deviations are genuinely such. He shows the lay apostle where disagreement can be legitimate: Lawful options are not to be targeted. This schema on what we can and cannot change should have been the preamble to renewal from the start.

Chapter 5 is the fruit of the author's personal experience. It covers the mechanics of organization. He carefully lays out the reasons for his preference for small groups (not to the neglect of tried-and-true larger organizations). This chapter is an extraordinary guide in group dynamics as seen through the lens of the current Catholic crisis.

The remainder of the book, nearly half of the total text, consists of critically valuable appendices: actual sample letters to various authorities along with their replies, each of which receives a perceptive critique; Fr. Fox's valuable list of orthodox Catholic sources with updating by the author; and much more.

May I take this opportunity to salute a brother priest? Though Gerard Morrissey remains anonymous, an insider has described him as a "non-academic parish priest." This and the two preceding volumes manifest deep pastoral experience, an ability to speak non-technically to the ordinary lay person, and a grasp of dogma and psychology that rivals anything the "academics" have so far produced. His now completed trilogy emerges as a potent remedy for the disease of dissent. It remains for loyal Catholics to begin the restoration. They should do so with these three books in hand.

What, then, is the prognosis? Will the disease be terminal in the Western Church? Only if we do not undertake the preliminary therapy that this book proves is both possible and urgent. The author is a "beloved physician" whose inspired labors can help us assist the divine physician, Who alone will be able to pronounce, "This sickness is not unto death."[2]

CHAPTER 32

ADVOCACY EXEGESIS

The New Biblical Theorists: Raymond E. Brown and Beyond, by Msgr. George A. Kelly (Ann Arbor, MI: Servant Publications, 1983).[1]

After penning two landmark analyses of the emerging "American Church" (both of which are sociological documentaries with volatile theological implications), Msgr. Kelly has once more returned to the battleground. This time, he penetrates beyond the frontline clashes to expose the ivory tower of American revisionist Scripture scholarship. He shows it to be a self-secured bunker in which is spawned much of the ideological strategy and weaponry now deployed in the battle for the Church in America.

Perhaps the most remarkable thing about this work is that Kelly himself is not an exegete. To reconnoiter and map out this exotic terrain must have seemed a Herculean challenge. In order to inform and alert the widest possible readership, he needed to offer a global view of the maze that is modern biblical criticism. And he needed to do *this* in accurate, comprehensible, and readable language. And yet despite the huge task, he has succeeded.

Kelly starts with an adequate introductory survey. Following this, his scheme is to focus on the sacrosanct labors of Fr. Raymond E. Brown as paragon of the long-dominant biblical "establishment" in the United States. This device of *unus stet pro pluribus*[i] is fully valid. Once the reader has studied Brown, he can approach his peers with comparative ease. Many of these are Brown's fawning disciples,

---

[i]   Latin for "one stands for many" (i.e., the example of one suffices to show how many [or the whole] behave).

while others, more independent, nevertheless share the same fatal basic presuppositions.

Kelly treats the major works of Brown *in extensor*. To list them is to recognize the seminal debates that have exploded from theory into practice, shaping the confrontational standoff within American Catholicism:

1. *The virginal conception and bodily resurrection of Jesus;*
2. Allied to it the context of the Infancy narratives, *The Birth of the Messiah;*
3. *Priest and Bishop*, echoing the Küng-Schillebeeckx assaults on ecclesiology in general and hierarchical institution in particular.

Kelly also shows how Brown posits in *The Community of the Beloved Disciple* a contradictory pluralism within the very bosom of the apostolic Church in order to justify the dissent that prevails among us. Kelly includes elements of other books, addresses, and articles, particularly the early work *Jesus: God and Man* (1967), which triggered the crucial debate on the human consciousness of Christ.

Kelly first states Brown's positions and arguments. He does so by copiously quoting Brown's own words. He then cites authors pro and con, often non-Catholic scholars, and often with surprising results. Finally, he states the Magisterium's position, adducing official statements as well as other supportive arguments. This follows the pattern of Kelly's earlier books where primary source documentation proved so effective.

The book closes with a handy catalogue of Brown's major theses and hypotheses with yet another presentation of the obviously contrary thrust of authentic Catholic doctrine. An appendix that displays major excerpts from key magisterial documents on Sacred Scripture is a bonus that greatly enhances the value of Kelly's book.

Kelly's exposition devotes much effort to exploring Brown's peculiar methodology, which is, put briefly, methodical doubt camouflaged by semantics:

4. *Endless introduction of "new" questions*, each engaging and "reopening" core doctrinal issues. Kelly comments, "He merely insinuates a denial by asking repeated questions with negative answers built into the questions." Even Fitzmyer, a friendly peer, caustically observes, "Brown manages to avoid saying there is no historical evidence for the Davidic descent of Jesus, for the birth at Bethlehem, or for the virginal conception, at the same time affording ample evidence for the perceptive reader to draw this conclusion" (*National Catholic Reporter*, December 2, 1977).

5. *Speculation and theorizing are extensive*, with heavy use of qualifiers and disclaimers such as "likelihood," "it may mean," and "I suspect." Kelly notes, "Guesswork and speculations are important limitations on the value of any research which purports to read biblical documents differently from those commonplace from the beginning of the Church."

6. *Brown consistently claims for himself "the rhetorical middle,"* the "centrist" theology, with nary a blush that this places the pope, the foundation rock of Catholicism, far out in right field.

7. *Brown intermingles homiletics and exegesis.* He increasingly targets the educated non-specialist faithful rather than the restricted circles of his fellows, thus clearly assuming the mantel of advocacy exegesis. He thereby challenges response in the public forum, yet shows himself paranoid over criticism from "non-scholars." Silent disdain on the one hand or gratuitous insults on the other are trademarks of a wounded Brown.

Kelly makes an important observation: Brown has never faced thorough scrutiny or evaluation by his peers (whatever their stripe). The "establishment" is a mutual protection clique, while nonmembers, however great their competence, rarely get a forum under its control. When Cardinal Sheehan, in this a refreshing exception among the hierarchy, issued his telling series of critiques, he used *Homiletic & Pastoral Review*, not the inside trade journals.[ii]

Some orthodox scholars have produced similar articles and monographs (John Sheets, SJ, John Mulloy, et al.). Fr. William Most's *The Consciousness of Christ* and Fr. Manuel Miguens' several books and essays have clearly (if not explicitly) provided full-dress critiques of Brown's positions. Yet establishment types have blithely ignored these eminently scholarly works. For Brown, master of the mountain, response is beneath his dignity. Even last year's penetrating critique by Abbé René Laurentin, hardly a redneck by anyone's standards, got no notice outside orthodox circles.

Now, for the first time, Kelly has published an encyclopedic analysis. Perhaps silence will yield to vituperation since the readership will be much wider and the indictment more comprehensive and damning. Yet Kelly is fair, civil in tone, even indulgently temperate throughout, and these qualities only enhance the effectiveness of the critique. He simply lets Brown pontificate in his own words, while the juxtaposition of magisterial positions is stunning in its effect.

Kelly also exposes the fundamental methodological error in Brown's approach, one that has disqualified him and many of his establishment colleagues from the category of Catholic exegete. He deliberately refuses to use the analogy of faith. This has always been the Church's requirement *sine qua non* for her faithful biblical scholars. Most recently, the Church in *Dei Verbum* forcefully and repeatedly demands that the exegete work within the indissoluble triad of Tradition, Scripture, and Magisterium. Catholics such as Brown who evade this liberating principle must come to their study of the Bible with many presuppositions and biases that blind and shackle with no claim to divine guidance. To understand this, I strongly suggest that one first read *Dei Verbum* and then compare Brown's works with the related responses of Fr. Manuel Miguens, OFM.[iii]

[ii]   Lawrence Cardinal Sheehan, cardinal archbishop of Baltimore, 1961-74.

[iii]   To compare and contrast Brown with Miguens, it is worth noting Kelly's own words on the latter: "Fr. Miguens had studied Scripture in Rome and

I find a few areas of weakness in this otherwise excellent book. The only major reservation I have comes within Kelly's otherwise valid perception of "early" and "later" Brown. Kelly renders a charitable assessment of "early" Brown in *Jesus: God and Man*.

Here I must agree with Fr. Most. Already in this volume, Brown is "later" than Kelly thinks. I concede that the language is cautious, the "questions" and hypotheses are more nervously tentative than in more recent works, but the fatal methodology so well catalogued by Kelly is precisely the same: systematic insinuated doubt, endless open-ended questions, without a breath of the analogy of faith. I think Msgr. Kelly has been too benign here.

Nor am I at ease with his rather truncated assessment of magisterial stands on the "human consciousness" of Christ. I stress this single point since I am convinced that this matter of the revival of the "ignorant Jesus," a leitmotif of classical modernism, has denatured current catechetics, liturgy, and devotional life. For this,

---

Jerusalem, held doctorates in both Sacred Scripture (SSD) and Sacred Theology (STD), taught for thirteen years at Jerusalem's Studium Biblicum Francicanum and for six years at The Catholic University of America, where he was the highest degreed professor in his field, well-accepted by his students, and praised to me by the head of his department. He was the author of two books: *The Virgin Birth: An Evaluation of Scriptural Evidence* and *Christian Ministries*. "After his six successful years at Catholic University, Fr. Miguens was denied tenure because he was a critic of modern historicist exegesis as practiced, and of Fr. Brown. A Spanish-born visitor to the American Church, a private personality without powerful friends, he later came to St. John's University in New York, but never again taught students worthy of his intellect or his learning. The very academic freedom proposed in theory to protect unpopular opinion was no help to the modest Miguens. If his likes could be driven so easily from a bishop-owned university without defense by anyone in authority, and Charles Curran given tenure in the same period, the Catholic world was itself in a 'squirrel cage.' Miguens, a victim of politics, was himself uninterested in the politics of self-defense. He left CUA quietly" ("A Wayward Turn in Biblical Theory," an address delivered by Msgr. George A. Kelly on November 12, 1999, at a conference on the Bible and the Church).

Raymond Brown must bear the onus. His *Jesus: God and Man* has been the catalyst of this caricature of Jesus, the Word made Flesh.

The major thesis of Kelly's *The Crisis of Authority: John Paul II and the American Bishops* comes to the fore near the end of this new book. He highlights what is an ominous scandal: Many American bishops (among them some who otherwise merit respect for maintaining Catholic standards) adulate, patronize, and protect Brown. Does the aura of scholars mesmerize these bishops (seeing as how the establishment mutually fosters each)?

When the Faith is undermined (even by indirection and suggestions, as Brown prefers to do it), a bishop should rise up to defend his flock by his instinct of faith and his grave duty before Christ, who revealed *truth*, not contradiction and doubt.

It is imperative that our burdened bishops take a day or two off to ponder Kelly's indictment of Brown. One of the first qualifications for a good shepherd, after all, is the willingness and ability to detect a wolf in sheepskin clothing. Any sincere bishop who does this will surely discover that the colossus has clay feet.

CHAPTER 33

THE PETRINE COMMISSION[1]

And On This Rock: The Witness of One Land and Two Covenants, by Stanley L. Jaki (Manassas, VA: Trinity Communications, 1987, 2nd ed., rev. and enl.)

The courtship between faith and science has had a stormy love-hate history. It is rare that one finds the couple harmoniously wed in their acquisition of natural and supernatural truth. Fr. Jaki is one of those exceptional geniuses whose intellect is happily at home with science and faith. He has won the attention and acclaim of his peers for prestigious works and lectures directly bearing on the physical sciences, which cogently demonstrate the compatibility of science with theology.

But in two remarkable books (each focusing on the text of Matthew 16), it is the theologian who initiates the study, while the scientist follows up with his specific methodology to illuminate the imagery of the core Petrine passage. The results are stunning.

In his book *The Keys of the Kingdom*, he brilliantly explicated the phrase, "I will give to you the keys of the kingdom." This year the phrase, "on this rock" (and with it the allied image of the "jaws of death" or "gates of hell"), receives an archaeological-geographical study.

The introduction is an intriguing and indispensable entree into the mind and motives of the author. If it is, as Fr. Jaki admits, a very personal exposition of how he was introduced to the central theme of his study, the rest of the work, while more "objective," sparkles with personal observations, not least of all in the magnificent footnotes.

Throughout, Jaki is puzzled, if not scandalized, by the failure of previous exegetes to appreciate the pivotal importance of the geographical setting of the Petrine commission text. Often purely ideological biases can explain the neglect. He notes we can see the anti-papal animus of Hans Küng in his *Structures of the Church*, in which the text receives only a passing reference, with not even one mention of Caesarea Philippi.

Chapter 1, "The Scene of the Rock," introduces us to the imposing background of Matthew 16, the massive rock Banias (aka Panias), abutting on Caesarea Philippi from where it is dominantly visible. At some 200 feet high and 500 feet wide, it forms the *Sitz im Leben* of Christ's words to Simon Peter.

Fr. Jaki quotes Josephus'[i] description of Caesarea Philippi:

> ... [A] splendid pagan city lying in clear sight of a huge wall of rock. At the top of that wall, there glitters the white marble of a temple dedicated to Caesar. At its bottom, there is an outwardly idyllic sanctuary of Pan. Immediately to the left of that sanctuary, there is a fathomless cavity full of water, one of the three sources of the Jordan [River].

Fr. Jaki meticulously presents the geographical, archaeological, and historical aspects of this site and compellingly links them to Matthew 16. The "rock" is self-evident, but the gaping mouth of the cavern is such an integral, visible, and preternatural facet of the scene that it offers a likely visual aid for the reference to the "jaws of death" or "gates of hell." The numerous illustrations and photos included in this book are effective in convincing the reader of the author's thesis.

There follows a chapter on the divine title of "Rock," applied uniquely to Yahweh in the Old Testament. It is a splendid thematic review, a running exegetical commentary on the qualities of "Rock," which serves to illuminate its astonishing transmission in the New Testament to the all-too-human Simon.

---

[i] Flavius Josephus, Jewish historian of the first century AD.

Chapter 3 then gives an excellent biography of this apostle named "Rock." The change of name has always been one of the preliminary data in the exegesis of Matthew 16. Biblical theology well establishes the Semitic significance of such a change. Beyond that, Fr. Jaki stresses that before its application to Simon, "Rock" was a uniquely divine title. (He proves Isaiah 51:1-2 is no exception.)

I might adduce another observation of this "sharing in divine prerogatives." When Peter walks on the water at Christ's bidding, the apostle is doing what only Yahweh does in the Old Testament and Jesus in the New. Fr. Jaki deplores the efforts Cullmann makes in his work on Peter to downplay the background of Caesarea Philippi (to the extent that he actually transposes the site to the Last Supper). Cullmann sees this as a more "spiritual context" for the pronouncement, and thus shows, as Jaki dryly comments, a "puzzling disregard for the geographical context."

Chapter 5, "The Shadow of the Rock," surveys the humanly inexplicable bi-millennial "weathering" of the Rock. The text is a rich tapestry of history, theological commentary, and rarely presented testimonies from hostile witnesses. The limits of this review allow for only a few examples. Thus, speaking of the papal claim of infallibility in *Saint Joan*, G.B. Shaw says:

> [B]y far, the most modest pretension of the kind in existence. Compared with our infallible democracies, our infallible medical councils, our infallible astronomers, our infallible judges, and our infallible parliaments, the Pope is on his knees in the dust confessing his ignorance before the Throne of God, asking only that as to certain historical matters on which he has clearly more sources of information open to him than anyone else, his decision shall be taken as final.

Jaki speaks of "our own virulently anti-papal times," and this quote suggests Shaw might have added "infallible modernist theologians," et al.

The author also cites a letter of Karl Barth to Pope Paul VI. [ii]Barth wrote the following to His Holiness two months before his death in 1968:

> You may be sure of my great respect for what might be called the heroic isolation in which, Holy Father, you now find yourself.

The reference was to the fallout from *Humanae Vitae*. Jaki points out with admiration the restraint of Pope Paul in not making this letter public. It appeared only when published by Protestant authors in 1981. This illustrates a major contention of Fr. Jaki, what he calls the "long-suffering" or "redemptive suffering" of the papacy. He sees this as a historical virtue of the Rock:

> Long-suffering can ... be taken for "failure of nerve" by those "loyal" among the sheep... The strength of one's nerves is never proven better than under the stress of trial, which can take on historic dimensions...

Several times Jaki locks horns with the chimera of "dialogue":

> [It] can be a vehicle not only of brotherhood, but also of reaching out for power by those who mistakenly feel themselves excluded from the sharing of power and turn their dialogue with those in authority into filibuster...
>
> Dialogue is not debate, let alone filibuster. Even in political life, only those engage in filibuster who know deep in their hearts that they shall not prevail. Nor shall the jaws of hell.

---

ii   The so-called Father of the Neo-Orthodox movement, Barth was a Swiss Calvinist theologian and committed opponent of modernism. Although initially he spoke of Catholicism as the "Roman heresy," his views grew more temperate over time, and he became prominent in the ecumenical movement. Because of the profound respect many had for him, he was invited as an observer to the Second Vatican Council (illness prevented him from attending). He died in 1968.

The final chapter, "Divine Origin of the Papacy," is a profound meditation. Here, especially, the focus is on the magisterial role of the papacy in the tumultuous post-Vatican II era. His motif is that the Rock and its infallibility are ever "faithful to type" (Newman's criterion for true development of doctrine). Again, he uses striking anecdotes and citations. For instance, Jaki relates how Pope John XXIII, whose wit and optimistic joviality were legend, nonetheless often used a particular expression to warn his collaborators of his intense determination to preserve doctrine and discipline: *Facciamo da Papa*.[iii]

Typical of the reflections in this final chapter is the following:

> Historically, the Church, both the Church of the Old and the New Covenant, existed before their Holy Scriptures came into existence. As to the Bible, its witness is very clear about the priority and primacy of the Church over Holy Writ. To be sure, the Scriptures are divinely inspired codification of the authoritative self-reflection of the Apostolic Church, and they function as norms for a similar reflection in the post-Apostolic Church. Anything that contradicts Scriptures cannot be regarded as part of the *depositum fidei*.
>
> The dogma of infallibility is not only not contrary to the Scriptures, but once it is rejected in the name of the Scriptures, there remains no consistent basis for vindicating the infallibility of the Scriptures themselves.

In his work on the Keys, Fr Jaki had given an *in extenso*[iv] critique of Karl Rahner. He returns to this critical evaluation here, speaking

---

iii   It would depend on the context, but this could mean one of two things: 1) What we make and do derives from the Father (also Papa) or 2) What we do is in keeping with the Father and should be!

iv   *In extenso* means "at full length."

of Rahner's "bottomless transcendental Thomism" à la Kant.[v] He would require every theologian to name clearly his "favorite philosopher," and discerns false epistemology as the basis of modernist theological aberrations. "They all follow Ockham into the morass of Nominalism whatever the label they put on it," he writes.[vi] He quotes Bultmann as telling Rahner, "How fortunate you must be to be able to appeal to the Pope; appeal to the Lutheran synods merely leads to greater disunity."

A biblical scholar will soon realize how these studies, *And On This Rock* and *The Keys of the Kingdom*, seemingly limited to two images, serve to shed light and life on the whole of what we might call "Petrology." Never in the future will a truly Catholic exegete be able to deal adequately with Matthew 16 without referring to and relying on the seminal concepts of Fr. Jaki on the imagery of "Rock" and "keys."

---

[v]   Immanuel Kant (1724-1804), hugely influential German philosopher. He believed the only things we could truly know with any certainty were those things we could test and experience (e.g., math, science). We could only speculate about whether God existed; we could never really have any certainty of His existence.

[vi]   Jaki here refers to William of Ockham (1288-1348). He was a proponent of nominalism, which one dictionary defines as "the doctrine holding that abstract concepts, general terms, or universals have no independent existence but exist only as names." It is also the philosophy that certain objects given the same name have nothing in common but that name.

CHAPTER 34

BORN OF PRAYER

Behold The Pierced One: An Approach to a Spiritual Christology, by Joseph Cardinal Ratzinger (Translated by Graham Harrison, New York: Ignatius Press, 1986).

Appointed as watchman over the Congregation for the Deposit of the Faith, Joseph Cardinal Ratzinger periodically addresses various constituencies of the universal Church. He selects themes that in his judgment most advance a positive explication of neglected or contested doctrines.

The present volume, one of a series published by Ignatius Press, makes accessible to all of us what otherwise would have remained restricted to a fortunate few. The subtitle, *An Approach to a Spiritual Christology,*[i] serves to bind three major addresses and three liturgical homilies together. This is no mere publisher's artifice, either, for each part pursues an organic continuum. Each part also centers on the restoration of prayer and devotion in the Church, and it is precisely these things that will provide the pressing and positive antidote to the malaise of spirit widely experienced in the Catholic world today.

Christology

The first lecture, "Taking Bearings in Christology," was given in Rio de Janeiro in 1982, and subtly but pointedly corrects the liberationist errors in this field.[ii] The Cardinal Prefect explains:

---

[i]   Christology is the study of Christ.
[ii] Father here refers to the so-called theology of liberation.

> [M]y task and aim was to present in some way the inner
> totality and unity ... of Christology. For the loss of such a
> total view is the real central problem of the contemporary
> Christological debate, and it cannot be met except by
> renewed attempts to embrace this totality.

It is a short but densely elaborated review from an excitingly fresh angle.

Having examined the New Testament titles of Christ and analyzed the critical ploy of separating the "Jesus of history" from the "Christ of faith," he locates "Son" as the core title:

> [T]he title "Son" comes in the end to be the only com-
> prehensive description for Jesus. It both comprises and
> interprets everything else.

This title is studied in seven progressively probing theses. According to Ratzinger, the relation of Son to Father is most perfectly manifested in the *prayer* of Christ, an uninterrupted communion-communication. This reaches a climactic intensity in his thesis that "Jesus died praying," thus unifying Christology and soteriology[iii] and identifying cross and Eucharist.

The ecclesial dimension insists that this prayer of Christ must be the interior life of all conjoined to Him in His Body, the Church (thesis 3). To know and understand Jesus, we must participate in His prayer. A special thread binding all three lectures is Ratzinger's preoccupation with the Third Council of Constantinople, seen as unfolding and crowning the dogma of the Council of Chalcedon.[iv] His treatment of the "problem" of two wills in Christ is also most illuminating. A bonus in this lecture is the commentary on the historical-critical method of

---

iii   Soteriology is the study of the doctrine of the biblical salvation.

iv   The Council of Chalcedon took place in AD 451 to combat the heresy of
      monophysitism. This held that Christ had one nature, divine, and that His
      divinity overwhelmed and absorbed any humanness like the sea overwhelms
      and absorbs "a drop of honey." Chalcedon corrected this and posited that
      Jesus was fully human and fully divine.

exegesis (p. 43). This first lecture ends with the challenging sentence, "Christology is born of prayer or not at all."

Sacred Heart

Delivered in 1981 at the Sacred Heart Congress in Toulouse, the second lecture falls chronologically and conceptually prior to the others. Ratzinger sees the current eclipse of devotion to the Sacred Heart as instigated by the intellectual purism and classicism of the early liturgical movement. The dominance of head over heart is a major derangement of our era. It is obvious that unless the two collaborate in tandem, the head becomes a non-human, soulless computer.

The modernist coup has driven the liturgical movement, which in turn has virtually killed this traditional devotion. However, it has sought to banish not only devotion to the Sacred Heart, but all traditional and popular devotions—primarily Marian piety. In this vacuum of the heart, ersatz enthusiasms have germinated. Ratzinger credits Hugo Rahner[v] for pioneering efforts to restore Mariology and the cult of the Sacred Heart through his patristic research.

The cardinal lauds Pius XII's 1956 encyclical *Haurietis Aquas* (On Devotion to the Sacred Heart) for demonstrating a new rationale for devotion to the Heart of Jesus, one rooted in both Scripture and Tradition and built on an anthropology and theology of bodily existence. Ratzinger then displays the thesaurus of the biblical theology of "heart."

I alert the prospective reader to precious critiques on pages 54 and 60 of the stoical *apatheia*[vi] of the opponents, reminiscent of *The Ratzinger Report*.

---

[v] German Catholic Jesuit and theologian (1900-68) and brother of Karl Rahner.

[vi] One source defines this as "being objective or having clear judgment." Others define it as "freedom from passion" and even letting go of the problems over which you have no control and letting God handle them.

Communion

The last of the trilogy of studies deals with ecclesial spirituality under the contemporary dynamics of the biblical theology of *koinonia* (communion). This profound and perennial ecclesiology was highlighted at the Dutch Synod in 1980 as the key doctrine for confronting the chaotic alienation in Holland. Since then, it has assumed recurring stress in the teaching of Pope John Paul II. It emerged as a major motif in the Extraordinary Synod of 1985, again as an *idée-clé*[vii] for resolving the grave, now universal, misdirections in ecclesiology.

Ratzinger marshals all the basic biblical loci [i.e., centers of attention]. He pursues the general theme of this trilogy by centering the mediating nexus of communion (between Trinity and Church) in the Person of Jesus Christ, the God-Man. *Koinonia* weds the exterior to the interior aspects of the Church. In other words, we can have no community without Communion! Once more, therefore, we find ourselves engaged with spiritual Christology in a manner so essential to a restoration of orthodox Catholicism.

Homilies

In the three homilies—they can surely be called sermons—the cardinal draws on the richness of Eastern liturgical themes. He focuses on the Paschal Mystery, the core of these addresses. He calls the faithful to "behold the Pierced One," whose excruciating wounds, received in prayer on the cross, have become gloriously resplendent in the Resurrection triumph over sin and death. These homilies bring home to us, who are members of His Body, our sharing in the spiritual Christology of the *Triduum Sacrum*.

Ratzinger the man

In the current storms, a good bishop must be a lightning rod, not a weather vane. Paradoxically, therefore, one of Cardinal Ratzinger's

---

vii   French for "key idea."

greatest tributes is that the "right people" have selected him as the object of their vilification, a vilification that is often orchestrated and vitriolic, visceral rather than cerebral. The final beatitude comes to mind. We all know that the real target is not the Cardinal but the Pope. The dissenters thus acknowledge the spiritual and intellectual bonding of the two.

Ignatius Press adds to its growing prestige by publishing this collection of Ratzinger's studies on issues that stand at the heart of our crisis. Surely, those who admire His Eminence will eagerly seek further to absorb his wisdom.

But dare we dream the improbable and challenge his opponents to read this volume? They will discover the razor-sharp faculties of analysis and synthesis characteristic of German scholarship. But deeper than the method—and here they might possibly be touched—they will discern in the heart of Joseph Ratzinger a man of piety, charity, sincerity, faith, and conscience, the compelling motives for his fierce ministry of defense.

CHAPTER 35

THEOLOGICAL REFLECTION

Our Father's Plan: God's Arrangements and Our Response, by Fr.
William G. Most (Manassas, VA: Trinity Communications, 1988).

Fr. Most has produced many books and articles on particular
themes, ranging in style from popular to densely erudite. This work,
however, is the crowning testament of his long career. What is its
genre? Catechism? Systematic theology? Biblical exegesis? Devotional
treatise? Ascetical or mystical theology? Homiletic source book?

All of these and more!

This book is a virtuoso performance by one of America's eminent
theologians and philologists. It unintentionally reveals the brilliance
of a scholar who has suffered through the ersatz "renewal" with
orthodoxy and humor intact.

Fr. Most wrestles here with vexing theological questions
and displays a sophisticated acquaintance with scientific and
psychological data, as well as a mastery of patristic sources,
magisterial pronouncements, Greek mythology, philosophy, classics,
and intertestamental literature.

Yet no prospective reader need cringe. Nothing he writes is
obscure. Everything is accessible to the average individual. This book
gives us the singular privilege of sharing the inner life of a holy priest,
a genuine man of the Church. Once the dry dust of dissent is whisked
away, history will be enthralled by this genius and wonder why he
was largely ignored and seldom consulted. Then again, the crowds
always prefer Barabbas, don't they?

The subtitle *God's Arrangements and Our Response* exposes its
twofold structure. First, the author gives us an enthralling, startlingly

fresh presentation of the mysteries of divine revelation, which is the basic "plan" of God's economy of salvation. Midway, the author focuses on man's proper response, moving us from faith to action, thus exploring the dynamics of grace in the soul. The traditional stages of the spiritual life are carefully discussed by one who obviously has understood them not only in abstract theory but from personal experience. In passing, Most makes perceptive comments on transcendental meditation (TM) and "centering prayer."

Along the way, he tackles perennial theological debates with zest and gives them convincing solutions (e.g., predestination and free will; justification and the doctrine of merits; Mary's role as "co-redemptrix" and "mediatrix"; the consciousness of Christ; the precise sense of "*extra ecclesiam nulla salus*";[i] the concept of "lay-priesthood"; the unity of love/obedience, death, and heaven).

Appropriately published in the Marian Year, a deep love for Mary pervades *Our Father's Plan*, and it stands as a filial priestly tribute. Most covers the Presentation of the Infant as an "offertory" in relation to the Cenacle and the Cross; Mary's active relation to the Mass; the knowledge of Mary. The majestic refrain at strategic points of the book echoes the words of Pius IX from *Ineffabilis Deus* (On the Immaculate Conception), which describes the love of Mary for her Son: "None greater under God can be thought of, and no one but God can comprehend it."

In his thrilling description of heaven, Fr. Most refers to one who sees Mary there, and he cites a remarkable passage of Pius XII:

> Surely, in the face of His own Mother, God has gathered together all the splendors of His divine artistry... You know, beloved sons and daughters, how easily human beauty enraptures and exalts a kind heart. What would it ever do before the beauty of Mary! That is why Dante saw in paradise, in the midst of "more than a million

---

i   Latin for, "Outside the Church, there is no salvation," the exact meaning of which has caused great controversy in some circles.

> rejoicing angels ... a beauty smiling—What joy! It was in
> the eyes of all the other saints"—Mary![1]

Jewels like this adorn the whole volume and breathe the spirit of its priestly author.

As such, priests will discover here a mine of homiletic outlines. For example, the astronomical descriptions of the physical universe that show forth the glory of the Creator are pages that rival similar texts of Pascal. Teachers will also find rich resources for their lesson plans.

The only niggling criticism this reviewer might risk concerns the book's title. It fits the author like a glove: clear, logical, unpretentious, modest. But couldn't he have chosen some more eye-catching, alluring title? It is my prayer that this review can draw attention to what will come to be recognized—in spite of its understated title—as a classic of theology and spirituality.

I also pray that the thirsting People of God will welcome access to one of the rare oases in the sterile desert of the post-conciliar "American" Church.

CHAPTER 36

SURRENDER TO TRUTH

Faith and Certitude, by Thomas A. Dubay, SM
(San Francisco: Ignatius Press, 1985).

A few years ago, I attended a required event that afterwards featured a dinner. I sat at table with three older priests whom I had not seen for some years. The occasion prompted us to express our opinions on the state of our Church. Our *Tischreden*[i] soon revealed diametric opposition between us on essentials of the Catholic Faith.

This, in itself, came as no surprise since conversations among priests in these latter days have become routinely "ecumenical." What really shocked me was that whenever I pressed them on any of these substantive matters ("Now doesn't this make a difference? Is it tolerable that we priests don't agree on this?"), they refused to admit that it was important, all the while insisting vehemently that *I* was hopelessly "wrong" not to agree with them.

As we were, mercifully, led in grace after the meal and were about to go our truly separate ways, I begged them to at least agree that we did not agree on some important points. They angrily refused to admit even that! I traveled home that night in deep sadness and utter exasperation as how ever to reach these aging priests (who echoed a majority of younger men). I recall fuming over the core of that refusal: They had wiped out the "principle of contradictories"! I recall fuming because their logic was so bad they didn't see that distinctions or contradictions are of any consequence.

---

[i]   The literal translation is "table talk," and the sense it carries is that of an informal discussion. It is also the name of a book by Martin Luther.

They had committed semantic, intellectual, and spiritual suicide! They had ruled out any rational discourse but continued to demand "dialogue"!

In this masterful book, Fr. Thomas Dubay, SM, adroitly reveals that the roots of our crisis germinate in this sort of basic epistemological muck. As we survey the acknowledged chaos in the Church, we tend to isolate piecemeal the surface derangements in catechetics, biblical criticism, liturgy, religious life, the seminaries, and so on. The exceptional genius of Fr. Dubay is that he is a diagnostician-surgeon. He recognizes these separate "crises" as symptoms of a pervasive and lethal disease.

He then moves to exploratory surgery at the level of the underlying common sources: errors in epistemology, logic, and "natural theology"—the now deplorably neglected foundations of pre-metaphysical philosophy courses.[ii] He does not neglect to describe the surface symptoms but does so only to demonstrate their interconnection and to lay bare their common causes, which stem from the *will*. He skillfully probes the motives that seduce and pervert the will. His chapter, "The Causes of Error," responds to the dilemma of how my priest tablemates could so blandly reject the first principles of rational functioning. He concludes, "The taproot of most human errors is the will" (p. 83).

Having done this, however, Dubay returns to his main concern, which is to heal and restore. To do this, he describes (or rather "prescribes") the graduated processes that lead the human thinker from the sane first principles to the threshold of the act of faith, those luminously reasonable steps that prepare for and fully justify the embrace of divine revelation moved by the supernatural, transcendent, free gift of grace. When one concludes this book, he should be firmly convinced that our act of faith is not absurd; it is not

---

[ii]   Metaphysics, says the *Catholic Encyclopedia*, is "that portion of philosophy which treats of the most general and fundamental principles underlying all reality and all knowledge." So if you get metaphysics wrong, you will get so much else wrong as well.

a blind leap into a black hole; it is precisely a *rationabile obsequium*, a logical and loving surrender to truth incarnate.

As one might expect, the organization of the book is admirable in the relentlessly logical development of each of its 14 chapters; here we can mention but a few.

Dubay begins with a telling description of "existential boredom," the pandemic symptomatic malaise of modernity. He catalogues the causes and points out the remedies (recovery of faith and certitude, healing and correction of the intellect and will), themes which he pursues throughout the chapters that follow.

While not attempting to write a book on fundamental theology or an updated apologetics text on issues of revealed faith, Dubay clearly shows that theological errors stem from epistemological errors. His chapter "Scholarship, Doubt, and Certitude," documenting the enormous contradictions of experts from their own peers' testimonies, is a liberating and crucial preamble to the next two chapters on biblical exegesis.

Chapter 9 offers an excellent and balanced analysis of the current critical methodologies. Dubay subjects these schools to the test of perennial Catholic principles for genuine biblical studies, especially citing the analogy of faith required by the Council's *Dei Verbum*. He willingly accepts what is valid in historical-critical studies but excises their lethal flaws. He then proceeds to bring this down to the experience of average lay Catholics and their often-confused teachers and pastors in Chapter 10, "Biblical Criticism and Pastoral Practice."

Space allows for comment on only one other exceptional section of what is an exceptional book, Chapter 13, "Another Case: Theism" (pp. 215-326). In presenting motives for belief in a personal, omniscient, and omnipotent God, Dubay uses the data of modern science to describe the breathtaking wonders of the macrocosm and the microcosm, the infinitely large and the infinitesimally small. This chapter merits being called a classic of theodicy. These enthralling pages evoked for me the essay of Pascal in his *Pensées* on the "*Disproportion de l'homme.*" Fr. Dubay has given us an updated (and possibly superior) version worthy of the original.

On rereading my comments thus far, I realize I may have given the impression of a stifling, complex, forbidding text. Far from it! Fr. Dubay is one of the best writers in the Church today. His style is limpid, almost entirely accessible to the moderately educated layperson. He explains with striking imagery, colorful language, and readily grasped examples. Indeed, he says his target audience is the average person, not just those in the academic or theological establishment.

I marked page after page with items to be quoted but finally gave up—on *every* page there are those precious commodities, so rare today: facts, clear and compelling statements of truth, and citations of other great minds to show convergence along the path to certitude and faith. He writes incisively but with charity. He seeks to convert, not to conquer.

I kept thinking, "If only every bishop would read this and then urge it on his priests, religious, diocesan staff, seminarians, and the faithful at large."

If read by a large public, this book alone could restore sanity and common sense to the Church, for here are the premises to faith, the antidotes to our severe "crisis of faith."

The only nitpicking point of complaint I have is the title. It sounds flat and unappealing. It disguises what is a golden book of wisdom, a book of healing for tormented minds and souls. But whenever I try to concoct a more captious title, I come up empty. It is, like its author, logical and straightforward. Long known for his writings on religious life and for his retreats and conferences to Religious women (one can almost detect where he has been welcomed by the health and stability of the communities he has served), Fr. Dubay has given the Church at large a book that has to be read to be believed—despite the title. His is one more masterpiece in the increasingly vital repertory of Ignatius Press.

CHAPTER 37

THE VIRGIN OF THE VISITATION

Those Who Saw Her: The Story of the Apparitions of Mary, by
Catherine M. Odell (Huntington, IN: Our Sunday Visitor, 1986).

> In those days, Mary arose and went with haste into
> the hill country, to a city of Judah, and she entered the
> house of Zechariah and greeted Elizabeth. And when
> Elizabeth heard the greeting of Mary, the babe leaped
> in her womb; and Elizabeth was filled with the Holy
> Spirit and she exclaimed with a loud cry, "Blessed are you
> among women, and blessed is the fruit of your womb!
> And why is this granted me, that the mother of my Lord
> should come to me?"[1]

The account of the Visitation records the loving, concerned
initiative of Mary and the ecstatic response of her cousin. Mary
arises "with haste" to make a long, perilous journey through the
hill country. Elizabeth utters the Spirit-prompted benediction,
questioning in stunned humility, "How is this that the mother of
my Lord should come to me?"

Catherine M. Odell has compiled an anthology of major
apparitions—visitations, if you will—of Mary in our troubled
times. With the exception of Guadalupe, the accounts included here
have occurred in the past 100 years or so, several in our apocalyptic
twentieth century. And, aside from a closing chapter on the events
at Međugorje, currently under Vatican study, they have all received
the approval of the Church in one form or another.[i]

---

[i]   To this day, more than 20 years after Father penned this book review,
the Church has not definitively ruled on the validity of the Međugorje

In her Introduction, Odell states her decision to narrate the amazing facts in a non-technical, unpretentious manner. This she does, yet with touching beauty and in spellbinding sequence. The effect is a book that will captivate those who know the stories, as well as those learning of them for the first time.

Three preliminary chapters discuss the historical person of Mary of Nazareth and her earthly mission as mother of Christ, and they present an exposition of the attitude and prudent response of the Church in discerning the genuineness and credibility of the claims. Odell then begins to recount the apparitions themselves: Guadalupe, Rue de Bac, La Salette, Lourdes, Pontmain, Knock, Fátima, Beauraing, Banneaux, and—with a question mark—Međugorje.

Only with the introductory chapters do I have some critical reservations, a few of which I feel obliged to mention.

I suggest that the wording, "To humor the boy [Jesus] struggling to learn [carpentry]," is misleading. Jesus, it is true, learned the art in an experiential manner, but that He needed to be "humored" or to "struggle" recognizes neither His theoretical knowledge (cf. the intricate question of the *communicatio idiomatum*) nor the singular perfection of His human nature.

The English version Odell chose for citing Scripture presents us with a neuter "it" to designate the one who will crush Satan's head (Genesis 3:15ff.). The triumphant "offspring," whatever the gender, is surely personal. Even more regrettable, when discussing the

---

apparitions. What local bishops have said is that "it cannot be established that one is dealing with supernatural apparitions and revelations." That said, some very prominent people in the Vatican have expressed their support, including, reportedly, John Paul II and then-Cardinal Ratzinger. Also, Preacher of the Pontifical Household Fr. Raniero Cantalamessa, OFM Cap, was scheduled in summer of 2007 to preach at a priestly convocation in the Bosnia-Herzegovina hamlet but cancelled when refused permission by the local bishop, ostensibly because it might imply Vatican acceptance of the apparitions, when no formal determination has been made at the local level. In September 2006, Vinko Cardinal Puljic of Sarajevo, Bosnia-Herzegovina, announced the formation of a commission to review the alleged apparitions.

Immaculate Conception, the author cites Luke 1:28 in the modish but obscure "highly favored daughter" version inspired by Zechariah 9:9. The traditional and highly defensible "full of grace" would have more directly illuminated her discussion of the dogma.

Later, Odell says that belief in apparitions is "quite optional." Here she makes an important point, but does this phrase adequately convey what should be said? Further on, there is an incorrect statement that "no claimed apparitions" have received "an approval from the Church since 1947." Some, in fact, have received explicit approval from local ordinaries.[ii]

This leads to a final appreciation. This wonderful book serves as an excellent introduction to the phenomena of apparitions— of Christ, Mary, saints, and angels. For those who wish to probe further, may I suggest Fr. Albert Hebert's recent compendium, *Prophecies*, which displays a veritable constellation of apparitions, many very recent, some approved, others now under study by Church authorities. We may prudently consider such claims unless and until the Church renders a negative verdict.

[ii]   Of the roughly 80 reported apparitions of Our Lady since 1947, three have explicit approval by the local ordinaries and thus the Church. These are These are: Zeitun, Egypt (1968, approved 1968); Akita, Japan (1973, approved 1984); Betania, Venezuela (1976, approved 1987); Cuapa, Nicaragua (1980, approved 1982); Kibeho, Rwanda (1981, approved 1988); and San Nicolás, Argentina (1983, approved 1990). Similarly, the Church has expressly disavowed six alleged apparitions. These are Necedah, Wisconsin; Bayside, New York; Naju, Korea; the false apparitions given to Vassula Ryden of Switzerland; and the false apparitions given to Maria Valtorta in Caserta, Italy, who wrote down what she claimed to have received in the Vatican-condemned book, *Poem of the Man-God* (it was placed on the Index of Forbidden Books in the early 1960s, and that censure has since been reaffirmed). The sixth and most recently rejected "visions" were condemned on September 24, 2007, and concerned a group in London called the Community of Divine Innocence. On September 14 of the same year, the Vatican also excommunicated a Canadian group called the Army of Mary, whose foundress claims to be the Virgin Mary and divine.

The Virgin of the Visitation continues to come in haste to our menaced planet. She does so with greater frequency to warn a rebellious world and to give solace, instruction, and hope to her beloved, beleaguered children.

Catherine Odell has done us the service of opening the jaded eyes of a materialistic, anti-supernatural age to the reality of our heavenly home, where a mother's heart keeps vigil.

CHAPTER 38

THE ANALOGY OF FAITH

The Catholic Church and the Bible, by Fr. Peter M.J. Stravinskas
(Huntington, IN: Our Sunday Visitor, 1987).

The Catholic Church and the Bible is a handy beginner's
introduction to the appreciation of the Church for her own
"constitutional" book, the Bible. Fr. Stravinskas is a masterful
apologist, which is so welcome and providential during this turn-of-
the-millennium crisis of faith. Many will recognize him because of
his regular contributions to the *National Catholic Register*, in which
his thematic discussions of central positions of faith serve to fortify,
illuminate, and enrich believing Catholics of America.

The present work displays the same qualities. The style is simple
but stimulating; the content is meaty and orthodox.

The author begins with an introduction to the nature and
origin of the biblical literature, and he presents the basic doctrinal
hermeneutical concepts. The Vatican II Constitution on Divine
Revelation, *Dei Verbum*—so often neglected by dissenting
theologians—is cited and relied upon by Stravinskas to clarify the
functional relations and interdependence of Tradition, Scripture,
and Magisterium, the analogy of faith.

Chapter 1 concludes with a rousing *apologia*[i] to counter the
accusations of the fundamentalists and thus bolster the confidence of
Catholics. He indexes the preservation, transmission, and extensive
use of the sacred books in Catholic life to vindicate his claim that

---

[i]   Greek for defending one's position on a subject against attacks.

"[T]he Catholic Church is not only a 'Bible-based' Church, but *the* 'Bible-based' Church."

Chapter 2 gives a very rapid survey of the books of the Old and New Testaments. The next two chapters, a third of the text, demonstrate the biblical theology of the Mass. This is apologetics at its best. But it will also remedy those theological currents that seek to separate word and Eucharist, to the detriment of the latter. This section would be especially enlightening to average Catholics who may know little of the Jewish roots of the liturgy.

An entire chapter analyzes the Mass texts, line by line, showing the biblical texts and allusions from which they are drawn. The final chapter, "What About...?" answers specific fundamentalist challenges in the best tradition of Rumble and Carty.[ii]

Having given the book a strong endorsement, I must nevertheless state some reservations and cautions.

First, there is no formal introduction to the book. It would have helped to know the author's intended goals and audience. I judge that Fr. Stravinskas seeks to aid Catholics in the current struggle with fundamentalists. This would explain certain "silences," but Catholics are equally threatened, often from within the Church, by neo-modernist biblicists. There is no hint of this other ominous side of the pincer movement that assaults Catholics from the left as well as from the right.

The author's roseate assessment of current Bible study among Catholics lacks a balance of critical realism, and I would question some of the entries in the appended resource list. I would have

---

[ii]   Rev. Dr. Leslie Rumble, MSC, and Rev. Charles M. Carty. A convert from Anglicanism who had been raised to despise the Catholic Faith, Fr. Rumble hosted a radio show from the 1920s through the 1940s that was broadcast all over New Zealand and Australia, during which he answered listeners' questions about Catholicism. At the same time, Fr. Carty broadcast a similar program from St. Paul, Minnesota. They learned of each other's work and collaborated to compile many of these questions and their answers in a three-volume set titled *Radio Replies*. TAN Books still publishes these excellent apologetics books.

preferred *A New Catholic Commentary on the Holy Scripture* (Nelson) to the *Jerome Biblical Commentary* and would not have been so generous in endorsing the New American Bible. I would have added some caveats to the citations of Raymond Brown.

The brief survey of biblical books leaves a few statements hanging in the air that require clarification on key points. It might also have helped, especially when targeting fundamentalists, to have mentioned recent scholarly reactions to Markan priority, source criticism, and late dating.[iii]

But I offer these few reservations only from a scrupulous sense of duty that a reviewer assumes. Catholics today hunger and thirst for the word of God, but they often receive stones and dust. Fr. Stravinskas has given them one more truly Catholic delicatessen where pure bread and invigorating wine are not only in abundant supply but are enticingly displayed.

[iii] The Markan priority refers to the belief that of the synoptic Gospels— Matthew, Mark, and Luke—Mark came first. This is because Mark is comparatively spare, and Matthew and Luke appear to build off of it. However, in writing his Gospel, why would Matthew—an apostle—have relied on the work of Mark (who may or may not have been an original disciple)? Also, recent books such as *Eyewitness to Jesus* (New York: Doubleday, 1996) have made a compelling case that Matthew was indeed written first. In any event, the early Church placed the Gospels in the order in which the Fathers thought they had been written, namely, with Matthew first. Source criticism seeks to discern the Bible's original sources. It begins with the notion that the scriptures combine what originally were distinctly written documents. Source critics attempt to learn as much as possible about these original sources and their authors.

The late dating of the New Testament refers to the belief of some scholars that the New Testament books were actually written later than the first century (and sometimes much later). Thus they would not have been written by the apostles but by people claiming to be them or of their school.

CHAPTER 39

THE NARROW WAY OF THE MASTER[1]

Protestant Fundamentalism and the Born Again Catholic, by
Robert J. Fox (Redfield, SD: Fatima Family Apostolate, 1989).

Many people see Fr. Robert J. Fox as an author, lecturer, and
a leader in the Fátima apostolate. He is all of these, but first and
foremost, he is a parish priest whose primary work is the daily care
of souls. We cannot appreciate this latest of his prolific efforts except
in the context of his zeal as a pastor.

Fr. Fox expresses what all pastors urgently need to recognize:
"The time for a revival of apologetics is long overdue."[i]

"Revival!"

Since Vatican II (and clearly not because of it), the perennial
Catholic art of apologetics of "fundamental theology" has been
shelved (if not consciously jettisoned). And while we have neglected
the "fundamentals" of our Faith, and although our people are no
longer able "to give a reason for the faith that is in them,"[2] others
"whose own the sheep are not" have been ravaging Christ's flock. It
is ironic that the latter are known precisely as "fundamentalists."

---

[i] Father wrote this review before the modern apologetics movement had really
gotten underway. While Catholic Answers (the first modern apologetics
organization) had been around for a decade, Karl Keating's groundbreaking
Catholicism and Fundamentalism had only been out for a year, and the first
modern apologetics magazine *This Rock* was still several months away from
seeing its first issue hit the stands.

All too recently, the American bishops have noted the crisis with alarm. Fr. Fox records the evidence from a recent survey: 33 million (or 40 percent) of all homes in the US watch at least one of the ten best-known TV preachers at least six minutes once a month. Some TV evangelists and all Protestant fundamentalists boast that 30 percent of their financial support comes from Catholic viewers.

In addition, thousands of Catholics take part in fundamentalist Bible study groups and attend their rallies. The bishops have now publicly acknowledged the vast leakage of membership to these and other churches.[ii]

For over a decade, however, some zealous, informed Catholics have been producing a number of excellent handbooks to meet the challenge of the proselytizers. With his ardent concern for souls and his long years of pastoral experience, Fr. Fox has contributed a superlative addition to this crucial cause.

The book covers all the bases. After brief introductory notes on the historical background of the fundamentalist movement, an exposition of its methodology, and a survey of the major targets of

---

[ii]   This is still happening. Indeed, it is a widely held truism that a majority of many Evangelical and fundamentalist congregations are made up of lapsed Catholics. Estimates are that 30 percent of the Evangelical and Pentecostal churches membership in this nation are comprised of lapsed Catholics. According to a 1986 Gallup poll, a similar percentage of this nation's 17 million Hispanics are Protestant, with 64 percent of these coming from the Catholic Church.

This is not simply an American phenomenon either. In the world's largest Catholic country, Brazil, 15 percent are now Protestant. The figure is 20 percent in several other Latin American countries, and the figure is thought to be as high as 50 percent in Guatemala, which would make it Latin America's first majority Protestant country. Of course, in Europe, people have largely stopped practicing Christianity altogether, regardless of the denomination. Mass attendance in Ireland is still relatively strong, but even at 62 percent, it is drastically down (by over 20 points, according to some estimations; some surveys, however, put weekly Mass attendance at just 35 to 48 percent). Mass attendance over the last decade in Great Britain has dropped from 37 to 17 percent. Only 20 percent of people attend Mass in Germany. It is just 5 to 12 percent in France (depending on the survey).

its assault against Catholicism, the author admirably presents and vindicates the core doctrines of the Church. He tellingly exposes how the fundamentalists, with their vaunted insistence on literal biblical interpretation, have conveniently refused to apply this principle to the abundant pivotal passages that forcefully state the Church's case. In doing so, he discusses the authority and unity of the Church, the papacy, the Holy Eucharist, the sacramental system, the full splendor of sanctifying grace, true devotion to the Mother of Jesus, and more.

In most of the book, Fr. Fox addresses himself to the fundamentalists as respected and sincere Christian souls. He reveals extensive knowledge of "where they are coming from" and adapts much of their characteristic terminology. He states their arguments with courageous integrity. A striking feature of the book is the frequent, lengthy quotations of Jimmy Swaggart, who epitomizes the fundamentalists' contempt for the doctrines and institutions of Catholicism. The author's patient and charitable, but bluntly devastating, point-by-point rebuttal demonstrates apologetics at its best.

This is a big book, and I would recommend that anyone daunted by its dimensions should "sample" a chapter or two. I might particularly suggest the brilliant chapter on Mary, which is at once rigorously scriptural and sublimely lyrical, redolent of the tender love of the author, whose priestly life is consumed with the devotion to the Mother of Christ. Once the reader tastes such a "sample," it will be hard to resist devouring the volume from its beginning to an appendix, which offers responses in catechetical style to the polemical questions most often raised.

Fr. Fox does not disguise the fact that the greatest allies of the fundamentalists are all too often modernist priests and dissident theologians who have eviscerated the authentic doctrine of the Church and "demythologized" the inspired texts of Scripture, confusing the faithful to the brink of despair. But in his delicate charity, he does not explicitly indict the guilt of some converts to fundamentalism. Catholicism, correctly understood, is rigorous in its moral and disciplinary demands. Many Catholics today retain their attachment to religion but are allured by the false assurances of a once-for-all salvation that will cloak over their sins without the life-long struggles required by the sacramental means instituted by Christ, especially the humble confession of sin. The Church of Christ demands of her children that they work out their salvation without presumption and that they daily take up their crosses to follow the narrow way of the Master.

As noted, Fr. Fox addresses this book to fundamentalists. As such, Catholic pastors and friends should offer it to them. But in reality, the most important and wisest readership will be those good pastors and people who have never forgotten that the primary business of the Church is to "save souls."

PART V

Fr. Gilsdorf as Biblical Scholar

CHAPTER 40

GOSPEL PARADOXES[1]

The Servant-King

In St. John's Passion account, in the place we might least expect it, we discover the most powerful assertion of our Lord's kingship and authority. This paradox is one of several in the Gospels we will explore in the next few issues.

Because we hear it proclaimed solemnly each Good Friday, the text is so familiar that we may have overlooked this astounding theological statement: The King-Messiah (so patiently and eagerly longed for by the Jews) is, in fact, the Suffering Servant.

The Messianic prophecies in prophets and psalms gave a triumphalist portrait of one who would exercise royal might, gain conquering dominion, and usher in an era of prosperity and peace. In this reign, Israel would rule supreme, and naturally, such notions were easily accepted.

But the clusters of hymns in Isaiah concerning the Suffering Servant were equally valid, prophetic in the truest sense, yet their message became muffled, passed over in embarrassment or confusion. In fact, some liturgical translations (*targums*) even "corrected" the text's clear assertions.[i]

---

[i]   A *targum* was an Aramaic translation of the Old Testament. After the return from the Babylonian exile, ca. 538 BC, the use of Hebrew progressively fell into disuse, and Aramaic became the *lingua franca* of the Jewish people (although Hebrew was still the official liturgical language). The analogy would be the Church's continued use of Latin as its official language. The Jews effected Aramaic translations so that the people could understand the scriptures proclaimed in the synagogues during their liturgies. Of course, as

Since the Passion account is so familiar, a few words will suffice to highlight how both the King-Messiah and Suffering Servant are reconciled and fulfilled in Jesus. The reader can later read the full context in John 13:18-19. Meditation will then reinforce the few items listed here:

1. The mockery in the praetorium, where the soldiers robe Christ, bloodied by the scourging, in "royal" purple. They place a reed (used to beat Him) as a scepter in His hand. They crown Him with thorns. Having spit in His face, the jeering soldiers kneel and salute, "Hail, King of the Jews!"

2. There ensues the dialogue with Pilate: "You are, then, a king?" "You have said it. I am a king, for this was I born..." Pilate then displays Jesus in His pathetic regalia to the crowd, asking them, "What shall I do with your King?" Agitated by their religious leaders, the people retort, "We have no king but Caesar!"

3. Next comes the way of the Cross, a parody of a royal procession. Christ is enthroned and elevated—on a cross. The scroll above His head gives the cause of execution: "King of the Jews." When His enemies protest this declarative sign, Pilate, his hands freshly washed, gives the laconic reply, "What I have written, I have written."

What we shall call a "paradox" here, is an extended example of what Scripture scholars call "Johannine irony." There are many occasions in St. John where a statement, usually on the lips of the enemy, bears a double meaning that, to the faithful, yields a true but opposite sense never even considered by the speaker. As a result, the irony is drawn out and includes not only words but also dramatic actions. We cannot overlook the importance of this paradox for John.

Father alludes here, this occasionally led to corruption or bad translations, much as in our own day.

We should make one more pivotal point to which we will return: We more or less completely find the elements of kingship in the first three Gospels' Passion accounts as well. They are historical facts. John does not just dream these up to fit his theological perspective.

In this paradox, there is a profound and enduring lesson for all times. We can already see the root in Jesus' action at the Last Supper when He washes the feet of His apostles. He does here the menial task that slaves or servants performed. "You call Me Teacher and Lord; and you are right, for so I am. If I then, your Lord and Teacher, have washed your feet, you also ought to wash one another's feet. For I have given you an example, that you also should do as I have done to you. Truly, truly, I say to you, a servant is not greater than his master."[2]

Authority in the Church is exercised as a service and often enough as a suffering service. The hierarchical service of pope and bishops is a service of authority, that is, by teaching and governing ... "Teacher," "Lord." This office was poignantly evinced in the reign of Pope Paul VI, who was truly a suffering "servant of the servants of God."

With relentless speed, the role continues, and Pope John Paul II shows us he, too, is a true vicar of Jesus Christ. With courageous humility, he speaks with authority, not as the scribes and Pharisees. Once more, it is our present day scribes and Pharisees who frantically stir up the people to reject him and all he stands for. Of old, they said, "Jesus is an idealistic illusionary from provincial Galilee." Today, they say, "John Paul is a likeable illusionary from the Slavic ghetto—Catholicism."

Having said this, they take their polls and claim that so many are rebelling that the Pope has lost his authority. They well understand that if the Pope has no authority, why worry about the authority of any bishops? The assault from the beginning has been against the keys of the kingdom.

In this tempest of rebellion and dissidence, we need to gaze calmly again at the hours of the Passion. Did Christ lose His authority when Judas betrayed, when the apostles (His first priests and bishops) denied and abandoned Him? Did Christ lose His authority when His own people mocked Him or rejected His kingship? Did Christ nailed to the Cross lose His authority in the consummation of His death agony? Indeed, did Christ lose His authority in the tomb?

On the contrary, in this wonderful paradox, it is precisely here that the kingly authority of Jesus the Messiah triumphed over all opposition, even over death. If today the Pope (in union with faithful Catholics whom the pollsters facilely number as a small minority) exercises his authority as suffering servant, does he lose his authority?

On the contrary. The resurrection, the restoration of all things, divine vindication is near at hand. Heaven and earth will pass away, but the final judgment is for eternity, and of this kingdom, there is no end.

The Shepherd-Lamb

At the beginning of the Gospels, John the Baptist heralds Jesus: "Behold the Lamb of God." Later, in John 10, Christ explicitly identifies Himself: "I am the good Shepherd."

We have become accustomed to both titles from childhood, so much so that we may have never pondered the paradox. But let us look at the two: How can the Shepherd also be the Lamb?

Let us first look more closely at our Lord's self-description as Good Shepherd. The Jews would immediately have caught the prophetic messianic sense. Both the prophets and psalms foresaw the Messiah as the ideal shepherd of his people. Once Jesus speaks of the hireling (and He does so repeatedly), Ezekiel's long discourse would surely have flooded their minds and given them a fullness of context we can easily overlook.

For us, the hireling (who works only for pay, whose own the sheep are not, who turns tail at the prospect of peril) is just a kind of conventional literary foil against which to spotlight the ideal shepherd.

To get the full thrust of Ezekiel, one must read the whole, emotionally-charged Chapter 34, a bold invective against the bad shepherds of Israel. Toward the end of this indictment comes the splendid promise on the lips of Yahweh: "I, Myself, will be the shepherd of My sheep... I will seek the lost, and I will bring back the strayed... And I will set up over them one shepherd, My servant, David, and he shall feed them."

The promise of the Good Shepherd is set against the black background of treason and apostasy on the part of the religious leaders. God Himself will come, will visit His flock, and will serve as the good shepherd of His sheep.

In John 10, our Lord also shows us that the Church is His sheepfold. He makes the glorious promise: "Other sheep I have who are not of this fold; these also I must gather, and there shall be but one fold, one shepherd."

We note again that these are not contrived sayings put in the mouth of Jesus by John to create a theological premise. In his Gospel of mercy, Luke also gives us words of Jesus that stem from Isaiah and Ezekiel, and he sketches the tender picture of the shepherd seeking the one stray lamb and carrying it home on his shoulders.

Because of repeated use of pastoral imagery by Jesus in the Gospels, the rest of the New Testament shows the early Church already applying to her ministers the titles of shepherding. They are pastors of the Church; they are "overseers" (*episkopoi*, Greek for "bishops") of the flock.

It is commonplace in recent times to resent this imagery, idyllic and evocative as it is. "Mature Catholics," as they like to style themselves, prefer to shy away from the confines of the herd and corral. The ecclesial image of fold and flock are "time-conditioned," we're told, and need to be "reinterpreted into modern idiom." The People of God are now, after all, at long last conscious of their dignity and maturity. It will not do to tag such privileged souls as sheep. Sheep, it is said, are docile, if not imbecile. They are jostled about and mindlessly come and go at the bidding of their masters.

Yet Christ is Himself a Lamb! He not only laid down His life for His flock but also first "emptied Himself," taking on our nature. While we do not like to think about it, lambs in biblical times were prime designees to be sacrificial victims. While Mary cradled the Infant in the manger of a stable, the flocks of sheep around Bethlehem stood in the final staging area before functionaries led them to the Temple for sacrifice.

In John 19, we see that this was indeed the destiny of the Lamb of God. The Evangelist makes it plain that this is his vision of Christ on the Cross. The Good Shepherd has laid down His life for the sheep, but He dies as one of them, a Victim-Lamb. Christ bleeds on the Cross during the very hours of the Passover slaughter of lambs at the Temple. There the priests were lined up at the altar of sacrifice while lamb after lamb was slain—one for each household. Their work was fast and almost furious. According to legal norms, those who slaughtered the sheep drained the blood into vessels, which they then rapidly passed from priest to priest until at last they poured out the blood at the base of the altar.

By the time of Jesus, this Passover sacrifice, which memorialized the night of liberation in Egypt, had concentrated within itself all the themes of the liturgical feasts and all the motives of the other biblical sacrifices: atonement, adoration, thanksgiving, reconciliation, reparation, communion, and petition.

When St. Longinus pierced Christ's heart on the Cross, St. John, the theologian of the Sacred Heart, calls our attention to Exodus 12, the rubric of the annual sacrifice of the Passover Lamb. With extraordinary emphasis, John gives witness that the last drops of blood drained from the master's heart. His witness strikes home with the force of an oath. The significance of this is that the rabbinic writings tell us the priests broke open the heart of the Passover lamb to drain out the last reserve of blood.

In the last pages of the Bible, we encounter the Revelation theme—a Johannine theme—of the Lamb, epitomized in the central vision as slain, but standing. We see then that the Good Shepherd, who so loved His flock that He took on their nature in order to lay down His life for them, takes up that life again. In this, He sets the perfect model for all shepherds of His Church, and in a preeminent way to the one whom He commissioned to feed all His lambs and all His sheep.

The Priest-Victim

In the Old Testament, the priest who offered the sacrifice was distinct from the victim whose life-blood he offered. The priest usually imposed his hands on the victim.[3] The precise meaning of this liturgical gesture is contested. Some say it shows a simple declaration of ownership since the layperson who presented the victim sometimes performed the imposition: "This belongs to me, and I now offer it in sacrifice for my intention." Others hold for a sense of substitution: "I offer this life as a sign that I offer my own life wholly to You, Author and Sustainer of life." We cannot dismiss this notion.

At any rate, the specifically priestly role began later at the "receiving" (or catching) of the blood. If, however, the priest did impose hands, and if this was in the sense of vicarious substitution, this was the closest the priest of the Old Law came to identifying himself with the victim.[ii]

The Letter to the Hebrews most fully develops the priesthood of Christ and thus the New Covenant. It is implicit but clear throughout the New Testament as a whole. The eucharistic discourse of John 6 and the Last Supper institution formulas of the first three Gospels are vividly sacrificial in terminology. The Passover context fortifies this understanding of the Eucharist.

Even in the Infancy narrative, St. Luke uses priestly technical terms for the presentation of the Infant in the Temple. Thus, the Letter to the Hebrews merely makes explicit what was the conviction

---

[ii]   See Lev 16:20-22.

of the first followers of Jesus: He is the eternal High Priest and Mediator between God and man by His sacrifice.

We saw that the Jews expected a King-Messiah. The Semitic word *Messiah* translated into the Greek of the Gospels as *Christos*. Both mean "the anointed one." Soon the word became a proper name for Jesus though, some still refer to Him as "Jesus the Christ."

In the Old Testament, there were two anointed personages: the king and the priest. So it is not surprising to find a strong, new messianic current at the time of Christ. This asserted the Messiah would be both King and Priest (or even that there would be two Messiahs, one to fit each function).

What is truly new and constitutes one of the major paradoxes of the New Testament is that the Priest *is* the Victim. He no longer offers the blood of substitute animals, but He enters the Holy of Holies with His own Blood![4] The letters of Paul show this vision of the Blood of Christ. In one controverted passage,[5] where Christ is said to "be made sin," the more logical sense for Paul the Rabbi would be that Christ "is made sin-offering," the atonement sacrificial Victim. From our vantage, we see why one of the magi offered the newborn Messiah the bitter gift of myrrh.

We have already discussed the paradox of Shepherd-Lamb. All that has been said there of Jesus, the Lamb of God, reinforces this proclamation by the New Testament that our eternal High Priest is also the Victim who, on the altar of the Cross, offers His own Blood drained from His own Body as the unique and perfect Sacrifice of the new and everlasting Covenant.

Archbishop Sheen frequently repeated this epochal insight into the priesthood. Since Christ is both Priest and Victim, so must be His priesthood in the Church. Those who are priests today are "personal instruments" of the unique and indivisible priesthood of Christ, the sole Mediator. The Church has always taught that priests act *in persona Christi* ("in the person/place of Christ"). It is Jesus Himself who offers the one sacrifice.

Now the implications for priestly spirituality are enormous: The priests of the Church must also be sacrificial victims. The consequences of this victimhood, which is inseparable from the priestly ministry, were, of course, in Archbishop Sheen's mind. Goodbye "self-fulfillment." Goodbye "arbitrated assignments" and "grievance committees." Hello "obedience," hello "humility," "self-emptying," and "mortification."

While we speak first of the ministerial priesthood, we quickly extend this sound spirituality to every member of Christ's Body, the Church. All the baptized share in Christ's priesthood and are baptized into His death. How urgently our times require "victim souls."

We have now surveyed three of the major Gospel paradoxes: the King who was Suffering Servant, and the Shepherd who willed to become a Lamb of His flock so that, finally, the Priest might be Victim. Our King-Shepherd-Priest is at once our Servant-Lamb-Victim.

Is this, then, the end of the story? Do these paradoxes stand alone? A paradox is, after all, only an *apparent* contradiction. It seems an impossible assertion, but for one who holds the key, it is not. As we might expect from divine revelation, such a key that unlocks the mystery of our three paradoxes exists. Furthermore, the key constitutes a new and fourth paradox, which we will now consider.

The key

We have previously studied three "paradoxes" of the Gospels. Jesus the Messiah is King and Servant, Shepherd and Lamb, Priest and Victim. On first glance, the terms *seem* to be impossible pairs, but affirmed as they are in the inspired Word of God, we know that they find full compatibility in Christ.

If we put the paradoxes in these words, "The King *becomes* Servant, the Shepherd *becomes* Lamb, the Priest *becomes* Victim," we find ourselves a step closer to the resolution of the enigma. The key is, itself, a fourth paradox: the Word *becomes* Flesh. The second Person of the Trinity "empties Himself," assumes our nature, and "takes on the form of a slave, being born in the likeness of men."[6]

The key, then, is the Incarnation. Jesus is God-Man; true God assumes our lowly nature and becomes true man. In what theologians call the hypostatic union, the divine nature unites to the human nature in the one Person of Jesus Christ.

This is most apparent in the paradox of the Shepherd who becomes Lamb. A superior nature assumes a lower nature while ever remaining Shepherd. This is true also of Priest-Victim since the victim was of a lower nature than the offerer.

But here there is no substitution. Rather, there is identification. In the King-Servant paradox, we see a higher dignity condescending to assume a lower function. The hymn of Philippians 2 again comes to mind: "He emptied Himself, taking on the form of a slave...." But in context, it is evident that for all three paradoxes, the Incarnation is the key.

There is another very timely lesson for us in the area of interpretation of the Gospels. While discussing the King-Servant theme, we noted that John was presenting an intricate theological statement on the reality and nature of Christ's kingship. But, we pointed out, he did not invent or concoct episodes to do so. As a witness, John was closest of the evangelists to the detailed events he records, which are historical facts, not "myths." The three synoptic evangelists include much the same factual material in their Passion accounts. The difference lies in the editing done by John. He marshals the facts and stresses them, thus making as clear as possible his inspired understanding of the kingship of Jesus, which remained less explicit in the synoptics.

From the modern approach of form criticism there is a spin-off method called redaction criticism. The latter is a study of what the editor (redactor) did with the source material from which all the Gospels were composed and why he did it. What was his original contribution, his personal theological message? John's use of the material, as indicated above, serves as an example.

Form criticism (with all its spin-offs), however, is good news and bad news—and "bad news" should have nothing to do with the Gospel! Church authorities have granted that some insights of this modern approach are valid and useful, but they have pointed out grave errors and inherent pitfalls in the process. An anti-supernatural and anti-historical bias in many of its prominent practitioners vitiates the premises, applications, and conclusions of form criticism. The Pontifical Biblical Commission has, therefore, set the limits within which faithful Catholic scholars are free to use the method.[7]

We cannot here review all the arguments against the abuses of form criticism, but let us observe from our study of the paradoxes just one point.

Simply because we detect a deep theological theme underlying any text of the Gospels in no way makes us suppose that the evangelist (redactor) contrived events and forged statements to force-fit his theme. On the contrary, we must assume that he has used raw historical data, and that God inspired him to lead us to their deeper sense. We assume God intended this deeper sense, this fulfillment, and that Christ so spoke and acted that the inspired writers had only to show us its significance.

There are many such theological themes in the Gospels, and the trend now is to dismiss the supporting facts as inventions of the sacred authors in order to present the "developed" beliefs of the "community." These creative ideas of post-Resurrection Christianity are "myths," they tell us, and so to get down to the historical skeleton, we must "demythologize."

After the scholarly piranhas have finished their work, only a few scattered chewed-up bones are left. The Infancy narratives are but the first targets of this anti-historical (and ultimately anti-supernatural) zealotry. Some sincere Catholics who too readily concede this first assault find to their discomfort that not just the Infancy narratives but also the whole fabric of the Gospels are also "theologized" and must then be demythologized—mysteries, miracles, and, with them, the cornerstone of the Resurrection.

But this is preposterous. The faithful know that Sacred Scripture has the Holy Spirit as its primary Author. To assume that anyone but Jesus of Nazareth fulfilled these themes in the words and deeds of His life and that anyone but the Holy Spirit inspired the recording evangelists to discern this fullness of revealed truth would lead us to a question that not one of the demythologizers has ever faced.

Just who were these anonymous spiritual, literary, and theological giants who conceived such sublime vistas of immortal beauty? No one identifies these surpassing geniuses, who, as individuals, conjured up these masterpieces in the womb of primitive Christianity and yet did so in such a way that their separate creations stand harmonized and unified in the mosaic of the New Testament. The believing Christian calmly names the revealing God who fulfilled and inspired.

PART VI

FR. GILSDORF ON OUR LADY

CHAPTER 41

OUR LADY APPEARED IN GREEN BAY, WISCONSIN, AS ... MOTHER AND TEACHER[1]

About 15 miles north of the Wisconsin city of Green Bay, in the heart of what is called the "Belgian peninsula" and just a few miles from the first historical immigrant Belgian colony (now called Champion but commonly known by its earlier name of Robinsonville), there stands a small, unpretentious brick chapel. Nestled amongst the farms, it stands on the spot Our Lady chose to appear over 100 years ago, where she gave a message seemingly reserved just for our times.

Every Sunday of every month, the "Chapel," as it is known, fills with devout people who have traveled miles here since 1970 to participate in the Rosary Crusade Holy Hour. Here they renew their faith and adjust their spiritual bearings by praying the Rosary, hearing sermons, singing hymns, and worshiping the Christ in Benediction. In May, there is also a special annual Mass, a eucharistic procession around the small grounds, and Benediction with the Blessed Sacrament.

The great celebration of the year

But the great celebration of the year is the Feast of the Assumption. On this day, a thousand or more assemble from near and far in pilgrimage as they have for over a century. The priest celebrates the principal Mass of the day at an outdoor altar. Now and then, the bishop or a prominent diocesan official is the chief celebrant. A eucharistic procession follows Mass. Participants recite the Rosary, sing hymns, and engage in eucharistic adoration and benediction. The procession winds along the fences of the chapel land, a fact that reminds older pilgrims of an event we will mention later.

And all this is but a faint image of more faith-filled days when many thousands of pilgrims assembled, often having made their way on foot through the night of the vigil. Why? Ask any one of these pilgrims, past or present, and they would tell you a story that is unique in the annals of Church history in the United States.

The story

On October 9, 1859, a year after the apparitions of the Blessed Mother at Lourdes, a young Belgian lady, Adèle Brice, age 28, was walking to the gristmill at Robinsonville with a sack of wheat on her head. Her journey of some four miles followed an old Indian trail. The land was newly settled, and the countryside was still a wilderness of hills and forest.

In this second week of October, the Wisconsin woods were ablaze with the scarlet and gold of autumn. At a spot where the chapel now stands, Adèle was astounded to see a beautiful lady dressed in white looking at her from between two trees, a maple and a hemlock. After several awe-inspiring minutes, the vision disappeared, leaving for a moment a cloud of white mist. Shaken, Adèle finished her errand and returned home. There she told her parents of her experience, and they conjectured that it might be a poor soul in need of prayer.

On the following Sunday, accompanied by her sister Isabel and a neighbor lady, Adèle took the same trail on the way to Mass. The nearest church then was at Bay Settlement, 11 miles distant. At the exact spot as before, the lady in white appeared again. Adèle exclaimed in agitation, "Oh! There is that lady again!" Her companions saw nothing, but they witnessed the fear that visibly gripped Adèle. Again, the vision remained a few minutes and then disappeared in a white cloud.

After Mass, Adèle went to confession to the pioneer missionary, Fr. William Verhoeff, OSC. She told him about the lady and sought his advice. He asked her to speak about it outside the confessional. (Adèle herself gives this information.) Fr. Verhoeff told her that if the messenger was from heaven, it would not harm her, and she should not be afraid. She should ask "in God's name who it was and what it desired of her." Then the three women made their way home accompanied by a man of the parish.

Let us now, for the sake of accuracy, follow verbatim the account of Sr. Pauline La Plant, who often heard Adèle tell her the story as a child and who has providentially recorded the event for posterity. Sr. M. Dominica, OSF, wrote an excellent and thorough history of the Chapel that relates this account:

> As they approached the hallowed spot, Adèle could see the beautiful lady, clothed in dazzling white, with a yellow sash around her waist. Her dress fell to her feet in graceful folds. She had a crown of stars around her head, and her long, golden, wavy hair fell loosely over her shoulders; such a heavenly light shone around her that Adèle could hardly look at her sweet face. Overcome by this heavenly light and the beauty of her amiable visitor, Adèle fell on her knees. "In God's name, who are you, and what do you want of me?" asked Adèle, as Father had directed her.
>
> "I am the Queen of Heaven, who prays for the conversion of sinners, and I wish you to do the same. You received Holy Communion this morning, and that is well, but you must do more. Make a general confession and offer Communion for the conversion of sinners. If they do not convert and do penance, my Son will be obliged to punish them."
>
> "Adèle, who is it?" said one of the women. "O, why can't we see her as you do?" said another, weeping.
>
> "Kneel," said Adèle. "The Lady says she is the Queen of Heaven."

Our Blessed Lady turned, looked kindly at them, and said, "Blessed are they that believe without seeing."

"What are you doing here in idleness," continued Our Lady, "while your companions are working in the vineyard of my Son?"

"What more can I do, dear Lady?" said Adèle, weeping.

"Gather the children in this wild country and teach them what they should know for salvation."

"But how shall I teach them who know so little myself?" replied Adèle.

"Teach them their catechism," replied her radiant visitor, "how to sign themselves with the sign of the Cross, and how to approach the sacraments; that is what I wish you to do. Go and fear nothing; I will help you."[2]

Sr. Dominica concludes the story: "Wrapped as it were in a luminous atmosphere, Our Lady lifted her hands as though she were beseeching a blessing for those at her feet. Slowly, she vanished from sight, leaving Adèle overwhelmed and prostrate on the ground and the dense woods as solemn as before."

Contemporary accounts tell how joyously and energetically Adèle fulfilled this mission entrusted to her by Our Lady. She often made her way through the forests as far north as Little Sturgeon, some 50 miles from home. She suffered from rain and cold, from the driving Wisconsin snow, from fatigue, and from the ridicule of those blind to the signs of divine grace. The little lady with rather homely features (one side of her face was slightly disfigured) went from house to house, taking on chores without being asked, and all she requested in return was permission to instruct the children in the rudiments of the Faith.

Sr. Pauline wrote, "I remember well as a child; she would come with her little band of children to Bay Settlement, kneel at the foot of Our Lady's altar, and sing hymns with them in French... I would kneel behind her with a burning desire to follow her... [So] many times we would gather around Adèle and have her tell us of the apparitions of our Blessed Mother. She would always tell us in the self-same way how she saw her twice without Our Lady saying a word, but that the third time she spoke to her and gave her the message of instructing the children in their religion, lest they should lose their faith."

What was the Church's attitude?

What was the Church's attitude? In such cases, there is usually an official investigation by Church authorities, following which the diocesan ordinary (i.e., bishop) either accepts the claimed apparitions as genuine (in the sense of allowing the faithful to put human credence in them) or rejects them as spurious.

The so-called "Chapel" visions are unique in this because the diocese never instigated a canonical investigation. Thus, no one has ever pronounced official ecclesiastical approval or disapproval. By the same token, the bishops of Green Bay never discouraged the faith and piety that Adèle's claims aroused in the vast majority of the people.

On the contrary, this credence was greatly, if tacitly, stimulated by the participation of the bishops and high diocesan officials in the annual pilgrimages to the chapel subsequently built over the ground where Adèle claimed Mary touched the soil of Wisconsin with her motherly feet.

Only for a short interlude was there a problem, long since forgotten, when a bishop temporarily banned the August 15 pilgrimage because of the scandal of commercialism and the carnival (or should we say "Kermiss"?) atmosphere created by hawkers who took advantage of the crowds for personal gain.[i] Once the scandal was eliminated, the pilgrimages resumed as before.

---

[i]   In his book *The History of the Belgian Settlements in Door, Kewaunee and Brown Counties* (Brussels, WI: Belgian-American Club, 1974), Math S. Tlachac describes the Kermiss this way: "After the harvesting had been completed, it was customary for the people in Belgium to attend Mass to give thanks to the Lord for a bountiful harvest. This was followed by feasting and dancing. Some of the Belgians are musically talented, and in most every community where a Kermiss was observed, a local band was formed to play

Therefore, it seems safe to believe in this truly wonderful visitation of the Mother of God and the vital message she delivered in the deep woods of the rugged "Belgian peninsula." While there are many Marian shrines in the United States, including the massive National Shrine of the Immaculate Conception in Washington, DC, here, in a modest chapel in the heartland of our nation, there gently burns the tradition of a genuine apparition of Our Lady—which took place just a year and a half after Lourdes!

Let us now consider its two-fold message.

First, there is an ominous note, coming from the motherly Queen of Prophets.

> Make a general confession and offer Communion for the conversion of sinners. If they do not convert and do penance, my Son will be obliged to punish them.

We encounter here a refrain found in all modern apparitions of Mary and with what striking intensity if we consider the vision of hell shown the children at Fátima! But what of Our Lady of Green Bay? Here again the events prove unique and have, I believe, a "multiple fulfillment" (to borrow a phrase from the exegetes). In the annals of American history, the great Peshtigo fire ranks as one of the most tragic and destructive of its kind. This fire raged to the west of the Bay, gradually building up to what was described as a "hurricane of fire," and it ravaged land, buildings, cattle, and people.

On October 8, 1871, a violent wind, which some say swept the fire over the waters of the Bay, ignited the Peninsula for miles, engulfing acres of fields and forest. The wind of fire roared out of a deathly silence on that day, driving hundreds of families from their homes, destroying everything in its path (including many people). And the Chapel stood squarely in its path.

---

at dances. The Kermiss usually lasted three days." Keep in mind that the Green Bay area has a very large concentration of descendants of Belgian immigrants.

Safe in Mary's chapel

Instinctively, the people ran to the Chapel with Adèle. Here they would take their refuge and make their final stand. Here they awaited what many truly believed to be the end of the world. They prayed and kept vigil all night while the storm of fire raged around them. Then, toward the morning of October 9, the twelfth anniversary of the apparitions, there came a torrential rain that soon extinguished the conflagration.

After prayers of thanksgiving, the harried people went outside. The Chapel's grounds stood fresh and green. All that lay outside the holy precincts was smoldering and charred. When the people examined the fences of the ground, they discovered that the outsides were charred, but the sides facing the Chapel were untouched.

Is there any need to spell out the lesson? Was this not, perhaps, a small-scale rehearsal of warning of the "annihilation of entire nations" spoken of later by Mary at Fátima? And at any rate, is it also not a great promise of hope to those who take refuge in Mary in this world now smoldering in sin and blasphemy? May we not have full confidence under the mantle of the Refuge of Sinners?

The second part of the Green Bay message is equally urgent and equally prophetic. Once it had meaning for just one small area, but now it applies to the whole nation, a nation dedicated to Mary Immaculate.

Listen to it again:

> Gather the little children in this wild country and teach them what they should know for salvation... Teach them their catechism, how to sign themselves with the sign of the Cross, and how to approach the sacraments; that is what I wish you to do. Go and fear nothing.

And add to it the precious comment of Sr. Pauline, no doubt enshrining in her memory a further remark of Mary to Adèle: "The third time she spoke to her and gave her the message of instructing the children in their religion, lest they should lose their faith."

Fr. Robert Fox has frequently spoken of Our Lady of Fátima as "Mary the Catechist." That is a powerful insight! And reflection on the manifold modern day apparitions of Mary shows clearly that this is a prime motive of her visits: Mary comes as Mother and Teacher, *Mater et Magistra*. As Mother and Model of the Church, she looks upon her ignorant and confused (but so tenderly loved) children and longs to have them "learn their catechism, lest they lose their faith."

See how simply her few heavenly words cut through the forest-like sophistry of so much of the present, almost demonic confusion of tongues passing for "religious education." Our Lady of Green Bay is preeminently "Mary the Catechist." Here alone in modern apparitions she *explicitly* defines catechetics as her message and mission. Her words are for America and for the world today. The few specific items she gives—basic prayers, sacramental preparation, doctrine that must be learned and taught—are, incredibly, hardly deemed worthy of attention today in certain professional religious educational circles. The phrase "for salvation," the word "catechism," and even the concern about "losing their faith," these are now taboo in more than a few areas.

She conquers by her gentle presence

The appearance of the Messenger herself confronts and demolishes the assumptions of revived modernism. It is no wonder that those infected with modernism studiously ignore apparitions and miracles, for once we admit that the supernatural has asserted itself in our world, the whole materialist, secular-humanist, evolutionist, and agnostic construct collapses like the sand castle it is. Admit La Sallette, Lourdes, Fátima, or the Chapel at Green Bay, and the Woman has conquered![ii] And she does so by mere gentle presence.

[ii] Mary has often been seen as the "woman" of Scripture (cf., Gen 3:15; John 2:4; Rev 12:1).

We are much like the companions of Adèle, who do not personally see. But the comment of Mary to Adèle applies also to us: "Blessed are they who believe without seeing." The mission is now ours to pursue, and it is more urgent than ever before: "Teach the little children." And for those who feel unqualified to teach their holy Faith to others (as Adèle did): "Go and fear nothing; I will help you."

CHAPTER 42

WOMAN AMONG ALL WOMEN[i]

Besides revealing a relative independence from magisterial moorings, the recently issued Catholic bishops' pastorals on peace and the economy also signaled a stylistic departure from previous pastorals, and this may likely become a precedent for the future.[ii]

Namely, they exposed a division between binding, magisterial doctrine and non-binding, unofficial majority opinion. This has resulted in confusion for the less-than-careful readership and in exploitation by biased educators seeking to equate the two.

In the first draft of the pastoral on women, "Partners in the Mystery of Redemption,"[iii] methodology has degenerated even further: A pastoral has now become "reportorial." Witness the indiscriminate, nonjudgmental raw quotations of the so-called "voices of alienation" and acid complaints almost entirely from the radical feminist camp. Although these "voices" challenged the Church's perennial teachings and firmly stated decisions, they go untouched by any effective comment or disclaimer. Elsewhere,

---

[i] This originally appeared in the May 1989 issue of *The Mindszenty Report*, named after the remarkable Servant of God József Cardinal Mindszenty (d. 1975) and dedicated to promoting his memory and the cause for his canonization.

[ii] The US Conference of Catholic Bishops issued "Economic Justice for All" in 1986, and "The Challenge of Peace: God's Promise and Our Response in 1983." As noted by George Weigel and *First Things* editor Fr. Richard John Neuhaus, both documents demonstrated a tendency to make unqualified, absolute claims outside the bishops' main area of competence, faith, and morals. In recent years, the bishops have largely gotten away from this.

[iii] This pastoral was so problematic that the full body of bishops never approved it.

passages on key matters (contraception, women's ordination, and so on) receive evasive treatment, which could provide opponents with a subliminal undermining of the papal positions.

Contrast this draft document with John Paul II's long-awaited apostolic letter, *Mulieris Dignitatem* (On the Dignity and Vocation of Women), dated August 15, 1988, Feast of the Assumption, the closing of the Marian year, which became public in October 1988. We now have on the table a papal document and the National Conference of Catholic Bishops' (NCCB) draft pastoral on the same volatile topic. One focuses on Mary, the other Eve. The draft has undergone revisions, and the diocesan listening sessions have ground through the now-familiar process. In reference to the Pope's letter, a member of the drafting committee has said of "Partners" that "we are in agreement on every point."

I beg to differ.

I hasten to say I am aware the second draft of the pastoral has now been completed. After complaints from women, the title no longer names them "Partners"; now they are "Friends." Also, the "voices of alienation" have been dropped, and there has been some firming up on those contested passages. Yet our earlier remarks are justified.

The fact remains that the select drafting committee that produced the defective "Partners" published it far and wide *moto proprio*[iv] and allowed the media to misrepresent it as a final document of the NCCB. Furthermore, it did all this before review and critique by the body of bishops, whose national meeting was only a short time away. It seemed like a rush job to pre-empt criticism.[v]

There are several points worth making:

[iv]   i.e., "on their own initiative."

[v]   Indeed, the April 25, 1988, edition of *TIME* noted that the draft "was written by a panel of six bishops chaired by Joseph Imesch of Joliet, Ill., with the assistance of five scholars and two staffers—all women." It also repeatedly referred to what "the bishops" as a body had said with this document without any acknowledgment that this was a draft—and only a draft—and thus had no standing or force. And of course, absent the will of the individual diocesan ordinary, these documents have no juridical force.

1. The Pope insists that Mary, Virgin and Mother, is the obligatory model of Christian feminism.
2. The papal letter comes as a doctrinal coronation of the Marian year.
3. It is consistently based on scriptural anthropology.
4. The axial concept of complementarity is insisted in this eloquent assertion of "the original unity of man and woman."
5. It builds on John Paul's epochal "Theology of the Body" and sections of *Redemptoris Mater* (Mother of the Redeemer), the inaugural encyclical of the Marian year.
6. It introduces several new insights: e.g., that male and female are "mutually subject" to the dominion of Christ.

First, then, let us review the revealed scriptural and anthropological data.

Where to begin? I suppose there is no place like the "beginning," the real beginning, *bereshith*[vi] (i.e., Gen 1:26): "Let us make man in Our own image."

In 1:27, we read, "So God created man in His own image, in the image of God He created him; male and female He created them. And God blessed them, and God said to them: 'Be fruitful and multiply and fill the earth and subdue it and have dominion over the birds of the air and every living thing that moves upon the earth' ... And God saw that it was very good."

This look of God was a look of infinite love for what was good. He loved all creation, but above all, He loved man, male and female. Before further comments, let us remember that Genesis 2 gives us a second creation account. This time, Genesis 2 highlights the specific creation of woman:

7. v. 21 "So the Lord God caused a deep sleep" and took a rib from Adam's side.

[vi]   This is the Hebrew word for Genesis, i.e., "In the beginning."

8. v. 22 "and the rib which the Lord God had taken from the man He made into a woman and brought her to the man."
9. v. 23 "Then the man (*ish*) said, 'This at last is bone of my bones and flesh of my flesh; she shall be called woman (*ishshah*) because she was taken out of man.'"
10. v. 25 "Therefore, a man leaves his father and mother and cleaves to his wife, and they become one flesh."

In our days, we can never again read these texts without hearing the resonance of the exalted and profound teaching of John Paul II's "Theology of the Body."[vii] I admit I asked at the time, "Why?" Why devote several years of weekly addresses (in effect publishing a book by installments) to how God wrote the nuptial language of the body into our very beings? With all the doctrinal and disciplinary crises in the Church, why this?!

Now with "Partners" squarely confronted by *Mulieris Dignitatem*, I think I have a partial answer. He has discussed this because the anthropological crisis undergirds all other crises.[viii] I should have realized from the start: The *Holy Spirit* moved the Pope, and we, in our own time, have gradually begun to see the full reason for this prophetic emphasis on the Theology of the Body.

[vii] Starting in 1979 and continuing through 1984, the Servant of God John Paul II dedicated each of his weekly General Audiences to the topic of "Theology of the Body," a theme he had worked at developing for over 20 years. The basic thrust in this development of Church teaching is that nothing about the way in which God created man and woman is accidental or random or arbitrary. There are profound reasons for men being men and women being women. Our bodies have specific meanings, and these communicate very powerful truths about God and our relationship with Him, His love for us, and our purpose in life. Indeed, our bodies are the key to unlocking the very meaning of life. An excellent source of information on this body of teaching is the Theology of the Body Institute (www.tobinstitute.org).

[viii] Keep in mind that anthropology concerns human nature, especially as contrasted with the nature of God. If we get God wrong, we get humanity wrong. And if we get humanity wrong, we get everything else wrong.

Now for a few comments on the text. God created man (Adam). Here "man" indicates the nature. Then we read that "male and female He created them." In other words, our one human nature has a two-fold expression. There is a radical equality but not identity.

Thus, there exists in mankind a two-fold complementarity. We were created in God's "image and likeness," and to us He gives dominion: "Let them have dominion." Here, too, there is equality. This image and likeness entails sexual differentiation, but I would include the traditional exegesis that it also refers to intellect and free will. How else could God entrust dominion to them?

Here we see the mystery of the Godhead mirrored in "man." The "image and likeness" is a Trinitarian reflection, the room of all "communion," the analogue of the equality, and differentiation among the Persons of the Trinity.

In Genesis 2, we learn about what Pope John Paul calls the "original solitude" of man. What a dramatic, haunting scenario! Here the sacred author shows us one solitary human standing on the newborn earth, surrounded by the vast universe. Man cries out for his complement.

We note the derivative origin of woman. Adam is *ish*, she is *ishshah* (i.e., taken from man). But understand, this derivation is not demeaning. On the contrary! Adam is from the dust; Eve is from man, a far nobler origin. She is not from the lower elements but from *ish*. Again, the sacred author shows and stresses equality of nature.

Finally, in verse 24, God declares the nuptial meaning of this complementarity: The two shall become one flesh, and this communion shall institute the primordial family. This echoes the words of Genesis 1:28, which reads, "Be fruitful and multiply, and fill the earth and subdue it." We could not have a more clear statement of the inseparable bonds of love that live in spousal communion.

Before moving on, let us take one last glance. We see how Genesis 3:20 links the name Eve to life. The woman is the "mother of all the living."

Divine revelation cuts through the sophistry of our muddled days: Equality in dignity but not identity. One in nature, diverse in function; equal but different. The more one explores the Holy Father's "Theology of the Body," the more one appreciates the mystery of the distinct spousal "gifts," that vast gamut of the positive and fruitful complementarity, which encompasses also the psychological, intellectual, affective, emotional, and truly spiritual dimensions of human nature.

Those today who demand sameness in every respect (and call this equality) destroy womanhood. The amazons do not really hate man they hate woman. They despise *being* women. They tell the whole world they regard men as superior *per se.* They reveal a self-destructive inferiority complex. They believe the only way to be equal to man in dignity is to be equal or identical to him in identity. In the "battle of the sexes," they concede the victory to the males.

This attempt to eradicate all differences is an effort to "masculinize" women. Hence, the remarkably strong lesbian presence in radical feminism is a dead giveaway. Radical feminism's perversion also reveals itself when it so readily allies itself to anti-life and homophile causes. Here we see the bared, cloven hoof.

How far has this revolution progressed? When some Catholic religious women flaunt their pathetic secularity, mouth pro-abortion and homosexual anti-gospels, rage against their Mother the Church, and vilify the person of Christ's vicar … the reflection of the demonic in the pool of their actions freezes the heart.

With the fraudulent promise of liberation, the father of lies tempted the first woman, Eve. (The psychoanalysis of Genesis is matchless!) It is woman who speaks for all creation, freely to assent or dissent. When Eve, lured by the prospect of being equal to God, rebelled against His will, the stark and sudden results were enslavement, alienation, and death for body and soul. The cosmos of Genesis 1 and 2 reverted to the chaos of Chapter 3.

In our waning century, the surrogate of Satan, his godless apocalyptic beast, stalks out one constituency after another. It "raises their consciousness," convinces them that God is the tyrant, that the

Church, His kingdom on earth, is the prison, and that its leaders and faithful believers are the slave-masters. The beast then promises liberation. And all it asks in return is for them to rebel against their religion, against revealed truth. As one pundit put it, "Women—offended, 'hurt' by the Pope, the Church, and the Bible—seek power, not equality." Their goal is "empowerment" in ministry and theology.

The phenomenon of the "women's liberation movement" should cause us to shudder in admiration of the perverting power of demonic intellect. Here we witness a jugular strike at creation itself: woman, family, human life, and chaste procreation. Genetic scrambling is a symbol of it all. Next comes an incursion into the sacred precincts of consecrated religious women and thereby an assault against the whole order, discipline, and faith of the Church.

Referring to the life led by some women religious, we learn of some cases hardly discernible from those of radical feminists: worship of the goddess, witchcraft, Wicca, the Eucharist invalidly consecrated by "priestesses," lesbianism, women's ordination, and pro-abortion activism. Of course, there are also documented suggestions of covens in the convent. The instrument orchestrating this primeval revolution is the Marxian beast, but the personal source of the power and cunning is the same as in Eden.

"In the beginning" (i.e., Genesis), he was the serpent; in the end (Revelation), he is the red dragon.[ix] We must see clearly that the two recent Vatican declarations on liberation theology[1] respond not only to political but also to all "liberation" fronts. So-called women's liberation emerged from the more extensive sexual revolution of which gay liberation and abortion rights are spin-offs. Priests and male religious have also constructed their own infrastructures for liberation from the Petrine keys.

Our Lady clearly prophesied these revolutionary ferments at Fátima:

---

ix   Actually, the Hebrew word *nahash* used for "serpent" in Genesis can be translated as "dragon."

> Russia will spread her errors throughout the world, fomenting war and revolutions.

Given how she described these errors, we see that their precise definition is "dialectic materialism." We should meditate on this deeply: What do we see increasing in every aspect of Church life in the West? We see materialism, secular humanism, the denial of the spiritual, and the rejection of the supernatural order.

Is this not purely and simply a denial of the transcendent God and His grace? And how do they implement such an apostasy?

Recall that "dialectic" is a cognate of "dialogue," a word now twisted by the Enemy to mask his *non serviam*." Once the constituencies are roused to class struggle, we again hear that ancient cry, "I will not serve! I will not obey!" [x]

Then there is consciousness-raising, which is the chief stratagem in what is called the "theory of rising expectation," a social theory

---

[x]   We often hear from those who dissent from the Church's teachings of their bewilderment over the Church's refusal to "dialogue" with them. "Ok, you don't agree with us, but why won't you at least dialogue with us? What's wrong with dialogue?" Of course, they do not actually seek dialogue but capitulation. And because they do not receive capitulation, they respond with *non serviam*. Witness the case of "Bishop" Pat Friesen. A Dominican nun, she burned to be a priest. In graduate classes in Rome, she even insisted in sitting in the confessor's chair during mock sacrament of penance exercises with her male priest classmates. But both Paul VI and John Paul II definitively shut the door on the possibility of her ever attaining her dream. By her own admission, she raged at this "discrimination," and, when the opportunity presented itself, consented to being illicitly ordained to Holy Orders. Then, she says a retired bishop approached her and offered to bestow upon her episcopal consecration. Now she goes around the world ordaining women to the priesthood. Because the Church would not capitulate, she said, "*Non serviam*" to the Church, to whom alone Christ gave the power to bind and loose (cf. Matt 16:18-19 and 18:18; 1 Tim 3:15). The ironic thing about Friesen and her group, Roman Catholic Womenpriests [sic], is that she says they are "non-hierarchical, non-clerical, and inclusive." And yet she ostensibly is a bishop (which implies hierarchy) who ordains clerics, and they have failed to include Scripture or the Magisterium in their considerations.

originally applied to political revolutionary situations. Compare this to the questions of celibacy and women's ordination. When we open Pandora's Box, we will find ourselves face to face with the specter of an "anti-creation." We will find ourselves transported back to "Paradise Lost" and reminded of the original sin—the ultimate rebellion. We will see pathological attempts to feminize terms regarded as "patriarchal."

People who should know better are milking dislocated texts that attribute to Yahweh spiritual maternal qualities to insist, "She is our Mother." It is beneath contempt that some who have theological degrees actually seize on the grammatical gender of certain words (*ruach, racham, rechem,* or *chochmah*) to establish a female biological gender.[xi] The feminist campaign to expunge the divine title of Father is a dead giveaway.

Apparently, their only understanding of gender is its earthly human, corporal, genital expression. They seem not to have the slightest hint of the sublimity conveyed by the supreme expression of paternity, that divine, purely spiritual, transcendent generation from which all fatherhood on earth derives its name.

The human male analogously reflects the reality of God's fatherhood in its purest spiritual essence. All men and all women are sons and daughters of this one Father. The core of the Son's revelation, as so many contemporary exegetes have insisted, is *"Abba-Abbenu."*[xii]

Let us add one more consideration as we mention the New Testament. If Jesus, the eternal "Son" of God, elects to appear as

---

[xi]   For those of us who speak English, it is hard to keep in mind that virtually every other language has both masculine and feminine tenses in its grammar. This is certainly true with Hebrew. These words Father references—*ruach* (breath, spirit), *racham* (mercy, compassion), *rechem* (womb, because God's mercy is "wombful" in its protection, and in being merciful, God gives birth to something new; see Deut 4:31), and *chochmah* (wisdom)—are all feminine in tense.

[xii]   *Abba* is Aramaic for Father, and some say it is the equivalent to our "daddy" or "papa." *Abbenu* also means "our Father."

male when made incarnate in time, should this not give pause to those who trifle with the title of "Father"?

At this point, it is necessary to insist that there are, in fact, two diametrically opposed feminisms. We have dwelt on the revolutionary liberationist feminism of the anti-creation, which when pursued to its logical end is atheistic and nihilistic. However, we herald the dawn of a new Christian feminism, which centers on Mary.

Mary, *mediatrix* of graces, is mother and virgin; the Church is mother and virgin.[xiii] Mary is full of grace; the Church is and must ever be "full of grace."

On the other hand, those apostate sectors—still calling themselves Catholic but who are secularized and reject the supernatural order—are proven to be cancerous, schismatic, and, indeed, non-Catholic. They are no longer "full of grace"; they are grace-less.

Note that these antibodies (which represent whole sectors within but no longer of the Church) begin instinctively by rejecting Mary and extinguishing devotion to her [note how they began with the Rosary, starting shortly after World War II and accelerating with a vengeance after the Council]. They have evicted the Mother from our family home, the Church. Theirs is a motherless church. It is precisely in these Mary-less zones that radical feminism germinates. We can understand this and every other disorder in the Church in the light of the truth that "Mary does for the Church what a mother does for the home."

What does a mother do that makes a house a home? Among many other things, she brings:

> love, tenderness, warmth, beauty, radiance, order,
> cleanliness, purity, nourishment, clothing, healing, care,
> nursing, defense, shelter, refuge, peace, reconciliation,

---

xiii   To understand the concept of Mary as mediatrix of all graces, it is best to read Fr. William Most's article on the subject at www.ewtn.com/faith/teachings/marya4.htm.

harmony, devotion, piety, fidelity, unity, smiles, laughter, joy ...

Mary brings all this and more to the Church. Think what is lost when some evict her from their spiritual lives! The most powerful and effective remedy for the ills in the Church will be for women of faith to vigorously restore devotion to Mary in their homes and parishes and, we must not fail to add, in their convents! Religious Sisters are the special reflections of Mary among us. They must work with her to do all those things that mothers do for our home in the Church, the family of God.

Mary is the Woman of assent and of faith; the true Church will always be the Church of assent. Again, the counter-Church is known for its endemic dissent. The Church is the parlor of familial dialogue but never the arena of dialectics. Catholic dialogue can never be filibuster as Fr. Jaki once remarked. The Catholic says *fiat*; the modernist says *non serviam*. *Fiat* is the key to salvation.[xiv]

In creating all things visible and invisible, God pronounced *fiat*. The first woman was tested by a fallen angel and spoke dissent, and all the living became ever after cursed as a result. An angel of the Lord tested the Woman of the Gospel, who in turn voiced assent, and all the living became ever after blessed. Mary's assent was to the redemption. The redemption is the Christian liberation.

By her *fiat*, Mary assented to the truth, and the Truth incarnate made her free and gave mankind the keys to the kingdom that unlocks the chains of ancient bondage through her. Mary, then, is the liberated and liberating woman.

In the spiritual sphere, man depends on the image of woman, her leadership, and her "ministry of intercession" to initiate him into

---

xiv   Theologians speculate that when Satan fell, he said, "*Non serviam*" ("I will not serve")! In other words, he would not do God's will. He chose his own way over God's, which is the essence of sin. St. Luke in his Gospel tells us that when the Angel Gabriel appeared to Mary and presented her with God's plan of having the Word made Flesh conceived within her, she responded, "*Fiat mihi*" ("Let it be done unto me").

the spiritual life. Woman—the model of creation (responding to the covenant of the Creator), the life-giver—is the voice of consent, of communion.

Any confusing of the physiological with the transcendent dynamism of grace might seem to favor the eunuch syndrome of androgyny. As never before, therefore, we need men to be men and women to be women. We need priests to be priests, Sisters to be Sisters. In this respect, however, we have a very special favor from the Mother of the Church: We have John Paul II.

Karol Wojtyła is the incarnate answer to the conundrum of how a man can be a real man but also be a perfect reflection of Mary without the slightest confusion. Let men look to Pope Wojtyła to realize how manly it is to have consuming tender devotion to Mary, blessed among women. The more men love and revere and imitate Mary, the more they will respect, cherish, and honor all womankind.

Mother is also teacher: *Mater et Magistra*. Childbirth involves education in the fullest sense. In the Church, the Magisterium objectifies this maternal role of *magistra*. However, all those who teach in union with the Magisterium also communicate that role (especially mothers and consecrated women). Here again, Mary is the supreme analogue. In Scripture, the heart is the center, the "core" of inner life, the source and seat of all forces and functions of soul and spirit.

In the heart dwell feelings, emotions, desires, and passions. But the heart also houses the rational functions: intellect, understanding, thought, and reflection. It also is the residence of the will, the wellspring of resolutions, and the focus of decision-making. The heart came to stand for the whole inner being of man in contrast to the external side, the *prosopon*.[xv]

It is the symbol of the person, the inner citadel. It is the parlor where God meets us in intimate conversation, the supreme center

---

[xv] This is a Greek word for *persona*, "mask," what we see on the outside or the face we show to others.

in us to which God turns, in which religious life flourishes. It is the active, though concealed part in which all of life can concentrate and perdure.

These descriptions paraphrase the entry in the *Theological Dictionary of the New Testament*, which adds, "What man sees and especially hears enters the heart." The heart must keep what it has received. "Memories and divine commandments are written on the tablets of the heart."

To summarize, the heart is the arena where God meets man and man meets God. In a truly receptive sense, it is the repository of memories, the storage place of the treasury of God's word and revelation.

In announcing the Marian year, the Holy Father addressed Mary in prayer:

> The evangelist says of you: "Mary treasured all these things and reflected on them in her heart" (Luke 9:19). You are the Church's Memory. The Church learns from you, O Mary, that to be a mother means to be a living memory, means to treasure and reflect "in the heart" on all the events of men and people...Yet how many events, how many hopes, yet how many threats, how many joys, yet how many sufferings what great sufferings. We must all, as a Church, treasure and meditate on the events in our hearts. Just like the mother.

This is a striking new theological title for Mary: "the Memory of the Church," and it derives from the biblical theology of the heart.

On analysis, we see the heart displays feminine characteristics: receptivity, deep emotive and affective resonance, intuition, and contemplation. St. Luke tells us that it was in her heart that Mary "pondered all these things," recorded them, held them fast, and treasured them.

Who could have given a better witness than Mary?

Who could have observed, pondered, and preserved more perfectly? Her eyes were the purest, her ears the most open to God's word. And more: She was a mother, endowed to be the Mother of God. Surely Mary's witness, which began with Christ's Infancy, continued to the Ascension.

Who could have seen more accurately the events of Christ's ministry, His Passion and death (she stood *juxta crucem*), His Resurrection and Ascension? Who could have heard more intently every word of the Word made Flesh in her womb? Among all women, who could be more receptive? Like Mary, the Church is *magistra* (i.e., "teacher"), witness to the Tradition, and perfect relator of the words and deeds of Christ.

With Mary, the Church ponders all these things in her heart. In her numerous modern apparitions, Mary acts as teacher of and catechist to her children. She acts as witness to her Son's gospel. It is significant that she so often refers to her Immaculate Heart. In a sense, we dare say that Mary is the mother of the Magisterium. She is not Christ the Priest, but she is mother of Christ. She is not the Magisterium, but she is mother of the Magisterium.

In addition to recognizing Mary as mother and virgin in relation to the Incarnation, we recognize that she is daughter of the Father, mother of the Son, and spouse of the Holy Spirit in her relation to the mystery of the Trinity. In a word, she is the quintessential woman, prototype of creation, and the great sign of history's climax. In the eschatological perspective of the Apocalypse, this woman "clothed with the sun"—dare we recall Fátima?—is the one who prepares the world and the Church for the Son's *parousia*. She who perfectly prepared the First Advent is destined to be the woman who prepares the Second Advent. Mary is "the woman of two Advents."

In our own times, we see her busily at this task, doing what we would expect a good mother to do in these circumstances:

11. visiting her children in peril, weeping tears, even of blood
12. warning them prophetically of impending crisis, or errors, of pseudo-liberations

13. guiding them to a safe refuge
14. fortifying them with supernatural signs and teaching them the salvific elements of the catechism, the basic doctrines of faith and morals
15. admonishing them to shun sin and do penance and leading them to the sacraments, God's sublime channels of grace
16. promoting prayer (especially the Rosary) and promising them peace and an ultimate holy triumph through the medium of her Immaculate Heart

In the afterglow of the Marian Year, this promise seems to be nearing its fulfillment, the beginning of the time of the triumph and a peace the world cannot give. This triumph will be a final and definite exorcism. The woman will crush Satan's head (cf. Gen 3:15). In this great battle, this purification of world and Church, this to-the-death struggle against the red dragon of godless materialism in both its Eastern and Western forms, women have an eminent role in union with Mary.

The masterpiece of Satan's perversion is the corruption of woman. In union with Christ's vicar, women, reflecting Mary, the woman of Revelation, are clearly the providential sign of Mary's conquest. In the end, her Heart will triumph!

CHAPTER 43

MARY: WOMAN OF THE TWO ADVENTS[1]

Personally present at the first divine Advent, Mary has helped us prepare for the second and final Advent by her apparitions at Lourdes and Fátima.

In the Gospel of St. John, Christ twice addresses His mother as "woman." The interpretation of this address has always exercised Catholic apologists. The use at Cana is compounded by the Semitic expression, "What [is it] to me and to thee?" which, even in the most benign translation, heightens the apparent harshness for English ears.

But it is the second use of *gyne*, woman, on the lips of Christ on the Cross—in His dying moments—that presents even more of a dilemma. Priests and theologians are all familiar with the older commentaries where the novelty of *gyne* is illustrated from classical usage. This illustration was valid, but it never seemed to satisfy. What *is* satisfying is the paradoxical truth of the matter, that by calling her "woman" instead of "mother," Jesus raised Mary to heights of dignity and splendor that thrill the truly Catholic heart, and His doing this also gave her the title of "Mother of all the living."

St. John has recorded these two vocatives, "woman," at two crucial moments of his Gospel: Cana and the Cross. And as we know, the Cross in Chapter 19 is the denouement where all the intricate Gospel themes are resolved (though in retrospect, the Cana episode hints at our answer, as well).

The Fathers have generously commented on the Genesis content of the Cross: The new creation with the new Adam on the tree of life in the sleep of death giving issue from His open side to the new Eve, the Church. The Fathers did not invent this exegesis: It is all there in the Gospel account, but to show this would involve unraveling, for example, the theme of Christ as the new Temple, thus fulfilling the messianic vision of Ezekiel, where the living waters—with all the qualities of Eden's river—are seen to flow *e latere dextro templi*.[i]

Nor did the Fathers contrive their designation of Mary as the new Eve, the new mother of all the living. In any event, I believe our modern Mariology has sufficiently clarified the relation of Mary to the Church to allow us to state simply that Mary is the image, the epitome, the personal summa of the Church, which is both virgin and mother.

Mary prepares

In the text of Revelation 12, we again encounter the term "woman," the *signum magnum*[ii] clothed with the sun, her crown of twelve stars indicating the new Israel, the Church founded on the Twelve. Even if some exegetes will deny that John of the Gospel wrote the Apocalypse, this "school," if we could call it such, would not betray the master on this key word. The twofold address of Mary as "woman" here is further interpreted at the summit of revelation history. Here, too, I strongly hold the convergence of Woman-Mary-Church. The context is overwhelming in its allusion to Genesis 3:15, the "proto-evangelium."[iii] For those of us who believe in the divine inspiration of all Scripture as a body and in its unity of sense deriving

---

[i]   This comes from Ezekiel 47:1 and formed part of the *Vida Aquam*, which was sung in place of the *Asperges Me* from Easter to WhitSunday in the old High Mass. "I saw water coming forth from the Temple on the right side, alleluia: and all those were saved to whom that water came, and they shall say: alleluia, alleluia."

[ii]   Latin for "great sign," Rev 12:1.

[iii]   "I will put enmity between you and the woman; and between your seed and hers." Then, depending on what translation you have, it reads, "He/She/They shall strike at/bruise your head, and you shall strike at/bruise His/her/their heel."

from the primary authorship of the Holy Spirit, we readily accept that here, too, in this instance, Scripture interprets Scripture.[iv] John is clearly asserting that the mysterious, triumphant woman of Genesis is fulfilled in Mary, archetype of the Church.

Furthermore, I believe it can be shown that this woman clothed with the sun bears the constant Johannine bivalence of what Dodd called "realized eschatology" (but in a sense he would not endorse): *both* then, *in illis diebus, and* in the future. The event has been accomplished, the victory has been won, but it will be realized also in the consummation of human history through the mystical Body of Christ (i.e., in the strict eschatological sense). This "multiple fulfillment" is typical of New Testament eschatology. Consider the interweaving of temple destruction and end-time *parousia* in the dominical discourses.

For these and other reasons, I see Mary as the "woman of two Advents." She most perfectly prepared the first coming of Christ and stood there *juxta crucem* to merit the motherly title of woman. God's plan has also designated her to prepare the Church and, mediately, the world for His glorious Second Coming.

A second labor begins

Once these premises are posed, I would like to suggest that the "visitations" of Mary in modern times, her apparitions, bear an eschatological sense: She is preparing the Church and the world for

---

iv   We must point out that Father did not mean "Scripture interprets Scripture" in the same sense as some Protestant exegetes use the phrase. These people mean it to say we have no need of a magisterial authority or a final interpreter of Holy Writ because "Scripture interprets Scripture." Obviously, this can lead to problems when discerning what the Bible ultimately says about baptism, the Eucharist, salvation, or any number of issues that have led to the creation of 30,000+ denominations. For almost all of these bodies use Scripture as their only authority, and those that do all believe that, clearly, "Scripture interprets Scripture." For a greater sense of this, see Acts 8:26-39 and the episode between Philip and the Ethiopian eunuch.

the *parousia*, the second Advent. We, of course, "know not the day nor the hour." If one is inclined to be sanguine, this may be a quite remote preparation. But before we dare to pursue this hypothesis, so keenly relevant to priests, gripped as we are in the apocalyptic birth pangs of our days, a further cautious apology is required.

In his panoramic *Christianity in the Twentieth Century*, Fr. John Hardon, SJ, analyzes the decline of devotions in general; in the course of which, he cites the debunking of Marian apparitions. He sees as basic causes:

1. A false ecumenical irenicism that scuttles anything deemed an obstacle to the separated brethren; and
2. A sociological acculturation to a secularized worldview.

These are unquestionably root causes. I would add another: Supine acquiescence to modernist propaganda against the supernatural and miraculous (indeed against any transcendence).

Keep in mind, if we accede to this often unspoken ploy, we forfeit a potent weapon against modernism, a weapon offered us by heaven itself. Granted that these phenomena occur, it must be the divine intent to show this world another world, to unveil and reveal the existence of the transcendent, the supernatural, and the miraculous (indeed against any transcendence).

For if people witness these occurrences in our godless twentieth century, how can the modernist ever convince them that the same did not happen in the days when the Son of God trod His earth? How, in a word, could these revisionist theologians ever "demythologize" the Gospel? No wonder they strive to stifle all reference to apparitions.

Can God still intervene?

In the above references, Fr. Hardon is speaking of those of little faith. But what of orthodox priests and theologians who experience discomfort or remain studiously reticent when encountering these phenomena? We are, one might argue, engaged in a bloody battle to defend the Deposit of Faith (i.e., the fullness of the divine revelation that was sealed with the death of the last apostle). Will not talk of modern apparitions open the door for the theories of Process Theology with its ongoing revelation?[v]

The overriding questions are:

3. Can God still intervene in history?
4. Does the closing of Divine Revelation prevent God from *reaffirming* His existence, His demands, His good news, His mercies, His warnings, or His omnipotence?

To ask the questions is to answer them. And "reaffirming" is the crucial word. Pius XII called Fátima, for instance, the "reaffirmation of the Gospel." Some may still object, "If it is not new doctrine, why

---

[v]   Fr. Hardon says this theory, derived by Tielhard de Chardin and others, "is that view of reality, including what Christianity calls God, which sees everything still in the process of becoming what it will be. But nothing really is. It is called 'theology' because it is a form of evolutionary pantheism, which postulates a finite god who is becoming perfect. But this god is not (as Christians believe) an infinite all-perfect God from all eternity. It is called 'process' because it claims that the whole universe, including God, is moving toward completion. But process theologians do not identify either what this completion is or when or whether it will be reached. [For this reason], nothing is stable, nothing is certain, because *nothing really is*. There are no definite moral laws, no absolute norms of conduct, no certain principles of thought, and no means of knowing anything with certitude." Thus it denies the supernatural and original sin. For process theologians, redemption means a better earthly life, and eternal life essentially means the same thing. In this framework, religion largely becomes a function of working for and achieving social justice because achieving the kingdom of God is equated with creating a better temporal world. Redeeming the eternal soul takes a backseat (if it is needed at all) because often the only real sin is not doing absolutely everything possible to see that others have their needs met. Unfortunately, this notion is somewhat prevalent in the Church today.

bother? We have the Gospel." But the Gamaliel reply is, "If this be of God ... why does *God* bother, why does *He* deem it to be salutary?"[vi]

The guidance of the Church and the examples set by the sovereign pontiffs must be the criteria for our proper attitudes in this, as in everything.

In this spirit, the following guidelines emerge:

5. Study the decrees of Urban VIII and Benedict XIV.[2] Clarify fully, as they do, the difference between Divine Revelation strictly so named and those apparitions approved by the Church. Know precisely that the latter are based on human grounds of credence; that we cannot and must not regard them as articles of Catholic Faith; that approval does not entail some kind of "canonization" of attached messages, prophecies, and so on. This, in turn, must be made clear to the faithful. We may be surprised how adequately the *sensus fidelium* already grasps these distinctions.

Discern, refute, foster, and heed

6. Immediately reject and refute whatever false claims the Church has condemned. I might add, however, be *sure* the Church has condemned them. There are currently some claims of apparitions, messages, and so forth, which are under careful study by Church authorities and which bear some preliminary tokens of favor. The Marian Movement of Priests, with its messages Don Stefano Gobbi says he receives from Mary, comes immediately to mind. At the risk of controversy, but for the sake of personal honesty, I might

---

vi   Grandson of the great Jewish teacher Hillel the Elder and himself teacher of the Apostle Paul. See Acts 5:34-40 and 22:3 for the important role he played in the early Church. Some traditions claim he secretly became Christian after having received baptism at the hands of Peter and John although this theory is suspect for several reasons. His remains supposedly rest in Pisa, Italy.

give the opinion, reached after years of careful research: The events at Garabandal, Spain, are still under the scrutiny of the Church. They have not received what could be called a final adjudication, much less a condemnation from the Holy See nor from the present local Ordinary.[vii] We might also mention the alleged visions of Mary to a soldier in Vietnam, unfolding these past few years.[viii]

7. On the other hand, there are also numerous alleged apparitions so crude, so grotesque, so obviously in conflict with magisterial teachings, that only the starvation of confused souls too long deprived of genuine piety can explain their success. We should *expect* such diabolic deceptions whenever true apparitions are present. After Lourdes, for example, many alleged apparitions, some with plainly preternatural elements, were immediately reported during the canonical process. The minions of hell scramble to smother the genuine. They pose as angels of light to confound the undiscerning. But in those cases not ruled on finally and officially (and which are not obviously perverse), we should adopt an attitude of prudent openness, not automatic rejection. Needless to add, we should use the greatest reserve and caution in our comments on them.

8. Do not deprive the people of what the Church clearly has approved. Priests should accept and foster what the

---

[vii] The Church has not yet made any definitive pronouncement regarding Garabandal. The results of the three investigations into Garabandal at the local diocesan level are with the Vatican.

[viii] The closest thing the editors were able to find was the alleged apparition(s) to a Vietnamese soldier named Stephen Ho Ngoc Anh in Binh Lo, Vietnam. In 1974, the Virgin allegedly appeared to Ho Ngoc Anh, a paratrooper who the Communists held and tortured. Then, in 1975, she allegedly appeared to him again to complain about children dying and to ask him for a lot of prayer and sacrifice in order to avoid a "major disaster" that would otherwise come on mankind. No competent authority has ever ruled on either the validity or invalidity of these apparitions.

Church accepts and fosters. How can priests be justified in withholding from souls the salutary, consoling, and providential impact of Guadalupe, Lourdes, and Fátima (not to mention the many other apparitions and prodigies) and their wholesome devotions, to which the Church has long given her solid favor?

9. Be directed in this admittedly delicate area by the example of the popes, our supreme pastoral guides. Even a casual reading of the official papal documents[3] will impress us with the seriousness and frequency of the popes' free discussion of these apparitions and other such phenomena.

We can give only two of many examples here. The first shows the treatment of an apparition already approved, and is from Pope John:

> After the example of the Pontiffs, who, for a century have exhorted Catholics to give ear to the message of Lourdes, we beg you to listen with simple heart and right mind to the salutary warning of God's Mother. Furthermore, let no one be surprised at hearing the Roman Pontiffs insisting on the important lesson passed on by the child of Massabielle.[ix] Since the Pontiffs stand as the appointed guardians and interpreters of divine revelation contained in Holy Scripture and Tradition, they also have the duty of commending to the faithful's attention—when after mature deliberation they judge it opportune for the general good—the supernatural lights it has pleased God to freely grant to certain privileged souls. This they do, not to propose new doctrines but to guide our actions: *Non ad novam doctrinam promovendam, sed ad humanorum actuum directionem* (St. Thomas IIa IIae q. 174, a.6, ad3). This is the case of the Lourdes apparitions, upon which excellent historical works have recently thrown conclusive light.[4]

[ix] St. Bernadette of Lourdes actually came from this village.

The second, from Pius XII, is of special interest for us since he treated of a phenomenon (the weeping Madonna of Syracuse) which had not yet received approval at the highest level:

> It is true that up to the present, this Apostolic See has not in any way made known its judgment concerning the tears said to have been shed by an image of her in the humble house of some workingman. Nevertheless, it was with lively emotion that we read the unanimous declaration of the Episcopate of Sicily of the reality of the event. Without doubt, Mary is eternally happy in heaven and suffers neither pain nor sadness. And yet, she does not remain there insensible, but rather feels love and pity for the suffering human race, to which she was given as a Mother when she stood sad and weeping at the foot of the Cross to which her Son was nailed. Will man understand the mysterious language of those tears? Oh, the tears of Mary! On Golgotha, they were tears of compassion for her Jesus and of sadness for the sins of the world. Does she still weep for the wounds produced anew in the Mystical Body of Jesus? Or does she weep for her many sons whose errors and sins have extinguished the life of grace and who gravely offend the divine majesty?[5]

In her apparitions and messages, Mary is not delivering a new revelation. She is eminently mother-catechist. Consider Fátima, for instance. Here, Mary is a mother teaching her poor, neglected children all the major points of the Catechism so subject to attack in our times, and she does so in a fresh and compelling manner, . A corollary is that only the children, only the simple and open souls respond and benefit. As Christ declared to His Father, "You have hidden these things from the learned and the clever and have revealed them to the merest children."[6]

The Immaculate Heart will triumph

We have mentioned previous popes, but is it not true that our present Holy Father [John Paul II] is our most impressive and immediate example of Marian devotion? He leads us by profound words that open up creative horizons of mariological insight. He hardly gives a speech that does not contain a Marian jewel. His actions, however, are equally instructive. He makes Marian shrines the magnetic centers of his journeys, and in these shrines he does not hesitate to affirm his belief in apparitions, miraculous images, cures, and prodigies. Consider his trips to Knock, Jasna Góra (aka, Częstochowa), Pompeii, the *Consolata* in Turin, and the Virgin of Aparecida, Brazil.[x]

Of the Guadalupe image, he says with emotion, *"Ella mi llama."*[xi] He is not embarrassed. He does not fear ridicule or worry about compromising his reputation for scientific scholarship. He is like a child, this wondrous Pope. He intimates by example what we priests should think of the mystical phenomena of our times, those frequent, astounding messages of Mary, this woman, Queen of Angels, Queen of Messengers.

There is an eschatological, apocalyptic configuration to this modern series of visitations:

10. Guadalupe: the Woman with Child, clothed with the sun, crushing with her feet the emblem of the serpent god;
11. Knock, with its tableau from the Johannine Apocalypse (i.e., the Book of Revelation);
12. The great sign in the sun, which shook and fell from the heavens at Fátima, and the woman who stood regally beside the solar disk to utter prophetic words of war and peace, of persecution, and even annihilation of nations.

---

[x]   Space does not allow for a description of each of these miraculous (and approved) sites, but information on them is readily available online (e.g., www.apparitions.org).
[xi] Spanish for "She calls to me."

If space allowed, we could fortify this thesis with many details, but even these few should surely give pause to those exegetes who blithely reject any literal sense to the apocalyptic discourse of Jesus. Even with all the caveats we have insisted on, how else should we read these signs of our time? Is it not a powerful argument, at least *ex convenientia*,[xii] that Mary is also the woman who prepares for the second Advent when Christ will present His kingdom-Church to the Father? St. Louis de Montfort foresaw the apostles of the latter days when Mary's children would be like heels—abased, stepped on, ground in the dirt, but heels for all that which would crush Satan's head.

And Pope John Paul's coat-of-arms is a visual reminder of the *mater stans juxta crucem*. The blank space at the right of the Cross was the place of the newly ordained John, but by implication, it is the station for Karol Wojtyła and for every priest. "From that hour the disciple took her unto himself."[7] The Holy Father has done so; he powerfully suggests we do so, as well.

The Church, too, in all her members, is engaged in an eschatological combat. The Church, too, must live through the Passion, the agony of mind and spirit, the betrayal of Judas, the dispersal of disciples, the mockery, the derision, the darkness of that hour from which John took Mary unto himself. But just as surely, the Church will experience the final victory at the consummation of the age: "In the end, my Immaculate Heart will triumph."[xiii]

It is the lot of priests to imitate the Holy Father and be with the woman, virgin and mother, "from this hour," renewing our *adsum*[xiv] and *libenter*,[xv] willfully engaging ourselves in this escalating warfare, preordained to culminate in the greatest victory of cosmic history. To do this, we should make our own the motto of John Paul II: *Cały*

---

xii   i.e., from fittingness
xiii   This is what Our Lady said at Fátima.
xiv   "I am here."
xv   Willingly, cheerfully.

twój, Totus tuus, the core of his consecration to Mary: "O Mother, I renounce myself, I am *all thine*, and all that I have is thine."

CHAPTER 44

THE WOMAN OF ASSENT[1]

Introduction

It is constant Catholic affirmation that, from the beginning to our own days and into eternity, Mary is *model* of the Church. But we must hasten to say she is not an abstract, absent, passive model. We must add the descriptive synonyms: Mary is the personal summa of the Church, its living icon, its archetype and epitome, its intensely active mother. The Church is a *mystery*. The mysteries of faith—including Mary's role in the economy of salvation—resemble precious jewels. Therefore, we can never fully understand in this life, we can never exhaustively apprise how Mary reflects the mystery of the Church.

As a jewel, she has multiple facets. We must turn the facets, one by one, and contemplate them, probing, seeking to penetrate more deeply. And though we will concentrate on one facet, we must never forget or neglect the numerous others. We must try to grasp and correlate all the myriad facets of Mary. The more we succeed, the more we will begin to understand the Holy Church whose image she mirrors. As St. Bernard lovingly proclaimed, "*De Maria, numquam satis.*"[i]

What Mary is, the Church is (and the faithful should be). And what the Church is, Mary shows us. Mary is virgin and mother. The Church is virgin and mother. The Church is *mater et magistra* (mother and teacher). Mary is likewise mother and teacher. We distinguish the *ecclesia docens* (the Church teaching) and the *ecclesia*

---

i   "Of Mary, one can never say enough."

discens (the Church learning). The Church is both teacher and disciple. To call the Church *discens* means she is *discipula*, disciple.

The disciple is pupil, student, and learner. We shall note in passing Mary's special relation to the Magisterium (i.e., the hierarchical teaching authority of the Church), but we will focus on that other facet.

Mary is the first and most perfect disciple of Christ, "the Teacher come from heaven." As Pope John Paul II has so often said, "She leads us on the pilgrimage of faith."[ii] In our discussion, we seek to emphasize that Mary is the first of all believers, the first and most perfect Christian, the first disciple of the Lord. To the degree we approach her exalted union and perfection, to that degree we become true, genuine Christians and disciples.

The woman of assent

The Church hails Mary as the woman of assent and of faith. In this, she is the mandatory model of the Church, which will always be the Church of assent. Assent is the essence of the act of faith. Since faith is the basis of Christian discipleship, so too is assent. Today a cancerous counter-church has as its brand an endemic *dissent*. The Church is the parlor of familial *dialogue*, but never the arena of dialectics. As Fr. Stanley Jaki once observed, Catholic dialogue can never be filibuster. The Catholic disciple says *fiat*; the modernist boasts in *non serviam*. *Fiat* is the hallmark of discipleship, learned from Mary. *Fiat* is the key of salvation. In creating all things, visible and invisible, God pronounced *fiat* (i.e., "Let it be"). In creating all things new in Christ, He accepted the *fiat* of the new Eve, "Mother of all the living," in the new creation of grace. The devil tempted the first woman, and she spoke dissent, and all her children became cursed. An angel tested the Woman of the Gospel, and she voiced

---

[ii] For a beautiful reflection on this, see the late Holy Father's General Audience address of Wednesday, March 21, 2001, available at the Vatican website. www.vatican.va.

assent, and all her children became blessed. Mary's assent was to the Incarnation and redemption.

The heart

Again, we must pause for background. For the disciple of Christ, there is the matter of the heart. In Scripture, the heart is the center, the "core" of inner life, the source and seat of all forces and functions of soul and spirit. The heart generates feelings, emotions, desires, and passions, but it is also the seat of the rational functions such as intellect, understanding, thought, and reflection. What modern man locates in the brain, the biblical man attributes to the heart.

In addition, the heart is the residence of the will, the wellspring of resolutions, and the locus of decision-making. The heart, therefore, has come to stand for the whole inner being of man, in contrast to his external side. It symbolizes the *person*. It reveals the center of life. It stands as the inner citadel of the individual. The heart is the *parlor* where God meets man in intimate conversation, the supreme center in man to which God turns and calls and appeals, the hub where religious life and experience flourishes. It is the active part of us in which all of life can concentrate and perdure. It includes concepts that, for us, are vitally relevant to the vocation and mission of a disciple and eminently so in the role of Mary, mother and first disciple: "What man *sees* and especially *hears* enters the heart."[2] The heart must keep what it has received. "Memories and divine commandments are written on the tablets of the heart."[3] Our eyes, ears, and touch directly transmit data that registers in the heart, where it is pondered and stored.

To summarize: The heart is the place where God meets man and man meets God. In a truly receptive sense, it is the *repository* of memories, the storage place or treasury of God's word and revelation.

In announcing the Marian Year of 1987-1988, the Holy Father addressed Mary in prayer:

> The evangelist says of you: "Mary treasured all these things and reflected on them in her heart" (Luke 2:19). You are the Church's memory. The Church learns from you, O Mary, that to be a mother means to be a living memory, means to treasure and reflect "in the heart" on all the events of men and people... Yet how many events, how many hopes, yet how many threats, how many joys, yet how many sufferings ... what great sufferings. We must all, as a Church, treasure and meditate on these events in our hearts. *Just like the Mother.*

Here we have from the vicar of Christ a striking, new theological title for Mary: "The Memory of the Church," and it derives from the biblical theology of the heart. The Pope describes how we as *disciples* must imitate Mary, who was her Son's first disciple.

In biblical times, a rabbinic disciple was admonished to be like a sponge, absorbing every drop of his master's teaching. He was also exhorted to be like a sealed *cistern*, storing the "drops" of his master's teaching without loss.

The connection of these images with the heart is obvious and comprehensive. But with the disciples of Jesus, we must store in our hearts the total Person, Who is the Word. His Sacred Heart is the sign of His person. The hearts of His disciples, therefore, are not vaults in which to store the words abstracted from their Master. Every deed, every event, every action and reaction, every emotion of Jesus must also be observed and stored. Christ's disciples are witnesses to His Person. They are not merely secretaries of His words, not functionaries; they are witnesses. Here we see the fullest operation of the heart as Scripture portrays it.

The heart and women

On analysis, we observe that the heart displays characteristics in which women excel: receptivity, deep emotive and affective resonance, intuition, and contemplation. Who better knows her child, the fruit of her womb? And what mother could rival Mary in this key role of discipleship?

In the second chapter of his Gospel, St. Luke frames—deliberately—his Infancy narrative with references to Mary's heart, which I will translate very literally:

1. Immediately after the departure of the shepherds on Christmas night: "Now Mary guarded together all these happenings, tossing them around together in her heart...." (Luke 2:19).
2. And after the finding of the child Jesus in the temple: "And His mother thoroughly guarded all these happenings (words) in her heart" (Luke 2:51).

Midway between, Simeon prophesized that a sword would pierce her *psyche* (also tantamount to heart) so that thoughts from many hearts might be revealed. We see the cost Mary pays to lead and form all Christian disciples. Even in the Infancy narrative, her heart, so finely attuned to scriptural allusions, discerns touching, pathetic signs of the Passion: her infant Son stretched out on the wood of the manger, which prefigures the Cross, the "sign of contradiction" mentioned by Simeon at the Presentation.

Luke loads this passage in particular with technical terms of priestly and sacrificial import. Note also how Luke alludes to the connection between Mary and the Ark of the Covenant, which is the locus of sacrificial blood atonement. The blood will be her Son's, the Suffering Servant; Mary will stand as the suffering handmaid.

Pondering them in her heart

We mentioned that the data impressed on the senses are transmitted to the heart. We should explore this further in the case of Mary. Luke tells us that she "pondered all these things" in her *heart*, that she recorded them, held them fast, treasured them. Who could have witnessed better than Mary? Who could have observed, pondered, and preserved more perfectly? Her *eyes* were the purest; her *ears* the most open to God's word. And more: She was a *mother*, endowed by God to be the mother of God. Surely, Mary's witness began with her Child's birth, because Luke first tells us how Mary kept all these things in her heart. We consider "all these things," the moment of birth when her eyes gazed into the infinite depths of His eyes. This moment is experienced by every mother with every child, but more so with *this mother* and *this Child*, her Creator and Savior.

Nor should we fail to account for the memories stored and pondered during the nine months that began from the Annunciation and Incarnation. The evangelists do not explicitly record the details of Mary's pregnancy, but what we do see are profound and inevitable realities based on the fact of a mother conceiving, bearing, and giving birth to her child. Luke's reference to Mary's heart also suggests she was his major source in his account of the Infancy.

Mary's witness—moreover, her careful attention and her unfailing memory—began at the Incarnation, continued to the Ascension, and continues even now in regard to Christ's Body, the Church of which she is Mother.

The words of Luke concerning Mary's observing, receiving, preserving, and pondering demonstrate her constant service as the first disciple of Christ. Earlier, we mentioned the "cost of discipleship." We think of the seven dolors (i.e., sorrows) and Mary's title as Mother of Sorrows and Queen of Martyrs.[iii] It was her maternal witness under the cross, specifically *juxta crucem*, that fully demonstrates the cost that Mary paid.

On Calvary, what did her eyes see? The blood of scourging and nailing and the piercing of that Sacred Heart that was her life. What

---

[iii]   Mary's seven sorrows are: 1) Simeon's prophecy; 2) the flight of the Holy Family into Egypt; 3) the loss of the Child Jesus for three days; 4) Jesus and Mary meeting on His way to Calvary; 5) Mary watching her Son suffer and die by crucifixion; 6) Longinus piercing Jesus' side with his lance, taking Jesus down, and placing Him in His mother's arms; 7) Mary seeing her Son buried in the tomb.

did her ears hear? The violent blows of the hammer, the curses and taunts, the groans, the last words, and the expiring shout of her Son. When His body lay in her lap where she laved His holy wounds and reverenced them with her kisses, could she fail to recall that night of Christmas when she first cradled Him in her arms?

The discipleship of Mary is concentrated in her heart. We who wish to be true disciples of Jesus must so unite ourselves with her that we may see with *her eyes*, hear with *her ears*, receive, ponder, and react with *her heart*. If we must make our hearts like unto Christ's,[iv] there is no surer or more perfect way than to make our hearts like unto Mary's. Her Sorrowful and Immaculate Heart is the summit of human communion with Jesus.

---

iv   Father alludes here to the prayer, "Jesus, meek and humble of heart, make our hearts like unto Thine." In turn, this is an allusion to Matt 11:29, where our Lord says, "Learn from Me, for I am meek and humble of heart."

Part VII

Fr. Gilsdorf's Other Writings

CHAPTER 45

THE EUCHARISTIC MYSTERIES:
THE TWO TABLES OF THE LORD[1]

During Holy Week of 1981, in a move not seen since Pius X simultaneously issued *Pascendi* and *Lamentabile*, Pope John Paul released two documents.

One was *Dominicae Cenae*, a profound profession of the Faith mingled with a grieving assessment of the grave loss of that faith and resultant abuses. The other was *Inaestimabile Donum*, a catalog in syllabus form of some major abuses that existed at the time. (It stands as an indictment of the alienation of the "American Church" from the vicar of Christ that these same abuses—and many more—still exist today!)

However, I want to draw your attention to Part III of *Dominicae Cenae*, which discusses "The Two Tables" of the Mass, namely the Table of the Word and the Table of the Eucharist.

The Fathers of the Church repeatedly note this two-fold division, which corresponds to the Passover Seder with its scriptural and homiletic prelude, followed by the solemn offerings and the consumption of the sacrificial lamb. (It also reflects the synagogue service of word and worship.)

Some exegetes also see a parallel in the eucharistic discourse of John 6, which begins with the "words" or teaching of Christ as a symbolic nourishment and ends with the explicit revealing of the eucharistic mystery of faith.

At any rate, the discourse ends with Peter's confession in the name of the apostolic college.[i] Peter and his successors are always the supreme custodians of the Eucharist. In our times, witness Pope Paul's monumental encyclical *Mysterium Fidei*, as well as the two documents of John Paul II now under discussion.

In *Dominicae Cenae*, the sections on the Two Tables are relatively brief and are primarily disciplinary, a correction of specific abuses. Behind and between the corrections, however, lie the doctrinal foundations of the whole text. Since the Holy Eucharist is the "mystery of faith," *Mysterium tremendum et fascinans*,[ii] I know you will sympathize with me if I state the obvious.

Therefore, I will focus on one aspect of each Table, aspects I consider to be central to the element of the "sacred" and which are under assault by current errors.

The Table of the Word

First, we will consider the Table of the Word. Hebrews 4:12 reads, "The Word of God is living and active; it probes the thoughts and motives of our heart." Each morning during the Council there took place a brief but impressive ritual action. The Gospels were borne in solemn procession down the aisle between the tiers of Council Fathers and were then enthroned and incensed near the papal altar. Thus, venerated by the Fathers, they remained there, a visible, silently eloquent witness of every thought, act, and emotion of the assembly.

Since the Council, we have seen this veneration of the Gospels in televised solemn papal Masses, as well as in other less elaborate liturgical actions. It has been flanked by candles, kissed, elevated,

---

[i]   "After this many of His disciples drew back and no longer went about with Him. Jesus said to the twelve, 'Will you also go away?' Simon Peter answered Him, 'Lord, to whom else shall we go? You have the words of eternal life; and we have believed (and have come to know) that you are the Holy One of God'" (John 6:66-69).

[ii]   The fascinating and full-of-awe mystery.

enthroned, and honored with incense. One might compare these ancient "baptized," imperial rites granted to the Book with those given the celebrant of the Mass (who acts *in persona Christi*) and, indeed, to the eucharistic species. Because of the similarities in how each is treated, we intuit a deeper connection between the Liturgy of the Word and that of the Eucharist.

The parallel fascinates the mind. It is almost as though this book were somehow a living person, as though this impressed *word* of God were somehow the *Presence* of the Incarnate Word of God.

How far is such an intuition valid? How far is this whimsical observation grounded in fact? May we not see in these traditional ceremonies surrounding the scriptures an invitation to regard them not only as a science for us to study, but also as a mystery for us to contemplate?

In the eucharistic encyclical *Mysterium Fidei,* Paul VI spurs on our musing when he distinguishes the various "presences" of Christ in the Church. Among these he numbers "the Gospel which she (the Church) proclaims as the Word of God, which is not preached except in the name of Christ, by the authority of Christ, and with the assistance of Christ, the Incarnate Word of God."

Bultmann tried to construct an "existential encounter" of Christ in the word. However, by his demythologizing, naturalist premises, he cut off the contemporary Christian from the historical and supernatural roots. But if we supply supporting premises that are orthodox, the concept of "existential encounter" has authentic potential.

As we probe the mystery here, we will posit two premises.

The first premise

The first is that Christ is *simultaneously* and *perfectly* conscious of every human act, internal as well as external, of every human being, past, present, and future. Therefore, from the moment of His conception in Mary's womb, this all-embracing consciousness conditions His entire public ministry: His recorded words, emotional responses, and internal and external acts. For the magisterial texts that confirm this, we need only refer to the precious collection found in Fr. William Most's *The Consciousness of Christ*.

As just one example, however, look at one of the most illuminating and mystical passages of Pius XII in *Mystici Corporis*:

> Now, the only-begotten Son of God embraced us in His infinite knowledge and undying love even before the world began. And that He might give a visible and exceedingly beautiful expression to this love, He assumed our nature in hypostatic union... But the knowledge and love of our Divine Redeemer, of which we were the object from the first moment of His Incarnation, exceed all that the human intellect can hope to grasp. For hardly was He conceived in the womb of the Mother of God, when He began to enjoy the beatific vision, and in that vision all the members of His Mystical Body were continually and unceasingly present to Him, and He embraced them with His redeeming love. O marvelous condescension of divine love for us! O inestimable dispensation of boundless charity! In the crib, on the Cross, in the unending glory of the Father, Christ has all the members of the Church present before Him and united to Him in a much clearer and more loving manner than that of a mother who clasps her child to her breast, or than that with which a man knows and loves himself.[2]

We are involved here with the complex discussion of the *communicatio idiomatum*. We are well aware of the controversies. But as Pius XII asserts, Jesus knew who He was from the time of His conception. And along with the perennial authoritative witness of the Magisterium, we also affirm the fact of Christ's comprehensive consciousness.[iii]

[iii]   In other words, the human Jesus always knew He was God the Son. As we will soon see, some theologians such as Fr. Raymond Brown, etc., would have

From this first Christological premise, we see that in the Gospels, all of *Christ's* words and deeds are "conditioned" and "influenced" by the full existential complex of *my own* needs and *my own* human personal response. In other words, I am in His mind. He sees me. He addresses me. The Gospels are, indeed, an historical record of the past, but in this manner, a connatural encounter is effected *here and now*. Christ, in His historical agony, for instance, is affected by *me*, both as an individual and as a member of His Body, either toward consolation by my sympathy, my conversion, and my adherence, or toward a sharpening of His agony by my indifference, my sin.

Gethsemane may well illustrate what is meant. The mental agony of Jesus simultaneously registered in His consciousness the love and hatred, the fidelity and apostasy, the salvation and damnation of every soul from Adam to the *parousia*.

The same dimension of awareness enters into every word and act of Jesus the Gospels record. I say "act," because an act is also dramatically and efficiently a "word." Therefore, my whole existential situation and being share in prompting and formulating each word of Christ in its final Gospel expression. Thus, I am actively involved in this "word" that never passes away. I live in and act upon the pages of Scripture. And what we label "I" here embraces every "I" of every human soul, created or yet to be created, however ignored or unappreciated by history that soul may be.

Second premise

The second premise is this: Christ *transcends* time. In the divine hypostasis of Christ, there is no past or future, only an eternal all-comprehensive *now*. If our first premise moves us "backward" toward an engagement with the past, this premise moves those same historical events "forward" to our own moment in time.

---

us believe otherwise, and as a result, such views have become commonplace amongst average Catholics. The Church, however, rejects this notion.

In fact, our two Christological principles complement one another. They form an interdependent polarity. The mysteries of Christ's Incarnation, birth, preaching, miracles, Transfiguration, Passion, death, Resurrection, and Ascension are present to Christ, who lives them *now*. These mysteries are now and forever. Our incorporation into His Body through the sacraments lifts us above and beyond the life of nature and outside of time. As members of His Body, we also live these same mysteries in timeless solidarity with Christ our Head.

From these two briefly sketched premises, there emerges a vision of the Gospels as a relevant, living, ever-present "epiphany" of the Lord. In no way do we imply a strict and substantial identification of Christ with the material scroll of Scripture. There is, however, a parallelism by analogy. Somehow, we do encounter Christ Himself in the Scriptures, and this is an engagement with the living Person, Who is the Word—*semper vivens*.[iv]

Thus we can see how the Table of the Word comes into its fullness in the Table of the Eucharist. For the Christ living in the Gospel accounts is the living Christ. The same Jesus manifested and proclaimed in the Scripture is the living Person of the risen Jesus made present, sacrificed for us, and communicated to us really and substantially—Body, Blood, Soul, and Divinity—in the Table of the Eucharist.

Although consciousness of this fact was precisely the sort of thing called for by the Council, do we see any awareness of this amongst average Catholics? No. Why? Because we live in a time when many deny the principles of Christ's "consciousness" and divine transcendence. Who denies this? The modernists. Indeed, this denial is the very essence modernism, and so it is no wonder that the long-condemned errors of the modernists have spread like contagion. It is no coincidence that these have become dominant in catechesis, seminary courses, pulpits, and seminars. And, therefore, it is no coincidence that we have seen the private and communal

---

iv Latin for "forever living."

devotions of the Church all but obliterated. The modernists have extinguished devotion, the furnace of the Church, and we all shiver in a malevolent coldness as a result.

These lethal errors of our day are precisely the same old heresies diagnosed and condemned by St. Pius X in *Lamentabile Sane*. In that good Pope's time, the average Catholic was inoculated against this contagion because it was not taught in seminaries and thus priests did not teach it to their flocks. Today, however, through the immediacy of the media, it has spread in virulent fashion. As a result, the demonic assertion, "Jesus was just a man, a 'human person,'" has infected many of the faithful, and the same with the notion that "Jesus didn't know who He was," and so on. The whole package has been tagged the "Ignorant Jesus" theory.

We note here in the strongest possible terms that the denial of either or both of these interdependent doctrines (i.e., the transcendence and the consciousness of Christ) annihilates devotional and liturgical life in any genuine Catholic sense.[v] The all-embracing consciousness of a transcendent divine Person, true God as well as true man, is the vital breath that animates all Catholic spiritual life. To choke off that breath is to asphyxiate the life of devotion and liturgy. Should we be surprised by the pestilence that sickens and demoralizes us?

Relationship of the "Two Tables"

The intimate connection of Scripture to liturgy is obvious. If we read the Gospel as just another (albeit inspired) book, a tome of merely historical perspective, a literary record of past events, then we will doom our understanding of the Mass and the liturgical cycle of Mysteries that it enshrines as a mere commemoration of the past, a lingering at the tomb.

---

[v]   To see an example of this phenomenon in our own day, read the article "In Holland, They're Inventing Their Own Mass" here: http://chiesa.espresso. repubblica.it/articolo/170066?eng=y

Instead, we must understand the Mass as the true *anamnesis*, an existential commemoration and re-presentation that the context of Scripture and the Tradition of the Church demand. The Eucharist must be the central action in which this sacred symbiosis is realized.

At the Table of the Lord, we break out of our space-time reference, our *nunc fluens* ("floating now") of the human condition, and enter in to the eternal *nunc stans* (the "standing now") of Christ. To experience the existential encounter with the Eucharist, we need a deepened sense of Christ truly living and present in His Gospel. To regard the Gospel as a disconnected memoir of words and deeds long past, with but a lingering moral or suasive influence here and now, is to relegate the eucharistic liturgy, suffused and pregnant as it is with the word of God, to a flat, horizontal, remote, historicist review that has no ability to "engage" us, to touch us. In a sense, the Table of the Eucharist is the existential fulfillment of the Table of the Word. As we stated earlier concerning private devotion, when we deny the consciousness and transcendence of Christ, the Mass becomes an empty husk, a secularized spectacle.

As we have noted, the eucharistic sacrifice fully actualizes the Table of the Word. The eucharistic Real Presence, the encounter *par excellence*, animates the liturgical cycle in such a way that we truly live in the pages of the Gospel and participate in the mysteries of Christ here and now.

Paul VI, when treating the eucharistic presence in *Mysterium Fidei*, states:

> This presence is called "real" not to exclude the idea that the others are "real" too, but rather to indicate presence par excellence, because it is substantial and through it, Christ becomes present whole and entire, God and man.[3]

As we will observe later, Pope John Paul in *Dominicae Cenae* insists that the Table of the Eucharist is the *mensa* of an *altar* (and we must never succumb to the error that the Eucharist is "just a meal"). The Mass is a sacrifice.

The Table of the Eucharist

The one central point we select for our reflection on the Table of the Eucharist is the need to restore a sense of *awe*. Awe is the proper response to theophany, man's perception of the divine Presence.

It would be easy to cite numerous other accounts of awe in the Old Testament. However, let's race ahead to the fullness of time when God manifested Himself in His Son, when the Word became flesh and dwelt among us.

When God did this, He mercifully "emptied Himself," restraining His "glory" so that men could tolerate the light. The Gospels, however, recount how Christ occasionally manifested His divinity to some degree, and when He did, the response was awe:

1. On Tabor, the chosen three "fell on their faces, and they were filled with awe" (Matt 17:6).
2. This awe on the other occasions also overwhelmed the disciples and the crowds: "And amazement seized them all, and they... were filled with awe" (Luke 5:26).
3. "They were overcome with awe" (Mark 5:42).

Unfortunately, we cannot take further time to draw out the rich marrow of these texts, but they underscore the fact that when a person of faith senses the presence of God, awe is the spontaneous response.

Thus, when faithful Catholics contemplate the Eucharist, they see with the eyes of faith the real, divine Presence. And with that, they behold a stunning vista of the mystery of "transcendence and condescension" which is at the heart of the Incarnation. And whenever God grants us the grace to perceive it to some degree in our contemplative adoration, our genuine response must be a holy and inebriating awe.

The ordinary approach to eucharistic devotion is to emphasize the truth of the transcendence, the infinite splendor and glory of Christ, the divine Person, real, living, omniscient, and omnipotent before us. And this truth must never escape our mind. Yet we must also thrill to the heart-rending spectacle of the divine *condescension*. This is an inseparable truth based on the mystery of the Incarnation, the *anabasis* and *katabasis* of the creative Word made Flesh.

Let us now consider with awe the incredible fact that God has stooped to conquer our hearts.

1. In the Incarnation, the Word became flesh and emptied Himself, taking on the form of a slave. We shall see that at each degree of condescension there is a deepening and corresponding "risk." And note the risk: Christ delivered Himself to the mercy of men, and see what we did to Him in the Passion.

2. Still this was not enough. Christ took a second step. In the Eucharist, that bread He gives us is His own flesh. Note the greater concomitant risk of love: The flesh and blood are the fruit of His *sacrifice*. Under the humble species of bread and wine, He is even more "helplessly" vulnerable to the perversion, unbelief, and negligence of men. In these days of eucharistic outrage, we should often reflect that "host" derives from *hostia*, victim.

3. Could Christ possibly stoop lower than this? Incredibly, yes! There is more to this awe-inspiring epic of the divine Beggar Who bends to us for love, the divine Gambler who does not hesitate to risk His glory. Christ remains present in the *fragments*, the ultimate in divine condescension! A *crumb*! A *drop*! And the risk? How often today do those who should know better heedlessly disregard and casually abuse these fragments?

St. Thomas Aquinas summarizes the constant tradition of the Fathers in discussing a "Doctrine of the Fragments" that extends to our own days. (In *Memoriale Domini*, for instance, Pope Paul warns of five ways we could lose the fragments when distributing Communion in the hand.) Let us at this point recall two lines of the hymn *Adoro Te*:

> *Tantum esse sub fragmento, quantum totum tegitur...*
> (There is as much under a fragment as is contained
> in the whole...)
> *Cujus una stilla salvum facere, totum mundum quit ab*
> *omni scelere.*
> (Of which one drop is able to save the whole word
> from every crime.)

A signal service to the faithful will be a priest's solicitude for "gathering up the fragments." How beautiful a moment in the Table of the Eucharist should be the adoration of the remnants as we purify. How much salutary, mute admonition can we give our people, how much reparation to Christ for the cavalier carelessness of our times if priests slowly and adoringly purify the sacred vessels with awe?

The Benedictine preparing our deacon class at St. Meinrad Seminary to celebrate Mass several times admonished us, "You can tell a good priest by how he cares for the fragments."

That was in 1956. I believed it then; I believe it now. Our crisis today is largely reflected in a failure to respond to this eucharistic condescension and to defend, as courageous custodians, our "vulnerable" Lord with all our energies. On these tiny fragments stands or falls the doctrine of Transubstantiation and, with it, the mystery of faith.

In *Dominicae Cenae*, Pope John Paul addresses priests:

> Upon all of us who, through the grace of God, are
> ministers of the Eucharist, there weighs a particular
> responsibility for the ideas and attitudes of our brothers
> and sisters who have been entrusted to our pastoral
> care. It is our vocation to nurture, above all by personal
> example, every healthy manifestation of worship toward

Christ present and operative in that sacrament of love. May God preserve us from acting otherwise and weakening that worship by "becoming unaccustomed" to various forms of eucharistic worship that express a perhaps "traditional" but healthy piety, and that expresses above all that "sense of the faith" possessed by the whole People of God, as the Second Vatican Council recalled.

CHAPTER 46

THE HEDGE

The rabbis spoke of placing "a hedge around the Torah." We routinely scorn the Pharisees for their multiplication of secondary laws. Jesus' indictment of excesses was surely merited. Yet if kept within limits, the concept of the "hedge" was and is logical and pious.

The idea was to surround the central laws of God with peripheral laws. They insisted on these latter, which formed a protective hedge and prevented the violation of the sacred Torah.

Similarly, for centuries, the Church had always seen the wisdom of surrounding her greatest treasure, the Most Blessed Sacrament, with a hedge of protective legislation.

To see how this played out in practical terms, let us transport ourselves back some 30 years. We are in a church at the time of Communion: The people kneel at the Communion rail; they cover their hands with the starched linen Communion cloth. The servers carefully attend the priest with the paten extended under the recipient's chin to catch any fragments of the Host.

On returning to the altar, the celebrant purifies the sacred vessels and his consecrated fingers that he had held together since the consecration. "Soiling of the hands" was a rabbinic phrase indicating that touching the scroll of the Torah "contaminated" the hands with the sacred. Thus, they washed their hands before and after handling the sacred Scripture.

We see this mirrored in the *Lavabo* and purification rites. "*In illis diebus*," no one touched the chalice, ciborium, or monstrance except with a cloth and only if necessary. The priest or deacon pre-washed the purificators and corporals before sending them to the laundry. They deposited water in the sacrarium.

Additionally, the faithful had the sacredness of the Eucharist instilled in them by frequent Benediction and exposition, by practice of the First Fridays, by Forty Hours Devotion in every parish, and the bittersweet hours of adoration on Holy Thursday. A holy serene silence reigned in the House of God, and when the liturgy called for music, it was always God-centered. One learned awe by respecting the rubrics of the hedge. No one dared dream of profaning the Holy of Holies.

Fast forward back to today. Do we still have such care taken? Who or what was responsible for the sudden and drastic dismantling of the hedge (a dismantling that came without debate)? It began with a few concessions, a few mitigations to update our worship. But overnight we jettisoned the ramparts, so that today many churches have become meeting halls for casual visiting.

Even during Mass itself, the churches are more like theaters. Entertainment, not worship, is on the bill. Pastors and architects now design churches to be "multipurpose." Polka Masses and Gay Masses are featured. The polka Mass is a big crowd drawer in the Midwest, a sure fund-raiser advertised as the centerpiece of parish picnics. More and more churches no longer have kneelers—a revolutionary coup which precludes any form of eucharistic adoration! Add to this the fact that the sacrament of penance is almost extinct in some areas and one can repeat the problem raised by the Holy Father: How can everyone always receive Communion and seldom, if ever, go to confession? Do they not "eat and drink judgment on themselves, not discerning the Body of the Lord?"

Today the Holy of Holies stands exposed to the abuse, contempt, blasphemy, and sacrilege of any and all. Who has brought us to this brink? Is there anyone here who doubts we are facing a satanic assault? The direct assault against Jesus Christ in the Eucharist is the quintessential sign of diabolic action. We need to meditate on Second Thessalonians and its prophecy of the mass apostasy. We need to ruminate on the apocalyptic phrase, "The abomination of desolation standing in the Holy Place."[1]

I will not fully describe the shambles left once we saw the hedge uprooted. Perhaps it is better for each of us to agonize through our own experiences of the desacralization and desecration of our churches and our most sacred acts of worship. Once they removed the hedge, every abuse centered directly on the Person of Jesus Christ. Once again in this "Passion of the Eucharist," His enemies spit in His face.

How did we lose the response of reverence, let alone awe? One might recall the powerful influence of Harvey Cox's *The Secular City*. Its theme was that there is no distinction between the sacred and the secular. Therefore, nothing is sacred. The concept spread like a tidal wave in seminaries and convents and thence to parishes, sweeping away traditional signs of reverence.

There were immediate disastrous effects on the liturgy, from desacralization to trivialization to loss of faith to outrage. We might add that since the Eucharist is the architrave of the sacraments, when *it* is desecrated, *all* the sacraments are affected and ravaged. It is essential, then, that we regain the sense of awe as we discern in the Table of the Eucharist, our *Inaestimabile Donum* ("gift beyond price"), the source and summit of all Christian life.

What can we do? Everything necessary to promote a restoration of reverence. In this matter, even the good may have been innocently beguiled. We should, for instance, reconsider the "options" we have chosen. Have we chosen what most expresses our appreciation of the sacred? Have we made an effort to know what the preference of the Holy Father may be?

Also, we should increase our visits to the Blessed Sacrament and seek more extended periods of adoration. All these efforts will be painfully counter-cultural and a constant source of humiliation and reparation.

Finally, even those who prefer the *novus ordo* (i.e., the new Mass) should give strong support to *Ecclesia Dei*. We see the Pope's clear intention. By sheer comparison with what transpires in many parishes, the revival of the Tridentine rite will help correct abuses and infuse a spirit of reverence.

I recall hearing a story that can console us amid our lamentations. If memory serves me, my source was Archbishop Nicholas Elko,[i] though some of the details are blurred. It concerns a prelate (probably Archbishop Elko himself) who, before the last conclave, visited a Polish Franciscan monastery situated on a hill near Rome. He arrived late at night. A friar led him to his room on the second floor.

The prelate went to the choir loft before retiring well after midnight. As his eyes adjusted to the dark, he discerned by the dim sanctuary lamp a figure of a man stretched out prostrate on the floor before the tabernacle. Were his eyes deceiving him?

The next morning, he asked the friar about it, who told him, "Oh, that's Cardinal Wojtyła. He stays here often, and we know he frequently spends the night in adoration of the Blessed Sacrament."

We are in pain. We are languishing in this desert of secularization, the great apostasy of the West. But this is our Pope! This is a eucharistic saint! And he knows what we know, and he suffers far more than we suffer. If we doubt this, we need only go back to *Dominicae Cenae*. Let the Holy Father conclude and summarize for us:

> As I bring these considerations to an end, I would like to ask forgiveness—in my own name and in the name of all of you, venerable and dear brothers in the Episcopate—for everything that for whatever reason, through whatever human weakness, impatience, or negligence, and also through the at times partial, one-sided, and erroneous application of the directives of the Second Vatican Council, may have caused scandal and disturbance concerning the interpretation of the doctrine and the veneration due to this great sacrament.

---

[i] Eastern rite auxiliary bishop of Cincinnati, who helped make radio broadcasts to Catholics behind the Iron Curtain (i.e., Eastern Europe). He passed away in 1991.

> And I pray the Lord Jesus that in the future, we may
> avoid in our manner of dealing with this sacred mystery
> anything which could weaken or disorient in any way
> the sense of reverence and love that exists in our faithful
> people.[2]

And let us hear once more some key sentences from the
document in a section titled "The Sacred Character of the Eucharist
and Sacrifice":

> There is a close link between this element (of *Mysterium*)
> and its sacredness ... the Eucharist is a holy and sacred
> action. Holy and sacred, because in it are the continual
> presence and action of Christ, "the holy one" of God...
> The Eucharist is a holy and sacred action, because it
> constitutes the Sacred Species, the *Sancta sanctis*...
>
> The sacredness of the Mass, therefore, is not a
> "sacralization," that is to say, something that man adds
> to Christ's actions in the Upper Room... The sacred
> character of the Mass is a sacredness instituted by
> Christ... This sacred rite can in no way lack its sacred
> character and sacramentality since these are willed by
> Christ and transmitted and regulated by the Church.
> [Nor] can this sacred rite be utilized for other ends. If
> separated from its distinctive sacrificial and sacramental
> nature, the eucharistic mystery simply ceases to be.
> It admits of no "profane" imitation, an imitation
> that would very easily (indeed regularly) become a
> profanation. This must always be remembered, perhaps
> above all in our time, when we see a tendency to do away
> with the distinction between the "sacred" and "profane,"
> given the widespread tendency, at least in some places, to
> desacralize everything. In view of this fact, the church
> has a special duty to safeguard and strengthen the
> sacredness of the Eucharist.[3]

The Pope is always the supreme confessor and custodian of the Eucharist. He struggles to maintain the hedge against the efforts of those who want to uproot and destroy it. At the end of the eucharistic discourse, challenged to profess his faith in the mystery just revealed, Peter says with some degree of awe, "To whom else shall we go? You have the words of eternal life."

So we turn to Christ's vicar Peter, living among us, and we echo, "To whom else shall we go? You have the keys. Against this rock the gates of hell shall never prevail."

Let us join our eucharistic Pope in the prayer with which he sealed *Dominicae Cenae*:

> In order that our unity and the constant and systematic collaboration that leads to it may be perseveringly continued, I beg, through the intercession of Mary, holy spouse of the Holy Spirit and Mother of the Church, that we may all receive the light of the Holy Spirit.[4]

Amen.

CHAPTER 47

QUESTIONABLE RESPONSES: COMMENTS ON A RECENT BOOK BY FR. RAYMOND BROWN: PART I[1]

Although his work is not in line with Catholic Tradition and the Magisterium, this has not stopped many from seeing Fr. Raymond E. Brown, SS, as our day's premier Catholic exegete. Indeed, given his radical departure from Catholic orthodoxy on so many points, this reputation is difficult to understand. Nonetheless, it is what it is, and this fact provides more evidence of an "American Church" that has progressively become severed from its universal roots.

I mention this because Fr. Brown has recently produced another book, *Responses to 101 Questions on the Bible (101 Questions)*.[2] The paperback resembles a small catechism, yet, as I will suggest later, it has an exceptional value and merits the utmost scrutiny. It gives a compact summary of the major topics Brown has treated *in extenso* in previous works.

Now many make the distinction between "early Brown" and "later Brown," whereby the early Brown was orthodox, and later he became progressively squishy in his theology (to put it charitably), because around 1970, he began to adopt new positions that clearly contradicted his earlier views.

Julia Grimes, a knowledgeable laywoman, sent a letter that appeared in the January 1, 1981, *National Catholic Register*, where she demonstrated from Brown's own writing his about-face from his previous writings. She referred extensively to a booklet he wrote in 1960 where he defended "the very doctrinal truths he is now either disputing or 'nuancing'—namely, the physical Resurrection of Jesus, the foundation of the Church by Christ, and the divine mission of the Apostles." She concludes by asking, "What are we to think? How much credibility can he preserve when his thinking on such serious issues can change so radically...?"[i]

Brown says he wrote *101 Questions* to answer questions he received from people during his workshops and lectures. As such, the writing gives the impression of simulating spontaneity.

Don't be fooled. Brown has given himself every opportunity to elaborate and refine his responses with meticulous reflection. And this is true not only of his responses, but of his self-crafted "questions," as well.

Most of the preliminary responses are unexceptional, standard statements of statistical fact. But these are non-theological for the most part and aren't necessarily problematic. Once theology is injected, however, the controversial elements come glaringly to the fore.

Critical observations

We cannot comment here on everything objectionable about this book (there is just too much). Even less can we nitpick peripheral points, however much they help complete the picture. Therefore, we will limit our scope to a few general observations on Brown's basic methodology and some of his controversial assertions.

We should begin with Brown's assertion that, "Fortunately, in my life, and in recent Roman Catholic experience in general, in the *biblical field*, there has been no tension between scholarship and official Church teachers. That is not true of other fields of theological endeavor" (Q. 16, p. 26).

---

[i] In the original article, Father inserted this endnote, quoting Msgr. Kelly in *The New Biblical Theorists*, "Shortly after Vatican II, Brown himself, writing in the *Anchor Bible*, identified the author of the fourth gospel as John, the son of Zebedee, one of the Twelve" (pp. 108-9. See other examples on pp. 116-21).

Now this is ridiculous, and Brown fully knows this. To call his statement disingenuous might be charitable, but it would not be the truth. He *knows* better. He has read *Divino Afflante Spiritu* (Pius XII's 1943 encyclical, and Brown's self-proclaimed favorite), *Humani Generis* (Pius XII, 1950), Vatican II's *Dei Verbum*, and *Sancta Mater Ecclesia* (an instruction issued by the Pontifical Biblical Commission [PBC] on April 21, 1964, under the English title *The Historicity of the Gospels*), and they all contradict him.

We could cite other documents and allocutions, but in every case, Brown makes them say what he wants them to (as opposed to what they actually say). He never even hints at the stern admonitions they give to exegetes to submit to the Magisterium and to observe the analogy of faith as the basic methodology of Catholic scholars.

I am not the only one to have noticed this, either. Many others have often remarked how, in citing the "three stages" of redaction criticism in *Sancta Mater Ecclesia*, Brown recasts the language to lend support to his own interpretations. Furthermore, he stops precisely short of the restrictions, cautions, and commands the PBC has set for Catholic biblicists. This cafeteria, pick-and-choose exegesis reaches the outrageous when he says *Humani Generis* supports the theory of evolution and says Pius XII offered the possibility that man descended from apes.

Aside from failing to give his readers the context of Pius' thoughts on these two points, Brown shows an extraordinary lack of candor by ignoring *Humani Generis*' strong indictment of errors in biblical criticism and theology (not to mention its summons to Catholic scholars to adhere to approved methods).

We shall further see that his scholarship is opposed by eminent peers in the field: Manuel Miguens; René Laurentin; John McHugh; William Most; the Mariological Society of America and Fr. Juniper Carol, its first president; the Fellowship of Catholic Scholars; and not least by Lawrence Cardinal Shehan. These men's credentials for scientific biblical scholarship are as evident as their firm adherence to magisterial directives. Brown knows these critics and their expertise, but he resorts to his usual tactic of dismissing them with silence or contempt.

For example, in Question 17, we read:

> There are a small number of vocal ultraconservative Catholics who think their interpretations of Church doctrine are official and [that] they constitute a Magisterium that can judge scholarship—this is a group I often call the third Magisterium, consisting of self-appointed vigilantes who have no real status to speak for the Church.

Such diatribes are typical (and the above is rather mild). Note the reference to a "third Magisterium." But isn't this the pot calling the kettle "black"?

One of Brown's persistent ploys is to claim that *he* is the "centrist." He thereby paints anyone who dares to dissent from his opinions as an "eccentric" to the right or left. However, when one studies Brown's positions and contrasts them with those of the papal Magisterium, it becomes evident that he no longer considers the pope as the center. No, instead Raymond Brown occupies that place (cf. Q. 22, p. 31; Q 33, p. 46; Q. 39, p. 55).

In a June 4, 1981, *Wanderer* article, John Mulloy comments:

> Has there ever been an age in the history of the Church when a theologian or Scripture scholar who rejected the scriptural basis for a) the Virginity of Mary, b) the Divinity of Christ, c) the Resurrection of Christ, d) the fact that Christ Himself established His Church, and e) the fact that Christ instituted the priesthood and the episcopacy (the list could be continued) [could possibly] call himself a centrist theologian? In fact, it [shows] the immense theological rot and degeneration which has taken place in the Church ... that a man of Fr. Brown's views and teaching can lay claim to such a position.

Proving false his claim to hold the center, Brown reportedly made statements that represent an astounding departure from Catholic orthodoxy (see *The Wanderer*, May 7, 1981). Charles R. Pulver covered a speech by Brown given to the NCEA at the New York Hilton Hotel on Wednesday, April 22, 1981. One might quibble that the reporter was slanting the intent of the speaker, but pay special attention to the direct quotations, Brown's own words:

> He immediately set up a distinct dichotomy between the "centrists" and the "rightists" within the Church. (In the past, he has termed these groups "moderates" versus "ultra-conservatives." His central theme was this: *both groups are perfectly legitimate and acceptable to the Magisterium of the Church.*
>
> These groups exist, he said at the outset of his speech, because *they do not understand official doctrine in the same way.* He contended that even a list of basic teachings is not self-explanatory, for there can remain "the difference between the doctrine and a way of understanding the doctrine."
>
> Here he "insisted" that "whether or not those involved recognize it, there are *no major differences between the Catholic center and the Catholic right in matters of official Catholic doctrine*" (emphasis his). "But there are sharp differences in the way doctrines are understood, and the right wing generally argues that its understanding of doctrine *is* doctrine. Often the rightist understanding is arrogantly titled 'orthodox' with the not-too-subtle implication that any other interpretation is heterodox or heretical."

The reader of *101 Questions* will be able to assess how fundamental the differences are between Brown's responses and the perennial teaching of the Church. And here we see laid bare an assumption that screams for attention: What kind of hermeneutics says Catholics have unity if they profess by rote the formulations of doctrine, yet differ radically in their understanding of the message revealed? The opposite premise might be acceptable, but unity of faith insists on unity of meaning. Is it any wonder that Brown finds broad commonality between Catholic and Protestant biblical scholarship?

The victim here is the truth. If Brown's opinion becomes widely accepted, we would be a schizoid, bicameral institution, and perennial teaching will be susceptible to change. Even more to the point, his work would obliterate the Magisterium's authority to say a certain position is objectively in error. How does this match up to Vincent of Lerins' dictum, "*Quod ubique, quod semper, quo dab omnibus*"?[ii]

The analogy of faith

Occasionally, after presenting novel or controversial ideas, Fr. Brown assures us that, despite the absence of biblical evidence, he does accept the Catholic doctrine on the grounds of Tradition and Magisterium. But having suffered the mind-numbing effects of negative arguments, the reader comes away with the impression that Tradition and Magisterium independently assert doctrines that might not agree with Scripture or (as the negative arguments suggest) might even contradict the written word of God. One could be excused for seeing Brown's deferential bows to be cautionary lip service intended to disarm his audience and/or ecclesiastical censors.

Brown alludes to *Dei Verbum*, which is precisely the document that insists on what we call in modern times the "analogy of faith." This is, of course, the perennial Catholic "rule of faith." In Brown's favorite encyclical, *Divino Afflante Spiritu* (*DAS*), Pius XII follows

---

ii   "In the same Catholic Church, care must above all be taken that we hold fast to that which is believed everywhere, always, and by everyone."

the directives of Leo XIII's *Providentissimus Deus*, by insisting on the analogy. Paragraph 24 of *DAS* must unnerve Brown.[iii]

Dei Verbum defines the analogy:

> Sacred Tradition and sacred Scripture make up a single sacred deposit of the Word of God, which is entrusted to the Church... So, in maintaining, practicing, and professing the Faith that has been handed on, there should be a remarkable harmony between the bishops and the faithful.
>
> But the task of giving an authentic interpretation of the Word of God, whether in its written form or in the form of Tradition, has been entrusted to the living teaching office of the Church alone. Its authority in this matter is exercised in the name of Jesus Christ. Yet this Magisterium is not superior to the Word of God, it is its servant. It teaches only what the apostles have handed on to it. At the divine command and with the help of the Holy Spirit, it listens to this devotedly, guards it with dedication, and expounds it faithfully. All that it proposes for belief as coming from divine revelation derives from this single Deposit of Faith.
>
> It is clear, therefore, that, in the supremely wise arrangement of God, sacred Tradition, sacred Scripture, and the Magisterium of the Church are so connected and associated that one of them cannot stand without the others. Working together, each in its own way under the action of the one Holy Spirit, they all contribute effectively to the salvation of souls.[3]

Catholic scriptural scholars must operate within these parameters. Brown doesn't. Despite his protestations, his methodology seems more in harmony with the Reformation "rule of faith" (*sola scriptura*) if we consider his various statements. Indeed, for all his contempt for

---

iii   This essentially says that the analogy of faith and, thus, the Church's teaching authority must remain paramount with Catholic scriptural scholars.

fundamentalism, one even notes how Brown is quite ready to use it himself. His "proof-texting" can rival that of any literalist.[iv]

All of this becomes abundantly clear when one compares Brown's major hypotheses to the work of prominent Catholic exegetes who treat the same subjects in full adherence to the analogy of faith. For example: Brown and Manuel Miguens on the virgin birth; Brown and René Laurentin on the Infancy narratives; Brown and William Most on the knowledge of Jesus; Brown, Cardinal Shehan, and Miguens on the New Testament ministries.

It is no secret that these opposing studies were stimulated as critical responses to Brown. What differentiates them from his work is that they set out to clarify and defend the doctrinal positions of the Church, harmonizing Scripture, Tradition, and Magisterium. Never do these critics bend the scientific limitations of the scriptural texts, yet their conclusions, justified by rigorous exegesis, emerge as positive and supportive in contrast to the universally negative and minimalist conclusions of Brown.

Miguens, for example, in his *Church Ministries in New Testament Times*,[4] adds a corroborative addendum on the major extra-biblical witnesses, especially Sts. Clement and Ignatius. He notes that their *Frühkatholizismus*[v] is, in fact, consonant with first century apostolic tradition and praxis. Brown's critics carry out the "sublime office" of biblical scholars defined by Pius XII in *DAS*, namely, "To scrutinize, explain, propose to the faithful, and defend from unbelievers the very Word of God, communicated to men under the inspiration of the Holy Ghost."[5]

The analogy of faith is not some unscientific intrusion on a genuinely scientific and historical exegesis. Quite the opposite. It is a liberating principle that frees the exegete to explore the productive

---

[iv] Father's original endnote here says, "See *101 Questions*, Q. 91, p. 120; Q. 98, p. 130. Brown interprets likewise in *Humani Generis*, where he quotes no nuances of Pius XII. In fact, he uses this approach whenever it promotes his argument."

[v] German for "early Catholicism."

lodes in the mine of Scripture. It shows where one can successfully probe for and find the ores of truth. This enables the scholar to avoid potentially years of intense labor with only fool's gold to show for it.

Therefore, the faith convictions of a Catholic exegete are not ungrounded assumptions that are exempt from rigorous and honest scientific method. Indeed, the history of biblical criticism shows that no biblical scholar approaches his studies without assumptions. The question, however, is whether one bases these assumptions on personal biases and doubts or roots them in the deposit of faith grounded in Tradition and expounded by the Magisterium.

Benchmarks of Brown's flawed methodology

Numerous critics have pointed out the fatal flaws that consistently mar Raymond Brown's work. While these critics have independently treated one or several of these flaws, we should perhaps credit the most systematic cataloging, description, and refutation of these characteristics to Msgr. George A. Kelly in his monumental study, *The New Biblical Theorists: Raymond E. Brown and Beyond.*

Given Brown's influence in the world of biblical studies, anyone who wants to understand the crises of our times should conscientiously study the Kelly critique (especially those bishops who support, admire, and protect Brown).

What follows then is a short list of these methodological cachets that readers will find in abundance in all of Brown's "later" books and speeches, and which he has woven into the fabric of *101 Questions*. Notice how a number of these features overlap and complement one another.

The first is *reductionism*. In this, the witness of Scripture is reduced to the "scientifically controllable biblical evidence." Brown dismisses texts the Church (i.e., Fathers, Councils, Magisterium) has used throughout the ages as her evidence of basic Catholic doctrines. He does so on the grounds that the Church has defined few if any biblical passages.

In this, of course, he relies on a statement of Pius XII in *DAS*. However, he twists it by nuancing the sense of "defined." Thus, he voids the apologetic force of texts the Church has consistently employed.

For example, take the texts traditionally used by the Magisterium to support Petrine primacy and the sacraments of the Eucharist and penance. He also reduces the "authenticity" (in the technical sense of attribution of authorship) of, for example, much of the Pauline corpus.

This gives him the ability to later discredit the historicity of traditional interpretations. This further enables him to consequently view them as witnesses only to later conceptions and practices rather than as contemporaneous with Paul himself.

Similarly, he downplays the historical value of Acts. Together with the assumption of late dating in the Gospels themselves, this opens the floodgates to "retrogression," which we will mention later.

In *101 Questions*, one hears Brown echo the sad refrain of his conclusion that "the scientifically controllable biblical evidence leaves the question of the virginal conception unresolved."[6] So he says, but the opposite is claimed in *The Virgin Birth* by Miguens (among others).[7] Would Brown say this question of scriptural evidence is merely an example of magisterial formulation that two factions "understand differently"?

Next is one of Brown's favorite crutches, his *nuancing*. Put another way, he engages in "plausible deniability." We can best perceive the gist of the term by reading a small sample of the nuancing technique he demonstrates in *101 Questions*:

> Q. If the person who celebrates the eucharist [sic] was not designated in a regular way in New Testament times, does not this mean that we would be free today to have a certain flexibility about who celebrates the eucharist [sic]?[8]

R. Let me remind you that I stressed our ignorance of New Testament times. Our documents do not give us the information to state that the celebrant of the eucharist [sic] was determined according to a rigidly fixed pattern; but I did not affirm that no such pattern existed. We simply cannot document the situation ... but suppose you are right, and there was no pattern rigidly fixed in all the churches as to the celebrant of the eucharist [sic]. There still must have been some type of church recognition...

Now to understand the perplexity of the invented questioner, we need to read the whole context of the excerpt above, including Brown's reply to the preceding question:

[The Twelve] ... could hardly have been present at all the eucharists of the first century, and we do not know whether a person was regularly assigned to do this task and, if so, who that person was. (I should emphasize this point because various modern writers sometimes assert with remarkable surety that the head of the household celebrated the eucharist. That is a guess; we have not a single text in the New Testament that indicates that.) In *Didache* 10:7,[vi] we find that, despite a suspicion of wandering prophets, the author insists that they cannot be stopped from "eucharistizing." If that means "to celebrate the eucharist" rather than simply "to give thanks," then in some places the prophets may have had a role in the liturgy (see also 13:1-2)...[9]

In these quotations, the word so frequently on Brown's pen is not used, but we see what nuancing does for clarity. If the straw questioner (i.e., Brown) seemed confused before, how does this

---

[vi]   The *Didache*, also known as "The Teaching of the Twelve Apostles," was written in the latter part of the first century. As such, it is the oldest extant non-scriptural Christian writing. It contains instructions for such sacraments as baptism and the Eucharist.

hedged circumlocution give him relief? It would take a staff of corporate lawyers to decipher his ultimate meaning.

In the full context of Questions 93-94, Brown insists some things we cannot know from Scripture, whereby we then see him offer his own opinion. We note, too, how he reaches beyond the "scientifically controlled scriptural evidence" to cite the text of *Didache* and thus grasp like a fundamentalist at the term "eucharistizing," which he has to admit could have a non-germane sense. And always the obscurity is due to the sleight-of-hand of "plausible deniability." He relates negative suggestions, and then inserts sentences to presume the authority of the Church and thus offer personal opinions that allow him to say, "But notice I said." After all the verbiage, he leaves doubts and arguments hanging in foggy air.

Another favorite Brown device is to pose the rhetorical questions of "others," leaving it suspended without response. Or, alternatively, he gives a nuanced and qualified treatment.

In Q. 101, p. 134, for instance:

> Perhaps the proper way of phrasing an answerable question pertinent to the '60s is not "Would the Christians of that period have looked on Peter as the Pope?" but "Would Christians of that period have looked on Peter as having roles that would contribute in an essential way to the development of the role of the papacy in the subsequent church?" I think the answer is yes, as I tried to explain in response to a previous question where I pointed out the roles that Peter had in his lifetime, and the symbolism attached to him after his death. To my mind, they contributed enormously to seeing the bishop of Rome, the bishop of the city where Peter died, and where Paul witnessed to the truth of Christ, as the successor of Peter in care for the church universal.

Brown then cites an ecumenical book on Peter (that he helped edit) as coining the formula of a "Petrine trajectory":

I think that is a good term, for it conveys the image of a long line of development starting out in Peter's lifetime and continuing into the subsequent church.

He then mentions the weaknesses and failures of Peter, his chastisement by Jesus for not understanding, his denials of Jesus, and adds:

That can be very helpful to us Roman Catholics who believe firmly in the pope as the vicar of Peter in carrying out Christ's care for the church.

We need to place this response in a context where the Petrine texts (Matt 16; Luke 22; John 21) are sapped:

Let me emphasize that the Gospels of Matthew, Luke, and John were all most likely written after Peter's death and that therefore texts in them concerning Peter have an importance in revealing the mindset of the last third of the first century pertinent to this figure...[10]

His conclusion:

All three passages written for different communities confirm the ongoing symbolism of Peter as the embodiment of faith, proclamation, pastoral care, and continued support in the church.

Significantly, in citing Matthew 16, Brown truncates the text to omit the conferral of the keys and the power of binding and loosing *ad personam* to Peter. We note the nuancing of questions, the repeated use of the word "symbolism" (which he doesn't define), the reference to development, and the deliberate use of "vicar of Peter" rather than the traditional title "Vicar of Christ," to name just a few.

Another device he uses is *citation*, what "others" say, for example with the Infancy narratives.[11] The questioner (having heard a highly nuanced foreword) asks whether, since the Nativity stories are not historical, are they then folklore?

He receives this response:

> Forgive me for rather bluntly insisting that you pay attention to what I said. I did not say that the birth stories are not historical. I gave reason why scholars think that some of the events in those stories may not be historical. I think there are historical details in the birth narratives, although neither Matthew's nor Luke's narrative is completely historical...[vii]

What a web he weaves in his dual role as questioner and responder. To illustrate further would require reproducing the whole book.[viii] We will see this method in passages that follow. Again, one must remember that this whole book focuses on questions crafted by Brown himself. Here he "rather bluntly" rebukes himself!

Next there are his *assumptions*, such as with the Markan priority and the late dating of New Testament books. He follows again the classical liberal concept which allows any texts ascribed to Christ or the Twelve to be seen as developments and creations (albeit Spirit-generated) of the post-Resurrection Church community, even to the turn of the second century. We shall see that his Christological stance on what Jesus knew and foresaw offers him an additional argument in this scenario.

Once more, we find ourselves haunted by the liberal Protestant theories of the distinction between the "Jesus of history" and the "Christ of faith" (not to mention the contrivance of a creative theologizing role of the community).[ix] The appeal to "retrogression"

[vii]   i.e., "This is not an exhaustive list of problems that raise doubts about the historicity of the infancy narratives" (Q. 57, p. 79) ...

[viii] For more examples in his previous works, see Kelly, op. cit., on "inferential doubts," p. 153, p. 46 on "infallibility," and p. 98 on "cultic priests and sacrifice."

[ix]   Some liberal scholars believe that there is a difference between the "Jesus of history" and the "Christ of faith." Namely, while there was a historical

is a universal solvent.[x] One can use this to question the force of any problematic text that stands in the way. This acidic assumption permeates *101 Questions*.

Then he *popularizes* and *politicizes*. Usually, theologians and exegetes test their more controversial findings among their peers. Brown, however, will not dignify the most qualified or dissenting peers with a serious intramural debate. (So much for the right to dissent!) Thus, the selection of his topics often takes on the coloration of ecclesiastical partisan politics. This would be bad enough if he confined his audience to his peers. However, he disturbingly seems to target a general readership who (more often than not) cannot discern wheat from chaff. (We will return to this in our conclusion in Part II.)

---

person named Jesus, this man didn't do all of the things attributed to Him by people who believed (i.e., had faith) He was the Christ. However, the Church rejects this theory.

[x]   In other words, Brown is saying that later, post-Resurrection Christians made up things about the Savior, etc., that weren't true.

CHAPTER 48

QUESTIONABLE RESPONSES:
COMMENTS ON A RECENT BOOK BY
FR. RAYMOND BROWN: PART II[1]

Christological assumptions

Logically, Brown's revisionism of the traditional theology of inspiration and inerrancy are fundamental problems in his approach. However, these items are mere "fallouts" from the other radical priorities he espouses.

In all theology, Christology is central. There has been no academic groundswell to endorse Brown's variation on the theme of the F.C. Baur dialectic of Pauline versus Petrine churches.[i] For his part, Brown concocts a Johannine versus Petrine struggle resulting in a compromise synthesis. This new construction posits a clash between "high Christology" and "low Christology." *101 Questions* highlights this Brown hypothesis, first elaborated in his *The Community of the Beloved Disciple.*[2]

What has emerged as the nucleus of Brown's Christology concerns the human knowledge of Jesus. Included in his familiar description of Jesus as a Galilean Jew of the early first century is the supposition that Jesus did not know and did not foresee anything beyond the limits of the human mind. This theory has been tagged, indelicately but tellingly, the "ignorant Jesus" position [i.e., that Jesus

---

i   A nineteenth-century German theologian, Baur said that the early Church was basically one big struggle between St. Paul's universal Christianity and those who wanted to keep the Faith more purely Jewish. This tainted his view of the Bible, because he said this conflict altered its formation.

did not know He was divine]. Brown himself nuances "ignorance" to mean lack of knowledge, while conceding to Jesus a superior intellect and insight.

At issue here is what we call the *communicatio idiomatum*. In the present book, Brown does not clearly discuss the Person of Jesus in its Chalcedonean formulation.[ii] It is Catholic dogma that Jesus Christ is one divine Person, the eternal Son of God Incarnate.

The problem of the *"communicatio idiomatum"* arises concerning the relation of the two natures hypostatically united in the one divine Person. One cannot deny that the divine Person in His divine nature is omniscient. One must also acknowledge that the human mind of His human nature is *per se* limited. The dilemma: How can Jesus not know in His human nature what He knows in His divine nature? We are obviously in the presence of an ineffable mystery. In such a case, the theologian must rely in humility on the Magisterium for illumination.

So what does the Magisterium say?

The traditional Christological solution has been to posit some manner of infused communication of knowledge. The prevalent magisterial position attributes the beatific vision to the human mind of Jesus. The most thorough study of the question, clearly directed against Brown's stance, is that of Fr. William G. Most, *The Consciousness of Christ*. We especially refer the reader to the section that presents a thorough review of patristic and papal Magisterium on the subject. For our purpose, we will single out texts of the more recent popes.

First, we consider the syllabus of condemned errors of the modernists, St. Pius X's *Lamentabile Sane*. All 65 entries would bear comparison with Brown's positions in *101 Questions*, but on the issue of the human mind of Christ, we will cite the following, stressing once more that *the following are condemned errors*:

[ii]   Recall the earlier explanation of the Council of Chalcedon.

No. 32: It is impossible to reconcile the natural sense of the Gospel texts with the sense taught by our theologians concerning the conscience and the infallible knowledge of Jesus Christ.

No. 33: Everyone who is not led by preconceived opinions can readily see that either Jesus professed an error concerning the immediate Messianic coming, or the greater part of His doctrine as contained in the Gospels is destitute of authenticity.

No. 34: The critics can ascribe to Christ a knowledge without limits only on a hypothesis which cannot be historically conceived and which is repugnant to the moral sense. That hypothesis is that Christ as man possessed the knowledge of God and yet was unwilling to communicate the knowledge of a great many things to His disciples and posterity.

We will add here a few other condemned errors since they are allied to Brown's responses:

No. 40: The sacraments had their origin in the fact that the apostles and their successors, swayed and moved by circumstances and events, interpreted some idea and intention of Christ.

No 41: It was far from the mind of Christ to found a church as a society which would continue on earth for a long course of centuries. On the contrary, in the mind of Christ, the kingdom of heaven together with the end of the world was about to come immediately.

Again, one could find a fair number of the errors condemned by *Lamentabile* in *101 Questions*. Does Brown suggest that some Vatican official has told him that *Lamentabile* has also been rescinded? In fact, St. Pius X issued a decree, *Praestantia Scripturae*, on November 18, 1907 (shortly after he issued *Lamentabile*), in which he levels the penalty of excommunication on those who endeavor to weaken the force of *Lamentabile*.

Since some theologians ignored even this decree, the next Pope, Benedict XV, approved another one on July 5, 1918, declaring that the following propositions *cannot* be safely taught:

> Prop. 1: It is not certain that the soul of Christ, while He lived among men, possessed the knowledge which the blessed have in heaven (Denz. 2183).[iii]
>
> Prop. 2: Nor can the opinion be called certain which states that the soul of Christ was ignorant of nothing, but that from the beginning, knew all things in the Word, past, present and future, or everything which God knows by the knowledge of vision (Denz. 2184).
>
> Prop. 3: The view of certain recent persons about the limited knowledge of the soul of Christ is not less to be accepted in Catholic schools than the view of former theologians about His universal knowledge (Denz. 2185).

We shall see that Pius XII, Brown's own liberating champion, will make these positions abundantly clear.

First, however, we should make a major point here: Once Brown posits the ignorance of Jesus (and I accept the word in Brown's benign definition), all subsequent responses take a drastic and tragic turn. This theory of ignorance is the trigger of his radical departure from other perennial Church teachings. The reader must understand that

---

iii   "Denz" refers to the *Enchiridion Symbolorum et Definitionum* (known as "Denzinger," for its author's name), which the *Catholic Encyclopedia* says was "a handbook containing a collection of the chief decrees and definitions of councils, list of condemned propositions, etc., beginning with the oldest forms of the Apostles' Creed. It has often been republished, with considerable additions, of which the most important are part of the Bull defining the Immaculate Conception (*Ineffabilis Deus*, 1854), the Syllabus of 1864, and the [First] Vatican [Council's] decrees."

the quotations that follow are but a few representative samplings from Brown:

> Q. 77, p. 105: If one posits revelation without limitations in human knowledge one imagines a Jesus who foresaw all that would happen, including the full outline of the church [sic], how it would develop, where it would be proclaimed, and various details of its liturgy and life. In short, one pictures a Jesus who gave us a blueprint for the church, and that is often quite close to the way the foundation of the church was understood in times past. [And on p. 106, discussing Matt 16:18, "On this rock"] ... a statement that many think had post-resurrectional origins. Thus there really is no Gospel evidence about detailed planning for or of the church, and [the] burden of proof has to lie on those who assume Jesus had thought about all that.
>
> Q. 78, p. 106: The foundation of the church need not mean that Jesus had detailed knowledge of what the church would be like or that he could have drawn up a blueprint for it.
>
> Q. 79, pp. 106-107: What about sacraments? Does not our understanding of the sacraments imply direct institution by Christ?
>
> Brown answers:
>
> I think that question uses precisely the right term: "by Christ." The previous question spoke about the founding of the church by Jesus, and I did not object, because I think there is continuity between what Jesus did in his lifetime and the resultant church. Nevertheless, the classical formulations for relating church realities to Jesus of Nazareth would have them stemming from Christ. The church teachers responsible for such formulations were not thinking simply of the Jesus of the ministry, i.e., exactly what Jesus said and knew before his crucifixion.

They were thinking of the whole New Testament presentation of Jesus as the Christ, the Messiah, with post-resurrectional insight... Institution by Christ means that those actions we call sacraments are specifications and applications of a power that Jesus Christ gave to his church in and through the apostles...

Q. 80, p. 107: One does not have to hold that, sitting at the Last Supper, Jesus foresaw all that would develop from His statements about the bread and wine that he declared to be his body and blood [sic]. One does not have to think that he foresaw liturgical developments, the full practice of the eucharist [sic] in Christianity, or that he could speak about transubstantiation.

Q. 85, p. 113: I hope you see that my answers in regard to baptism and the Eucharist are related to the non-blueprint approach that I took toward the origins of the church. Immediately after the resurrection, Christians did not have a total view of all aspects of baptism or of the eucharist, no matter how soon they began to perform those actions. Only over a period of time through the work of the Holy Spirit were they led to see different riches in what they regarded as gifts of Christ.

Q. 86, pp. 114-115: The Jewishness of Jesus and of the first to believe in him helps to explain the lack of a blueprint for the church. New structures did not need to be established because Judaism had its own structures: it had its priesthood, sacrifices, liturgy, feasts, and administration. Jesus did not have to think about such issues.

Q. 92 p. 121: (How is ordination instituted by Christ?) Earlier ... I pointed out that "instituted by Christ" did not necessarily mean that in his lifetime Jesus had carefully thought out the sacramental system, or had foreseen the exact specification into different sacraments of the sanctifying power he gave to the church in and through the apostles. What he did at the Last Supper was the root, not only of the sacrament of the eucharist [sic], but also of the sacrament of ordination.

The center

The reader will surely have observed that Fr. Brown expounds almost verbatim the modernist errors condemned solemnly by Pius X and to which he attached the penalty of excommunication (e.g., compare Q. 77 with condemned proposition no. 34 of *Lamentabile*).

So what we have here is an implicit invitation by Fr. Brown to weigh his credentials and charisms against those of Pope St. Pius X (or, for that matter, Benedict XV). We are to decide whether Fr. Brown or the Petrine Rock represents the center of Catholic orthodoxy.

Now we must ponder the following passage from Pius XII, one of the most stirring and profound expositions of the Christological roots we have discussed.

I know I have used this quotation several times before, but one will readily see from the following passage how Pius XII's understanding of biblical interpretation contradicts Brown's concept of an ignorant Jesus. Every Catholic needs to meditate deeply on the significance of this text (And Fr. Brown, who has quoted *Humani Generis,* will know very well how the same Pius XII insists on the binding authority of an encyclical):

> Now the only-begotten Son of God embraced us in His infinite knowledge and undying love even before the world began. And that He might give a visible and exceedingly beautiful expression of this love, He assumed our nature in hypostatic union: hence—as Maximus of Turin with a certain unaffected simplicity remarks—"in Christ our own flesh loves us." But the knowledge of love of our divine Redeemer, of which we were the object from the first moment of His Incarnation, exceed all that the human intellect can hope to grasp. For hardly was He

conceived in the womb of the Mother of God, when He began to enjoy the beatific vision, and in that vision all the members of His Mystical Body were continually and unceasingly present to Him, and He embraced them with His redeeming love. O marvelous condescension of divine love for us! O inestimable dispensation of boundless charity! In the crib, on the cross, in the unending glory of the Father, Christ has all the members of the Church present before Him and united to Him in a much clearer and more loving manner than that of a mother who clasps her child to her breast, or than that with which a man knows and loves himself.[3]

We should also cite an earlier passage of the same encyclical that discusses the *pleroma* of Christ:

"In Him it hath well pleased the Father that all fullness should dwell" (Col 1:19). He is gifted with those supernatural powers that accompany the hypostatic union, since the Holy Spirit dwells in Him with a fullness of grace than which no greater can be imagined. To Him has been given "power over all flesh" (cf. John 17:2); "all the treasures of wisdom and knowledge are in Him" (Col 2:3) abundantly. The knowledge which is called "vision" He possesses with such clarity and comprehensiveness that it surpasses similar celestial knowledge found in all the saints of Heaven. So full of grace and truth is He that of His inexhaustible fullness we have all received (cf. John 1:18).[4]

The Petrine Magisterium has taught us through these passages how to probe the pulsating core of Catholic life. We most fraternally beg Fr. Brown and those bishops who endorse him to realize what they are doing by rejecting the human consciousness of Jesus. Here is the cancer in *101 Questions*, one spawned in Brown's earlier and lengthier *Jesus: God and Man.*[5]

Pius XII's Christology eloquently expresses the consensus of saints, Fathers, Doctors, mystics, and simple pious Catholic faithful of all ages. He sees his interpretation of the consciousness of Jesus Christ as the genuine witness of the New Testament. For a Catholic, here is the centrist position.

All-embracing consciousness

Consider the text of Hebrews 4:12: "For the Word of God is living and active ... a discerner of the thoughts and intentions of the heart." The Bible is unlike any other book. In what sense is it "living and active?" We think of the Church's liturgical veneration of it (e.g., incensation, candles, kisses), and how that closely parallels the veneration accorded the Eucharist. Why?

The Gospels offer the clearest insight. They show how each of us—each "I"—lives in the sacred pages. Recall the teaching of Pius XII: When Christ speaks and acts, I am present before Him in the crowd. Why? Because He has me in mind. He sees me. He knows me. This knowledge conditions what He says and does.

I use the subject "I" to stress that the *individual* is not just in an anonymous crowd, but in the mind of Jesus. The "I" here, as Pius XII attests, refers to every "I" of every created human person of all ages. Christ, the living Word, knows our response. "The Son of Man knows what is in the heart of man." On our part, we are not merely reading an account of 2,000 years ago.[6]

For our purpose here, we will very briefly consider two Christological premises:

1. Christ is simultaneously and perfectly conscious of every human act, internal as well as external, of every human being, past, present, and future. Therefore, Christ's recorded words, emotional responses, internal and external acts, from the moment of His conception in Mary's womb, throughout His entire public ministry, and indeed, forever, are conditioned by this all-embracing consciousness.

From this first premise, we come to realize that when I read or hear the Gospel, all the words, deeds, and affections of Christ are "conditioned" and "influenced" by the full existential complex of my own needs and my own human personal response. The Gospel is, indeed, an historical record of the past, but it also effects a connatural encounter in this dimension, *here and now*. Christ, in His historical agony, for example, is affected by *me*, both as an individual and as a member of His Body, either toward consolation by my sympathy, my conversion, and my adherence, or toward a sharpening of His agony by my indifference, my sin. Indeed, I live in the pages of the Gospels.

Again, we contend that the consciousness of Christ is the linchpin of all devotions in the Church. When this doctrine is obscured or, worse, denied, that extinguishes the furnace of piety, and coldness grips all aspects of Catholic life.

The second premise is this:

2. Christ *transcends* time. In the divine hypostasis of Christ, there is no past or future, only an all-comprehensive *now*.

If our first premise moves us "backward" toward engagement with the past, this step moves those same historical events "forward" to our own moment. In fact, the two Christological principles complement one another. They form an interdependent polarity. The mysteries of Christ—Incarnation, Nativity, preaching, miracles, Transfiguration, Passion, death, Resurrection, and Ascension—are *present* to Christ who lives them *now*. The mysteries are now and forever. By our incorporation into His Body, we are lifted above and beyond the life of nature and outside time reference.

As we shall see, this is effected through the sacramental-liturgical life, which, for those in a state of grace, actualizes the events recorded in the Gospels. Being members of His Body, we also live these same mysteries in timeless solidarity with Christ our Head. The living transcendent Christ, the "same yesterday, today, and forever," stands before me here and now.

The reader might wonder if, after this admittedly lengthy discussion, we have lost track of Fr. Raymond Brown and *101 Questions*. No. There is a connection.

The rash, modernist novelty of Fr. Brown's pale, unknowing Jesus has incubated the "ignorant Jesus" plague that has swept seminaries, lecture halls, and classrooms at all levels. Preachers have insinuated it from pulpits, and publishers have printed it in catechisms and popular religious texts (almost always without the nuances and plausible deniability of the original).

In the end, what has Fr. Brown wrought? For many, he has facilitated the obliteration of faith in the Jesus described by Pius XII. In turn, this has contributed to the suffocation of devotional, liturgical, and contemplative life. How do we recover this? Only in the dynamic of Pius' Christology. Only in this way can we hope to reverse the sterility and horizontalism that devastate the American Church today.

The 102nd question

What, then, is the responsibility of Fr. Brown and his devoted colleagues? It is crucial to be clear concerning Brown's targeted readership. In his introduction, he states, "I want to alert readers that this is a people's book, not primarily a scholar's book."[8] On the first page, he elaborates:

> I suppose I have spoken a thousand times to groups of all sorts who were interested in hearing about the Scriptures. They have included assemblies of bishops, clergy of Catholic dioceses, clergy of churches other than my own, orders of sisters, and the many, many people who attend summer schools, institutes, congresses, and conferences.

We also need to raise the question: What is the responsibility of those bishops who lionize and defend Brown? After all, he strategically cites his lectures to bishops and their invitations to speak in their dioceses. Their receptiveness may be largely due to the current "wisdom" that Brown is "untouchable."

We note, too, that *101 Questions* bears the *nihil obstat* and imprimatur. These are supposed to give assurance that "a book or pamphlet is free of doctrinal or moral error." We respectfully urge our bishops to make an effort to read the two installments of the incisive critique of Brown by their late colleague, Cardinal Shehan.[9] We can offer but one paragraph of the Cardinal's findings:

> Instead of the Church *actually established* by Christ, he proposes a Church which *stemmed from Christ*; and in place of a Eucharistic Sacrifice which was *actually instituted by Christ*, he proposes a sacrifice and a priesthood which *gradually emerged* some 70 years after the public life, Passion, death, and Resurrection of Jesus and the coming of the Holy Spirit.

These are prominent propositions, by virtue of "retrogression," which Brown offers in *101 Questions*.

Therefore, bishops and Fr. Brown must pose the ultimate "102nd Question": Even after being filtered through all Fr. Brown's nuances, what will be the inevitable "message" conveyed to all the impressionable non-specialists who read his books or sit at his feet? How do they in turn pass this new theology along to others? What are the effects on priests who, on ascending the pulpit, must ask, "What can I honestly preach?"[10] How does this alter the traditional convictions of Religious? And not least of all, what does this do to the faith of the many "ordinary" Catholics, the lambs and sheep of Christ's flock?

Some modest measures

What can faithful Catholics do to control the damage and to reverse the tide of these vaunted "assured results of modern biblical criticism"?

1. While I obviously would not recommend the works of Fr. Brown to the general public, I urge those who do read them to arm themselves beforehand with an open-minded reading of Brown's critics. Begin with Kelly, then Shehan, Miguens, Most, Laurentin, et al.

2. There are many other excellent critiques of Brown that are not easily accessible. One thinks of Mulloy, Morriss, Carol, Myers, Pulver, and Marshner among others. Other critics with high credentials of scholarship have published their assessments in the *National Catholic Register*, among them Hallett, Most, and Hitchcock.

3. Bishops should read these critical works and ponder their overall effects on their flocks.

Regardless, the bishops have a duty to protect the Catholic faithful by informing them that Fr. Brown does not transmit the Faith in union with the Magisterium. They should weigh in the balance words of Fr. John Meier, an exegete ally of Fr. Brown:

> Ray Brown still takes all kinds of vicious attacks— not from learned conservatives but from the sort of Neanderthal know-nothing types. If they ever knew what some of the rest of us are doing, they'd have a heart attack... Ray has become the lightning rod. One might say he has taken our scholarship upon himself and has borne the weight of us all.[11]

But since there is a division of mind among the bishops, we may also have to hope for guidance from Rome. The following texts are grounds for an appeal to such guidance.

Joseph Cardinal Ratzinger

In addition to his address at the 1990 World Synod of Bishops, in which he deplored a facile acceptance of the false assumptions of

Protestant exegesis as a cause of crisis among priests,[12] we hear earlier words:

> In keeping with the Sermon on the Mount, the Christian faith is and remains the defense of the simple versus the elitist presumptions of intellectuals. At last, the totally democratic element at the root of the duty of the ecclesial Magisterium comes into view here. The Magisterium has the task of defending the faithful folk versus the power of intellectuals. Its task is to give voice to the simple wherever theology no longer explains the profession of faith and wherever it takes possession of it and sets itself on a plane above the simple words of that profession of faith. When faced with intelligent theories of intercultural communication, the Magisterium must hold to simplicity and to easy comprehensibility of the fundamental terminology of the Profession of Faith. When faced with the contrivances which denounce the literal understanding of faith as intolerable ingenuousness, and when they go as far as to tell us that certain formulations really mean the same thing (when they express the exact opposite), the Magisterium must adhere to the literal understanding, to the oneness of the common, fundamental profession of faith...[13]

Here the Cardinal echoes the words of Matthew 11:25-27 where Christ thanks His Father for having hidden these things from the learned and the clever and having revealed them to the little ones.

Pope John Paul II

> Defend authentic doctrine against suspicious silences, deceitful ambiguities, mutilating reductions, subjective interpretations, deviations which threaten the integrity and purity of the Faith...[14]

Considering the words of Fr. Meier, considering the unequivocal and pertinent statements of Cardinal Ratzinger and the Holy Father, we pray for guidance. Fr. Brown will undoubtedly insist he is in full accord with the Catholic Faith. Is he right? How much can we rely on this teaching? Are his claims to orthodoxy valid? Is he a safe guide, or, as I would judge, a major contribution to the befogged wasteland of an "American Church," progressively alienated from its divinely constituted center?

CHAPTER 49

HOLINESS—THE BIBLICAL WITNESS TO THE HOPE WITHIN US[1]

In the pages that follow, I invite you to join me in reliving the experience of one of the pivotal moments, correctly understood, at the "center" of Old Testament tradition. And let us do so not primarily as exegetes, but as human beings transported into the awe of theophany. Doing this little dramatic exercise will not only place us in God's Presence but identify us with the prophet Isaiah.

The year is 742 BC. We stand in the Temple before the altar of incense, before the veil that separates us from the Ark. Isaiah speaks, "I saw the Lord sitting on a throne, high and lofty: and the hem of His robe filled the Temple. Seraphs attended upon Him: each had six wings: with two, they covered their faces, with two, they covered their feet, and with two, they flew. And one called to another and said, 'Holy, holy, holy is the Lord of hosts: the whole earth is filled with His glory.' The pivots on the thresholds shook at the voices of those who called, and the house filled with smoke.

"And I said, 'Woe is me! I am lost, for I am a man of unclean lips: Yet my eyes have seen the King, the Lord of hosts.' Then one of the seraphs flew to me, holding a live coal that had been taken from the altar with a pair of tongs. The seraph touched my mouth with it and said, 'Now that this has touched your lips, your guilt has departed and your sin is blotted out.' Then I heard the voice of the Lord saying, 'Whom shall I send, and who will go for us?' And I said, 'Here am I, send me.'"[2]

The threefold "holy" (aka, the *trisagion*, the eternal hymn of the angels that we echo in every Mass) reveals to us that the very essence

467

of God is His infinite holiness. This repetition is grammatically understood as a superlative used in Semitic languages, though many Christians instinctively assume a *sensus plenior*[i] that foreshadows the Trinity.

From earliest times, scholars used the Greek *hagios* (i.e., holy) to signify the separation of all things and persons involved in the cult from the realm of the profane. The biblical Hebrew term for "holy," *qadosh*, also indicates separation, here in a more exalted sense of "consecration," a setting apart of anyone or anything dedicated exclusively for worship of the one true God. They become the exclusive possession of the God Who is *Qadosh, Qadosh, Qadosh,* the all-Holy.

Thus we see in this passage the mortal fear Isaiah exhibits in the Presence of the Lord, Who is a *Mysterium tremendum et fascinans.* We see here how God is at once tremendous, threatening of a sinful mortal's life, yet magnetizing, fascinating; how He throws us into awe, but an awe that is filled with ecstasy.

Isaiah knows he is not worthy to be in His Presence, and he voices his fear, saying, "Woe is me! I am lost. I am a man of unclean lips." He is neither consecrated nor ritually qualified for cult in a professional sense. He therefore needs the assurance that comes with the purification administered by the seraph, the angel of fire. But he also senses the overwhelming ethical and moral demands entailed in the mission given him. Unlike other prophets, however, he accepts the mission without hesitation. This inaugural vision, his call, dominates his whole book. Isaiah is the great prophet of the "Holy One of Israel."

At this point, we should note and must reject the polemical Protestant effort to divide the priestly and liturgical institutions from that of the prophets. They falsely depict the priestly and liturgical institutions as only concerned with an external, legalistic holiness. They then depict the prophets as insisting on interior, subjective, and moral holiness, in bitter opposition to the Temple worship.

---

[i]   Latin for "the fuller sense."

First of all, such a dichotomy never existed. The "Code of Holiness" of the priestly book of Leviticus echoed the whole history of the Sinai Covenant. It said all must avoid sin, as well as obey, serve, and fear, yes, but also love God.

Thus the words of Leviticus 19:1-2: "The Lord spoke to Moses, saying: 'Speak to all the congregation of the people of Israel and say to them: You shall be holy, for I, the Lord your God am holy.'"

Other commandments—both positive and negative—follow. The holiness demanded in these is far removed from the calumnious fabrication of a purely ritual purity. Despite this, Reformation theology eagerly fostered the notion of warfare of moral prophets against priests and their "legalism." The fact, however, is that despite isolated instances, a close collaboration between priests and prophets existed in the Old Testament (as even recent Protestant scholarship has candidly admitted).

In any event, we must correct the damage done by the longstanding, Reformation-inspired myth amongst Catholics, and we must recognize the devastation it has wrought in the Church, not least among seminarians.

It was with the keenest understanding of this perversion that infects many of our seminaries and the theological institutions that Cardinal Ratzinger extensively attacked this canard in his masterful intervention at the 1990 Synod of Bishops on the priesthood:

> Such views (derived from modern exegesis) somehow presuppose hermeneutical decisions developed in the period of the Protestant Reformation and endow them with new force. A basic key in the new reading of Scripture that has been born in these times must be found in the opposition between Law and Gospel that was deduced from Pauline theology. The Law that has been abolished is opposed to the Gospel. Priesthood and cult (sacrifice) would seem to belong to the category of law; the Gospel is said to express itself in the figure of the prophets and in the preaching of the Word.

For this reason the categories of law-priesthood-sacrifice-cult acquire a negative connotation because [in the Protestant view] they lead man to the letter that kills and to works that cannot justify. The essence of the Gospel, on the contrary, would consist in the hearing of the Word and in faith, which alone can render a man just.

Thus, the figures of the prophet and of preaching alone are congruent with the Gospel, while "faithful Christians" would thoroughly exclude priesthood from the Church of the New Testament since priesthood pertains to the Law.

It was this perspective that thoroughly determined the course of modern exegesis, and it shows through at every point. From it, the above terminological observations took their force. Catholic theology, which has accepted modern exegesis almost without argument since the Council, was unaware of its hermeneutical key and thus was unable to respond to the great questions to which it would give rise.

And so the crisis we spoke about at the beginning was born. In the meantime, the work of the theologians is beginning to acquire a more balanced view of these questions. It should not be forgotten that already in the sixteenth century, after the initial conflicts, the beginnings of a new balance appeared.

The Cardinal Prefect here fingered a live scriptural nerve that those probing the roots of today's crisis in the priesthood may easily overlook. Regardless, the dichotomy of priest and prophet is a myth.

We must also insist that the stereotype of a mechanistic ritual purity, a legalistic "cultic qualification" in the Old Testament theology of holiness is also unjust, if not calumnious. In his comprehensive article on the subject, Otto Proksch[ii] has some lines dedicated to

---

[ii]   Early twentieth-century Scripture scholar and theologian.

the interior piety of the genuine Jewish believers. He credits the Temple and the sacrificial system as the ambience that stimulated the devotion and interior spirituality of faithful Jews. God forbid that we forget the saints of the Old Testament!

Therefore, as we survey the intertestamental literature and those rabbinic sources that derive from pre-Christian times, we observe a waxing "spiritualization" in Jewish thought, not least in the motives of the sacrificial cult.

Having stated all this, we must admit that the atonement and reconciliation of the Hebrew feasts, rites, and sacrifices still retained (in theory, at least) the aspect of an external purification (as, for example, a close study of Yom Kippur will evidence). Thus, we can understand the judgment of the Letter to the Hebrews:

1. Since the law was only a shadow of the good things to come and not the true form of these realities, it can never, by the same sacrifices that are continually offered year after year, make perfect those who approach. Otherwise, would they not have ceased being offered, since the worshipers, cleansed once for all, would no longer have consciousness of sin? ... For it is impossible for the blood of bulls and goats to take away sins (10:1-4).

2. But when Christ came as a high priest of the good things that have come ... He entered once for all into the Holy Place, not with the blood of goats and calves, but with His own Blood, thus obtaining eternal redemption. For if the blood of goats and bulls, with the sprinkling of the ashes of a heifer, sanctifies those who have been defiled so that their flesh is purified, how much more will the Blood of Christ, who, through the eternal Spirit, offered Himself without blemish to God, purify our conscience from dead works to worship the living God! (9:11-14)

We have invoked the name of the Lamb Whose Blood was drained out in sacrifice on the cross. Jesus Christ has inaugurated the new and everlasting Covenant, has purified the consciences of the contrite, has infused souls with divine life, and has redeemed all who believe in and embrace Him. "Who do you say that I am?" This question, addressed to the apostles—and, as always, answered by their spokesman Peter—is also addressed directly to every human soul.

It is not enough to mouth what others say. Instead, in order to attain holiness, each of us must go back to the most pivotal moments in the history of the created universe. It is little wonder that St. Paul speaks of the Incarnation as *kaine ktisis*, a "new creation." Again, the scene is set and the veil is pulled back, which, incidentally, is the literal translation of the Greek "apocalypse" and the Latin "revelation." Before this veil, the maiden at prayer is hailed by an angel who names her "full of grace." Heaven and earth are suspended on her fiat. She is told that the "Holy One who is born of her will be called Son of God."

So, Jesus Christ is the Son of God the all-Holy, and He Himself is called "Holy One."[iii] With this beachhead of the Word made Flesh in a fallen world, the thrice-holy Godhead unites with the clay of human nature. As a result, not only do we discern the theological concept of the holy, but the holy is now a new reality, a new creation.

Now, the New Covenant is the dispensation of *grace*. When announcing to Our Lady that she will conceive and bear the Word made Flesh, St. Gabriel names the Virgin *kecharitomene*, literally meaning "perfectly and fully endowed with *grace*." The key noun is *charis*. The angel does not use the name "Mary," but rather names her "the one perfectly filled with *charis*" [i.e., grace]. The most important task we now face is to define this word.

One is tormented by the sophistic semantics used in some Bible translations (even Catholic!) to avoid saying it: "grace." Thus, Mary is "favored one" or "highly favored daughter." "Favor" is itself highly favored by those who, for reasons of their own, reject the

---

[iii] Father's original footnote reads, "We will come back to this, the pivotal drama in all of history, but right now, we want to continue this pursuit of holiness' theological meaning."

perennial Catholic usage. They argue that *charis* simply equates with the Hebrew Old Testament sense of *hen*.[iv] In their reading, the Incarnation has added nothing interior to the sense of holiness.

But *charis*, infrequent and vague in Greek usage, had already been appropriated in Christian usage to convey all that the Church means by "grace." It is crucial to recognize the *concept*, even when expressed in other words and figures. Thus St. Paul, so closely linked to St. Luke, uses *charis* when speaking of grace, but also employs many other synonyms, such as filiation, regeneration, new man, new creation, new Adam, incorporation, "in Christ," and so on. St. John describes the "mutual indwelling" (*meno*), as well as filiation, the *succus divinus*, the divine sap of the vine vitalizing the branches.

One of the most striking lines of the Gospel of St. John is where Jesus states the essential purpose of His mission, in effect answering the "*Cur Deus homo?*"[v]

"I have come," Jesus declares, "that you may have life and have it to the full."[3] But everyone born into this world already had life. Why would God's Son have assumed human nature and suffered death for us to offer us a gift we already possessed?

He did not offer *bios*, but *zoe*, that is, not biological, bodily life, but a pledge of immortality, a share in *everlasting*, divine life. And, see, here is the connection between what I was talking about before and grace: The *essence* of divine life is holiness, and *grace* is the carrier and substance of that divine life.

Here precisely lies the astounding and awesome newness of holiness in the New Testament. No wonder the Church refers to the created gift of participation in the life of the Trinity as "sanctifying" grace.[vi] One of the most damning indictments of modernist catechetics (i.e., religious education) is its refusal even to mention, let alone teach, the incredible but true good news of sanctifying grace.

---

iv   Hebrew for "favor, mercy, kindness, graciousness."

v   "Why did God become man?"

vi   The root of "sanctifying" is the Latin *sancta*, which means "holy." So what Father is saying here is "holy-making grace."

To appreciate the splendor of this free gift, we should reflect on the grievous error of Luther. There he was, all tangled up in his rationalized scrupulosity. Because of this, he rejected the Catholic dogma of sanctifying grace. Instead, he injected the virus of pessimism that stamps Protestant anthropology and soteriology. Because of him, hundreds of millions who claim Christ believe the nature of man is essentially and irremediably corrupt. They believe Christ's death only saves us by placing a cloak over that inner corruption. As a result, they hold, man is declared by an external fiat to be justified, but he remains forever *simul iustus et peccator*.[vii] There is only that impermeable cloak wrapped around him.

At this point, one cannot help but reflect on the words about whitewashed sepulchers. What every Catholic needs to review or, for that matter, learn for the first time is that unspeakably thrilling doctrine of sanctifying grace. The Church teaches that grace justifies the interior. The heart, soul, and mind of man are purified, vivified, transformed. God comes into the soul. Father, Son, and Holy Spirit abide there, but not merely to remain there passively. In fact, in the words of Christ, God lives in us and we live in Him. He invites and enables us to enter into the life of the Most Holy Trinity.

It is encouraging to see some gradual recouping of this truth on the part of serious Lutheran and Evangelical exegetes and theologians. We notice recognition of some key elements in the Catholic position on the specificity of the word *charis* as distinguished from the legal imputation of justification or "favor." There is acknowledgment that the causative verb form in question does not always support Luther's position.

---

vii   Latin for "At one and the same time both righteous and a sinner." The famous (and possibly apocryphal) formulation by Luther for this was that man was a heap of dung, and that Christ's atoning sacrifice covered us as snow covers dung, so that man appears to be righteous (i.e., grace is merely imputed). Still, underneath the snow, the dung remains. The Church, however, has always taught that Christ's death and Resurrection transforms us so that we don't simply appear to be righteous (or justified) but actually are (i.e., grace is infused).

As Conzelmann states, "What God declares just, He makes just."[viii] He also observes that the word *hen*, "favor," was not only the gift of God but required that the object or recipient of God's favor be truly *de facto* beautiful and pleasing, literally "gracious" in His eyes.

We might observe that today's modernists have succumbed to the error of Luther and have weaned generations from the awesome fullness of the Catholic doctrine of sanctifying grace. And, in turn, the mainstream Protestant notion simply reflects a return to the externalism and legalism of the Old Testament condition in which ritual and sacrifice, in themselves, were unable to transform and purify the conscience, the heart, and the soul.

Interior holiness, that divine life which is grace, is mediated to the soul through the efficacious septenarium of the sacraments. Hence, true Catholicism thrives essentially on the sacramental system, which derives its power and efficacy from the atoning and life-giving Blood of the God-Man.

To this end, we find one of the most stunning passages of Scripture in 2 Peter 1:2-4:

> May grace and peace be yours in abundance in the knowledge of God and of Jesus our Lord. His divine power has given us everything needed for life and godliness, through the knowledge of Him who called us by His own glory and goodness. Thus, He has given us, through these things, His precious and very great promises, so that through them you may escape from the corruption that is in the world because of lust, and may become *participants of the divine nature*.

Let us absorb the staggering impact of these last words. To do so, we must look at the inspired Greek text: *theias koinonoi physeos*.[ix] Here we see the full splendor of what the Church means by the grace

---

viii   Hans Conzelmann (1915-89), German Lutheran theologian.
ix   Here translated "participants of the divine nature," but literally, "communicants of the divine nature."

mediated to us through the sacraments. We probably have heard the Greek word *koinonia*, which many have often loosely used in religious discussion. Perhaps the best and most accurate English equivalent is "communion." This word is recurrent in the teaching of Pope John Paul. We shall see that the grace imparted to sanctify (i.e., make holy) the individual soul effects a solidarity with all those who share the same divine gift. To understand this "com-union" (i.e., union together), however, we must briefly and schematically begin at the source. To do so, we find ourselves again contemplating the Thrice Holy.

The source and supreme paradigm of *communion* (*koinonia*) subsists in the Most Holy Trinity. We cannot here offer an extensive treatise on this central mystery of ecclesiology. We beg your indulgence to accept a few "shorthand" propositions without presuming to display the panoply of theological subtleties.

From all eternity, in the unchanging Now of the Godhead (*nunc stans*), the Father *knows* His divine essence and expresses it in a Word. This Word, limitless and infinitely perfect, is the Second Person of the Trinity. The Father begets the Word, His Son, in an eternally simultaneous act. The Word is the only-begotten, coeternal Son, the perfect image of His Father (cf. Heb 1). And in a similar coeternal act, the Father and the Son breathe forth their mutual Love. This mutual breathing (in Latin, *spiritus*) in its infinite perfection is the Third Person, the Holy Spirit.

Even this clumsy recital shows us that the relational acts of knowing and willing (along with their objects, *truth* and *love*) constitute the essence of this divine communion, which thereby constitutes a *community* of Three Persons. We also observe that *communion* entails *communication*, the interaction of intellect and will. And, again, the objects of these are truth and love, which, in the divine relations of the Trinity, are synonyms for the Godhead: God *is* Truth; God *is* Love.

The triune God—without beginning, without end—has freely willed to send forth, to communicate this interior communion into temporal, contingent[x] creation, which is crowned with men, rational creatures, themselves made in the image and likeness of their Creator. These men are therefore capable of knowing and loving and, when elevated by grace, sharing in the life of the Trinity. Thus, the temporal missions *ad extra* of Son and Holy Spirit are motivated by the goal of communicating the Trinitarian communion. The uncreated Persons of the Trinity bring *communion* to the human and angelic persons they created. Only between *persons* can communion exist.

Let us inject some most crucial and eminently practical questions:

1. Can we, dare we, imagine dissent, contestation, alienation, division, antinomianism, or anarchy among the Persons of the Holy Trinity?
2. Can we, dare we, suggest that such phenomena are healthy signs of any Christian community?

Such was the challenge Vatican II set before the Church. Thus, *Lumen Gentium*, having explained the communion of the Church, devotes all of Chapter 5 to the universal call to holiness. It opens with these words:

> The Church, whose mystery is set forth by this sacred Council, is held, as a matter of faith, to be unfailingly holy. This is because Christ, the Son of God, who with the Father and the Holy Spirit is hailed as "alone holy," loved the Church as His Bride (cf. Eph 5:25-26); He joined her to Himself as His Body and endowed her with the gift of the Holy Spirit for the glory of God. Therefore, all in the Church, whether they belong to the hierarchy or are cared for by it, are called to holiness,

---

[x]   Father here means contingent in its philosophical and metaphysical sense. As God is absolute (i.e., without beginning or end), man and all of creation are contingent (i.e., their existence is contingent upon someone or something bringing them into existence).

according to the Apostle's saying, "for this is the will
of God, your sanctification" (1 Thes 4:3; cf. Eph 1:4).
This holiness of the Church is constantly shown forth
in the fruits of the grace which the Spirit produces in the
faithful and so it must be.

In the turbulent backwash of the Council, many sectors of the
Church obscured this essential communion of holiness (when they
did not obliterate it) in favor of a horizontal return to the secular
and naturalistic commune of this world. Thus, the universal call to
holiness was a dominant and emphatic theme at the Extraordinary
Synod of Bishops in 1985.

At this vantage, it might be helpful to clarify that our topic
of holiness embraces *all* that we discuss here, for communion and
grace infuse and contain the holiness that subsists in the Thrice Holy
Godhead. "If we but knew the gift of God!"[4]

We have seen that the communion of the Church is Trinitarian
in its source. Every mystery is a gem, and to appreciate each, one must
contemplate its many facets, all of which contribute to a deeper and
fuller grasp of its unique value. We will now give a partial list of other
facets essential to the ecclesial communion which is the Church,
the Body of Christ, whose soul is the Holy Spirit, the sanctifier and
life-giver.

Catholic communion is *eucharistic*. The Bread of Life come
down from heaven imparts everlasting life. Christ dwells in us, and
we dwell in Him. He lives in us and we live in Him. St. Paul uses the
technical word in reference to eucharistic communion: "All we who
eat the one Bread are one Body... We are *koinonoi*, communicants,
in the Body and Blood of the Lord."[5] In eucharistic communion,
the mutual indwelling is nurtured, sustained, and consummated.
And the fuller the communion all have with Christ, the fuller the
communion all have with each other in His Body. No wonder this
most excellent sacrament is called, simply, Holy Communion.

Catholic communion is also *Petrine*. "Simon called Peter" by
Jesus, Who commissioned him head and spokesman of the Twelve

and the apostolic college, preaches in full ecclesial communion with him. Jesus designates him as the visible center and guarantor of the *koinonia*. One cannot knowingly bypass Peter and pretend to be living in communion with the Son of God's vicar.

As a corollary, we may note that the rabbinic word for *koinonia* is *haburah*. The family group that eats the Passover is called a *haburah*. Jesus and His disciples (i.e., rabbi and *talmudim*) are a *haburah*. Similarly, eucharistic communion is a family communion constituting the Church as the universal family of the Father, a paschal *haburah* of His sons and daughters.

Haburah in its prime sense of "bond" is also applied to the communion of husband and wife. As St. Paul notes, Christ is joined to His Bride, the Church, in an indissoluble bond precisely to make her "holy and immaculate." Our communion, then, is *nuptial*. And returning to Peter, he was the manager of a small co-op of fishermen. The Gospel speaks of "Peter and those who were with him." Again, the term *haburah* was applied to just such "co-ops." Thus, the boat of Peter, the flagship we may say, becomes the symbol of the Petrine communion of Christ's Church. Jesus traveled in Peter's boat. Jesus is in the same boat we are! This gives us an anchor of hope in these tempestuous times.

We cannot discuss the relation of this to the communion of saints, the eternal abode of those confirmed in holiness, but we should note that the apostolic usage commonly referred to those in communion with them as "the saints." Holiness is an essential mark of Christ's Church in time and in eternity.

Not least because mentioned last, we must return to the role of Mary, Queen of Saints. Since the *koinonia* is ecclesial, it is also *Marian*. Mary is model, mother, and personal summa of the Church. And, as Pope John Paul so beautifully named her, she is "Memory of the Church." The Church, as Mary, is virgin and mother. Mary's fiat is the nexus whereby all mankind is enabled to give consent to the influx of the communion of the Trinity. Time and eternity hinged on this maiden's "yes" to the communion of grace and holiness, which made her the woman of assent. She also has that "fullness of grace" that is the plenitude of Trinitarian communion: She is daughter of the Father, mother of the Son, and spouse of the Holy Spirit. To say "full of grace" is to say "full of holiness" and "full of communion." The angel Gabriel omits her given name and substitutes for it her essential name: *kecharitomene*. He salutes her as "full of grace." It is that *pleroma* of holiness, the essence of the Trinity, "the fountain of all holiness," communicated to us as a free gift from Christ, "from whose fullness we have all received."

In Mary, the first Christian, mother and *summa* of the Church, we discern the essential characteristics of the ecclesial communion in the will of God. Here we must limit ourselves to but a few of these signets of Christ's Church, so purely transparent in the person of Mary.

Mary was open to the transcendence of the all-Holy. The Marian Church, while serving mankind in this world, must never fail to proclaim the supernatural order and a Lord whose kingdom is not of this world. The Marian Church will always seek first the kingdom of God and His holiness because it imitates Mary, the "Woman of assent." Indeed, it must imitate her in her assent.

By contrast, the modernists are not open to the supernatural order and thus are closed to assent. They may mouth the name of God. They may even mouth fealty to His Church and assent to her teachings. But their practice and main focus is seeking a kingdom of this world, a secular commune, not true communion. The modernists revel in dissent and contestation.

Mary, the suffering handmaid of the Suffering Servant, stood by her Son's cross—*iuxta crucem*. The Church must likewise always stand *iuxta crucem* with all that the cross demands: sacrificial love, penance, mortification, and humility.

On the other hand, the modernists foment disobedience and antinomianism, and beneath a façade of pure concern for humanity, they recognize no binding authority beyond their own individual advantage. They vaunt their "liberation" from all restrictions, and ultimately reject the will of God with the ancient rebel manifesto, "*Non serviam!*"

Mary is Immaculate. The Church, modeled on Mary, must also be immaculate, unblemished. The modernists, who want the Church remade in their image, assault every aspect of moral absolutes, most prominently those of sexual purity. Anyone with any degree of love for God should hesitate to follow their clarion call for "renewal" and "reform."

So much more could be added, but it can all be summed up in saying that since Mary is full of grace, the Church must be full of grace. Without her, any dissenting conventicle is like a motherless house: disorderly, dirty, anarchic, and cold. And since the modernists have evicted Mary, they are quite simply "graceless." Their sacraments are regarded as mere "celebrations," rites of passage.

We have detailed the current crisis of faith by contrasting it with the genuine communion of the one and holy Church that is catholic and apostolic. How should we label this crisis that has divided us in canonical terms? Is it "heresy"? "Yes, but ..." Is it "schism"? "Yes, but..."

In my judgment, it goes beyond all that: It is apostasy. How did these infections and lethal viruses invade the Body of the Church? We can find the answer in Mary, who is the "Woman of faith."

She revealed at Fátima that Russia would be the scourge, that Russia would spread her errors throughout the world. The essential definition of communism is "dialectic materialism." Materialism excludes the spiritual, the transcendent, and the eternal. Therefore, it excludes God. Whether it goes public and professes this (theoretic atheism) or uses theist vocabulary while denying its substance (practical atheism), this is the root error of ideological communism. (By the way, we should not overlook the modifier "dialectic," which is a cognate of "dialog," and modernists never tire of insisting that the Church enter into dialogue with them. I leave you to your private musings on this.)

We have watched with mesmerized eyes as this exclusivist materialism slowly, inexorably infiltrated itself into world culture. It has conquered Western and American culture almost unperceived (and certainly with little resistance). Whole sectors of the clergy capitulated, as have Religious of both sexes and seminaries, and, through these agents, the not-so-innocent laity, which was all too eager to exempt itself from all guilt and restraint.

Furthermore (as if by a demonic coup), the modernists have contrived a forgetting of the saints, the "holy ones." The saints teach us that God wills that grace enable the soul so that it may ever grow in the mystical life, the thrilling exploration of "inner space." It is horrifying to see priests and nuns who have abandoned the Doctors of mystical theology, St. John of the Cross and St. Teresa of Avila, for example, to go scavenging among ersatz oriental gurus.

As Bishop John J. Myers of Peoria has commented, "It is sad to say that both official teachers and others with catechetical responsibilities have evidently been unable to introduce within our people the mysteries of an interior spiritual life. This would be the pastoral application of one of the most important and sadly neglected of dogmatic facts—the call to universal holiness."[6]

Thus, we see that the power centers, the "switch points" as Küng called them, are largely in the lock-tight control of the modernists. Regardless of the present and future of institutional Communism, the West has already succumbed to its lethal error of godless materialism.[xi]

At Fátima, one of her most endorsed visitations, Mary called for "consecration," which is the essential act of holiness. Mary is calling us to be sacred, to return to God as His own possession: "A holy nation, a people set apart."[7]

Our era is marked by the prolific and prophetic role of Mary. Prophecy delivers threats and warnings. We should have no doubt

---

[xi] Recall that at the time Father gave this talk, the fall of the Berlin Wall and the collapse of the Soviet Union were recent memories.

that the third secret of Fátima will give heaven's verdict on the crisis of faith and will pass sentence.

But the prophet is also the messenger of hope, and at Fátima, Mary—after all the chilling recital of woes—gave her children the infallible promise: "In the end, my Immaculate Heart will triumph, Russia will be converted, and a certain period of peace will be given to the world."

This unconditional promise is a beacon of hope that pierces the darkness of the apostasy and tells us that against all seeming odds, the materialism and practical atheism of all nations will receive the merciful "saints," and this hope is unconditional. As St. Paul tells us, "Love hopes for all things, believes all things, stands firm through all things."[8]

If we are truly consecrated, made a holy people set apart for the union with God Thrice Holy; if we have received a new birth into the supernatural life of divine sanctifying grace; if we recapture the sense of awe in the presence of the all Holy God; if we are closely bonded together in the communion of Christ's Church, a *koinonia* which is Trinitarian, eucharistic, Petrine, nuptial, and Marian, then (and only then) can we be fortified in the hope for things not yet seen, things God has in store for us, and which He has sent Mary to announce to our moribund, desacralized world. For Mary, full of holiness, is "our life, our sweetness, and our hope."

CHAPTER 50

THE POWER OF THE
KEYS IN SACRED SCRIPTURE[1]

By this time next year, God willing, the Holy Father will have visited our land for the third time as Pope.[i] He will focus his attention on the youth—our own and those of many nations. He knows well that they hunger for truth. We have seen the dramatic response these yearly gatherings have evoked. Often our youth have been like lambs without a shepherd. In their honesty, however, they recognize the voice of a good shepherd, a true father in faith, a champion and hero who will entrust them with the future of the Church in a new melanoma.

But all Americans will feel his presence powerfully during this trip, even if only through the media, and even if, as usual, the commentators give more than their fair share of time to some of his major detractors. The general public will see and hear him through any and all static. They will find their eyes riveted on this magnetic figure in white.

For us who already know him, his visit will strengthen and encourage us because we sense, as did Catherine of Siena, that the successor of Peter is "sweet Jesus on earth." For those who have been misled, they will realize how deceived they have been by those who vilify him. Many, the majority, will begin to gain a tentative appreciation of the man, which will only grow as time goes on. If nothing else, they will recognize a truly great world leader and man of exceptional historical impact, a charismatic personage, a spiritual

---

[i]   Father refers here to the 1993 World Youth Day that took place in Denver.

messenger, a moral prophet, and a mysterious man of destiny. For those who are so moved, the ultimate questions will eventually emerge: "*Who* is this man?" "*What* is this man?"

Here, I want to look at the scriptural evidence to clarify, "*What* is this man?" The biblical data confirms and elucidates the papacy as instituted by Christ, Who conferred the power of the keys on "Simon called Rock."

This review will be very brief. But the little we do say will show the convincing evidentiary fact of the papacy and *what* Peter and each of his 264 successors constitute for the Church.

I recall the thrill of seeing when I was a teenager movie news reels of the angelic Pius XII. Even then, I could not comprehend how any Protestant could dismiss the papacy. Today, I am even more mystified: How can one read the Bible without facing the fact that Christ built His Church upon the Rock of the papacy?

The name

When Christ called Simon the fisherman to be His apostle, He immediately changes his name. "Henceforth, you shall be called Peter."[ii]

In the Bible, whenever God gives someone a new name, it is most significant. The new name is seen as an indication of the essential function, the destined mission of the individual. Thus, Abram to Abraham, Jacob to Israel, and eminently, the name Jesus. In the case of Simon, the explanation is held in suspense. The others called are left with a nagging puzzle: "Why does He call Simon *Kepha*, the Rock?"

Christ the divine Teacher purposely wanted to keep them wondering. As Cullmann comments, "It is significant that it should have been possible to translate the word *kepha* into Greek. This confirms that it was not a proper name, for proper names cannot be translated."

---

ii   Father cited John 1:42 here.

In fact, a new Greek masculine form (*Petros*) has to be invented to convey the sense of a proper name. I believe it was Augustine who commented that *Petros* was from *petra*, not the other way around.

Peter, the leader

The apostles must have pondered not only the importance attached to this name imposed at the hour of vocation, but another factor, as well: The leadership or primacy of Peter over the twelve apostles. As proof of this, the lists of the apostles in the New Testament always begin with Peter (with one exception):

1. Matt 4:18-19: "Simon, who is called Peter," and Andrew, his brother, are told, "I will make you fishers of men."
2. Matt 10:2: "First, Simon also called Peter..."
3. Matt 3:16: "Simon, whom he called Peter..."
4. See also Luke 6:14-16 and Acts 1:13.
5. Mark and Luke use the revealing expression: "Peter and those who are with him"
6. In Mark 16:6-7, the angel tells Magdalene, "Go and tell Peter and the rest of [Jesus'] disciples."

Peter, the spokesman

Peter also acts as the apostles' official spokesman when the most crucial questions are posed (i.e., those that elicit their collegial faith). A prime example of this is in John 6, the "eucharistic discourse." When the sublime "mystery of faith" is revealed, many walk with Him no longer (even the outer circle of disciples). They protest, "This is a hard saying, and who can believe it?"

When Jesus is left with only the inner core of the Twelve, He challenges them, "Will you also go away?" Peter speaks for the rest, saying, "Lord, to whom shall we go? You have the words of everlasting life" (John 6:67-68). Later, we shall cite the moment when Peter confesses that Jesus is the Messiah and, in turn, Jesus entrusts him with the papal office.

The witness of Matthew's Gospel

Matthew is the "Gospel of the Church," the one which most fully documents the functions and structure of Christ's ecclesial institution. Three texts help illustrate the key role of Peter:

1. Matthew 7:24-27: The parable of the wise man who builds his house on rock as opposed to the fool who builds his house on sand. Violent storms, destructive winds, and raging floods assault the buildings, demonstrating the contrasting results of wisdom and folly. The same Jesus, wisdom incarnate, will not build on sand.
2. Matthew 8:23-27 and 14:22-23: The theme of the storm continues in two accounts of miraculous interventions by Christ. Both of these are ecclesial in nature. The boat on the Sea of Galilee in Matthew 8 is undoubtedly that of Peter and is a symbol of the Church. We will discuss this boat and its deeper significance later. Common to both pericopes is the presence of the apostles. Christ intervenes to save and instruct His chosen followers.

These two accounts, however, are not a doublet. The specifics and the basic lesson in each case lead us to see two separate historical events. The first deals with the care of the Lord for His disciples, and serves to elicit faith in His power to preserve them. The second (14:22-23) is of major impact on our topic since the function of Peter is highlighted.

Unlike the first episode, where Jesus is in the boat asleep and is called on by the apostles, here the scenario is advanced. During a storm on the lake, when shipwreck seems imminent, Jesus walks on the water toward the apostles, who are huddled and terrified in Peter's boat. "Walking on water" is something only Yahweh does (cf. Job 9:8; Ps 77[76]:20). Imposing one's heel on watery chaos (as Jewish lore depicted lakes, seas, etc.) and thereby bringing forth order demonstrates God's creative omnipotence.[iii]

Here, Peter brashly asks to come out and meet Jesus, Who then invites him to step out and join Him in this mystifying action. (This symbolizes how our Lord allows a frail creature to share in the divine prerogative of conquering infernal tempests.) Peter takes his first steps, his eyes riveted on the Master. Then he begins to realize the enormity of what he is doing. His eyes stray from side to side; fear engulfs him. He begins to sink and cries out in desperation to Jesus.

Christ then majestically and tenderly stretches out His hands and pulls Peter back to the surface. Over the 2,000 years of papacy, the countless crises confronting the successors of Peter have driven home the import of this moment.

3. In Matthew 18:18, the apostolic college as a whole gets a share in this power of binding and loosing, but *with* Peter and *under* Peter, who alone receives the keys and who first receives the awesome power of binding and loosing. And now at long last, the other apostles know why Christ changed Simon's name to "Rock." When visiting the headquarters of the World Council of Churches in Geneva, Pope Paul IV began his historical address, "Brothers, you know who I am. You know my name. My name is Peter."

"Confirm your brothers"

We turn now to the Gospel of St. Luke, where we find the precious text of Chapter 22, verse 31.

The setting is the conclusion of the Last Supper, and Christ has just instituted the Eucharist and the priesthood. After discussing

---

[iii]   This factor is crucial to an understanding of the parallel in John 6 and is deeply significant to validate Christ's eucharistic promise to change, to transubstantiate, the very elements of creation.

the distinctive type of leadership the apostles must exercise in the Church, Jesus turns to Peter.

"Simon, Simon," He says, "Satan has sought to sift you as wheat. But I have prayed for you that your faith may never fail (literally: "never be eclipsed"), and when you have turned again, confirm your brothers."

The original inspired Greek text shows the first use of "you" is plural, as in "all of you," but the subsequent uses of "you" and "your" are singular. So Christ here is telling Peter that Satan will assault the whole college, but He will singularly preserve Peter, whose faith will be the firm and infallible center of unity, communion, and orthodoxy for all.[iv]

We note also the vocative, "Simon, Simon." Jesus addresses the human weakness of the apostles as a group in contrast to the divine assistance guaranteed to the chosen Rock. Christ reverts to the native name of "Simon," since He knows that before Peter begins His papal ministry, He will be all too humanly fallible. After all, while walking on the water, he sank, and only the strong hand of the Master sustained Him. Jesus understands that later that night, Peter will deny Christ three times.

Peter and his successors still need the Master's strong hand. They remain human creatures subject to the fears and failings of our fallen nature in so many ways, excluding those areas of faith and morals protected by the charism of infallibility.

The conferral

In any event, Jesus made the promise to Peter. In John 20:3-9, we move to the moment of conferral. Here our Lord ratifies and fulfills the promise. We see young John with his green limbs easily

---

iv   This role is graphically illustrated whenever the pope, successor of Peter, visits nations in every part of the world. At these times, he gathers the bishops, successors of the other apostles. He does this specifically to strengthen and unify their witness in the historic—dare we say "apocalyptic"—tempest now raging around us. This is, after all, an era tested by an epidemic crisis of faith.

outrun Peter to the tomb. Nevertheless, once there, he steps aside to allow the repentant Peter to make the first official witness to the Resurrection, the cornerstone of all Christian faith.

Then, in John 21, on the shore of the Sea of Galilee (where the apostles were first called), we find them back again in their boats fishing. In the dawning light, the risen Christ calls out to them from the shore. Obedient to His directives, they make a miraculous catch.

Having recognized Jesus, and impetuous as ever, Peter jumps into the lake, hauling the teeming nets ashore. We recall that Christ likened His Church to an unbroken net, and that He told the apostles they would be fishers of men.

After the breakfast, Jesus takes Peter aside. Three times He asks him, "Simon, do you love me?" Surely implied here is a touchingly gentle call to atone for the threefold denial. Thus far, we have considered the thrice-repeated question. There remains, however, our Lord's crucial *responses* to each protestation of Peter's love.

First, we should note a special reason for the triple repetitions. The exegete Gaechter comments, "The solemn repetition of a formula engaging oneself, or entrusting some charge to another, or indeed expressing any binding decision, was, if spoken three times before witnesses, the seal of validity, giving the act a legal irrevocability."[2]

It moves us to recall that the conferral of the papacy remains the profession of love for the Son of God. Rome is forever the chair of love, as Ignatius of Antioch named her.

In the solemn responses of Christ to Peter, the ecclesial imagery shifts to that of the Good Shepherd whose flock is His Church, which John developed in earlier chapters (most notably John 10). After each affirmation of Peter, Jesus the Good Shepherd commissions him to "Feed My lambs... Shepherd My sheep... Feed My sheep..."[v]

---

[v]   The words for "feed" and "shepherd" in the Greek here are *boske* and *poimaine*, respectively. *Boske* has the sense of teaching, of feeding the faithful the truths that Jesus has given Peter to safeguard. *Poimaine* has the sense of "to lead, rule, or govern." When we consider this (and that the charge to

All the Gospel indications of the pastoral ministry are now given in trust to Simon Peter.[vi] Jesus ever remains the eternal Shepherd (overseer, "bishop") of His one fold under one Shepherd.[3] We are forever *His* lambs, *His* sheep.

Once His Presence is removed from earth, however, Peter will be His visible and universal (i.e., catholic) vicar in this world. Peter must know, love, and lead the whole flock, not just the humble lambs, but also the most prominent sheep. Just as Christ's flock is one and all-inclusive, so Peter's commission is universal and all-inclusive. Peter must feed the flock in green pastures. This "feeding" in the Church entails the heavenly nourishment of word and sacraments. He must shepherd Christ's flock. The shepherd feeds, leads, and guides. He maintains unity. He seeks out the strays. He defends the flock from predators even to the point of laying down his own life, an example supremely carried out by Jesus Himself.

At the end of this text, Christ prophesies to Peter that he must indeed pursue his love to the ultimate witness. The flock of Christ will have other pastors, but all must serve "with Peter and under Peter," who is now solemnly invested as bishop of bishops, chief visible shepherd of the Church on earth.

The evidence in Acts

In the Acts of the Apostles, Peter immediately shows he understood and vigorously assumed his special role in the nascent Church. He moves to replace the traitor Judas and thereby restore to the New Israel the plenary number of the Twelve.[4] Then at Pentecost, filled with the Holy Spirit and graced with a miracle of tongues, Peter

---

"feed" and "shepherd" was given to Peter alone, and not the other apostles), it gives pause when we consider the efforts of those who want to devolve papal authority.

vi   This is seen especially in the rich imagery of the Old Testament, particularly that of Ezekiel 34, in which God promises that He Himself will come to shepherd His sheep, and which contrasts the good shepherd with the hirelings.

delivers the inaugural sermon of the Church to pilgrims of many nations. Luke repeatedly tells us how "Peter stood up in the midst of the brethren" and gave the first papal addresses, witnessing to the risen Christ. We see him giving the opening speech at the apostolic Council in Acts 15, forerunner of the subsequent 21 ecumenical councils.

Peter's boat

The biblical theme of "communion," so stressed since the Council, centers on the Greek word "*koinonia*." The Aramaic equivalent is "*haburah*." Its root means "binding together." It is used to describe the marriage bond, the Passover Seder company, and, most typically, a family unit, but it can also describe a rabbi and his disciples. Thus, the Last Supper was a *haburah* of Jesus with His apostles.

The term was also used of a "co-op," typically of a fishing co-op. "Peter and those who were with him" formed just such a *haburah*. There are indications that the boat of Peter was the nucleus of a small co-op of which Peter served as the manager. It is in his boat that Jesus travels. This flagship of the *haburah* is depicted sailing the seas of history, ever threatened, ever preserved, straining toward the eschatological shores of mankind's ultimate destiny. This Petrine *haburah*, then, is the *koinonia*, the communion of the Church. Jesus sails in Peter's boat. When we are in Peter's boat, we are with the Master. In this co-op, we share in all of the Church's "goods." The validity and health of this ecclesial communion depends on all members being in effective and affective communion with Peter.

Reflections

Now let us shift gears a bit.

Having reviewed the witness of Scripture, we wonder how self-described Bible-based Christians can fail to see what Catholics see. However, confronting us in these past few decades is a far greater and far darker enigma: Catholics who fail to see what the Church sees. And it begs the question: Why do so many hypocritically persist in labeling themselves "Catholic" while spurning and despising the papacy?

Indeed, there is a small debate among orthodox Catholics about how to categorize the modernists' sin against faith. Most frequently, the reply is "schism." And the rejection by many in the West of communion with the pope makes this cogent.

Professor Hitchcock has articulated another view recently by saying the sin is not schism but "heresy." After all, schism usually means that the fabric of the Creed is kept largely intact. In this case, however, the alienation involves an implicitly global rejection of dogmatic and moral truths.

Perhaps, but I suggest it could more correctly be labeled "apostasy" (which in its total sense includes both schism and heresy). Apostasy entails a full rejection of the faith, a "turning away" from the supernatural dimension of Catholicism.

For that is the reality with the dissidents of today, isn't it? They have rejected the transcendent order. They have tacitly jettisoned grace, sacramental life, the miraculous, judgment, and life after death. Just read their catechisms!

At Fátima, Mary spoke of Russia's errors spreading through the world. The error of Russian communism preeminently was materialism, that is, the denial of the supernatural order and the God who created both nature and grace. It may seem brutal and not "TC" ("theologically correct"), but American radicals, for all their semantic camouflage, are subcutaneous atheists. As St. John says in 1 John 2:19, "They have gone out from us, but they were not of us."

Now it becomes obvious that the obstacle to their primary target, their "future church," is the successor of Peter, because he is the "*rock*" bottom obstacle between them and their objective.[vii] Neither reason, nor Scripture, nor Tradition, nor Magisterium will dissuade them,

---

vii   Father is using a buzz phrase employed by dissidents to describe their movement. There is even an organization that agitates for women priests called FutureChurch. According to its website, "FutureChurch is a national

for they are allies of the legions of the "gates of hell." But the good news is that we have read the book, and we know how the story will end: They will not prevail.

Eternal Rome

When a visitor enters the huge portals of the Basilica of St. Peter in the Vatican and passes through the great vestibule, he stands in awe at the vast expanse of this central church of Christendom. It is hard to take in its immensity, its grandeur, its wonder, and words do such a poor job of describing the effect on him as he sees it for the first time.

Far down the nave, his eyes discern the papal altar, at which he arrives after a long walk. Above him is Michelangelo's magnificent dome, and looking up he sees written at its base the words of Jesus in both Latin and Greek: "Thou art Peter, and upon this rock, I will build My Church... I will give to thee the keys of the kingdom of heaven."

Peering down, he next sees the *confessio*, the semicircular aperture in front of the papal altar. At the bottom of the lantern-bedecked staircase lies the tomb of Peter the Rock. Nearly 2,000 years ago, about 100 feet southeast of this spot, the Romans crucified Peter, and his friends buried him here in a simple grave.

Following the Edict of Milan in 307, Constantine erected the first basilica on the spot. Over the centuries, this edifice was embellished and often restored and then, beginning with the pontificate of Julius II, it was torn down and replaced with the present monumental marvel of the late Renaissance and early Baroque eras.

On October 16, 1978, the world awaited the appearance of Peter's two-hundred-and-sixty-fourth successor in the *piazza* outside. In the moonlight and following the announcement *Habemus papam*!—"We have a Pope!"—a white- and red-clad figure emerged

_____

coalition of parish-centered Catholics who seek the full participation of all baptized Catholics in the life of the Church [i.e., women's ordination]."

on the basilica's loggia of blessings (i.e., balcony). Astonished crowds from all nations watched from below and via television as they first encountered this man from Poland.

John Paul then spoke, and all nations and peoples heard and understood his inaugural words, "*Sia lodato Gesucristo*! Praised be Jesus Christ!" People asked, "Who is this man? *What* is this man?"

These are the questions that 20 centuries of the faithful, the curious, but also sincerely seeking souls have asked. These are the questions we, too, must ask and answer.

We know him. We know his name. His name is Peter.

CHAPTER 51

OUR PRIESTLY IDENTITY[1]

Good, faithful, well-formed Catholics have never doubted the "identity" of their priest. They know the priest is another Christ. And in more serene times, priests with faith echoed in Latin: "*Sacerdos alter Christus.*"[i]

And despite appearances to the contrary, Vatican II actually revived an ancient theological formula that gives precision and depth to the more popular expression. In the aftermath of the Council, and with the emergence of the pitiful phenomenon of a priestly "identity crisis," the humbling but thrilling truth that the priest acts and exists *in persona Christi*[ii] has been persistently explained and developed by Pope John Paul II, doubtless as an antidote to what is a radical erosion of faith in the supernatural.

During his Holy Year Celebration homily for priests, the Holy Father said in part:

> Let us open our eyes ever wider—the eyes of our soul—in order to understand better what it means to celebrate the Eucharist, the Sacrifice of Christ himself, entrusted to our priestly lips and hands in the community of the Church.
>
> Let us open our eyes ever wider—the eyes of our soul—in order to understand better what it means to forgive sins and reconcile human consciences with the infinitely holy God, the God of Truth and Love.

---

[i]   The Catholic priest is another Christ.
[ii] In the person (i.e., place) of Christ.

> Let us open our eyes ever wider—the eyes of our soul—in order to understand better what it means to act *in persona Christi*, in the name of Christ: to act with his power—with the power which, in a word, is rooted in the salvific ground of the Redemption.
>
> Let us open our eyes ever wider—the eyes of our soul—in order to understand better what the mystery of the Church is. We are men of the Church!
>
> It is precisely he who has made shepherds of us, too. And it is he who goes about all the cities and villages (cf. Matt 9:35) wherever we are sent to perform our priestly and pastoral service.
>
> It is he, Jesus Christ, who teaches [and] preaches the Gospel of the Kingdom and heals every human disease and infirmity (cf. ibid.), wherever we are sent for the service of the Gospel and the administration of the Sacraments.
>
> It is precisely he, Jesus Christ, who continually feels compassion for every tired and exhausted person, like "sheep without a shepherd" (cf. Matt 9:36).[2]

In another speech, directed to seminarians at the Roman Pontifical Seminary, the Holy Father compares *in persona Christi* to the title "vicar of Christ." The speech is remarkable for an unusual treatment of a most delicate *theologoumenon*.[iii]

> It is said—and this is true—that the Pope is the vicar of Christ, and I accept it with all humility. I accept it more easily since Vatican II because the conciliar documents apply this same definition of vicar of Christ to all bishops: Each bishop is a vicar of Christ for his local Church. The Pope is vicar of Christ for the universal Church. Certainly, it is a powerful title, a title that makes one tremble. I must tell you that I prefer not to use this title,

---

iii   A valid but optional opinion on a Christian dogma; a theological argument.

and to use it rarely. I prefer to say "Successor of Peter," yes; but I prefer better still to say "bishop of Rome." That other title must be reserved for [the] most solemn [of] moments where the Church must present herself in her Christological dimension as the Body of Christ. On this occasion and in this context also the title "vicar of Christ" seems more justified.

But I have said all this in order to tell you yet another thing: If it is true that the title "vicar of Christ" is so demanding for the Church, there is another title which is still more powerful and which refers to each of us as priests. This title tells us that we must act *in persona Christi*. It is much stronger to say *in persona Christi* than *vicarius Christi*: There is more identification, sameness, intimacy.

This refers to each one of us as a priest or as a future priest: to act *in persona Christi*... All of you, all of us, are called to act *in persona Christi*, and you must prepare well and deeply for this fascinating reality—you can't imagine a greater fascination—which is also a tremendous reality, *mysterium fascinosum et mysterium tremendum*, which intersect in Christ, *in persona Christi*, in the most effective way possible. These are my wishes, and for this annual meeting of ours we have had under the eyes of Our Lady: Mary of Confidence, Mother of Confidence.

One last thing: If it is true that the seminary is "the apple of the bishop's eye," I, as bishop of Rome, feel very happy that this seminary is found under the gaze of the Mother of Christ, that it grows spiritually and also numerically under these eyes. I trust in this maternal glance, in these eyes that have followed Jesus Christ in person. These same eyes, in a spiritual and moral way, must follow each one of us who are called to act *in persona Christi*, to be an *alter Christus*.

When I was a young seminarian, a Lutheran lady kept writing me long letters trying to dissuade me from my goal of the priesthood. Among the many other texts she harped on were 1 Timothy 2:5[iv] and Romans 6:9.[v]

I spoke about these texts to our saintly Capuchin rector, Fr. Gerald Walker. His face lit up as he told me, "It is true that there is but one mediator and that Christ suffered only one death. And that is the sublime beauty of the priesthood and the Mass. Those we name priests on earth are the personal instruments of Christ the One Priest. And the Mass is not another death of Christ. It is one and the same death made present to us in an unbloody manner."

I never forgot that germinal insight, and it is overwhelming to see it expressed *in persona Christi*, a phrase never discussed in those pre-conciliar days when *alter Christus* sufficed.

The corollaries open vistas of the mystery, "Only one priest":

1. At the altar of sacrifice: Christ is always the celebrant—"My Body ... My Blood." The priest is the instrument of Christ, but he is a personal instrument. This causes us to pause. From all eternity, God foresaw and called us with all our weaknesses and strengths. The character of priesthood does not suppress our personality, we are not inert, irrational tools, but Christ has chosen to work in us, with us, and through us! As we act in His divine Person, He acts in our human persons.
2. In the tribunal of mercy: It is Christ who raises His crucified hand to absolve and to apply His own Blood shed on the Cross for the remission of sins and the healing of all wounds, however mortal.

But it is not only in these central acts of priestly ministry! We are not speaking of a merely transitory, extrinsic, ministerial function.

[iv] "There is but one mediator between God and man, the Lord Christ Jesus."

[v] "Christ has died but once, now He dies no more."

The character of priestly Orders effects an interior, permanent, ontological configuration and transformation of the total existence and being of the priest—continuously in his every thought, word, and deed. His whole person exists *in persona Christi*. The priesthood is not a profession; it is a consecration.

It is, then, *in persona Christi* that the priest serves as teacher, revealer, preacher of good news (evangelist), minister of the sacraments, and, at these functions' source and summit, offers the eucharistic sacrifice. He mercifully dispenses the forgiveness of sins. He stands as healer, counselor, shepherd, prophet, and refuge. He loves and defends the poor, the outcast, the confused, the wounded, the scandalized, the aged, the little ones, the children, and the youth. In the pulpit, the classroom, and the office, he serves as evangelist and prophet. *In persona Christi*, he is the good shepherd for the sick and lonely, for the grieving, for the poor, and for the alienated. To children, he offers the hands, the voice, and the gentle heart of Christ.

Jesus is the unique eternal High Priest of the New Testament. He is unique also in this: Until Him, all priests of the Old Testament offered victims distinct from themselves. Christ, however, is both Priest and Victim.[3] It follows that, acting *in persona Christi*, priests of the New Testament must also be victims. This insight was one of Archbishop Sheen's greatest contributions to priestly spirituality. Notice how clearly it defines the lines of the post-conciliar crisis, not only among priests, but also amongst those in seminary formation.

One more corollary sheds light on the clerical malaise now eroding the life of the Church. As Paul tells us in Ephesians 5, Christ is married to the Church as His bride. This bride is immaculate and, though fertile, is virginal. Their bond is indissoluble; its purpose is holiness; its essence is sacrificial love.

Here we see the reason for the self-donation of celibate love, a love that is virginal but all the more potent and fruitful for being spiritual and supernatural. For *in persona Christi*, the priest is married to the Church. If there is a dearth of vocations, one certain cause lies in the failure to impress on potential priestly vocations this vision of the mystery of priest's espousal to the Church. Ecclesiology has imbued our young men with a warped caricature of the Church as stained, wrinkled, and the deserving object of caustic criticism. In such a circumstance, who could expect anything but rejection? What healthy young man would marry a woman he has come to despise?

This is why the Confraternity of Catholic Clergy eagerly seeks to influence seminarians with a genuinely Catholic witness of the priesthood. We hope to give them our vision, the vision of the Church as our spouse, the supremely beautiful immaculate virgin who, by our union with her *in persona Christi*, is also the fruitful mother of the living.

By our ordination, we are vowed to her, "for better or worse, for richer or poorer, in sickness and in health," and even death cannot us part, for we are priests forever.

Afterword

A Loyal Son of the Church: Fr. Richard N. Gilsdorf

When one reflects on the priests one has known through one's youth and adult years, there are a few that stand out like "lone stars in the night, who are more brilliant against the darkness" that now envelops the Church in America.

For me, Fr. Richard Gilsdorf was one of those priests. For those of us who knew him, he was a source of stability and wise counsel. We turned to him time and time again for spiritual direction and common sense answers as we contemplated and confronted the efforts within the Church to destroy a traditional and orthodox faith.

As you have seen Father explain in this book, there was a time in the Middle Ages when the term "papist" was a disparaging term used by traitors to the Church to label those priests and laity as enemies of the secular state.

Today, we still have "papists," those men and women who are loyal to the Holy Father, the divinely revealed truths of the Faith, and the authentic interpretations rendered by the hierarchical authority of the Church. On the other side are the modernists, those who despise the pope and embrace changing the unchangeable truths of the Faith, a false pluralism, and who believe in an ongoing revelation.

Fr. Gilsdorf was a papist. He wore the label as a badge of honor despite the "loud and angry criticism and condescending pity" he had to suffer the last 30 years or so of his life. He was one of the most articulate Scripture scholars, a former seminary professor, a sought-after lecturer, a devotee of Mary, and one who could have played a vital role in saving his diocese from the pitfalls of modernism. Instead, the powers that be relegated him to an isolated rural parish where it was thought his influence would be minimal.

But in His eternal plan, God had an assignment for him destined from the beginning of time, one that would afford him the opportunity for his God-given talents to influence a larger audience than would have otherwise been possible. Indeed, had he been pastor of a larger parish, would he have had the time for the efforts he made on behalf of Holy Mother Church?

Those of us who had the honor of calling him friend observed with admiration the loving tenderness shared between Father and his mother, Gladys, and his sister, Sr. Ricardo, OFM. We were struck with awe as we witnessed his loving attention during his sister's agonizing and painful last days, and the patience and kindness he showered on his mother as she, too, passed from this life into God's eternity a number of years ago.

His phenomenal ability to communicate the Faith to all, whether writing or speaking to the educated elite, to the average lay person in the pew, or to the little children in his small school and on the playground was a gift of God not possessed by many.

His contributions to the Church in his writings and lectures were truly noteworthy. For three decades he wrote prolifically, and two of his most popular articles were "The Plight of the Papist Priest" and "The Plight of the Papist Priest, Part 2" printed in the *Homiletic & Pastoral Review*. These two articles received more positive responses and requests for reprints than any other in the periodical's history.

The basic question he asked in these pieces was, what do papist priests do when they experience a conflict between the authority of the Holy Father and the authority of their local bishop? What do they do when ordered by their bishop or his officials to disregard repeated and insistent papal directives? Does he obey the bishop or the pope? As Father said, to state the question seems to answer it, but to know the answer in theory is not to solve it in practice.

These questions still remain. Our priests still need guidance from the highest authorities. What they needed then and still need today is moral direction for their consciences and pragmatically clear, pastoral guidelines.

Also worth noting is his address to the Twenty-fourth National Wanderer Forum in October 1991. There he blew the audience away with his special insights on attaining holiness, key to which was his devotion to Mary. "For Mary," he told us, "full of holiness, is our life, our sweetness, and our hope."

Then there were his book reviews and other articles, particularly those that exposed Scripture scholar Fr. Raymond Brown for the modernist he was (may God rest his soul). It is interesting that in these overviews of Brown's work, Father quoted both John Paul II and Cardinal Joseph Ratzinger, now Pope Benedict XVI, as they offered guidance to the faithful and expressed the need for a "defense of the simple versus the elitist presumptions of the intellectuals" represented in Brown's book. Indeed, Father would have rejoiced in Benedict's election to succeed Pope Wojtyła. This is especially true since the two were both so adamant on their insistence on looking at the teachings of the Council in light of Tradition, the so-called "hermeneutic of continuity," which Brown and his disciples actively worked against.

One cannot conclude this tribute without mentioning one of his life's greatest satisfactions: His part in founding the Confraternity of Catholic Clergy, a national organization of priests, deacons, and seminarians, an organization whose sworn purpose is loyalty to the Holy Father and the Magisterium in union with him. He served as president for a number of years.

In one of his newsletters to his priest associates in 1998, he offered a guarded optimism when he wrote, "We must never overlook the increasing shafts of light that presage the dawn of the day of restoration promised in all the biblical eschatology. These signs of a threshold of hope include individuals, foremost our heroic and saintly Holy Father, as well as the orthodox bishops now on the scene, some of whom have graced our national forums these past years.

"We are also heartened by movements and institutions: Catholic TV and radio, faithful new or revived religious communities and seminaries, vocations flourishing in dioceses where the bishops insist on Catholicism full and pure, the Fellowship of Catholic Scholars, the Catholic League, and many more, too many to list here—not least of which is the Confraternity of Catholic Clergy. We stand with all the children of light, facing the dawn and forcing back the veils of darkness."

As with his champion, Pope John Paul II, Fr. Gilsdorf suffered terribly from many ailments for the last 10 years of his life. Foremost among these was the onset of thoracic neuropathy, which periodically caused his body to shake uncontrollably, and which ultimately forced him to give up his parish work. He went progressively downhill after that, but always maintained his sense of humor and deep concern for the welfare of the Church he so loved.

One of his last real outings was the effort he made to attend my son's ordination to the priesthood on June 5, 2004. He was so proud to have been able to attend that blessed event. Now we pray he can join John Paul the Great in the heavenly liturgy, praising the Lord Jesus Christ Whom he so valiantly served all his life.

Jean Guitton, the great French Catholic who served as a lay observer at the Council, offered this image of what a priest should be: "Laymen today ask only one thing of our priests, and that is to give us God by means of their exclusive powers of absolution and consecration. We ask that they remain constantly mindful that we look up to them as representatives of the Eternal, as ambassadors of the Absolute. Starved for the Absolute, we need to have them in our midst as persons who will prove to us that He exists, and is, in fact, closer to us than we can image.

"This task requires, besides God's grace and guidance, priests on the highest level of commitment; generosity, selflessness, idealism, and unworldliness. We need priests [with] detachment from material wealth and worldly comforts and values, [who] boldly preach again the Sermon on the Mount; priests like St. Paul whose burning love for Christ transformed first him and then the pagan world around him."

That perfectly describes Fr. Richard Gilsdorf: A papist and an obedient and loyal son of the Church, a Scripture scholar, and a country priest.

May God grant him eternal rest and the reward he so richly deserves.

Patrick F. Beno

GLOSSARY

A

A fortiori – Literally "from the stronger." Loosely defined, this means, "It follows that" and "even more so."

Ad extra – Directed or oriented toward the outside of something. The sense in which Father uses the phrase in this book is the Holy Trinity going outside of its communion of three Persons in one God to man, typically through God the Son and God the Holy Spirit.

Advert – To call attention to, mention, point out.

Anamnesis – A remembrance or reminiscing.

Antinomianism – The belief that moral laws are either relative or made inconsequential as long as one has faith in Jesus.

Asseveration – From the word "asseverate," meaning to declare seriously or positively; to affirm.

Atavist – Someone who longs for the past. According to one dictionary, "Some social scientists describe the return of older, 'more primitive' tendencies (e.g., warlike attitudes, 'clan identity,' and so on. Anything suggesting the social and political atmosphere of thousands of years ago) as 'atavistic.'"

C

Ciborium – This vessel is like a chalice but it has a cover topped by a cross. It is used to hold the consecrated hosts.

Communicatio idiomatum – Also known as the "communication of properties." The 1913 *Catholic Encyclopedia* describes this as a "technical expression in the theology of the Incarnation. It means that the properties of the Divine Word can be ascribed to the man Christ, and that the properties of the man Christ can be predicated of the Word." Referring to this concept, Fr. Hardon says, "We may correctly say that Christ is God and that He is man, that God was born of Mary and that infinite Truth died on the Cross." Thus this phrase attempts to describe the relationship between Christ's two natures. For a fuller explanation, please see the online article on this subject at NewAdvent.org.

Connaturality – A participation of the same nature; a natural union or connection.

Conventicle – Meeting or assembly, especially of an illicit or non-conformist religious nature.

D

Dionysiac – Of or related to the Greek god of wine, Dionysius, and usually having a sense of the ecstatic or wild.

Diriment impediment – An impediment that nullifies marriage.

Dynamism - A process or mechanism responsible for the development or motion of a system.

E

Enchiridion – A manual or handbook.

Epistemology – The 1913 *Catholic Encyclopedia* says this is "that branch of philosophy which is concerned with the [nature, methods, limitations, and] value of human knowledge."

Epithalamia - A lyric ode in honor of a bride on her way to her marital chamber.

Eschatology – That area of theology that has to do with the end of the world.

Eschatological – Having to do with eschatology.

Essentialism – The view that, for any specific kind of entity, there are a set of characteristics, all of which any entity of that kind must have.

Ex nihilo – Latin for "out of nothing."

Exegesis – The 1913 *Catholic Encyclopedia* says this is "the branch of theology which investigates and expresses the true sense of Sacred Scripture."

Existential – Something that relates to one's experience of existence; what we can know by experience (rather than reason or theory).

F

Facticity – The contingent yet intractable conditions of human existence.

Form criticism – Sometimes called by the German word its originator Hans Gunkel created, *Formgeschichte*, form criticism is a way of critically looking at the writings in the Bible in order to discern and analyze the literary patterns they represent and to put them in some sociological context. Critics say this is a method to "deconstruct" and "demythologize" the Bible and thus can lead to people relativizing Scripture as merely the words of men. Proponents claim they are simply trying to get at what the writers meant. What did their words mean to them at the time as opposed to what they mean to us today?

Thus form criticism divides the Bible into segments, each called a pericope. Then the scholar scrutinizes the segments and sorts them into genres. Finally, he tries to derive the *Sitz im Leben*, or setting in life.

H

Horizontalism – The belief that authority in the Church should be more evenly distributed amongst the hierarchy, clergy, religious, and laity.

I

In extremis – At the point of death.

Irenicism – Promoting harmony, peace, and reconciliation amongst Christian churches and communions through reason and dialogue. A false irenicism would be a thirst for Christian unity at all costs, even at the expense of truth.

L

Laxism – The flip side of Rigorism. Laxism says an act is immoral unless we can know that it is morally good.

Leitmotif – A dominant and recurring theme.

M

Mensa – The altar slab on which the Eucharist is confected.

Metahistorical – According to Oxford University Press' Answer. com, metahistory is the "overarching narrative or 'grand récit' that gives order and meaning to the historical record, especially in the large-scale philosophies of history of writers such as Hegel, Marx, or Spencer."

P

Paten – A small plate made of precious metal that will hold the Host before and after the consecration. The word comes from the Latin *patena*, "a flat, open vessel," such as a shallow plate or bowl. This *patena* was used to collect the bread offerings from the congregation in the ancient Church.

Pentecostalist – Someone who seeks to emulate the apostles at Pentecost by being filled with the Holy Spirit.

Perdures – Permanently endures.

Pericope – A selected extract from a book.

Pleroma – Fullness.

Polygenism – An anthropological term indicating an origin from more than one ancestral line or species.

Polyvalence – The current state of things.

Prescind – "To separate or divide in thought; consider individually" (*The American Heritage® Dictionary of the English Language* [Fourth Edition, 2000]).

Prolix – Tediously prolonged; wordy.

R

Recapitulate – To restate or repeat principle points in a story or argument.

Redaction criticism – A school of criticism that examines the way biblical authors used earlier oral or written traditions. It also attempts to discern what motivated the biblical authors and to understand the historical context in which someone edited a particular text. For example, if, as many scholars believe, Mark was written before Matthew and Luke, why did Matthew and Luke seek to change the things they did?

Rigorism – According to *The American Heritage® Dictionary of the English Language* (Fourth Edition, 2000), a "harshness or strictness in conduct, judgment, or practice." Another definition is a theory that holds that the morality of an act has no objective quality, but is simply relative to the subjective knowledge of the person carrying out the act.

S

Sacrarium – The *1913 Catholic Encyclopedia* says this is a basin which drains directly into the ground, whose purpose is to "receive the water from the washing of the priest's hands, the water used for washing the palls, purifiers, and corporals, the bread crumbs, cotton, etc. used after sacred unctions, and for the ashes of sacred things no longer fit for use."

Septuagint – The pre-Christian Greek translation of the Old Testament. Whenever our Lord or the apostles quote the Old Testament, they quote the Septuagint.

Sine qua non – Indispensable.

Suasive – Having the power to persuade or convince; persuasive.

Subcutaneous – Under the skin.

Subjectivism – Any of the various theories that hold the only valid standard of judgment is that of the individual. For example, ethical subjectivism holds that individual conscience is the only appropriate standard for moral judgment.

T

Theophany – The visible manifestation of God to humans.

Trusteeism – Concerning the lay control of parish administration.

U

Ukases – An authoritative order, decree, or edict that has the force of law.

Univocal – Of one voice.

V

Vocative – Relating to grammar; relating to a way of calling someone.

INDEX

ENDNOTES

Chapter 1: *That All May Be One*

1   Father wrote this in 1959.
2   Matt 7:21
3   Cf. Ps 123[122]:2
4   Cf. John 1:14
5   Cf. John 14:6
6   John 10:30
7   John 14:15
8   John 10:16
9   John 21:15-17
10   Rom 10:15
11   John 17:20
12   Cf. John 21:15-17
13   Matt 5:17
14   Luke 10:16; Matt 18:17
15   John 20:21; Matt 28:16
16   Cf. John 3:2
17   Gal 1:6
18   1 Tim 6:20
19   Cf. 1 Cor 15:3; 1 Cor 11:23
20   Eph 4 *Passim*
21   e.g. Tit 1:9; 1:13; 2:1; 2 Tim 4:1-5
22   1 Cor 10:14
23   e.g., 2 Pet 1:19; 2 Pet 2; I Tim 1:3; 1 Tim 4; 2 Tim 4:1-5; Titus 1; Col 2; Eph 4:14; 1 Cor 15; 1 Cor 12:12; 1 Cor 1:10; 3 John 1:7; Jude
24   John 16:13
25   Matt 16:18; 1 Tim. 3:15
26   Eph 4:5
27   Cf. 1 Cor 12:15
28   Phil 2:5
29   Matt 18:17
30   Luke 11:23
31   Cf. Matt 18:7
32   John 17:21

Chapter 2: Tension in the Manger

1   This article originally appeared in *Emmanuel* magazine, December 1967.
2   Cf. Luke 2:15
3   Heb 10:7
4   Cf. Phil 2:8
5   Cf. John 4:34
6   Cf. John 3:16

Chapter 3: Signs of the Times

1   This originally appeared in *The Compass*, the newspaper of the Diocese of Green Bay, on August 29, 1969.

Chapter 4: Relevance and/or Faith

1   This originally appeared in *The Compass* on September 12, 1969.
2   John 1:14
3   John 1:14-16

Chapter 5: Corinth: The Secular City

1   This originally appeared in *The Compass* on September 19, 1969.
2   1 Cor 2:1-5

Chapter 6: First Corinthians 7: Procreation and the New Creation

1   This originally appeared in *The Compass* on October 3, 1969.
2   John 13:1
3   "*Mariage et virginite selon S. Paul,*" *Christus*, vol. 11, 1964.

Chapter 7: First Corinthians: Worlds Apart

1   This originally appeared in *The Compass* on October 17, 1969.
2   Gal 6:14
3   Gen 1:13
4   Col 1:20
5   Cf. John 3:16
6   John 19:36
7   John 15:18; 17:17
8   Cf. John 16:33
9   Gal 5:24
10 Gal 6:14

Chapter 8: "I Am, Indeed, a King!"

1   This originally appeared in *The Compass* on October 24, 1969.
2   Matt 27:11-14
3   Cf. 1 Cor 12:3, Phil 2:9, Rom 10:9

Chapter 9: First Corinthians 12: We Are One Body

1   This originally appeared in *The Compass* on October 31, 1969.
2   e.g., 1 Cor 11:28.
3   Cf. 1 Cor 14:36-40
4   1 Cor 12:14-22
5   Cf. Phil 2
6   Cf. Eph 1:10

Chapter 10: "Of All Things ... Invisible"

1   This originally appeared in *The Compass* on November 7, 1969.
2   Eph 6:10ff

Chapter 11: The Family of God

1   This originally appeared in *The Compass* on November 14, 1969.
2   Cf. *Ancient Israel: Its Life and Institutions*, vol. I, entry on "tribe," Fr. Roland Guérin de Vaux, OP.
3   Cf. John 3:16
4   John 4:34
5   Luke 22:42
6   Luke 23:46
7   Cf. Eph 1:20-23
8   Gal 4:4-5
9   Cf. Gal 4:1-7
10   John 14:20, 23
11   John 17:21
12   Cf. Luke 2:52
13   Luke 22:20; cf. Ex 24:8
14   Cf. 1 Cor 4

Chapter 12: Who are our Heroes?

1   This originally appeared in *The Compass*, date unknown.
2   *The Porter of St. Bonaventure*, James P. Derum, Fidelity Press, Detroit, 1997.
3   *L'Osservatore Romano*, September 29, 1968.

Chapter 13: From Peter to Paul

1   This originally appeared in *The Compass*, date unknown.
2   First Letter of Clement to the Corinthians, written about 97 AD.
3   *Lumen Gentium* (*LG*), "Dogmatic Constitution on the Church," no. 18, Second Vatican Council.
4   ibid.
5   ibid., no. 21-22
6   ibid., no. 25

Chapter 14: The Act of Faith

1   This originally appeared in *The Compass*, date unknown.
2   Rom 11:33
3   Cf. Luke 10:16
4   John 1:11-13
5   Luke 10:16
6   Eph 4:5
7   Acts 4:32f; 2:42f

Chapter 15: Simon Peter

1   This originally appeared in *The Compass*, date unknown.
2   Matt 16:13-19
3   Op. Cit., p. 138
4   Op. Cit., p. 139
5   Iliad V:646
6   Cf. *Strack-Billerbeck*, vol. 1, p. 733.

Chapter 16: The Sacrament of Healing

1   This originally appeared in *The Compass*, date unknown.
2   Matt 9:12
3   Matt 9:6
4   John 20:23
5   Is 53:5
6   1 Cor 11:27-29
7   *Sacerdotii Nostri Primordia*, "On the Priesthood," encyclical, John XXIII, no. 95, August 1, 1959.

Chapter 17: The Pirates of Penance

1   This originally appeared in *The Wanderer* newspaper on May 20, 1976.

Chapter 18: An Open Letter to Our Beloved Bishops

1   This originally appeared in *The Wanderer* newspaper on May 20, 1976.
2   This originally appeared in *The Wanderer* newspaper on August 29, 1974. The byline was "A parish priest." Obviously, Father felt he had to write this anonymously for fear of his own bishop's reaction.
3   Cf. John 10:12-13
4   1 Cor 14:8

Chapter 19: The Plight of the Papist Priest

1   This originally appeared in *Homiletic & Pastoral Review* in December 1981.
2   "Address to the Delegates of the Centre de Liaison des Équipes de Recherche," John Paul II, November 3, 1979.

Chapter 20: The Agenda of the NFPC

1   This originally appeared in *Homiletic & Pastoral Review* in July 1985.
2   *TIME* magazine, February 4, 1985.
3   "Circular Letter On Presbyteral Councils according to the decisions of the Plenary Congregation held October 10, 1969," Sacred Congregation of the Clergy. This letter was issued April 11, 1970, *AAS* 72 (1970), 459-465. One can find an English translation in *Catholic Mind*, v. 68 (December 1970), 53-58.
4   "Declaration on the Admission of Women to the Ministerial Priesthood," Sacred Congregation for the Doctrine of the Faith, October 15, 1976.

Chapter 21: Optional Catholicism

1   This likely appeared in *The Wanderer* newspaper sometime in 1977.

Chapter 22: Of Shepherds and Hirelings

1   This was written in November 1977, although where it was published is unknown.
2   Ezek 34
3   John 6:70
4   Cf. Matt 8:28-34
5   Jude 13

Chapter 23: The Doctrine of the Fragments

1   This originally appeared in *Homiletic & Pastoral Review* in February 1980.
2   Matt 17:6

3 Luke 5:26
4 Mark 5:42
5 Cf. Job 9:8; Ps 77:20
6 John 6:20
7 Mark 4:41
8 *Hymni et sermones*, IV, 4
9 *Dialogi*, III, 169
10 *Catechesis mystagogica* V, 21-22, PG 33
11 Session XIII, Ch. III
12 *Mysterium Fidei* (MF), "On the Holy Eucharist," no. 58, encyclical, Paul VI, September 3, 1965. Here he cites Origen, *In Exodum*, fragment, *PG* 12, 391.
13 *De Particulis et fragmentis hostiarum reverenter conservandis vel sumendis*, declaration, CDF, May 2, 1972.
14 *Theologia Moralis*, pars III, *De Sacramentis* (New York: F. Pustet Co., 1972), pp. 102-3, #102.
15 *Theological Investigations, Vol. IV: More Recent Writings* (Baltimore: Helicon Press, 1966), p. 314.
16 Cf. III, q. 77, a. 4
17 Loc. cit., p. 315
18 *Solemnia Hac Liturgia* ("Credo of the People of God"), no. 25, motu proprio, Paul VI, June 30, 1968.
19 From the same verse in John.
20 Loc. cit., p. 23, pp. 29-30

Chapter 24: *The Touch of Faith*

1 This originally appeared in *Homiletic & Pastoral Review* in April 1983.
2 *MF*, no. 36.
3 *Estúdios Bíblicos 19*, "*El simbolismo histórico del IV Evangélio*," pp. 329-348 (1960).
4 Front Royal, VA: Christendom College Press, 1980.
5 *Mystici Corporis* (*MC*), "On the Mystical Body of Christ," no. 75, encyclical, Pius XII, June 29, 1943.
6 Luke 24:5
7 Phil 2:5
8 Cf. Luke 8:45-46

Chapter 25: *Samoa and Sacred Scripture*

1 This originally appeared in *Lay Witness* in October 1983.
2 *The New Biblical Theorists: Raymond E. Brown and Beyond*, Msgr. George Kelly (Ann Arbor: Servant, 1983). Out of print.

3   Latin title: *Sacra mater Ecclesia* (*SME*), instruction, Pontifical Biblical
    Commission: *AAS* 56 (1964).
4   *Dei Verbum* (*DV*), "Dogmatic Constitution on Divine Revelation," no. 10,
    Second Vatican Council.
5   *DV*, no. 12
6   Heb 4:12

Chapter 26: Address to the Confraternity of Catholic Clergy

1   Father gave this address to the Confraternity meeting in 1986.
2   San Francisco: Ignatius Press, 1985.
3   Phil 3:18
4   "The Right Ordering and Development of Devotion to the Blessed Virgin
    Mary," apostolic exhortation, Paul VI, February 2, 1974.
5   Cf. Matt 11:29 and Phil 2:6-8
6   The closest cite the editor could find for this was the July 2000 *HPR* article,
    "Cardinal Ratzinger and Liturgical Music," by Michael J. Miller. There is
    also the article His Eminence wrote for the magazine *Communio*, "Liturgy
    and Sacred Music,'" v. 13, no. 4 (1986): 377-91 NC. The former is available
    online.
7   *Sapientia Christiana*, "On ecclesiastical universities and faculties," apostolic
    constitution, Pope John Paul II, April 29, 1979. This deals with those who
    teach theology in Catholic institutions.

Chapter 27: The Church as Communio

1   Fr. Richard Gilsdorf gave the following talk, "The Church as *Communio*"
    at the 1987 meeting of the Institute on Religious Life on April 23, 1987.
2   "The Pastoral Situation in the Netherlands," January 14-31, 1980.
3   Father Gilsdorf's original footnote, which is too long to place in the body
    of the text:

Note the significant remarks of the Pope to the Dutch bishops during his
May 1985 pastoral visit: "The particular Synod of 1980 that I mentioned
left all of us the charge to build this communion: communion of intentions,
of programmes [sic], of the bishops among themselves; communion of the
bishops with their presbyterate and with the individual priests; communion
of the pastors with their faithful, often divided not only by ideological or
political opinions, but also by contrasting views of the Church, by mutual
cataloguing, by positions of mutual exclusion; communion of particular
churches with their sister churches in the total makeup of the universal
Church, opening themselves to the breath and to the breadth of the universal,
which breaks what is too small and closed up in individual experiences. And

on this level, communion of the bishops with the bishop of Rome and with his *ministerium Petri* in the service of the particular churches and of the universal Church.

"But the communion that is inherent in the nature of the Church of Jesus Christ—we know—interweaves, exists, and perdures only around certain fundamental realities that are the concrete bond of this communion.

"These realities are centered on one person: Jesus Christ, the Eternal Word made man, Son of God and Son of Mary. Around Him, around the truth that He is and the truth that He proclaims, is communion in charity built" (Taken from *L'Osservatore Romano*, date unknown).

4   *LG*, no. 9

5   *On the Rubble of Renewal: a Pastoral Lament*, by Msgr. Nelson W. Logal (Chicago: Franciscan Herald Press; 1975).

6   John 17:31

7   Acts 2:41- 42

Chapter 28: *A Little Corner of Heaven*

1   This comes from one of Father's parish bulletins, date unknown.

Chapter 29: *The Paschal Mystery: Fount of Mission of the Church and Christian Culture*

1   This was written in 1988. No other information is available.
2   See no. 75.
3   Cf. Matt 26:30
4   John 17:1
5   John 13:1
6   *LG*, no. 11. It is also translated as "the fount and apex."
7   Cf. Father's article in *HPR*, April 1983.
8   *MC*, no. 75
9   Cf. Matt 26:45

Chapter 31: *The Remedy*

1   This review appeared in *The Wanderer* on an undetermined date.
2   John 11:4

Chapter 32: *Advocacy Exegesis*

1   This originally appeared in the Spring 1983 edition of *Reflections* ... The Wanderer *Review of Literature, Culture, the Arts.*

Chapter 33: The Petrine Commission

1   This originally appeared in the Winter 1988 edition of *Reflections* ... The Wanderer *Review of Literature, Culture, the Arts.*

Chapter 35: Theological Reflection

1   "Address to Italian Catholic Action Youth," Pius XII, December 8th, 1953.

Chapter 37: The Virgin of the Visitation

1   Luke 1:39-43

Chapter 39: The Narrow Way of the Master

1   This originally appeared in the Fall 1989 edition of *Reflections* ... The Wanderer *Review of Literature, Culture, the Arts.*
2   1 Pet 3:15

Chapter 41: Gospel Paradoxes

1   Father wrote the Gospel Paradoxes, but where (or even if) they appeared is uncertain. There is no date. We only have the original manuscripts. Therefore, instead of running them as separate articles, we have placed them all together to run as a whole.
2   John 13:13-16
3   Cf. Lev 16:21
4   Cf. Heb 9:12
5   Cf. 2 Cor 5:21
6   Phil 2:7
7   *SME*, "Instruction on the Historical Truth of the Gospels," April 21, 1964.

Chapter 42: Our Lady Appeared in Green Bay, Wisconsin as ... Mother and Teacher

1   This originally appeared in the November 1975 issue of *Immaculata* magazine.
2   These and other quotes come from the booklet *Our Lady of Good Help*, which is printed by the Sisters of St. Francis of the Holy Cross in Green Bay, Shrine of Our Lady of Good Help, New Franken, Wisconsin.

Chapter 43: *Woman Among All Women*

1   "Instruction on Some Aspects of Liberation Theology," Sacred Congregation for the Doctrine of the Faith, August 6, 1984, and "Declaration on Human Development and Christian Salvation," International Theological Commission, 1977.

Chapter 44: *Mary: Woman of the Two Advents*

1   This originally appeared in *HPR* in May 1981.

2   For Urban VIII, see *Sanctissimus Dominus Noster*, March 13, 1625. For Benedict, see *De Servorum Dei Beatificatione et de Beatorum Canonizatione*.

3   *Papal Teachings: Our Lady*, compiled by the Monks of Solesmes, Daughters of St. Paul edition.

4   Radio message for the closing of the Marian Year, given at Lourdes, February 18, 1959. See Papal Teachings: Our Lady, p. 474.

5   "Message to the Marian Congresses of Sicily," October 17, 1954, 1959. See Papal Teachings: Our Lady, p. 401.

6   Matt 11:25

7   John 19:27

Chapter 45: *The Woman of Assent*

1   This article is a condensation of a talk given by Father at a Marian conference in 1990.

2   Cf. Mark 7:17-23

3   *Theological Dictionary of the New Testament*, p. 627, edited by Geoffrey William Bromiley, Gerhard Friedrich (Grand Rapids, MI: Wm. B. Eerdmans Publishing, 1976). See also *Summa Theologica*, Q. 24, Art. 1.

Chapter 46: *The Eucharistic Mysteries: The Two Tables of the Lord*

1   Father gave this talk at a Wanderer Forum that took place October 6-8, 1989.

2   *MC*, no. 75

3   *MF*, no. 39

Chapter 47: *The Hedge*

1   Matt 24:15

2   *Dominicae Cenae* (*DC*), "On the Mystery and Worship of the Eucharist," apostolic letter, John Paul II, February 24, 1980.

3   Ibid., no. 8

4   Ibid., no. 13

Chapter 48: Questionable Responses: Comments on a Recent Book by Fr. Raymond Brown: Part I

1 This originally appeared in *The Wanderer* on May 23, 1991.
2 Mahwah, NJ: Paulist Press, 1990.
3 *DV*, no. 10
4 Arlington, VA: Christian Culture Press, 1976.
5 *Divine Afflante Spiritu (DAS)*, "On Promoting Biblical Studies," no. 59, encyclical, Pius XII, September 30, 1943.
6 *The Birth of the Messiah*, by Fr. Raymond E. Brown, SS, p. 572, cf. Qq. 63, 64 (Garden City, NY: Doubleday, 1977).
7 *The Virgin Birth: An Evaluation of Scriptural Evidence*, by Fr. Manuel Miguens, OFM (Westminster, MD: Christian Classics, Inc., 1975; republished St. Paul Books & Media, 1981).
8 Q. 94, pp. 122-123
9 Q. 93, p. 122
10 Q. 27, pp. 128-9
11 Q. 58, p. 80

Chapter 49: Questionable Responses: Comments on a Recent Book by Fr. Raymond Brown: Part II

1 This originally appeared in *The Wanderer* on May 30, 1991.
2 Mahwah, NJ: Paulist Press, 1978.
3 *MC*, no. 75.
4 *MC*, no. 48.
5 New York: Macmillan Pub. Co., 1967, 1973.
6 Father noted here, "I have treated this topic in more detail in an article in *Homiletic & Pastoral Review*" ("The Touch of Faith," April 1983, pp. 12-23).
7 See Col 1:24.
8 p. 3
9 *HPR*, November 1975 and January, 1976.
10 Cf. Kelly, op. cit., p. 146.
11 *National Catholic Reporter*, Feb 22, 1980, p. 20, cited in Kelly, op. cit., pp. 7-8.
12 Intervention, 1990 World Synod of Bishops, October 1, 1990.
13 Cf. *30 Days* magazine, March 1991, p. 69 (an abstract from a homily preached in Munich on December 12, 1979).
14 *Ad limina* address to the Spanish bishops, October 17, 1986.

Chapter 50: Holiness—*The Biblical Witness to the Hope Within Us*

1   Fr. Gilsdorf gave this talk at the 24th National Wanderer Forum in the Fall of 1991.
2   Isa 6:1-8
3   John 10:10
4   John 4:10; see also St. Peter Julian Eymard's tract, "Faith in the Eucharist."
5   1 Cor 10
6   "Pastoral Life and Catholic Doctrine," talk by Bishop John J. Myers, as published in *Proceedings*, National Convention, Fellowship of Catholic Scholars, September 1990, Philadelphia, pp. 129-130. Myers has since become Archbishop of Newark, New Jersey.
7   1 Pet 1:9
8   1 Cor 13:7

Chapter 51: *The Power of the Keys in Sacred Scripture*

1   This chapter is adapted from a talk Father gave to the 25th National Wanderer Forum, October 1992.
2   *ZKT.* 69 (1947) 328-54
3   Cf. 1 Pet 10:4
4   Cf. Acts 1:15-26

Chapter 52: *Our Priestly Identity*

1   This article originally appeared in the Newsletter of Confraternity of Catholic Clergy, v. XXIV, no. 3, May 1992.
2   "Homily for the Mass for the Conclusion of the World Jubilee of Clergy during the Holy Year of Redemption, 1983-1984," *L'Osservatore Romano*, February 23, 1984.
3   Cf. Heb 9

To order more copies at $19.95/copy, please contact:

Patrick Beno, Sr.
Esto Vir, Inc.
P.O. Box 11244
Green Bay, WI 54307

www.esto-vir.org

800-932-3826 for individual, parish, and bookstore orders